THE PRACTICE OF ESTATE AGENCY

THE PRACTICE OF ESTATE AGENCY

by
NIGEL STEPHENS
T.D., F.R.I.C.S., F.S.V.A.
with a Foreword by
P. N. BROOK
*Principal, The College of Estate Management,
University of Reading*

1981

THE ESTATES GAZETTE LIMITED
151 WARDOUR STREET, LONDON W1V 4BN

First Edition 1981
Reprinted 1985
Reprinted 1986

ISBN 07282 0053 8

Typesetting by Digital Graphics Ltd., 147 Wardour Street, London W1V 3T
Printed by lithography and bound in Great Britain at The Bath Press, Avon.

Acknowledgements

I have many to thank, among them John Murdoch, L.LB. of the Department of Law at the University of Reading, to whose book, "The Law of Estate Agency and Auctions", I often refer and who gave me very helpful advice; Paul Orchard-Lisle, of Healey and Baker, who assisted me in matters concerning commercial agency work and on whose drafts some sections have largely been based; Professor David Canter and the Housing Research Unit of the Department of Psychology at the University of Surrey, for access to their material; and John Vail, of L. S. Vail and Son, for his report on estate agency in Canada. I am grateful to my wife and family and my partners for their support; to many general practitioner colleagues at the Royal Institution of Chartered Surveyors; and to Peter Brook and his colleagues at the College of Estate Management for their encouragement. I thank my secretary, Beryl Stern, who typed it all at least twice and her husband for his tolerance. I am grateful to Peter Wilson and George Kirton of The Estates Gazette without whose patience and persistence this book would never have been completed. Lastly, but not least, I thank all those who directly or indirectly have helped me with my task and those to whose own writings I have referred.

Contents

Foreword

The gap in both education and literature on the practice of estate agency in the United Kingdom has been apparent for some time, and for this reason, if for no other, I am delighted to accept the invitation to write this foreword. Nigel Stephens is a man of many talents, and in his book he has made good use of his very considerable knowledge of valuation and law, and, indeed of all the other subjects which are necessary for the proper practice of estate agency, and he has harnessed them all to commonsense to produce a manual for practising estate agents and a text-book for those studying to become surveyors or estate agents.

The book displays not only the author's expertise, but also an enquiring mind which has reflected deeply upon the subject and carefully examined the criticisms which have been made of estate agency. The result is a fine balance of broad issues and practical detail, with a text which in size and scope is indicative of the importance of the subject. The appearance of the book is most opportune, because it is essential reading for all those studying for the Royal Institution of Chartered Surveyors' General Practice Final Examination, which includes the subject of Estate Agency.

I believe that this book, as well as being of inestimable value to all those who practise estate agency, will be the beginning of the proper teaching of real estate marketing in this country and the development of the subject as an academic discipline.

PETER N. BROOK
College of Estate Management,
Whiteknights,
READING,
Berkshire   3 December 1980

One

Introduction and Early Beginnings

Early auctions — Origins of today's profession — The auctioneers, the surveyors, the scriveners — Origins and growth of the professional bodies — British society prior to the Industrial Revolution — The effects of the Industrial Revolution — The creation and distribution of wealth and its effect on real property — Political interference in rented housing — Growth in house-ownership — Collective investment in the property market — The growth of the profession of the land.

The question as to whether estate agency is a profession or a purely commercial operation has often been debated, both amongst estate agents and between them and their critics. That estate agents are regarded with suspicion is beyond doubt. Their public image is not an enviable one. This book is not intended in any way to "whitewash" but does set out to examine the agent's role, not only in the market place but in the profession of the land in the wider context: to try to establish the principles that should guide his work. This is its first aim.

It is also intended to fill what many now see as a very real gap in the education and training of those who are to practise in the profession of the land. Of the various professional bodies allied to the profession, the Royal Institution of Chartered Surveyors represents the largest group of practising estate agents and the majority of the members involved belong to the General Practice Division of that Institution. To a greater or lesser extent the majority of these are directly involved in estate agency work, but not until now has estate agency or property marketing featured in the Institution's examination syllabus. Speaking at the last Oxford Conference of the Chartered Auctioneers' and Estate Agents' Institute in 1970, I made the comment: "In our student days they taught us something of the law concerning real estate, they taught us at least the basic principles of valuation, how buildings were constructed, something of Town and Country Planning, of public health and highways, of accounts, of rating and taxation, but estate agency as such barely featured ... if it involved a particular form of expertise we were left to pick it up in the jungle".

Since then attempts have been made by the Royal Institution to inform and instruct its members by publishing Practice Notes, and a member of the Incorporated Society of Valuers and Auctioneers published "The Art of House Agency". Neither set out to examine the role of the agent or to instruct in anything other than a limited section of a very wide market. The Centre for Advanced Land Use Studies at the College of Estate Management, Reading, have certainly recognised the need for training in estate agency and have provided courses. These have been able to reach only a relatively few practitioners and students and have been severely limited in the time given to the subject and therefore in content. If this book does anything to widen the professional and marketing knowledge of those who operate in the market place, then its second aim will have been achieved.

Marketing methods change, public demand and improved mechanical and electronic aids may dictate changes in approach and methods. New means of communication become available, staffing levels accepted for years may become uneconomic, consumer protection legislation — all these are factors that could dictate change. Estate agents ignore them at their peril, for they enjoy no monopoly in their chosen market. It is true that existing methods of operation have been established over very many years, and such changes as have taken place have been only marginal and certainly not dramatic.

It is my view that we have arrived at a time when dramatic changes in the agent's approach to marketing and many allied matters will have to be made if, and again I use the phrase in the widest sense, "the profession of the land" is not to lose control of one of its principal functions — that of marketing. In this context the house-selling operation is particularly vulnerable. If this book does anything to warn agents as to the dangers that lie ahead and give some guidance as to the fields in which changes are likely to come, then it will have achieved its third aim.

For reasons which I hope will become clear, I firmly believe that estate agency, if not in itself a purely professional occupation, is one that should be conducted by men and women with a background of professional knowledge who acknowledge and follow ethical standards prescribed by the leading professional bodies of the land. Any other outcome would not be in the public interest.

Concluding his report on a survey he conducted of the estate agent's role, Professor John Greve, then lecturer in Social Administration at Southampton University and now of the University of Leeds, said — "Estate agency is not simply a commercial activity, as one side claims; neither is it a non-commercial profession. It is a combination of the two and the elements of both salesmanship and professionalism should be combined systematically to the greater advantage of the consumer".

This particular survey, to which further reference will be made, was commissioned by the Consumers' Association but they chose to contradict this conclusion. They said: "We need not enter here into whether there should or should not be competition within the professions, because in our view estate agency is not a professional activity, but a commercial one". On the basis of the evidence before them such a conclusion could not have been an objective one. It was either simply emotive or it was intended to express their own predetermined view.

"The Public Interest" is the excuse often given by politicians and their administrators to deprive the public of their freedom of choice, or to excuse their own failures. It does, however, have a very real significance for any profession, or, if estate agency is not regarded as such, for any group of persons who, not enjoying the monopolistic position of some others, rely on the public for their livelihood.

Estate agents serve industry and commerce, but it is the public in the wider sense on whom they depend. If they fail to keep the interests of that public in the forefront of their thinking, they will fail.

It is unfortunate that those who have looked closely into the operation of estate agents, in particular the Monopolies Commission, the Consumers' Association and more recently the Price Commission, looked only to the residential market and even then only to the buying, selling and letting of houses. In doing so they, perhaps inadvertently, separated away what for many firms and individuals was only one part of a general practice. It follows that they ignored those fields, such as valuation, surveying, property management and town planning, where the professional training and knowledge of the general practitioner can be seen to be vital.

If I succeed in showing Professor John Greve's conclusion to be the correct one, I shall have achieved this book's fourth and principal aim. I believe also that I shall have achieved something in the public interest.

Limitations

No study of estate agency — principles and practice — could be complete without covering the law as it applies to the operation of the market and the agent's role in it, but it is beyond the scope of this book to deal with relevant law other than in the broadest terms. Estate agency, nearly always interpreted as "house agency", in practice covers a very wide field — houses and flats with vacant possession, factories, shops, offices, licensed premises, businesses as going concerns, hotels, farms and land. It covers the disposal by way of sale of both freehold and leasehold interests. It covers lettings of residential, commercial and agricultural property. In no field can an agent provide a competent service without a basic knowledge of the principles of valuation, or without a knowledge of the law as it applies to that field. It is highly questionable whether or not he is competent to advise if he does not have a basic knowledge of building construction, planning "blight" and the remedies open to any client affected. The basic compensation rules, town planning in both the local and regional senses, the Rent Acts and the basic principles of Capital Gains Tax, Capital Transfer Tax and Development Land Tax are other matters on which he should be, if not an expert, well-informed. These are questions that I may only touch on.

No one would deny the fact that little professional knowledge is required to market the standard dwelling-house not affected by "blight", with no unexploited development potential and basically sound, and some practising agents do little more than this. One would not deny the ability of the average house-owner to dispose of his own house. Many do so, but the reasons why the majority choose to use the services of an agent are matters to be considered.

Early Beginnings of Auctioneering and Estate Agency

A detailed study of the origins of the "estate agent" is certainly beyond the scope of this book, but to look briefly into the origins of the profession will, I believe, help to put the role of the agent into the right perspective and underline the principles of estate agency as I believe it should be practised in Great Britain.

The late D.H. Chapman, in his short history of the Chartered Auctioneers' and Estate Agents' Institute, opens by saying that auctioneering and estate agency is of no great antiquity, but, in partial contradiction, goes on to comment that auctioneering was practised in classical Greece. However, there is no reason to believe that sales of real property were effected in this way. The spoils of war and slaves probably constituted the lots, and soldiers the auctioneers. Chapman does, however, record the sale by auction in A.D. 193 of "the Roman World", "knocked down" to Senator Didius Julianos for 6250 drachmas, about 200 pounds sterling in terms of 1970 currency values. He does not tell us of what the Roman World then consisted, or what rights its ownership gave.

Samuel Pepys records an auction sale limited by the burning-time of a candle. A sand-glass was also known to be used to limit an auction by time.

Mr. Peter Ash writing on "The First Auctioneer" (Estates Gazette Supplement, 3.3.1958, at page 33) suggested that real estate auctions originated and developed with Christopher Cook of the Great Piazza in Covent Garden. His first sale announcement entirely devoted to land appeared in the London Evening Post in April, 1740. There is little doubt that following this he built a considerable practice.

Mr Chapman concludes that "estate agency" as defined by the Institute's Charter (a person who as agent buys, sells or lets property or any interests therein) is but shallow-rooted in the past. He comments that prior to the Industrial Revolution the buying, selling or letting of land were the province of no made-to-measure profession. The origins of the profession do, I suggest, go deeper.

Many believe that today's estate agent emerged from the profession of the law — from attorneys who developed the auctioneering sides of their practices, but Mr. Ash refutes this. He believes that estate agency grew from the old auctioneers, who were chattel men (but surely also agricultural auctioneers?) who, "turned eagerly to the exciting prospect of selling big landed estates", and that the expression "estate agent" was coined to describe the practitioner who did more of that class of work than he did auctioneering. In so far as it goes, this is undoubtedly true. Throughout the country one can readily identify firms of estate agents that grew directly from this source and who still combine the sale of real property with their earlier skills which indeed went, and still do in many cases go, a great deal further than auctioneering in its direct sense. The management of both rural and urban land and property valuation work of great variety, and newer skills such as dealing with town and country planning, now form an essential part of the general practitioner's overall function.

However, auctioneering was by no means the sole source of today's "estate agency".

Mr. F.M.L. Thompson in his book "Chartered Surveyors — the Growth of a Profession", throws another light on the early beginnings. He looks back to the sixteenth century. He quotes John Fitzherbert, whose "Book of Surveying" was published in 1523, as being the first English printed book to use the term "surveying" and tells us that it defines this function as "viewing the condition and situation of property and overlooking its management".

Although in earlier years the main role of the surveyor was the preparation of estate maps, used largely for the subsequent appropriation of land and its management, Thompson draws the conclusion that the overlooking of property (the French name for an overseer being "surveiour") "was and is the central function of surveyors, the core from which grew the profession and its many branches of the present day".

The employment by great landowners of persons to oversee their holdings, deal with tenure, rentals and many other matters on their lord's behalf goes back certainly to the Norman Conquest. It could be argued that these early stewards were among the progenitors of today's "general practitioner", and as most of today's practising estate agents can be so described, as being one of the origins from which they sprang.

Yet they really operated as managing agents and could not be said to have operated in a free and open market.

During this period the surveyor as such appears to have been a humbler being than the steward, his involvement being much more akin to that of a servant. His progress from this position was slow and certainly ill-defined. The actual link between "surveying" land and its subsequent valuation and management would appear to have taken many years to establish. As Thompson reports, "stewards remained superior and normally non-surveyors; attorneys, family friends, younger sons of gentry, successful farmers and the like". Nevertheless, the surveyor's influence and range of activities slowly grew.

In 1685 a best-seller was produced, "A Platform for Purchasers". Its author, William Leybourne, was a surveyor and his work set out "to guide purchasers of property, whether for residence or investment, in the intricacies of valuing different types of legal estate in land and calculating rates of return on purchase money". Clear evidence of a significant land market, but not necessarily evidence of a surveyor turned estate agent.

"Estate agency" as such was practised by a privileged few, in the main not surveyors, but primarily by the lawyers and in particular scriveners, the then equivalent of the conveyancing managers. It was they who had access to what property might be available and to those who could be interested in purchasing. In the late seventeenth century they began to keep lists of estates for sale and would-be purchasers, and became the first of the high-class estate agents.

The role of the surveyor, although still subservient, nevertheless grew, and landowners, purchasers, lawyers, and scriveners would appear to have become more and more dependent upon them for the facts on which to base value, and for the basic information necessary for the conduct of their transactions.

The hold of the lawyers or attorneys began to weaken, the ever-increasing demands of efficient management and husbandry made it more difficult for them to serve two masters — the surveyor's strength grew.

Over a considerable period two professions grew out of this confused situation — the surveyors and the land agents, the former with basic practical skills enabling them to carry out nearly all the tasks called for by an ever more active and complicated land market, and the latter more directly concerned with the management of agricultural land and good husbandry.

We shall later see from these sources — the auctioneers, the surveyors and the stewards — were to grow three clearly identifiable professional bodies — the Royal Institution of Chartered Surveyors, the Chartered Auctioneers' and Estate Agents' Institute, and the Chartered Land

Agents' Society. Other factors were to come into play before the three were to merge and become integral parts of the Royal Institution.

Throughout all this the lawyers, for all that they might have lost, retained a far from insignificant foothold. In Scotland they are still the strongest force in the residential estate agency market, and elsewhere even the provisions made to register all estate agents and to bring them under the control of the ill-fated Estate Agents Registration Council specifically exempted the lawyers and by implication acknowledged that they too practised estate agency.

There were, of course, others who were tempted into the property market — upholsterers, furnishers, builders, undertakers were amongst them, and again one can today identify some firms which originated in this way and some who continue to practise in both their old and new roles.

The Years of Change

It is perhaps hard for us to realise just how far-reaching have been the changes that have taken place in the whole structure of our society since the early days of the Industrial Revolution. Before that time Great Britain's economy, though stable, was an agricultural one. Wealth, of which land was clearly the most significant element, was vested in relatively few families and institutions. The Church, the colleges and a few trading concerns were exceptions. Home-ownership was rare, farmers were nearly always tenants. Education was the privilege of only a few. The economy was comparatively static. As a result of these factors the average citizen had no opportunity to improve his lot. Born into a community, he would grow up in one place, without formal schooling, would then take up agricultural work, or work in an allied trade. On marriage his home would be a cottage belonging almost certainly to the local landowner or his employer. There he would live and die, having aspired to nothing better. Perhaps today we should question whether in fact there was, or is, anything better to aspire to.

In the towns and cities of the land there were, of course, merchants who traded in the products of this simple economy. They were able to generate wealth and to own their own homes, but compared with their opposite numbers today, their lives were static, their contacts local. There were no telephones, the rail system had not come into being, travel by road was a major and arduous operation. The merchants' business tended to remain in their own families and as a result of these factors, their houses tended to be passed from one generation to another.

In such a society there was little need, or its leaders saw little need, for much control by legislation. The average citizen certainly had no need to seek expert help in the management of his property assets — there weren't any. Such real property as did change hands could easily be dealt with by the land agents, the lawyers and scriveners; even for most of these, negotiating the sale or letting of property was probably only a part-time occupation.

All this was summed up in a pamphlet issued by The Chartered Auctioneers' and Estate Agents' Institute — "The Rise of the Profession":

"Until the latter part of the eighteenth century the conditions governing the possession of real estate were vastly different from those prevailing today. Land owners were an exclusive and privileged, and certainly limited class, and land, so far from changing hands with any frequency, was held for the most part in large estates and by the same families from generation to generation. The burdens attaching to real property were by comparision negligible and under such conditions the business pertaining to real estate was comparatively free from modern perplexities".

The Industrial Revolution was to make drastic changes over, what in retrospect, was a very short space of time.

The mills and factories created new wealth and new employment. Workers were drawn from the land and they had to be housed, normally in poor, overcrowded dwellings hastily erected by their new employers.

Increased levels of trading demanded improved communications. Roads were improved, but more significantly, a railway network came into being, linking not only every town and city in the country, but linking these with the majority of small rural communities.

Almost overnight a simple agricultural economy had given pride of place to a highly productive manufacturing, trading and potentially mobile one. The new wealth this economy created, although still vested in relatively few, was much wider spread. The traders, the managers and the professionals who served them, wanted houses of their own. Unlike their predecessors, as they continued to prosper they were not prepared to accept a static "station" in life, but wanted to move on to bigger and better things. The inner suburbs of our major towns and cities still contain the buildings that this surge forward created. Converted into flats, private hotels, professional offices or falling into decay they may be, but the grandeur to which this newly prosperous section of the community aspired is still there to be seen.

Those involved needed a service. They wanted to buy land, to build, to sell and to build again. A new and much wider market in real property developed.

The long-held belief that real property was the safest form of investment was not eroded by the alternative industry now provided. As the newly-created wealth spread wider and wider not only did those who benefited seek their own homes, but in their turn they sought to invest their surplus money in real property. They built houses, sometimes a few, sometimes in rows and rows, and in doing so they created work for surveyors, architects and builders. Having built the houses, they needed tenants. As industry and commerce prospered, new workers were required. Managers, clerks and operatives had to be housed and a vast market in rented accommodation came into being. This too had to be serviced — lettings had to be negotiated, rents collected, repairs organised and bad tenants evicted.

Undoubtedly some not previously involved in the property field sensed the opportunity and set up to provide this service, but surveyors and auctioneers already involved extended their practices to take in "property management". Many practices relied on this sector of the market for the majority of their income. The majority of these practices have survived and to this day still manage some of the same houses. This notwithstanding the attempts of the politicians to destroy what should have been seen as one of the real benefits to come from the revolution — the wish of those who could afford to do so to invest in a way that could improve the life-style of others. The fact that so many of these houses were allowed to deteriorate, were not improved when the opportunity to do so was there, and were ultimately sold or demolished was not necessarily the fault of the owners. A few were undoubtedly at fault and as with the estate agents, as we shall later see, succeeded in getting all tarred with the same brush. This led to political interference — to rent control and slum clearance. More significantly, it was later to deter further private or institutional investment in this field, depriving the citizens of this country of a free market in rented accommodation — something most other developed Western nations still enjoy.

Intensification of this political interference in the years that have followed the Second World War has led to a polarisation. The majority of those who seek a home have either to provide their own or rely on subsidised housing provided by local authorities, with all the loss of mobility and freedom this entails. This polarisation, combined with the underlying belief that to own real property, albeit only your own mortgaged home, is to be free and secure, are the factors mainly responsible for the explosion in home-ownership that has taken place in recent years. This trend is one that all but a few would now appear to encourage.

Before the First World War rented housing was the only form available to the majority. It is true that most in the managerial groups, the successful shopkeepers and the professional men by 1914 owned their own homes, but the time had certainly not come when Mr. Average could aspire to do so.

In those years it is probable that the majority of those practising in the property market were dependent in the main for their income on their original skills and on property management. The selling of real property, the role now identified by the public as the principal, if not sole, role of the estate agent, would still have been secondary.

The Industrial Revolution not only changed an agricultural economy into a predominantly industrial one, it was to bring about far-reaching social changes.

As industry attracted more and more workers to the towns, greater national wealth led to the provision of more and more schools and to the building of hospitals, and to growth in services of all kinds, insurance, banking and accountancy.

The workers in these activities naturally wanted to be based close to the centres of population and wealth, and they too concentrated on the major towns and cities. The great majority sought not only to work in, but to live in the towns, and the pressures for property of all kinds increased — for factories, warehouses, offices, bigger and better shops and above all for homes. Our towns and cities did not grow by accident; demand had to be assessed, land identified, acquired and surveyed, buildings designed and constructed, potential value equated with estimated costs, buildings had to be let or sold; existing practitioners in the profession of the land were not slow in learning new skills and applying old ones.

It was in the years that followed the First World War and in particular from 1930 to the outbreak of the Second World War, that the significant change in the housing market took place. This was the age of the three up, two down "semi-detached" and of £5 deposits. The building societies as relatively new arrivals on the housing scene had established themselves and were there to direct public savings into the housing market. The possibility of house-purchase had arrived on the factory floor.

This dramatic change can be quantified. "During the 19th century the nation's housing stock increased five-fold, so that by 1911 the number of dwellings stood at 7.8 million. These were largely provided by private builders, and all but 10% were rented, the owners using housing as a source of income".

Before the First World War, therefore, only 10% of houses were owner-occupied; during the sixty years that followed, the number rose to well over 56% and between 1951 and 1976 the number of owner-occupied dwellings rose by a staggering 156%.

The increase in and movement of population as concomitants of the industrial revolution are well documented characteristics of 19th-century Britain. Population density centred around the towns and by 1901 nearly 75% of all people lived in the urban areas. Not only was this the age of the £5 deposit, it was also the age of the "mushroom" and uncontrolled growth of estate agency.

I have not attempted to carry out any research into the overall structure of the profession of the land during this period to try to establish just how many practices were started by persons who did not belong to any one of the then established professional bodies, but I would have expected to find it relatively small. Undoubtedly some did jump into what must then have been seen as a lucrative field, one that could be entered without qualification and without commitment to any set code of conduct. The temptation to use oppressive and what many see as unethical methods to get established was strong. The rogue estate agent was no doubt about and like the rogue landlord he tarred many with his brush.

The growth of the profession of the land and its standing today is the subject of another chapter, but I think it is beyond doubt that even in the 'thirties the majority of estate agency work, or what the public regard as "house agency", was in fact undertaken by members of established professional bodies, adhering to strict codes of conduct, who regarded this task as a natural part of the overall service they provided to those who wished to sell, acquire or let real property and those who wished to have it managed for them.

As we have seen, some argue that estate agency, or again perhaps one must be more specific, "house" agency, requires no special skill, no special knowledge, no special accountability and is a purely commercial operation. This is certainly the view the government and bodies such as the Consumers' Association would appear to take.

It is natural and right that the vast growth in home-ownership should bring with it closer scrutiny of those who rely wholly or in part on the house market for their livelihood. This scrutiny must cover not only the estate agent but the solicitor, the architect and the builder. Scrutiny will bring criticism but the scrutiny should be broadly based and criticism constructive if both are not to prove counter-productive.

Could it not be argued that one does not need to be a "professional" to teach in a primary school; was there not a time when surgery was regarded as something almost indecent; and was it not only a short time ago that you did not have to be qualified to practise dentistry? Who would today doubt the need for proper qualifications or the need for professionalism among practitioners in these fields?

To me it is inexplicable how so many can see nothing wrong in anybody being able to describe himself as a surveyor, auctioneer, valuer and estate agent without any proven knowledge or ability.

Other changes in our society also proved major factors in the development of the profession of the land.

Perhaps the most telling of these was the political demand for equality that led to a levelling out of wealth. Death duties in particular led to the break up of, or reduction in size of landed estates and more farmers became owner/occupiers. As landowners faced their difficulties, the newly acquired wealth of others needed to be invested — building societies and insurance groups grew.

The introduction of private pension schemes, unit trusts and bonds of many descriptions to absorb the savings of those who would not risk relying on their own judgement to invest in the share market followed. The Institutions came to hold vast wealth on behalf of many comparatively small investors. They turned to the property market. Many manufacturing and commercial companies preferred not to hold their own freeholds but to rent from others. The Institutions came in to finance and dominate the commercial property market.

The character of retailing changed, the more prosperous firms and individuals anxious to grow and prosper sought larger turnovers and accepted narrower margins. The national "multiples" were with us and sought to secure the best trading positions in our towns and cities. The old family traders came under pressure from the multiple retailing companies who could afford to accept narrower margins, from the Institutions, and from the developers who looked to the Institutions for their "out". Most found these pressures too great and sold out. The whole character of our shopping centres changed and indeed continues to change as we come into the age of the super and hyper markets.

All this provided work for the profession of the land, both for general practitioners and for those who chose to specialise in the commercial and investment fields.

There is yet another change that had a profound effect on the role of the property professional. Virtually every field in which he operated became the subject of endless changes in the law — Rent Acts, Housing Acts, Public Health Acts poured out of the bureaucrats. Town and Country Planning Acts became regular events, and taxation became a major factor.

Society demanded higher standards of safety and higher standards of accommodation in factories, offices and in the home. Last but not least came a welter of consumer-protection legislation. All these matters had a bearing on the value of real estate and on its marketing. It was necessary for the practitioner to keep in touch and if not to be an expert in every field at least to know where to look for trouble.

I have not attempted to write a detailed history of the growth of estate agency or the social changes that have brought those who practise it so much into the public eye. I have, however, set out to show how a clearly recognizable profession, that of the land, developed from a number of different sources and how the nature of this development was dictated, not so much by the practitioners, but by the economic and social changes that created today's society. I quote again from the pamphlet on "The Rise of the Profession" to summarise this period of growth:

"Real estate practice is one of a number of professions that have grown out of England's industrial development; and it is the upheaval of the nineteenth century with its redistribution of ownership and its multiplication of problems affecting property that can be traced to the vocation of auctioneers and estate agents.... It follows of necessity that the responsibility for the practical as distinguished from the legal business attaching to real estate gradually shifted from lawyer to layman, and, by the first half of the nineteenth century, real estate practice had reached a stage where it had attracted to it a considerable number of responsible workers especially identified with it. Thus, by slow degrees, was evolved the modern estate agent and auctioneer".

Wider knowledge and higher standards were constantly required. It is this background that has led to the fact that of those who practise "estate agency" the great majority are to be found in firms whose expertise in the property field goes far beyond the marketing of dwelling-houses. Relatively few estate agents are wholly without professional training and very few practise only "house agency", and yet it has been solely to this one aspect that those who claim to be concerned in the public interest have looked, and which has generated so much criticism. The state of the profession and the public image of today's estate agent are the subject of the next two chapters.

Two

The Profession Today

The Royal Institution of Chartered Surveyors — The Chartered Auctioneers' and Estate Agents' Institute — The Chartered Land Agents' Society — The development and growth of other societies — The Incorporated Society of Valuers and Auctioneers — The National Association of Estate Agents — The number of practitioners — Public image — Growth in the market — Market influences — Buyers' and sellers' markets — The agent's role as a market interpreter — The Price Commission Survey

As we have seen, the profession as we know it today grew from no one source. It was natural that each of the main groups from which it sprang, who in the early days practised their own particular skills in relative isolation, should have gathered together their practitioners, and from these groups a number of professional bodies were formed.

The oldest recognizable body is that now known as the Royal Institution of Chartered Surveyors, founded in 1868 as the Institute of Surveyors. As its name implied, its early members were undoubtedly limited to those whose task it was to survey land and buildings, to oversee, report on, and manage. The Institute was granted a Royal Charter in 1881, and in 1930 adopted the title of "The Chartered Surveyors' Institution". It did not adopt its present title until 1946. Its current constitution perhaps illustrates better than I have been able to do the wide range of activities covered by the profession of the land. The Institution itself is divided into no fewer than seven divisions, each with its own specialised role. They cover land agency, general practice, quantity surveying, mining surveying, building surveying, land surveying, town planning and development. Within the Institution each Division has its own Council, and indeed as a professional body it must be unique, for each Division has its own President.

Entry to Associate membership has for very many years been by examination. Before the Second World War, articled pupilage was common and the great majority of would-be practitioners had no alternative but to study for their examinations through correspondence courses. Articled pupilage ceased to be obligatory and after the war rapidly died out, but the educational standards demanded grew higher.

The demand grew for full-time educational facilities and the profession, principally on the initiative of the Chartered Auctioneers' and Estate Agents' Institute, established the College of Estate Management, in the early years based in Kensington, but now established on the campus of the University of Reading.

Universities began to take an interest, initially Cambridge, but others followed, and now many technical colleges and polytechnics in the country offer full-time courses leading to degrees in estate management or land economy. These degrees normally exempt the student from the need to take the Institution's final exam, but two years' approved practical experience, followed by a test of professional competence, is now required before associate membership can be sought.

Membership of the Institution is today in excess of 52,000. The majority of those practising estate agency are to be found in the General Practice or Land Agency Divisions. It is not possible to say with any real accuracy how many of that total membership are practising estate agents. The Institution believes it to be in the order of 17,500, but it must be remembered that estate agency is not practised only in the private sector, or indeed by the smaller firms that can be found in the High Streets up and down the country. Local Authorities, nationalised industries, the Property Services Agency of the Department of the Environment, and many of the larger public companies operating in many fields have their valuers' department, or their property departments, and many are in one form or another engaged in estate agency matters; engaged that is to say in the sale, acquisition, or letting of real estate.

The Royal Institution as we know it today is, however, the product of an amalgamation that took place in June 1970, between it, the Chartered Auctioneers' and Estate Agents' Institute and the Chartered Land Agents' Society. We earlier considered the source of these two bodies, which by 1970 were both very well established and highly respected. The former in particular had within its membership a very large number of practising estate agents. Entry to both was again by examination and both had played a part in the setting up of the College of Estate Management. There is no doubt that eight years later many members of the Royal Institution who came into that body via the Chartered Auctioneers' and Estate Agents' Institute, and many who had qualified as members of both, regret the passing of the Institute, for certainly in 1970 it was identified with, and therefore able to speak for, the general practitioner with perhaps a stronger voice than the others.

Although I have claimed for the Royal Institution the privilege of being the oldest of the professional bodies, Mr. Chapman in his history of the Chartered Auctioneers' and Estate Agents' Institute recalls the foundation in 1872 of the Institute of Estate and House Agents, a small body whose activities were limited to the then West End of London.

The Institute of Auctioneers and Surveyors of the United Kingdom was founded in 1886 but the Chartered Auctioneers' and Estate Agents' Institute as it existed at the time of its amalgamation with the Institution could not be seen to date from earlier than 1912 when an amalgamation between the Estate Agents' Institute and the Auctioneers' Institute took place.

The Chartered Land Agents' Society, formed in 1902, could perhaps also be traced back to an earlier date and to a meeting of six London surveyors at the Freemasons' Tavern on 27th June, 1834, when they formed "The Land Surveyors' Club". Its membership came in the main from those involved in the management of landed estates and agricultural property, but with the break-up of many of those estates, they too became involved in a wider range of activity and the merger of the three bodies in 1970, notwithstanding some of the ill-feeling it caused, could be seen as rational and inevitable.

As these three, ultimately chartered, bodies developed and came to demand entry only by examination, it was inevitable in a profession that in itself was not controlled and could not therefore lay down standards of entry that they left behind them in a vacuum those already practising and those who wished to practise but had neither set out to qualify as members, nor wished to do so. It was inevitable that these, and I trust I will not be taken amiss, "unqualified" practitioners should seek to form their own associations.

By the beginning of 1968, two were prominent — the Incorporated Society of Auctioneers and Landed Property Agents and the Valuers' Institution, by their very titles perhaps indicative of the pull that has always existed between those involved in the agency function and its commercial characteristics on the one hand and those who wished to identify with the professional aspects of the property world on the other. In practice both bodies were identified in the main with the house agency function.

Earlier discussions between the Incorporated Society of Auctioneers and Landed Property Agents and the Chartered Auctioneers' and Estate Agents' Institute failed to bring about a merger of these bodies, something which in retrospect many practitioners today see as a good opportunity lost. Many, seeing the Royal Institution as the leading body, with a decidedly professional bias and a "learned society" approach to life, had sought membership, but being dependent to a large extent in their practices on auctioneering and estate agency, had also chosen to seek membership of the Chartered Auctioneers' and Estate Agents' Institute, as a consequence facing the examinations of both, with many subjects common to both.

The good opportunity that many of today's practitioners see as having been lost was that of linking the Chartered Auctioneers' and Estate Agents' Institute with the Incorporated Society of Auctioneers and Landed Property Agents to form one body that would have represented the majority of those whom we now loosely call estate agents. They argue that had this amalgamation taken place there would have been a stronger voice in the land to speak about estate agency and for estate agents. This, in their view, would have been to the good both of the profession of the land and of the public. It was not, however, to be — in April, 1968, the Incorporated Society of Auctioneers and Landed Property Agents amalgamated with the Valuers' Institution, bringing into existence what is today the second strongest of the professional bodies — the Incorporated Society of Valuers and Auctioneers (I.S.V.A.).

Membership of the Incorporated Society today stands at something just under 8,000 and it is thought that the great majority of these are practising "estate agents".

The new Society set out to establish itself and increase its influence, and again entry is by examination and many colleges up and down the country provide both part and full-time courses. The Society on behalf of its members is currently contesting what they see as the privileged role of the Royal Institution and in particular seeking to have its own qualifications regarded as equal to those of the Institution when it comes to the appointment of central and local government officers.

The wheel, however, continues to turn, for the Incorporated Society as it set about strengthening its position left yet another void, a void that was soon to be filled by the National Association of Estate Agents (N.A.E.A.). This body had been formed in 1961 to represent those agents who did not belong to any of the other then established societies and who could be described as "unattached". The Association set no examinations nor sought any qualifications as a condition of membership, although it did seek to be satisfied as to the experience would-be members had obtained before admitting them.

In its turn, however, the Association would appear to have accepted admission on such an informal basis as being not wholly satisfactory, for it has set out in conjunction with the College of Estate Management to provide a course "for those who seek a formal qualification in estate agency, a course, based on the Association's philosophy, which provides complete coverage of background knowledge for those whose profession is or is likely to be the sale, purchase or leasing of freehold or leasehold property".

The Association in the introduction to its education programme states that since the Association's inception it "has held that the buying or selling of property is a purely commercial transaction which becomes a skilled craft and that the basic expertise and knowledge acquired in the hard school of commerce together with the understanding of the need to abide by a strong code of conduct are the requirements of the complete estate agent". The emphasis is decidedly in favour of the wholly commercial approach. But here there could be seen to be a contradiction, for in the very next paragraph the Association refers to the training of those who have chosen "as their profession what the man in the street understands as estate agency" and it later refers to the programme as providing for "a new generation of professionals who have a special skill and learning in some field of activity in which the public needs protection against incompetence".

Even those who see the buying and selling of property as a purely commercial transaction seem confused when it comes to describing the nature of their own members' involvement.

It should perhaps be stressed that the Association are not setting out to make the passing of their examinations mandatory. They have set out to create a new grade of membership of professional associates, as opposed simply to members.

Their syllabus is of particular significance, for it is the first time anybody has set out specifically to examine in the estate agency field. It covers such matters as the financing of house-purchase, accountancy, elements of law and property, landlord and tenant, and the law of contract, together with the more commercial and practical aspects of practice — advertising, and in particular salesmanship. This is a significant advance and to be welcomed.

Earlier the Royal Institution had established the Society of Surveying Technicians, in the hope that those in its General Practice Division, who were involved in the estate agency field, but who could not or would not aspire to being corporate members, might seek to train and join the Society, but in the general practice sphere it did not catch on.

It may well be that the National Association have, though one doubts whether it was intended, provided both an opportunity and the means for "unqualified" persons to acquire the basic knowledge that should be held even by those whose task is limited purely to house agency.

The National Association currently has only about 3,000, members but perhaps because its title identifies it with the country and with "estate agents" it has a disproportionate influence and this influence could be expected to grow.

When we come to consider the general principles underlying the respective Codes of Conduct, it will be seen that the Association's approach does permit what some might see as a more "aggressive" attitude to estate agency, than those of either the Institution or the Incorporated Society, which are to all intents and purposes identical.

There are those in these two major bodies who would not disagree with the Association's approach.

As I write this no one knows with any real accuracy just how many firms of estate agents there are practising in the country, or how many individual offices exist. The Monopolies Commission believed that in 1969 the total number of offices was in the order of 10,000 and the number of firms about 7,000, and in an article, "Estate Agents and House Purchase", in the "Times" of 20th March, 1976, an estimate of 25,000 was given. There is little doubt that rapid rises in house-prices, particularly in the late 'sixties and early 'seventies led to a considerable increase in the number of new firms setting up, and to existing firms opening branch offices, but to the writer, with an intimate knowledge of many towns in the South, an increase of 150 per cent in a relatively short period of time does not seem credible.

It would be wrong to leave the impression that practising estate agents are either "unattached" or belong to one of the three bodies, the Royal Institution, the Incorporated Society or the National Association. In the late sixties, as we shall later see, an Estate Agents Council was established. In October of 1968 it informed the Monopolies Commission that it had registered 3,626 firms of estate agents and of this total the majority were members of one or more of the national societies of estate agents, only 1,250 being "unattached". In addition to those that now form the three bodies already referred to, members of at least four other bodies were amongst those who sought to register. These bodies were the Rating and Valuation Association, the Incorporated Association of Architects and Surveyors, the Faculty of Architects and Surveyors and the Institution of Business Agents. These other professional bodies would no doubt acknowledge that estate agency is for them a minor role. They nevertheless thought their involvement sufficient to justify joining with the leading bodies in answering the Commission's public interest letter and giving evidence.

During 1978, a new body, the Corporation of Estate Agents, was advertising and seeking members, although little is known of its strength in numbers.

Mr. Simon Parkinson in 1978, when a final year student in urban estate management at the Polytechnic of Central London, commented in a dissertation on estate agency that in the last 20 years the number of estate agents had increased dramatically. He was no doubt relying on the widely differing figures given by the Monopolies Commission and later by the "Times". The Price Commission estimated that in 1979 there were about 6,600 firms of estate agents with some 11,500 branches in England and Wales, in practice very little change over the ten years. They also expressed the view that the agents as a whole have about 70% of the market of housing transactions — the "do it yourself" vendor accounting for most of the remainder.

Mr. Parkinson attributed what he believed was this increase in part to the price boom of the early 1970s, in part to a greater frequency in the number of times the average householder will move and to a growing demand for owner-occupation. "This demand can of course be in part attributed to the political 'killing' of the private rented sector and to the polarisation that has taken place as a direct result, i.e., owner occupation or subsidised local authority housing".

Mr. Parkinson went on to say that this vast increase in the number of agents over a short period was one of the factors, together with the vast increase in house prices in the early 70s, that had "exacerbated the latent problems of agency in the United Kingdom ... this has been reflected in the public image of agents which is very low".

He commented that in a survey carried out by the Law Society in 1973 estate agents ranked last out of the ten professions in public esteem. It is interesting to note that Professor Greve's survey reversed the order as between the estate agents and solicitors.

Before we go on to consider this apparently poor image and the estate agent's relationship with the public, it would be as well to consider one or two general matters referred to by the Price Commission in opening their Report. They dealt generally and briefly with some aspects of the estate agents' market. They (the agents) "operate mainly in a market for second-hand houses which has three principal characteristics — long run growth — uneven flow of business in the short term — and rising prices".

We have already noted the striking increase in owner-occupation since the First World War and in particular during the last 25 years. The Commission commented on the effect of this on the house market: "The number of second-hand houses coming on to the market each year throughout Great Britain rose from 685,000 in 1971 to 710,000 in 1976. Further growth to 790,000 by 1981 and 860,000 by 1986 is expected."

In that the great majority of estate agents adopt some form of "ad valorem" charging, a general rise in property values will lead to a corresponding rise in income per transaction. House prices do not necessarily follow closely the general price level — that they will ultimately reflect an inflationary trend is, of course, true, but there are factors affecting the house market that do not affect, or do not so directly affect, ordinary retail prices. To mention a few — the flow of moneys into the building society movement — house-prices rising more slowly than building costs and forcing a slowing down in the rate of supply of new dwellings — in some areas planning restraint sometimes coupled with abnormal external pressures, again causing a shortage and pressure on prices to increase faster than the norm.

The Price Commission illustrated these and commented generally — "There appears to be a long-term tendency for house prices to rise in relation to the general price level. In the short term, however, there are considerable fluctuations in the relationship between house prices and retail prices. For example, over the 10 year period 1969-78, house prices increased by 233 per cent and retail prices by 187 per cent but between 1973 and 1978 retail prices rose by 111 per cent compared with a 52 per cent increase in house prices".

There are two other aspects of the property (house agency) market that the Commission felt it appropriate to comment upon.

First, while acknowledging the underlying growth in the market, they recognised that in the short term this could be "overlaid" by considerable fluctuations in the volume of transactions. They saw a seasonal pattern as one of the reasons for this, but this would vary greatly from area to area. More importantly they identified a cyclical variation, by which they meant the regular tendency for the market to switch, sometimes very rapidly, from a "buyer's market" to a "seller's market".

From the agent's point of view the difference can be startling. In the former he is likely to be faced with a sharp increase in the number of instructions to sell, an increase in the number of houses on his registers, a much harder market in which to sell and possibly a level of transactions below what he would regard as acceptable. Increased instructions without increased sales means many more worried or even distrustful vendors to be serviced. The agent faces rising costs directly related to this increased workload without a corresponding increase in income.

Conversely a "seller's market" normally comes about when there is a reluctance on the part of vendors to sell and a shortage of houses available. The agent's selling task is easier, but prices are normally rising fast and accurate advice as to value is one of his difficulties. The tendency for vendors to sell direct increases, as do such problems as gazumping. Under these conditions high prices and therefore higher commission per sale are often countered by a smaller number of transactions.

It would seem the agent cannot win, but few would believe that. The Commission did not, for it commented: "At certain points a substantial supply of houses for sale is matched by demand and a surge in transactions occurs". These peak periods, which bring high income to most estate agents, typically last only a number of months.

Last, before considering the agent and his public image, the Commission went out of its way to give an answer to those who in periods of rapidly increasing prices blame the agents for inflaming the market and pushing prices up for their own benefit. In their summary they say — "There is no reason to believe that estate agents have any effect on the general level of house prices in the long term, although they may affect the speed with which prices adjust to a new, stable level after a change. The sharp increase in house prices in 1972 to 1974 was not a purely speculative boom engineered by estate agents, but was caused mainly by increased personal disposable income".

The agent's role as an interpreter of the market, its state, its values and the way in which it is likely to move is from the public's point of view as important, and indeed perhaps more important, than what many see as his sole function, the ultimate matching of vendor and purchaser.

Estate agency cannot be described as a "profession" in the same sense that we would so describe either medicine or the law. Its practice is not at present restricted by statute, although, as we shall later see, those practising it are subject to various controls. Entering it is easy, and requires neither qualification nor previous experience. No one professional body dominates it, although there can be no doubt that the great majority of practising estate agents are members either of the Royal Institution of Chartered Surveyors or the Incorporated Society of Valuers and Auctioneers and sometimes both. For a time these two bodies worked closely together to achieve a common approach as to the conduct of their members and as to the standards to be encouraged, but a proposal that they should jointly promote the image of the "qualified estate agent", although approved by general practitioners within the Royal Institution, was defeated by its General Council on the 3rd of March, 1980. That month a report by the Institution's Policy Review Committee, "Surveying In The Eighties", was published. It advocated an elitist and isolationist policy. It has caused deep divisions, not only in the Institution, and although the debate it has caused has only just started it is now difficult to see how any one of the professional bodies can effectively take the lead in estate agency. One hopes that second thoughts might ultimately prevail.

Both these bodies are open to criticism in one respect. Despite the fact that the majority of the members of the I.S.V.A. and the majority of the members of the General Practice Division of the R.I.C.S., practise estate agency in the "house agency" sense, neither has really set out to train and examine its potential members in matters directly, as opposed to indirectly, related to the sale and letting of real estate. The Royal Institution is now setting out to include property marketing in its examination syllabus, but "too little and far too late" is the view of many.

If the estate agent's role is not fully understood by the media and by the public one of the reasons must be that the leading professional bodies have done little to promote their own role in the field and to educate their members in marketing methods, by which I do not only mean methods of marketing houses, but, perhaps more importantly, marketing the services that they as professionals can give.

The Price Commission picked out this one particular point and in their conclusion expressed the belief "that agents could do more to inform the public of the services they offer, and as a first step in this direction, we would like to see each agent display prominently in his office the services he provides and the terms on which they are offered".

When we go on to consider in more detail the estate agent's role and his public image, the fact that the professional bodies have done so little to promote themselves, or indeed their members who practise estate agency, could be seen as significant.

Before leaving the profession today, one should perhaps comment on the "cut-price" estate agent. Many, believing that estate agency was a way to make easy money and believing that existing charges were too high, in which perhaps they were encouraged by the media and such bodies as the Consumers' Association, sought to set up in business charging in a variety of ways, but at a level significantly below that charged by the established agents in the area. Some charged lower rates of commission, others a set fee for a specific service. The property supermarket idea was one of the latter. In 1969 the Monopolies Commission found that such firms had either gone under, or had increased charges to the normal level. Many have tried in the following decade, but the picture remains much the same.

The Price Commission Consumer Survey showed a surprisingly high level of satisfaction with the services given by estate agents. This being the case, and given that estate agents enjoy no monopoly in the property, and in particular the house market, little change can be expected in the immediate future. If change does come it is likely in my view to come in the form of fewer but larger firms and computerisation. The Price Commission Survey showed that profitability increased dramatically with size, and the ability to out-advertise one's rivals is clearly an important factor in this. The age of the computer will not necessarily bring change in the basic methods of operating; it could, however, bring greatly increased efficiency and make it more and more difficult for the small firm to survive.

Three

Control of the Practice of Estate Agency

The law — The professional bodies — Local associations — Codes of Practice — Control by legislation and its history — Attitudes of the professional bodies — The Estate Agents Act — Consumer protection legislation

The general public, encouraged perhaps by the media, may be under the impression that there is little or no control of estate agency practice in this country. It may well be true that control is inadequate, but control there undoubtedly is and it is exercised at four levels.

First, and obviously, the estate agent is subject to the law, but not only common and criminal law. There has been a welter of consumer protection legislation that we shall be looking at in greater detail: The Misrepresentation Act of 1968, The Restrictions on Agreements (House Agents) Order of 1970 (the result of the Monopolies Commission Reference), the Consumer Credit Act of 1974. Larger firms also came under the eye of the now extinct Price Commission. We still have the Office of Fair Trading.

Secondly there is control over the behaviour of members exercised by the various professional bodies and this control we shall be looking at closely. The Royal Institution of Chartered Surveyors is answerable to the Privy Council.

There is a third and important level at which control is exercised in some areas. Although many property owners do move from one part of the country to another, the great majority of residential property transactions in a particular area take place between existing residents. Estate agency tends to be a much more localised business than many appreciate. Relatively few firms practising "house" agency do so on a national basis, and they tend to specialise in the higher price ranges. Agents either operate in one clearly defined neighbourhood or area, or — the larger firm with a number of branch offices — in adjoining areas. It is certainly because of these characteristics that local estate agents' associations came into being. Indeed we have seen earlier that one of the possible early origins of the Chartered Auctioneers' and Estate Agents' Institute was just such a local association formed in the then West End of London.

The Monopolies Commission in the late sixties identified no less than 79 local associations in England and Wales. There is little doubt that this number falls short of the likely total. Some associations operate very formally, publishing rules, holding annual general meetings, publishing reports, presenting chairmen with chains of office and assuming in their own right all the attitudes and authority one would normally expect of a professional body. Others, possibly known to nobody but their own members, are far less formal, but possibly just as effective. These associations lay down written and sometimes unwritten rules as to the behaviour of member firms, both in their dealings with the public and with each other.

The degree of co-operation between agents undoubtedly varies greatly from one part of the country to another, but in some areas it is significant, and to many firms, particularly the smaller, expulsion from membership of the local association could have very serious consequences. Their power is considerable and although the majority take the codes of conduct of the two main professional bodies as their guide, they seek even tighter control, for example, laying down rules as to the erection of agents' boards and in some cases effectively barring their use.

It is not unknown for an association to seek to try to control the amount of advertising space taken by its members. Although the Restrictions on Agreements (Estate Agents) Order 1970 prohibits any collusion with regard to the level of commission charges as between two or more agents, it is hard to believe, although in most areas there are variations between member firms, that local association members are not influenced in their level of charging by the majority view of their colleagues. In that in any one area house values are likely to be consistent and the level of wages paid to secretarial staff, and advertising rates in the local media, common to all, it would indeed be surprising if one found major variations.

Some associations are known to insist that members co-operate, for example by giving sub-agency instructions, only with other members; but at the same time insist that a firm must have practised in that town for a given time before being eligible for membership. Such an approach is clearly designed to make it more difficult, if not impossible, for a newcomer to get established.

Control by both professional bodies and local associations could be seen as negative and acting as a restraint against open competition. They would argue that such rules as they seek to enforce are there to ensure a high standard of practice and are therefore in the public interest. In some respects this would be true but in others it is questionable.

Whether or not such local associations are desirable two things should perhaps be stressed. They cannot enforce membership — they might make it harder for the newcomer, but cannot prevent him succeeding if he has the determination and resources to do so. Secondly, and in my opinion most importantly, if the service given by estate agents to the public is to be greatly improved, strong local groupings of agents are likely to prove vital — a few have already set about trying to make improvements based on a very high degree of co-operation.

Codes of Practice

No study of the control of estate agency would be complete without reference to the Codes of Practice, or conduct, prescribed by the leading professional bodies. I am in some difficulty here, for these are constantly under review and as I write, that of the I.S.V.A. is being considered by the Office of Fair Trading. The question it will endeavour to answer is whether or not it imposes restraint on free and fair competition, and there would appear to be fear in the professional bodies that their rules with regard to the attracting of business will be found unacceptable. Again we hear the question being asked: "Is estate agency a professional or purely commercial operation?" The question the professional bodies must, in the end, answer is whether their codes of conduct are intended to protect themselves from what they believe to be unfair competition or to protect the public, and if so from what?

We look briefly at the areas in which the professional bodies currently seek disciplinary control.

As the Price Commission found: "There is a clear distinction between the rules of the I.S.V.A. and the R.I.C.S. on the one hand and those of other representative bodies.

"The rules of the I.S.V.A. and the R.I.C.S. are effectively in two groups. Those that are intended to protect the consumer and those that seek to limit or control competition as between agents. The former tend to be positive in nature, designed to 'protect and promote the interests of clients'."

Examples include "a duty not to act for two parties to a transaction without their consent; the avoidance of conflict between commercial interests and the duty to the client; the confirmation in writing of terms of remuneration; a duty to disclose a personal interest to a client; and various rules concerning financial probity in dealing with the client." In these areas the rules of the N.A.E.A. appear to be similar in effect.

It is in the other group of rules that the conflict between the professional and commercial approaches to estate agency becomes apparent. The Price Commission said "In our view they tend to inhibit established agents from competing openly and aggressively with each other, and to restrict experiments in selling methods".

One asks if aggressive competition is likely to be in the public interest and it is a leading question, for if it is, then the rules of conduct in this group could be seen as protecting only the agents themselves. This is the question that the Office of Fair Trading has to answer in the context of the I.S.V.A's rules. The R.I.C.S. cannot be indifferent to that answer.

What areas then are covered by these rules? First, advertising: both the I.S.V.A. and the R.I.C.S. seek to ban advertisements concerning the achievements and successes of a firm, they seek to control the degree to which members mix advertisements with those of commerce or manufacturers. The most sensitive area is that of soliciting instructions and supplanting an agent already instructed. Both bodies seek to prohibit the soliciting of instructions, although some exceptions are made when this is done by letter and with a "saving clause" intended to prevent supplanting. Both forbid soliciting by personal call or telephone, and, as we shall later see, prohibit a practice that is not only acceptable in North America but positively encouraged. Both forbid the giving of inducements to a third party to secure instructions (bribes to the milkman are out!). Both again bar any attempt to secure instructions if another agent has already been appointed or if with reasonable care such an appointment could have been ascertained.

In these matters the N.A.E.A. adopts a different aproach. It seeks to prevent oppressive or aggressive methods but sees nothing basically wrong in going out to secure business.

The R.I.C.S. sees these rules as vital to its professionalism — but are they? It has applied to the Restrictive Practices Court on the grounds that it is exempt from registration, but what will its attitude be if that Court finds the I.S.V.A's rules in this context contrary to the public interest?

As I argue elsewhere, I believe this professional approach of the two leading bodies to be the right one and in the public interest, but their rules can only be acceptable for so long as they can be seen to protect that interest and not just that of their members.

Control of Estate Agents by Legislation

It is surprising that only in 1979 was legislation introduced that would enable any sort of control to be imposed on the practice of estate agency in Britain, for pressure to bring in some form of control had existed more or less continuously for some 90 years.

In 1888 a Colonel Duncan introduced a Bill to register architects, engineers and surveyors, but strong opposition forced the withdrawal of the Bill. The first attempt to provide for the statutory registration specifically of estate agents was not made until 1914, when Mr. Boyton introduced his Auctioneers and Estate Agents Bill. This was promoted and drafted by the Auctioneers' and Estate Agents' Institute and it aimed to make it a criminal offence for any unregistered person to practise as a valuer or auctioneer or to undertake any other function that the Act deemed as having to be exercised by a registered person. It visualised a registration board·of six members of the Auctioneers' and Estate Agents' Institute and six from the Surveyors' Institution, now the Royal Institution. Three further members were to be appointed by the President of the Board of Trade. This Bill failed to attract sufficient support and the matter lapsed.

Nine years later what became known as the Clarke Bill, formally the Landed Property Practitioners (Registration) Bill, was introduced by Sir Edgar Chalfield-Clarke. It was promoted again by the surveyors and auctioneers but this time with the support of the Land Agents' Society. It was very similar to its predecessor. It visualised a register administered by the Landed Property Practitioners' Registration Board, consisting of five members from each of the three promoting societies and five to be nominated by Government. Had the Act succeeded it would have become a criminal offence for anyone not registered to use the designation land agent, estate agent, surveyor, quantity surveyor, valuer, house agent or auctioneer. This Bill met considerable opposition, not only from agents unattached to any one of the three societies, but from lawyers. It lapsed due to lack of time and was never re-introduced. It may well, however, have acted as the spur that led the then unattached agents to form the Incorporated Society of Auctioneers and Landed Property Agents, later, as we have seen, to merge with the Valuers' Institution and become the Incorporated Society of Valuers and Auctioneers.

In 1928 a Bill was introduced by a Mr. Morley to set up a register of agents, but this met opposition from the three major societies and was defeated.

In 1934 the three societies issued a joint statement to the effect that they were opposed to statutory registration of estate agents on the grounds that it would not only be unworkable, but would not be of benefit to the public. The Incorporated Society in the same year made representations to the Home Office that led to the setting up of a select committee under the chairmanship of Lord Mersey to enquire into and advise as to whether or not changes in the law were needed to give the public greater safeguards against malpractice.

The Committee recommended setting up a central register, that would be open to public inspection; persons could be struck off and unsuitable persons refused registration. Registration was to be mandatory for those who wished to practise. A Bill based on the Committee's Report was introduced in 1936 by Sir Reginald Clarry, but it went further than just seeking to establish a register. It would have provided a guarantee fund and established a board of education for the profession. It did not receive sufficient support, and failed.

In 1945 both the Chartered Surveyors' Institution and the Auctioneers' and Estate Agents' Institute issued a statement in support of statutory registration.

Another seven years passed before Sir Henry Legge-Bourke introduced yet another Estate Agents Bill. This provided for the setting up of an estate agents' council that was to be responsible for ensuring a reasonable standard of competence. It would have laid down a code of conduct and maintained a register of practising estate agents. It called for clients' moneys to be kept in separate accounts and had it come into being the council would have set up a compensation fund to protect the public against the dishonesty of any registered person or his employee. Although supported by the House when introduced, this support was not sufficient to see it through its second reading.

Yet another attempt was made in November, 1965, when Mr. Jones introduced a Bill, this time with the support of the ten societies then recognised as being involved in estate agency. The ingredients were essentially the same and it also received the support of the House. It was, however, lost when Mr. Harold Wilson's Government resigned, and it was not re-introduced.

It was following this set-back that the professional societies attempted to resolve matters on a voluntary basis and the Estate Agents Registration Council was established and formally incorporated on 1st October, 1967. Again it was formed of representatives of the societies and nominees of the President of the Board of Trade. It also failed, although views as to why differ. Some appeared to believe that it was because many practitioners failed to register. Others believed that it failed because of differing views as to the code of conduct that should be adopted, again high-lighting the question as to whether estate agency is a professional or commercial occupation, with the Government's representatives tending to support the latter view. The leading professional bodies, not unnaturally, lost enthusiasm for a voluntary body that would not uphold their own codes of conduct nor insist on a reasonable standard of competence. It was felt by many that registration would give a cloak of respectability to many who did not deserve it, do nothing to protect the professional ethic and achieve little in the public interest that could not be achieved in other ways. (For example, the joint Indemnity Scheme run by the Royal Institution of Chartered Surveyors and the Incorporated Society of Valuers and Auctioneers to protect deposits held by members.)

The Government, however, remained interested and in 1975 the Department of Prices and Consumer Protection published a consultative document on the Regulation of Estate Agency, and later in

1977 the Government published its own proposals. In the event the Government did not introduce the Bill, but left it to Mr. Brian Davies to introduce it as a Private Member's Bill. This time it did receive a second reading and reached the Statute Book.

The Estate Agents Act 1979

The Act at least gives the prospect of some degree of control but is negative rather than positive and has been described as "negative licensing". It is the fourth level of control.

It is too early yet to know what controls envisaged by this Act the Secretary of State will seek to establish and I think it sufficient for us to look briefly at the machinery it provides and the nature of the controls that could be expected to follow.

First the Act relates only to those acting as an intermediary ("an agent") in the sale or acquisition of land and the definition of estate agency work is a wide one. It is not limited to residential work but covers all main sectors of estate agency work. One must assume it covers the work of the estate agent when he is acting as an auctioneer in seeking to sell real estate. It does not apply to the other functions of the general practitioner, such as management, valuing or surveying. As one might expect, it does not apply to solicitors acting as estate agents in the course of their practice.

Generally the Act permits anyone to practise; you do not have to register, you do not need a licence, you do not have to belong to one of the professional bodies and you do not have to pass a written examination. Although the Act gives the Secretary of State power to stipulate minimum standards of competence, any regulations made in this context *must* "prescribe a degree of practical experience which is to be taken as evidence of competence".

Once controls have been established by the Secretary of State, responsibility for operating them will lie with the Director-General of Fair Trading, who will have the power to make an order debarring an offender from practising if he considers him to be an unfit person.

The Act makes it a criminal offence for a person to practise as an estate agent if:

(a) The Director-General has made an order forbidding him to do so;

(b) if and when regulations are made under the Act as to minimum required standards of competence, he does not meet the standards demanded; and

(c) if he is adjudged bankrupt, although in such circumstances the individual may not be barred from working for an estate agent as an employee.

Certain requirements are imposed on an estate agent:

> He must keep clients' money in a Client Account, failure to do so being a criminal offence.
>
> He must inform clients as to his charges and the circumstances in which they will become payable and he must declare the nature and extent of any personal interest, whether as vendor or purchaser of any property. In this context personal interest would include the interest of a relative, an associate or any of that agent's staff.

The Act goes on to stipulate certain things an agent cannot do. He must not engage in any practice the Secretary of State has by order declared as undesirable.

An agent practising in England, Wales or Northern Ireland will not be able to accept any deposit unless he is covered by an insurance bond; if he practises in Scotland he will not be able to accept a pre-contract deposit in any circumstances. He will not be able to describe himself as an estate agent unless he displays whatever notices are prescribed in respect of indemnity insurance.

The ultimate sanction is a decision by the Director-General that an agent is unfit to practise. The circumstances under which he is empowered to consider an estate agent's fitness are, however, closely defined. He can only do so if: an agent has been convicted of an offence involving fraud, dishonesty or violence, and the conviction has not become spent under the Rehabilitation of Offenders Act — or has been convicted of an offence under the Act itself or breached any order made in pursuance of it.

The Secretary of State may by order specify any other offence, that need not be related to estate agency, as one which the Director-General could use as a "trigger" to instigate an enquiry into fitness. The fitness of an agent to practise could also be considered if he has committed racial or sex discrimination in the course of estate agency work or if he has infringed a specified provision of the Act which does not involve a criminal offence.

None of these circumstances are to be taken as proof of the estate agent's unfitness but simply as "triggers" any one of which could cause the Director-General to set up an inquiry into that agent's fitness to practise.

As in so many other matters an employer will be responsible for his employees' actions, and partners for each other's, although there would appear likely to be some latitude. It is clearly going to be important for employers to keep their staff fully informed as to provisions of the Act and orders made under it and to ensure that they are strictly followed.

We consider briefly the powers of the Director-General when he has concluded that an agent has acted in a way that renders him unfit to practise. He can issue a warning: "Do it again and I shall know you are unfit". His power to issue such a warning does, however, appear limited to minor breaches. In more serious circumstances this "light" option will not be available to him; he will either have to ignore the event or make a banning order. The nature of such an order can vary. At its most drastic it could prohibit an estate agent from doing any estate agency work at all, but it could be limited to one type of estate agency work — for example, it could prohibit that agent from accepting clients' money and it could be limited to a particular area. Thus if a branch office practised racial discrimination it does not follow that the Director need find the whole firm unfit.

I think it unnecessary to consider in any detail investigation by the Director when he has decided to enquire into a person's ·fitness, the proceedings that would follow and the appeal procedures. It is sufficient to point out that the Director is not confined to the "trigger" event or events, or to that person's involvement only in estate agency work. A person could be found unfit to practise estate agency because of "his conduct of business activities in a very different field".

If the Director-General wishes to make a prohibition order he must give the agent concerned twenty-one days' notice, giving his reason or reasons for doing so. The agent may make written representations in his defence, or request an oral hearing. Once an order has been made and comes into operation it is a criminal offence not to comply with it. There is a right of appeal to the Secretary of State and a further right of appeal, but only on a point of law, to the Court. The professional bodies exerted strong pressure for an automatic right of appeal to the Court, stressing the drastic nature of the punishment — the barring of a man from his means of livelihood — but they were not successful.

It remains to be seen how successive governments will use the powers given to them. They could be used positively by, for example, demanding a high level of competence but this would appear unlikely with a degree of practical experience being the minimum requisite. The totally inexperienced are likely to be barred, but apart from this the present state of affairs seems likely to continue. Could a government use its powers to attempt to deal with matters like gazumping, or could it seek to control the terms on which agents are employed? Ignorance of the way the market operates and of the agent's role has been a feature of government involvement up to now. The findings of the Price Commission were fair and one can only hope that they will be borne in mind. The powers of the Secretary of State are great, as is the power of the media to distort and sensationalise.

I described the Act as negative and I think rightly, for although it gives power to control, for example, accounting for clients' moneys and entry of the inexperienced, it gives little power to improve the present state of affairs. I do, however, advise principals or anyone contemplating setting up an estate agency practice to read: "The Estate Agents Act, 1979", by J.R. Murdoch.

Consumer Protection Legislation

It is perhaps appropriate to consider this subject when considering the control of estate agency in Britain. We are concerned about misrepresentation, misdescription, the negative control that exists with regard to estate agents' charges, and with the control of those involved in consumer credit. We shall be considering misdescription in particular more closely when we look at the preparation of property particulars and as to how this affects the estate agent who is selling as an auctioneer.

There is no doubt that we live and practise at a time when the need to protect the consumer is seen as a matter of paramount importance in the conduct of our businesses. The writing of this book has compelled me to read much that I would not under other circumstances have bothered to read and one wonders whether in fact anything has really been achieved by recent legislation in this field. The law, although there are always grey areas, appears to me to have been fairly clearly established prior to the Misrepresentation Act of 1967, and this Act and subsequent legislation may in my view prove counter-productive, in that all involved with "consumers" will become reticent and ultra-cautious and as a result under-estimate or under-play aspects of the commodity with which they are dealing, to the possible detriment of the consumer.

It would appear that in our society the consumer is anyone who buys anything from anybody, and that the vendor can never be right. The estate agent or auctioneer is torn two ways, for in that he is selling his services to the vendor, the vendor becomes the consumer and is entitled to expect the services he is purchasing to be performed in the best possible way. In that the service he is purchasing is the marketing of his interest in the property he has a right to expect it to be presented in the best possible light. On the other hand the agent he instructs to act for him becomes the agent of a "seller" and any prospective purchaser then becomes the consumer. Great care is needed if the right balance, in these conflicting circumstances, is to be struck.

We come first to consider the Misrepresentation Act 1967. It does not in fact define misrepresentation, but in another context we can take it as "a false statement of fact made by the vendor to the purchaser which induces the purchaser to enter into a contract of sale". It is important to note what can amount to a misrepresentation.

    (a) Half-truths or ambiguous statements can amount to misrepresentations.

(b) Statements which become false, although true when made, can amount to misrepresentations.

(c) It is possible to make misrepresentations by conduct.

(d) Mere silence cannot amount to a misrepresentation unless there is a duty in law to make particular disclosures.

(e) Only mis-statements of fact are capable of being misrepresentations. Mere opinions or "puffs" in advertisements cannot amount to misrepresentations.

(f) Only misrepresentations which are material are actionable, i.e., those which induce a sale, although the mis-statement relied upon by the purchaser need not have been the only reason for entering into the sale.

(g) Only mis-statements relied upon are actionable, e.g., if a purchaser relied upon his own independent structural survey he cannot then be said to rely upon anything said by the agent as to the property's structural condition.

It will, however, be no answer for the vendor or his agent to say that the purchaser had every opportunity of checking whether the statements were true or not, if in fact he did not do so.

We shall be considering the relationship between principal and agent, but we should note here the fact that an agent could render his principal liable by any misrepresentation he, the agent, made on the principal's behalf, although the agent may well become liable to the principal if the misrepresentation he made was made negligently.

An innocent misrepresentation, i.e., one made by a person who did not know it to be false, or who may have believed it to be true, could render a contract capable of rescission. This would apply even if the mis-statement had been incorporated into the contract itself, or if the sale had been completed, provided in this case that the purchaser would otherwise have been entitled to rescind the contract. The Act also provided for the award of damages for "negligent mis-statements", by which it meant statements made by a person who did not have reasonable grounds to believe them or who did not believe them to be true.

The Court may also award damages for an innocent misrepresentation in lieu of rescission where it would be "equitable" to do so having regard to the nature of the misrepresentation and its financial consequences, and further the Courts may restrict the right to rely on exclusion clauses in a contract that seek to limit responsibility for misrepresentation, except in so far as the Court thinks it is "fair and reasonable in the circumstances to do so".

The significance to the vendor and his agent is that any exclusion clause or caveat will not necessarily protect them; it will be subject, if challenged, to the test of reasonableness.

We must distinguish between this situation and that dealt with in the famous case of *Hedley Byrne and Co. Ltd,* v. *Heller and Partners Ltd* 1964. This dealt with the right to claim damages for false statements made in a situation where a duty of care exists. This duty arises "in all relationships where it is plain that the party seeking information or advice was trusting the other to exercise such a degree of care as the circumstances required, where it was reasonable for him to do that, and where the other gave the information or advice when he knew, or ought to have known, that the enquirer was relying on him."

In that the estate agent is seldom if ever likely to be a party to a contract of sale between the parties whom he has introduced, he cannot be liable to a third party, i.e., the purchaser, unless he owes that purchaser a duty arising independently from the contract. In the case of misrepresentation by the agent the purchaser's remedy will be first to sue the principal, to whom in turn the agent might be liable. But as Murdoch, in "The Law of Estate Agency and Auctions", says — "There are certain situations in which an estate agent employed by a vendor undertakes personal responsibility to the purchaser."

It would appear clear that the relationship between an estate agent and a prospective purchaser does fall within the principle of this case and it follows that any action taken by a purchaser against an estate agent who is the employee of the vendor, must lie in tort (negligence). In short, if an agent, although he be employed by his principal, gave advice or information to the purchaser knowing that that purchaser was going to rely on that advice, he would be liable to that purchaser if the advice proved negligent.

Liability might be avoided by a clear and expressed disclaimer to the effect that the information was given "without responsibility", but since the Unfair Contract Terms Act 1977 the position is unclear.

The *Hedley Byrne* case has wide implications for the estate agent, surveyor and valuer, for in the course of his work he frequently is called upon to give information or advice on which others are going to rely, often without realising that if the information or advice he gives is wrong he could be liable for negligence under the principle which the case established.

The Trade Descriptions Act 1968

The relevance of this piece of legislation to the estate agent dealing in land is perhaps not very clear. It originally applied to the sale of goods, but was extended to cover services, accommodation and facilities; it would not appear to apply to sales of land. Under its provisions any misdescription could be the subject of a criminal action if false statements alleged were made knowingly or recklessly. It would appear to be a defence to any such charge that the offence was due to a mistake or to reliance on information supplied, to the act or default of another person, to an accident, or to another cause beyond the agent's control, or that all reasonable precautions had been taken and all due care exercised to avoid the offence.

There is little more that need be said here, other than to stress the importance of what is said later as to accuracy in description and the need for great care in establishing, in so far as it is possible, the facts.

The Restrictions on Agreements (Estate Agents) Order 1970

This Order was the result of the Reference to the Monopolies Commission on estate agents' charges in the late 1960s. The Order did not apply to Northern Ireland, but elsewhere in Great Britain it abolished fixed scales of charging for the acquisition, disposal or letting of unfurnished dwellings. It must be stressed that it in no way affected scale charges in so far as they related to other forms of estate agency. It renders it an offence for any two or more agents to get together to agree a set or fixed scale of charges. It is an Order that has, as we have seen in looking at the development of estate agency, been of very little benefit to the public it was meant to protect, but it could be of great significance, for irrespective of what professional bodies an agent may belong to it enables him to seek business by undercutting the general level of charges in his area. There can be little doubt that some firms have become established by doing just this, even if they subsequently charged levels comparable with their competitors.

The Consumer Credit Act 1974

This again can be dealt with very briefly. It is aimed largely at hire purchase and various credit and hire agreements in relation to goods, but the Office of Fair Trading did publish a guidance note "Guidance Notes for Chartered Surveyors, Valuers, Chartered Auctioneers, Estate Agents, Mortgage Brokers and Insurance Brokers in Relation to the Consumer Credit Act 1974".

It dealt with six areas — Consumer Credit Business, Consumer Hire Business, Credit Brokerage, Debt Adjusting and Debt Counselling, Debt Collecting and Credit Reference Agency. For each field in which a firm or individual is involved a licence is required.

Credit Brokerage is the only case where an estate agent is specifically referred to in the examples given and clearly Mortgage Broking comes under this heading and a licence is required. Mortgage and Insurance Brokers are specifically referred to under Debt Adjusting and Debt Counselling, so a licence might also be required here. Strangely, property management or rent collection are not referred to under Debt Collecting, although one must question as to whether or not there is a point when the managing agent trying to collect arrears of rent or over-due service charges is in fact debt collecting as opposed to property managing. If in any doubt the practitioner should refer to the Office of Fair Trading.

Four

The Estate Agent, His Role and Public Image

Research by the Research Institute for Consumer Affairs — The Monopolies Commission — The Price Commission — Reports by "Which?" — Conclusions drawn, their relevance and effect — Insufficient appreciation of the agent's role in the market — A profession or commercial activity? — Ease of entry — Sole and multiple agency — Quality of service — Attitudes to commercialism — Principal criticisms — The need for improvement — Are there too many agents? — Methods of charging — The need to consider the future
The Price Commission Report of 1979 — Market Survey by the British Market Research Bureau — Its findings — Why vendors use agents — Relationships between vendor and agent — Conclusion — The need to explain the role of the profession

In describing early estate agency, Mr D. H. Chapman comments: "Not all its practitioners gloried in the name, witness Swithin ('Four in Hand') Forsyte [of 'The Forsyte Saga'] who was founded less on fiction than on the author's uncle. Here he is as we first meet him in 1886, aged 75, at the gathering of a family which opportunities seized had translated from yeoman beginnings to upper middle class prosperity:

'Over against the piano a man of bulk and stature was wearing two waistcoats on his wide chest, two waistcoats and a ruby pin ... and his shaven square old face the colour of pale leather, with pale eyes, had its most dignified look, above his satin stock.'

"In sum, the very pattern from which were stamped all who lived the right way, did the right thing, and echoed the opinion of other right people. And to achieve those ends, says John Galsworthy, 'He had made his own way and his own fortune'. His own way lay in the direction of estate agency ... 'Since his retirement from house agency, a profession deplorable in his estimation, especially as to its auctioneering department, he had abandoned himself to naturally aristocratic tastes'."

Perhaps today's estate agent has Galsworthy and his "Uncle Swithin" to blame for his dubious public image and not just the Consumers' Association. Perhaps they are to blame also for the fact that "estate agency" is today interpreted by the majority to mean simply "house agency".

There is little doubt that the estate agent's public image is a poor one. He is not alone in this, for was it not the great Dr. Johnson who said he did not care to speak ill of any man, but he believed that the gentleman who had just left the room was an attorney?

I think it beholden on everyone practising estate agency, on those, who while considering themselves to be practising on a higher plane, are nevertheless responsible for the conduct of estate agency practices, and above all on the students, to study the criticisms that have been made, to evaluate them and to endeavour to improve both the profession's approach to its task in this field and its methods.

Agents practising in the commercial field were in some vague way associated with what many saw as the grossly immoral boom of the early 'seventies, but in the main it is agency in the residential market that is "news" to the media and which has brought the criticism. This chapter is therefore directed to this market, but its subject matter may be, perhaps to a lesser extent, relevant in other markets and should not be lightly ignored.

If criticisms have been justified, there must be room for improvement. Recognition of faults is an essential step towards finding remedies.

I have not endeavoured to monitor or research general criticism made in the media, but have relied upon "Which?", the Consumers' Association's publication; on "Estate Agents, a Consumers' Assessment", published by the Research Institute for Consumer Affairs in 1963; on "A report on the supply of certain services by Estate Agents" prepared by the Monopolies Commission and printed by order of the House of Commons on the 20th February, 1969, and lastly on the Price Commission's Report, "Charges, Costs and Margins of Estate Agents" 1979 (Cmd. 7647). I also quote from Professor John Greve's Report referred to earlier.

Historically the Research Institute for Consumer Affairs publication came first. In the first two lines it acknowledged the very narrow view of the subject it was to take: "The estate agent is the man to go to for help with buying and selling houses. When consumers talk about estate agents that is what they have in mind". As a broad generalisation this may be fair, but it does not define a "consumer" nor the type of help he or she might be seeking. It, like the other publications issued by the Consumers' Association, sees buying and selling a house as "not a professional function" — "It is commercial". It seeks to separate the role of the general practitioner in this field away from any other skills he may possess. It is clear, the pamphlet says, "that a professional estate agent is likely to be qualified in many skills which do not directly concern the ordinary consumer". It lists some of them when it says he may be trained to advise on questions of rent ... repair ... valuation of property for sale, for probate, estate duty (Capital Transfer Tax) ... to conduct sales by auction or private treaty.

Who is the ordinary consumer? The house he (or she) is selling, or buying, may be let in whole or in part — he may want advice on rent. An owner's house may be in a bad state of repair and he may, and in practice often does, want advice as to what repairs if any he should carry out before offering it for sale and as to the likely cost of such repairs. A purchaser may wish to buy a house clearly in need of repair — is he "extraordinary" if he expects the estate agent he is dealing with to be able to advise him with reasonable accuracy as to the possible costs, or as to what work might be essential? The position of the agent acting for his vendor-client, but confronted with a purchaser wanting help is a matter we shall be considering.

Returning to the pamphlet, incredibly and significantly, in the same sentence we see that the undertaking of valuations of property for sale and conducting sales by auction are listed amongst those skills that are not the direct concern of the "consumer".

The very next paragraph of the pamphlet also makes one or two significant comments. The first could be seen as a direct contradiction of the earlier comment, for it acknowledges that the general practitioner may have specialist knowledge on which the ordinary consumer can draw — "surveying and again the valuing of property". It then makes the assumption that the "main" function of the general practitioner is the bringing together of vendors and prospective purchasers, lessors and prospective tenants and negotiating between parties. What is meant by "main"? Is it to mean that the majority of the practitioner's time is spent on this one function, or that the larger part of his income comes from it? It could also mean that they saw this as the most important of his functions as far as the public is concerned. It is another sweeping generalisation made irresponsibly and without foundation, for at that time no survey of the property profession was available to them.

I place great significance on these two paragraphs of the pamphlet. In my opinion they contain statements that not only go to the very root of the estate agent's role, but do so incorrectly, and draw assumptions that are contrary to the public interest and injurious to the profession. In two ways they show, whatever they may say later, that the estate agent's role was not understood.

"The bringing together of vendor and purchaser ... and negotiating between the parties" implies that the agent acts solely as a broker with no specific responsibility to either party. If this is his role, then his first aim must be to "pull off" the deal. I would not deny that some agents might take this short-sighted view, more often than not to their long-term disadvantage. It does, however, ignore what is a matter not only of fact, but of law, that an agent once instructed by a vendor owes a duty to that vendor and must thereafter act only in that "client's" best interest and, as we shall later see, use due care and diligence in doing so.

The Research Institute would, no doubt, argue that I have wrongly interpreted them, but this would not appear to be likely or even possible, for to separate, as they do, valuation for sale and the conduct of auction sales from the selling function itself as skills that do not directly concern the ordinary consumer can only be explained if one does see the agent simply as a "broker" or even "trader" in the market place. They acknowledge the specialist skills the general practitioner *may* have on which the ordinary consumer *can* draw, but by implication these skills are not seen as being necessary for the proper conduct of estate agency. It is on these vague and contradictory statements that they relied to draw the conclusion that the estate agent's role was not a professional one but a commercial one. Professor John Greve, who was consulted by the Institute, was himself later to disagree with this and drew the conclusion which I quoted in my opening chapter: "Estate agency is not simply a commercial activity, as one side claims, neither is it a non-commercial profession. It is a combination of the two and the elements of both salesmanship and professionalism should be combined systematically to the greater advantage of the consumer".

The confusion undoubtedly stemmed from the fact that the person who purchases, as opposed to sells, is regarded as the consumer. It cannot be too strongly stressed that it is the vendor who purchases the service of the estate agent and who, in the estate agency context, is the consumer.

It is impossible to say just what effect, if any, this erroneous conclusion drawn by the Research Institute was to have in the years that followed. It was doggedly followed by the Consumers' Association; the Monopolies Commission were directed to conduct their exhaustive survey only into the selling and letting of unfurnished dwelling-houses; and other bodies, notably the ill-fated computer-based National Property Register, failed to appreciate the degree of professionalism involved and indeed expected of the average estate agent.

The Secretary of State's direction to the Price Commission in 1978 again showed the narrowness of the assumed public concern. He directed them to report on — "Charges, costs and margins of estate agents with particular regard to charges, costs and margins in relation to sales and purchases of domestic property, and in this direction 'estate agent' means any person the nature of whose business includes this service of bringing together sellers and buyers of domestic property other than as a preliminary to some further service, and the 'sale and purchase of domestic property' means the transfer for a capital sum of property suitable for occupation by the purchaser as a dwelling."

In "Which?" published by the Consumers' Association in May, 1967, an article appeared under the heading, "Estate Agents". This followed the Government's instructions to the Monopolies Commission to investigate estate agents' charges — first to establish whether or not a large proportion of estate agents charged identical fees and, dependent upon this, whether or not a monopoly could be said to exist, and if so was it in the public interest? This is not an issue we need consider in any depth; a monopoly was held to exist. One or two matters raised in this issue of "Which?" do, however, need to be referred to, for they are relevant in any consideration of the estate agent's role and public image. First the object of the report, or article, for that is what it amounted to, must be challenged.

The first survey by the Research Institute for Consumer Affairs that led to the assessment already commented on was based on a sample of only 141 Consumer Association members. At that time they acknowledged the sample to be too small and tried to pre-empt criticism that their members, being clearly consumer-conscious, were not likely to be representative. They also referred to the further survey to be carried out, using a much wider sample. This survey was carried out by the R.I.C.A. using as their sample 781 house-buyers in South London, Bristol and Tyneside, who were questioned in detail about their experiences. This survey was never published, although "Which?" vaguely stated that it backed up the findings of the first one. There had to be a reason for the failure to publish and that reason appears obvious. Its findings did not support the emotive view they had already taken and its publication would have caused them embarrassment.

This unpublished report also contained findings that showed up the standard of service given by estate agents in a far better light than anticipated and it did not suit the Association. Despite John Greve's conclusion as to the unique role carried out by the estate agent, the Association's 1967 Report stated that "we think that as far as the buying and selling of houses is concerned estate agency is *not* a professional occupation". Two conclusions they had reached earlier, first that estate agents provided a rather inadequate service to people buying and selling houses, and secondly that estate agency did not seem a very efficient method of bringing buyers and sellers together, looked highly suspect.

The survey report says:

"Replies were classified on a scale which ranged from 'very good indeed' to 'very unsatisfactory'. Four-fifths of those who had been to agents had placed their agents in one of the two categories of approval and one-fifth thought the agents they dealt with were very good indeed." "Most vendors were satisfied with their agents. As a group they were rather more satisfied than the buyers, that is the applicants, but 88 per cent of these placed the agents they had dealt with in one or other of the two highest categories for quality of service — these being 'very good indeed' or 'reasonably competent'."

Dealing with the question of speed, "It was worth noting that only two buyers, (a very small fraction of 1 per cent) out of hundreds, thought that agents slowed down transactions.

"The degree of satisfaction with agents was both striking and encouraging. When compared with solicitors it can be seen that *they* still have some way to go."

One cannot fail to draw the conclusion that the Consumers' Association had already made up its mind, as it had on the monopoly issue, and did not intend to have it altered even by the result of a survey based on 781 members of its own Association. At best such a decision was irresponsible, at worst it was morally and socially bad.

Notwithstanding this, other matters were raised in the 1967 article which should cause the estate agent concern.

"A lot of house buyers don't realise that the estate agent is acting for the seller and treat the agent as a source of disinterested advice on all sorts of subjects ... It may be that they often get good advice, but the ice is obviously thin and the situation unsatisfactory."

Few would disagree with this statement. The majority of the general public do, I believe, see the agent as an impartial broker. Too often one hears a would-be purchaser say when submitting an offer of say £20,000 that he would go to £22,000 if he had to, in doing so putting the (vendor's) agent in a position of having to extract the higher figure if he is to do his duty by his client.

The Association suggests that "The commercial nature of the estate agent should be emphasised and attempts to professionalise them and limit competition will only confuse people all the more about what an estate agent really is — the agent of the seller (vendor) ..."

"The buyer will be better off if he understands clearly that the estate agent is *not* a disinterested professional adviser, but acting in the interests of the seller". The assumption that many buyers see the agent as a "professional adviser" may have been a slip of the pen but is worthy of note.

There is clearly a problem to be dealt with. Beyond doubt it is to his client, the vendor, that the agent has a duty to provide a service, but to do so it follows that he must also give an efficient service, albeit of a different nature, to all prospective purchasers with whom he has contact. It is difficult to see how increased emphasis on the commercial nature of the estate agent could possibly help. Is it not much more likely to strengthen the view that the agent is a disinterested broker? The opposite view could just as strongly be argued, for an increase in professionalism could lessen misunderstanding. At least the majority of the public who become involved in the property market would be aware that a professional man is one who normally acts for "a client", and that it is the client who pays him.

The report also refers "to limiting competition, now that scale fees as we knew them have been scrapped". "Limiting competition" can only refer to the limitations imposed by the various codes of conduct or to entry limited by examination or minimum standards of competence. The Association is unlikely to have been aware of the role played by local associations of estate agents and of the various ways in which they seek to limit competition.

The codes of practice of the leading professional bodies have been eased, particularly as far as advertising is concerned, but any relaxation that could leave the door open to harassing methods of obtaining instructions to sell or to agents obtaining signed contracts without the approval of solicitors and so on would be unacceptable.

The Monopolies Commission were later to attempt to prevent any restriction on entry and indeed relied on the "ease of entry" as a restraint against the general level of fees (or commissions) rising above the then levels. It is, however, difficult to see how ease of entry could in any way make the relationship between agent, vendor and prospective purchaser more widely understood. The new entrant, who need have no previous practical experience, who has to satisfy no one as to his competence and who need have no knowledge of the law of agency, may well not himself understand the true relationship that will exist between him, his vendors and would-be purchasers.

Responsibility for making the relationship clear to all concerned must rest in part with the professional bodies and local associations. They could certainly make more effective use of the media to get the message across. The task must in my view fall in the main directly on the estate agents themselves who, by better staff training, could ensure that any prospective purchaser calling on them had the agent's role explained to them. Similarly simple explanatory leaflets sent with all replies to written enquiries would help.

The second matter raised by this article also concerns purchasers rather than vendors. It questions whether in fact they are given an adequate service. The relevant paragraph I will quote in full, for it touches on yet another aspect of service to purchasers:

> "One difficulty is that there are such an enormous number of agents, most of them small local firms operating independently. So if one wants a comprehensive list of houses for sale in one

particular district, one has to go and see all the local agents — often
up to thirty, and conceivably up to a hundred. For most people
this just isn't practicable. Moreover, house buyers in the two
R.I.C.A. surveys [again one deplores the fact that the wider based
of these was not published] were none too impressed by the service
of the agents they did visit; they were often sent descriptions of
houses which did not at all correspond with what they asked for, or
which did not match the house."

The fact that a would-be purchaser has "to go the rounds" to get a
comprehensive list of properties that might suit him cannot be
disputed. It is a very serious weakness in the service that estate agents
collectively give. To the best of my knowledge only in two very
confined districts in the country has any real attempt been made to
overcome it. It is, in my opinion, capable of being overcome and will be
considered in depth later.

That many do receive descriptions (particulars) of houses which do
not correspond with the stated requirements is also undoubtedly true. It
is a less serious fault in the service and one more easily explained, and
perhaps easily forgiven, except when it results from sheer inefficiency.
It is, however, a more difficult fault to remedy, if indeed a remedy is
needed.

Particulars that do not, in the view of the would-be purchaser, match
the house they purport to describe are a fact of life. The particulars are
written by the agent of the vendor and within the limits set by consumer
protection legislation they are unlikely to describe the house in a way
that would be unacceptable to that vendor. It is likewise natural that a
would-be purchaser anxious to find a house that suits will, on receiving
particulars, read into what is not stated what he personally would like to
find.

In the conflict between professionalism and commercialism,
advertising and the circulation of particulars of houses, which must be
seen as a direct form of advertising, is one field in which the latter
prevails, for it is part of the marketing process that the agent is expected
to carry out for his client.

"Which?" returned to the subject of Estate Agency in November,
1969, when it reported on all aspects of "Buying and Selling a House".
This report, published after the Monopolies Commission Report, made
little reference to it, except to comment — "Some of the rules (of the
professional bodies) — and in particular those related to scale fees — are
in the agents' interests, but, according to the Monopolies Commission
Report on Estate Agents, operate against the public interest". In fact
the Commission dealt solely with the question of scale fees.

This latest report was based on a much more extensive survey than
either of the earlier reports. It used a sample of 8,000 members, again of

the Association, who moved house in 1967 and 1968. Despite the conclusions that it drew, it showed agents' services in a very much better light than perhaps was expected. Could it be that it confirmed the findings of the earlier unpublished report?

Having acknowledged that they had not been able to distinguish satisfactorily between the standard of service given by agents from each of the different societies, they did find that members got rather better service from agents recommended by friends than they had had, either after choosing an agent because of his advertisements, or when they appointed an agent because he had approached them. An indication perhaps that the standard of personal service given was more effective than pure commercialism.

The report then referred briefly to sole agency, multiple instructions and sole selling rights. This is a major subject, dealt with in another chapter. It is sufficient here to comment that a sole agent is the only agent instructed to sell; if he failed and the owner sold privately, he would have no claim to commission. Multiple instructions describes the practice of vendors instructing two or more agents to act independently, paying commission only to the one who succeeds. Sole selling rights are in most of Britain rarely given, although I believe not unknown in some districts. An agent with sole selling rights is entitled to commission whoever effects a sale if it takes place while his instructions are current. Multiple agency is a rare practice north of the line roughly drawn from the Wash to the Bristol Channel, but common practice south of this, although "mixed" agency would be a better description, for even in multiple areas, agents frequently are given sole agency instructions and the practice has been growing.

The subject is relevant in the context of this chapter for two reasons. First I believe that multiple agency instructions lead to confusion, encourage the much publicised problem of gazumping, and do much to harm the efficiency and public image of the estate agent. Secondly, an Association which one would expect to favour competition, almost regardless of cost, comes out clearly in favour of sole agency practice.

"By instructing one agent only you have a far higher chance of a quick sale — you make the situation worse for yourself the more agents you instruct". Again, "We recommend that you instruct one agent only, that you do *not* give him sole selling rights and that you limit his agency to two, or at the most, three months".

A general acceptance of this principle would not only increase the effectiveness of the agent's service, but do much to improve the operation of the market and, as a direct result, the public image of the agent, at present distorted by factors outside his direct control.

In acknowledging that one out of three of their members said that the agents had given them good service and the large majority had proved at least competent, the Association would appear to have accepted that their 1967 criticisms of inadequacy and apparent inefficiency were not justified. The overall picture, they now admitted, "is therefore quite good".

The agents were not, however, to be white-washed — there were complaints:

> * One in four said that agents had not made it clear in advance what their fees would be.
> * One in five found their agent's advice as to how much to ask for the house unsound — many suggesting an asking price below the amount eventually realised.
> * One in six were dissatisfied with viewing arrangements and that sometimes people were sent who were really looking for a completely different sort of house.
> * About one member in six felt that the agent was trying to persuade them to accept a quick sale at a much lower price than they expected.

The Association felt this last criticism to be perhaps the worst of them all and went on to suggest that the then "bottom heavy" scale of fees could be partly to blame, implying that the extra commission earned by the agent fighting for the best possible price was negligible. At that time the majority of agents were charging commission on a sliding scale, 5 per cent on the first £500, 2½ per cent on the next £4,500 and 1½ per cent on the residue being common in the south and south-east. The basis of charging now varies considerably between regions and between provincial and London practices, but there has been a move towards a uniform rate of commission.

Given that in some cases the agents were on their client's instructions asking more than advised and given that some may have been over-optimistic in their initial advice, one in six of a consumer-oriented sample is perhaps not significant. Nevertheless these criticisms have to be borne in mind in considering the practice of estate agency and ways in which improvements might be made.

Perhaps the most significant section of this report dealt with "Selling a house without an Agent". It has often been argued that there is no need to employ an agent, that they charge a ridiculously high fee for what they do and that there is little an agent can do that you cannot do for yourself. In this context the Association's findings were of considerable interest.

Of the 8,000 people in this survey, one in three *tried* to sell without an agent. Of these one in ten did not sell on the open market. Five out of ten did succeed in selling on the "open" market as a result of their own advertising. The other four resorted to an agent for help. If follows that only about 16 per cent of what is acknowledged as a consumer-conscious sample did in fact come on to the open market and sell without the use of an agent. What is not known is how many of those who did sell "privately" sought an agent's advice as to value and asking price or indeed as to what to accept either openly or covertly. It is not known how many may have sold privately after having sought an agent's advice and instructed him. A number, albeit small, are known to be prepared, by claiming a private sale, with the encouragement of the purchaser, to defraud the agent. The evidence shows that the percentage of houses sold with an agent playing no part whatsoever is very small. The Price Commission estimated that the estate agents as a whole have about 70 per cent of the market for housing transactions. Given that their evidence was obtained after a buoyant period in the market (early 1979) the agent's position under average conditions may be stronger and is certainly unlikely to be weaker.

"Which?" returned yet again to the subject in June, 1973, grouping agents with solicitors in "The Cost of Moving House". The object of this article was clearly to review the charges of both since the abolition of the agents' recommended scale of charges in 1971 and the solicitors' conveyancing scale in January, 1973. As to the agents, they concluded that "although the abolition of scales may have encouraged some estate agents to reduce fees, it also lets others increase them. There seems no pattern to the variation in charges — so you'll just have to be careful".

The fact that estate agents' charges had not dramatically fallen concerned them. It should have come as no surprise, for the Monopolies Commission had found no evidence that profit levels were in any way excessive. Despite the Association's more favourable report of four years earlier, their approach this time if anything became more critical.

"Ever since we started looking at estate agents, we have believed that their service is not necessarily the best way of bringing buyer and seller together. Nearly a quarter of the members we sampled were less than satisfied with the way their estate agents sold their houses". Surprising to me was the statement that the cost of selling privately "something under £20" in 1969 had dropped in four years to "less than £10".

The subject clearly fascinated them for they could not leave it alone. In June of 1975 came another report, (or would "article" be a more accurate description?): "Buying and Selling a House, 1975". The solicitors seemed to be its main target, but in looking at estate agents' fees it was stated that the situation had changed — "but for the worse", the proportion charging more than the old national scale having increased from 5 per cent to 18 per cent. Who, we might ask, was to blame for this? The Association had itself pre-empted the Monopolies Commission, concluding that a monopoly existed and advocating the removal of what were only recommended scales. When the Monopolies Commission Report was published the Government not surprisingly chose to ignore the minority report of the Hon. T. G. Roche, Q.C., and these scales were abolished. Faced with an economy in which operating costs rose faster than property values, agents were free to increase their commission rates in order to maintain profit levels. The belief that the abolition of scales would increase competition and efficiency proved initially to have been a fallacy, although it may have had a bearing on later developments. Had the old scales been maintained, it is most unlikely that the professional societies would have taken what would have been seen as a politically controversial step and increased them. It is equally unlikely that agents would have been allowed by those who instruct them, not only members of the public, but solicitors, bankers and accountants, to have charged in excess of them. The restraint that could have forced the adoption of more efficient methods and the weeding out of the least competent had been removed with the encouragement and approval of the critics themselves.

When considering the estate agent's role in the wider sense it should not be forgotten that he does not always act for the vendor or lessor. Very often he is acting for the purchaser or lessee to seek, advise and to acquire. This is indeed common in both the commercial and agricultural property markets, but it is certainly not unknown in the house market. An agent in his capacity as a surveyor and valuer might well be instructed to inspect a house on behalf of a prospective purchaser in order to advise as to structural condition, likely costs of repairs and as to value, and he might well then be asked to negotiate the purchase price on behalf of his "client". There can be no doubt that in carrying out this last task, he is acting as an agent for that prospective purchaser.

In the commercial market agents are retained by the Institutions, the multiple retailing companies and many other clients to look for premises on their behalf, to advise as to their suitability, on their structural state, as to value and to negotiate their purchase. Clearly, considerable knowledge of the market concerned and professional expertise are needed if these tasks are to be undertaken successfully.

The agent is therefore one who acts for a client and who looks to that client for remuneration at the end of the day. Seldom will he act between parties and if he does then only with their specific approval. He is not, or certainly should not be, a broker. There have been and no doubt still are some agents who as part of their day-to-day work acquire property either in their own name, or through nominees, for resale at a profit. If they do they are acting as dealers and not as agents. It must be stressed that most agents regard property dealing as conflicting with their proper role and deprecate it.

If one accepts that an agent should, or even that it is desirable that he should, bring to his task knowledge of such matters as building construction, town planning, compulsory purchase, rating, the Rent Acts and valuation, then one is acknowledging that both in his relationship with his client and in the knowledge that he should bring to that relationship he should be a professional man and not a businessman purely engaged in commerce.

We shall examine his role in more detail, but it is important at this stage to recognise also that there are many aspects of the agent's task that are commercial in nature, marketing of his client's property being the most obvious. Similarly, in a highly competitive field, the general practitioner, if he is to succeed, will need a degree of commercialism in the conduct of his own business and the marketing of the service he has to offer.

There are clear signs that many of the older-established firms are now adopting a much more commercial approach both in presenting their own firms to the public and in the conduct of their clients' affairs. This will continue, but certainly for the foreseeable future the nature of the firms, the individuals concerned and their training is such that the commercial role will remain secondary to the agent's prime function of giving his clients a service based on sound professional knowledge. There are firms who would not accept this view and it is perhaps doubtful if the National Association of Estate Agents would readily accept it as a premise, although they do not under-rate the need for experience and are clearly encouraging the acquiring of professional knowledge.

With no universally accepted code of conduct and no generally accepted scale of charges, it is inevitable that some firms have sought and continue to seek, to become established by a purely commercial approach. There is no doubt that some have succeeded and others will follow, but in general terms the position of the longer established general practitioners has not been seriously eroded, rather have the newcomers tended when established to adopt their attitudes.

Such evidence as there is clearly shows that the public image of the estate agent, if one defines the public as those who have used estate agents, is very much better than many, including the agents themselves, believe.

It is perhaps significant that notwithstanding the constant reference in the media to the unduly high level of the fees charged by agents who are selling (again limited only to the house market), the various surveys to which I have referred have produced little, if any, evidence to show that the public consider them to be unduly excessive, although the Price Commission did find that while most persons who had used estate agents were satisfied with the service they received they did not find it good value for money. Certainly neither the Monopolies nor Price Commissions found evidence of excessive profits being made.

It would, however, be foolish to consider that all is well. There are the 20-30 per cent of house-owners, for example, who set out to sell their own houses. Irrespective of whether or not they succeed, they must represent a criticism of estate agents and a belief either that there is nothing the agents could do for them that they could not do for themselves, or that the service they could expect was not worth what it would cost.

The fact that a would-be purchaser arriving in a town has to go the rounds of all the agents to compile a comprehensive list of houses that might be of interest to him is a serious criticism, for if the agents are not giving the best possible service to prospective purchasers, it follows that they must be failing to give it to their vendor clients. The most serious criticism of all is the quite obvious fact that the agent's role is not generally understood by the public, by those who have carried out the research and criticised as a result, or by the media. It is to these matters that we must direct our attention.

It was on the 1st September, 1966, that The Board of Trade made a reference to the Monopolies Commission for investigation and report on "The supply in England and Wales of the services provided by persons acting as estate agents in connection with the acquisition and disposal of unfurnished dwellings". They were instructed to limit consideration to conditions whereby two or more persons, supplying the service, charge fees or commissions at standard rates.

There followed the most thorough survey of the practice of estate agency in England and Wales yet carried out. During the course of their enquiry they took evidence from many sources. In that some of the witnesses' evidence was critical of the way estate agents operated, it is relevant in any consideration of the estate agents' role and their public image.

Not surprisingly, the Consumers' Association and the Consumer Council were amongst those who submitted evidence. This they did by way of a joint memorandum that was later to be supported by the National Federation of Consumer Groups.

What was surprising was that on this occasion their memorandum incorporated the findings of Professor John Greve, whose survey was acknowledged by the Commission to be "an unpublished survey of house purchase".

The very first sentence of the Commission's chapter summarising witnesses' criticisms stated that "some of the factors which contribute to the rigidity of the present system were the subject of complaints by a small number of agents." It is not the fact that some agents saw fit to make complaints to the Commission that is surprising, but the use of the word "rigidity". It is true that the Commission's initial survey showed sufficient agents charging at similar rates to bring their operation within the scope of the Monopolies and Mergers Acts of 1948 and 1965. This in itself was not sufficient to have justified the use of the word "rigidity" to describe the estate agents' methods of operating. In a field where entry can be made without qualifications or experience, where designations that would imply a degree of professional competence to the general public can be used without restriction, i.e. surveyor, auctioneer, valuer, land and estate agent, in a field where at the time the enquiry commenced no fewer than ten professional bodies were considered to represent estate agents, and even then by no means all, and in a field where neither registration nor licensing was necessary to practise, it is perhaps the lack of rigidity that is remarkable. Indeed one can see this lack of rigidity as possibly one of the factors that has led to the general misunderstanding of the estate agent's role and from that to distrust and to their reputed poor image.

Even a few members of the professional societies were said to have complained about their own society's rules concerning supplanting, canvassing, advertising and fee-cutting. Significantly all the complaints received from agents concerning the behaviour of the local estate agents' association were from non-members.

A typical complaint was that the local associations made observance of the leading professional societies' code of conduct a condition of membership and by so doing were said "to prevent almost any kind of competitive business promotion to attract instructions".

Two other main complaints from this source were that associations were able to exert pressure on local advertising media to the disadvantage of non-members and that members of local associations would not co-operate with non-members.

There is little doubt that these "closed shop" attitudes do exist. One cannot help but wonder, however, who would be the loser if the professional societies and local associations were to lose any degree of control over their members. Such a situation would no doubt favour the bigger firms. It is certainly possible that without this degree of control the unscrupulous, hard-selling "foot in the door" agent might prosper. But would it not be the smaller agent who ran his practice by professional as opposed to purely commercial standards who would be the loser? If this happened, the ultimate loser would be the general public.

One finds that there were "few complaints from the public about the lack of variation in estate agents' terms" and again that "there were only a few complaints from vendors about the general level of fees". Although much is made from time to time in the media with regard to the very high level of agents' charges, it is interesting that the Commission could find little evidence of dissatisfaction in this particular area.

It is the evidence of the consumers' organisations that is of particular interest — for, like so much of the criticisms they had made publicly, it was ill-informed, vague and unconstructive. They expressed the view to the Commission that the rigidity of the present system of estate agency was hindering reform of the system of house-transfer as a whole. One notes again the use of the word "rigidity", or is this perhaps where the Commission first found it? Many ideas have been mooted as to how the system of house-transfer might be improved. Here one must question what is meant by "the system of house-transfer".

Is this to be taken to refer only to the agent's role in the market, or is it meant in the wider sense to include the solicitor's role and house-transfer in both the selling and conveyancing sense? Both are relevant in any consideration of the estate agent's role, but the former is by far the more significant. Having for many years monitored the operations of estate agents, suggestions as to how their methods might be improved and, indeed, what should interest others attempting to break into the market, the adoption of new methods, one is forced to the inevitable conclusion that significant improvement could only stem from greater rigidity and not less. This we shall look at in more detail when we come to consider how in the years ahead methods of operating and the standard of service to the public might be improved.

The joint memorandum from the Consumers' Association and the Consumer Council referred also to the general lack of competition among agents, and this, with the fact that they operated in a sellers' market, together afforded agents no incentive to improve the system. The reference to the lack of competition surely shows complete ignorance of how the property market operates. It is also remarkable in the light of yet another comment made by these bodies, to the effect that there were too many estate agents and their excessive numbers led to the market being fragmented. Surely only if there were far too few agents dominating the market and handling more than they could cope with could they have justly referred to a general lack of competition.

The assumption that agents "operated in a sellers' market" was nothing short of naive, for although they normally in the house agency sense act for the "seller", as to whether or not the sellers or the purchasers dictate to the market is entirely dependent on the state of the market at the time and on supply and demand.

Professor John Greve went somewhat further on the subject of too many agents, saying that while the level of fees was often justified by reference to the costs of estate agency (including the costs of abortive work) it might be kept up . . . because there are too many agents, each of whom sell too few houses to permit a more reasonable commission to be charged. If there were fewer agents each on average would tend to sell more houses and the level of commission would come down!

He also thought that there was a case for re-organising estate agency charges so that what they receive is more clearly correlated with what they have to do to sell houses. Apparently many other complaints followed this line of thought; those from the public tending to the view that commissions were far too high where the agent had very little to do, i.e., where he was very rapidly successful; others, including some agents, felt that a *quantum meruit* basis of charging was more satisfactory. Charging for abortive work and separate charging for one or more of the services that agents rendered in a sale by private treaty were amongst other suggestions made.

It is not only from the consumers' organisations that complaints and criticisms have come. The media in the wider sense have missed no opportunity to join in. Their criticism has, however, been more objective and from time to time the more responsible critics have sought to inform the public as to how the market operates and to explain the agent's role.

The fact remains that the estate agent's public image remains a very poor one. As we have already noted, in a survey carried out by the Law Society in 1973 to establish where ten professions stood in public esteem and in relation to each other, the estate agents were bottom of the poll. The agents would argue that this ranking was not justified, that in the residential market, by which the agents always seem to be judged, property owners do not have to come to them to sell, and yet the majority do, and the majority of these are satisfied with the service they get.

They would argue that whilst their charges might on occasions be high in relation to the work done, overall profits are not excessive, a finding endorsed by the Monopolies Commission, and that in any event they only get paid when they succeed. They would argue that "gazumping" is in no way their fault, that they are only agents for the owners for whom they act. Those who belong to the professional societies would also argue that the rules of those societies are not there to protect the members, but to protect the public from the unscrupulous or oppressive. They would argue that the long delays between a sale being agreed and contracts being exchanged can in no way be blamed on them, but rather are the fault of the whole "subject to contract" procedure, the lawyers, the local authorities and the building societies. They would argue that their charges are lower than almost any others known in the Western World. Certainly the members of the two largest professional societies, the Royal Institution and the Incorporated Society, would argue that their professional approach is right. Many would indeed argue that "the present system" is there because that is the way the public wanted it, not the way they, the agents, made it.

There is no doubt considerable substance to these arguments, but for as long as the public image of the agent remains poor and criticisms continue, there can be no complacency.

It is therefore vital, if we are to consider estate agency methods, and the future of estate agency, that these criticisms be constantly borne in mind, for it is to those areas from which the criticisms come that we should first look to try to establish what is wrong, how improvements can be made, and indeed who is to try to bring them about.

First we should perhaps look to the control of estate agency and to the charge of rigidity, made not only as we have seen by the consumers' organisations, but by some practising agents. Are the Codes of Conduct laid down by the main professional societies self-protecting and do they unreasonably hinder a normal and healthy commercial approach to the estate agency task? If they do, how should they be changed? Are they equally applicable to the agency function in the commercial and residential sectors? For what might be healthy commercial competition in the former could very easily lead to oppressive methods and harassment in the latter. Are there too many professional bodies, resulting in lack of cohesion and co-ordination from the agent's point of view, and confusion in the minds of the public? Would both be better served by one very much stronger body, and could it lead more rapidly to improved standards and methods?

The Estate Agents Act now exists; how should the Secretary of State use the powers he has to invoke minimum standards of entry? This provision could have far-reaching effects and effectively reduce the numbers of agents, or were the Monopolies Commission right when they said that it was "important that the arrangements for the registration of estate agents should not be such as to restrict entry"?

Even if the professional societies could not, as I believe, be seen unfairly to hinder a healthy commercial approach and restrict open and fair competition, can the same be said of local associations? Many of these have become locally very powerful. Some undoubtedly succeed, notwithstanding the law, in controlling the general level of estate agency charges in their area. Some dictate the style that members' advertising is to take, and so on.

The professional societies can do little to punish their members for breaches of their codes of conduct, except in extreme cases and even expulsion would not, because of the very nature of the estate agency profession in this country, necessarily cause a member financial loss. The local association on the other hand, particularly in multiple agency areas where a newcomer may depend on sub-agency instructions to build up his practice, could, by withdrawing co-operation from that member, or denying him membership of the association, impose a severe financial penalty, restrict his growth or put him out of business.

As we have seen, in the residential field this power stems partly from the fact that estate agency is a localised business. I believe many associations do use their power oppressively and in a way that is not necessarily in the public interest. Having said that, my hopes for the future do rely to a large extent on the existence of these associations and on their continuing to be able to exert considerable power over their members.

In what might be called the control of estate agency we have three areas to look at: the power of Government following the Estate Agents Act and how it should be used; the role of the professional societies; and the role of the local associations.

The next main area of criticism to be looked at is that which concerns the direct relationship between the agents and the public they serve. Is the service given to vendors good enough? Is there sufficient competition between agents to ensure that it is? Is multiple agency as practised in the southern part of the country in the best interests of either the agent or the vendor, or does it lead to confusion, gazumping and unhealthy competition? How can our service to vendors be improved? Is the standard of service given to prospective purchasers adequate? Certainly in the residential field it is not. It may be that multiple agency gives a better service here than the sole agency basis of operating in the north of the country, but it still leaves a lot to be desired. Is our method of charging right and if it is right for the agent, is it fair to the public?

Last, but by no means least, is there not scope for a great deal more co-ordination and the use of more modern methods to bring about an improved standard of service?

Public Image: The Price Commission Report of 1979

Unfortunately this Report, although referred to earlier, was published when the text of this book was nearing completion. I could have set about re-writing all the earlier chapters in the light of its findings, for it not only investigated prices, costs and margins, but commissioned the British Market Research Bureau to carry out a consumer's survey (this they did in early 1979), but this would have been a major task and time was just not available to me for it. I have in places been able to amend the text.

This consumer survey did, however, confirm rather than contradict much of what had already been written and I have therefore felt it appropriate to deal with its findings and the conclusions the Commission drew from them, and in doing so will do my best not unnecessarily to repeat and bore my reader.

The keen student and, perhaps equally as important, the practitioner should obtain a copy of the Report and read it with care, for it goes into some matters much more deeply than I have been able to do and it deals with aspects of estate agency practice that I have not attempted to tackle.

When the Estate Agents Bill was debated in the House of Commons in November of 1978 many of the old criticisms were heard. Some M.P.s expressed concern about the lack of protection available to the public with regard to deposits, although I have not read Hansard to establish whether or not the existence of the Royal Institution and Incorporated Society's Joint Indemnity Scheme was mentioned.

Reference was made to the "unscrupulous minority of rogue agents who bring a bad name to the eminently respectable majority", an aspect of estate agency to which I have already referred, and of which the "eminently respectable" practitioner is only too uncomfortably aware.

Estate agents' charges were described as "grotesque" and reference was made to the lack of qualifications and "sharp professionals in expensive pin-striped suits". Why a professional, sharp or otherwise, should not be dressed in an expensive pin-striped suit was not mentioned; presumably a dull professional in a rollneck sweater and faded jeans would have been acceptable to the Member concerned.

The complaints received by the Price Commission from individuals again followed well known themes. Two are quoted in the Report:
(a) Cases where there was considerable delay in completing the transaction, often because first negotiations fell through and
(b) those in which a very quick sale was achieved and the vendor considered the charge was too high for the amount of work involved.

The Commission's Report was welcomed by the professional bodies, with some qualifications, and by most general practitioners. The Commission were given a remarkably short time in which to carry out their investigations and to report, and the thoroughness with which they did so, the fairness and objectivity of their Report deserve our congratulations. The political bias that one sensed in the reference to the Monopolies Commission ten years earlier and the attitude the members of that Commission adopted at the Public Hearing were in stark contrast with the fair, open-minded approach of the Price Commission. One must accept that the briefs were different.

Having said that, the Report was not entirely free of vague generalisations:

> "There is little reliable information about the attitude of the property-owning public towards estate agents. There appeared to be some degree of suspicion and discontent, which may be the result of particular incidents in personal dealings with estate agents, rather than as an outcome of a considered view of their role in property marketing."

This makes strange reading, for the British Market Research Bureau interviewed 699 purchasers and 499 vendors of domestic properties in England and Wales, who had effected property transactions during the preceding three years and the Report goes on to tabulate the results of the survey. In this context to say that "there is little reliable information" is perhaps surprising.

I intend only briefly to deal with the findings where I think they are relevant to the estate agent's public image and where they are important as a guide to the direction estate agents should be taking in the development of their practices.

First, and of particular interest, are the methods used by the 499 vendors to sell their houses. Eighty per cent went to estate agents, twenty per cent tried to sell through personal contacts, twenty one per cent through private advertisements, and seventeen per cent through private "for sale" boards or posters, three per cent used other methods. The total comes to well over a hundred per cent, for clearly some used more than one method, but the Report comments: "People tend not to be enterprising when selling their homes as over two thirds (68 per cent) tried one method of selling only". The proportion of those using each method who were successful could be significant: 73 per cent of those who instructed agents succeeded in selling through agents. Not surprisingly, a high proportion of those who relied on their personal contacts to sell succeeded, but less than half those who relied on private newspaper advertisements achieved their aim and only 4 per cent succeeded in selling by the use of private "for sale" boards or posters or other methods.

The Survey found that selling without the help of an estate agent tended to be more prevalent where property was cheaper, under £10,000. This would bear out the view expressed to me by a marketing consultant that estate agents' commission rates were too low at the top end of the market, where vendors required a very high standard of service, and at the bottom end of the market formed too high a proportion of the total proceeds of sale. This is a point that needs to be considered carefully when we come to look at possible future development in property marketing.

When those who decided to use estate agents were asked why they did so, they gave the following reasons and in this order: convenience, speed of transaction, coverage/access to buyers, "it is the normal (or only) way", "they are well equipped" or "they know what to do". A much more detailed analysis might be helpful in trying to establish the principal reasons why the property-owning public use agents, for there is clearly a lot of inter-play between the various reasons given, but convenience and speed are paramount. Of those who chose not to use agents the majority gave as their reason economy, a clear indication that the current level of charging is seen as too high by a significant minority, again, presumably, at the bottom end of the market.

A somewhat different result came from discussion groups that were organised. When some were asked to think more deeply about their choice of a method of sale, of those using agents, 61 per cent put speed in finding a buyer as their principal reason, 43 per cent getting a good selling price, and only 28 per cent convenience and negotiation.

"Speed and a good selling price clearly emerged as the main consideration, although the cost factor was important to many of those selling privately".

The agent's role in suggesting and agreeing asking prices was underlined, for of those who sold through agents, 70 per cent had either accepted the agent's advice as to price, or had agreed a price with the agent. Only 11 per cent decided to ask more.

Still looking at the relationship between vendors and estate agents, interesting responses were made when vendors were asked whether they were satisfied with the services offered. On all aspects but one the number who replied to the effect that they were very or quite satisfied bears out the earlier research that we have noted: 78 per cent were very or quite satisfied with the sales effort before an offer was received, 79 per cent with the advice they received as to price, 70 per cent with the effort made by the agent after an offer was received, 73 per cent with the overall service. What from the agent's point of view was serious was that despite this surprisingly high degree of satisfaction, only 45 per cent expressed themselves as satisfied that they had received value for money.

It will be of interest to note from the survey of 699 purchasers that 74 per cent in fact bought their houses through estate agents and 22 per cent direct from the vendor. Again, the survey found that the number of people not using estate agents was higher in the North, the Midlands and Wales, and where the value of the property was less than £10,000. Much of the information related to the service given by estate agents to purchasers will be considered later.

What I personally found surprising in view of the Consumers' Association's earlier criticism was that 74 per cent of the purchasers found the description of the property given by the agent was either very accurate or quite accurate and the widely-held opinion that agents tend seriously to distort appeared to have little foundation.

The conclusion the Commission drew from the Survey is, I think, of sufficient importance to justify setting out here in full:

"We conclude from this market research that the majority of estate agents' clients are reasonably satisfied with the services provided, which largely consist of a dissemination of property information from sellers to buyers. However, the public is not very well informed about the function of estate agents and their role in the marketing of domestic property and this contributes to a common feeling that charges are too high, for what is seen as little effort on the part of the agent. This suggests that estate agents and their professional bodies should make more considerable efforts to examine their relationship with the public and to improve customers' understanding of the services provided by estate agents."

"The evidence also suggests that sellers of property might well consider the possibility of attempting to market their property privately before placing it in the hands of an estate agent and possibly incurring considerably higher costs. They should take care, however, to ascertain the correct value of the property, particularly in a rising market."

The professional bodies will take what is despite their efforts, clearly a failure in public relations seriously, but if any real improvement is to be made in this area, it will be by individual firms. Local associations are not referred to in the conclusions, but remembering that estate agency in the residential sense tends to be very localised, they too could have an important role to play.

In suggesting that vendors might well consider the possibility of attempting to market their property privately before going to an estate agent, the Commission seem to be relying on the fact that 85 per cent of those who bought through estate agents offered a price less than that asked and were successful in obtaining some kind of reduction. It appears they said that a vendor's initial asking price is more likely to be reduced when the sale is through an agent, than when direct between vendor and purchaser. To rely on this to suggest that vendors might be well advised to try and sell privately is I believe very dangerous. At the time the survey was taken house values were rising rapidly and demand far exceeded supply. It is under these circumstances that agents will often find themselves advising asking prices in excess of those that would have been suggested by the vendor. The fact that such a high proportion of vendors agreed with the agent's price indicates that this was the case, and it would have been just as easy for the Commission to draw the conclusion that in times of rising prices vendors could be well advised not to attempt to sell privately. To an extent they made the point when they emphasised the need for care "to ascertain the correct value of the property".

This review confirmed that the standing of the estate agent and his public image is very much better than most people believe, but that there are certain fields where improvements can be made.

First, the criticisms revealed by the various consumer surveys are real and the professional bodies and individual firms must consider what can be done in these areas; in particular must agents find a better way of giving a comprehensive service to would-be purchasers. They must also find ways and means of explaining their role and the services they have to offer to the public, to counter the widely-held belief that however good and useful the service they give, it is not good value for money.

Five

The Relationship Between Principal and Agent — Subject to Contract Procedure

Types of agency — Creation of agency — Nature of agency — Sole agency — Multiple agency — Sole selling rights — The duties of the agent — Delegation — Sub-agency — The authority of the agent — Termination of agency — Relationship between vendor and agent in a multiple agency situation — The entitlement of the agent to commission — Duties of the parties — The importance of clear instructions — Circumstances under which commission is to be payable — Consideration of commonly used terms

Discussion of the operation of an estate agency practice involves considering the whole question of agency and differentiating between the various types of agency a practitioner could hold. Here we shall be dealing with the relationship between the vendor and his appointed agent or agents. It should not, however, be forgotten that a would-be purchaser or lessee can "retain" the services of an agent to seek a suitable property on his behalf and to negotiate the terms of its acquisition.

When one person appoints another to act as his representative, the latter becomes an agent and a contractual relationship comes into being. The person appointing the agent is normally referred to as the principal. The creation of an agency relationship as between a principal and his agent does not necessarily have to be by way of written appointment; oral instructions can bring the appointment about. If, however, the agent is to be given authority to execute a deed on behalf of his client, for example, actually to sign a conveyance, then a formal Deed of Appointment is required and the principal would in effect be giving his agent a Power of Attorney. There are some exceptions — an agent can without a formal Deed of Appointment grant leases for less than three years.

Whether or not the appointment was made in writing, where specific instructions are given to one person to act as an agent for another, the agency is said to be "expressly created".

An agency relationship can, however, come into being other than by expressed creation. It is rare, but an agency can be created as a result of the action or behaviour of the persons involved.

For example, a property-owner considering the possibility of selling his house but having taken no positive steps, and not having appointed anybody specifically to act for him, could hold out a person or firm as being his agent. If as a result of so doing that person or firm acted as if they had received formal instructions, an agency would come into being and the "principal" could be bound to the third party by that agent.

The relationship between a vendor and his estate agent is an agency relationship, but in a very limited sense. Almost invariably in agency matters the principal could become legally bound to a third party by his agent's acts. In estate agency matters almost invariably this would not be the case.

Agency

For no clearly defined reason two different methods of operating have developed in Britain and have become known as "sole" and "multiple" agency. Both terms are to an extent misleading and some amplification is necessary.

"Sole agency" as a method of operating in the property market means simply that only one agent is appointed to act for the vendor. In referring to sole agency areas one is referring to those parts of the country where this is the normal practice. It would not be unusual for two agents to receive instructions to act jointly, to co-operate in giving effect to the vendor's instructions and to share whatever fee is agreed; they would be joint "sole agents". In these circumstances it is usual for a higher fee to be shared between them than would have been received by one agent acting independently. The large country house, the agricultural estate and the commercial property are the sort where a vendor might feel it in his interests to employ both a local agent, who could be expected to have a more intimate knowledge of the area, its industry and inhabitants, and an agent operating nationwide, who might be expected to receive enquiries for property not limited to that particular district.

"Multiple agency" has been used to describe the practice, mainly common in the south of the country, where vendors may instruct more than one agent and often several, each to act independently of the other(s), with only the successful receiving the commission. Even this description is not strictly an accurate one. As we noted earlier, multiple agency areas could better be described as "mixed agency" areas, for some vendors within them do choose to instruct only one agent to act for them in a sole agency capacity, normally for an agreed period of time.

One must here differentiate between "sole agency" and "sole selling rights". An agent who holds sole agency instructions is, while those instructions subsist, the only *agent* authorised to act for that vendor. The vendor would not be precluded from selling personally, provided the agent could not be seen to have effected the introduction. The vendor having given sole agency instructions would only be precluded from selling through another agent if a valid contract giving sole agency rights could be seen to exist. Sole selling rights, or the sole right to sell, could preclude the owner from selling personally, unless of course he accepted the obligation to pay the agent commission at the rate agreed. We shall be looking at the whole question of agency, but in this specific context it is important to stress that for a sole agency agreement to "stand up" there must be present the elements of a valid contract. This would not necessarily have to be in writing, but it is clearly advisable for the agent to ensure that his instructions are so confirmed. Practice varies considerably, some expecting vendors to sign formal agency agreements either giving sole agency rights or sole selling rights, others write to confirm their instructions, but the latter would not in itself establish a contract of agency. Ideally, a reply from the vendor confirming acceptance of the terms and conditions set out by the agent should be obtained. A vendor could, however, act in a way that could amount to a recognition of a contract, i.e., if he himself held out the agent as one acting for him or clearly let that agent represent himself in that capacity.

It should, however, be noted that to be valid a sole agency contract should place some burden of responsibility on that agent. An undertaking by the agent "to use his best endeavours" may be sufficient. This is a grey area and any agent accepting sole agency instructions or sole selling rights would be most unwise not to take action that could be construed as his "best endeavours".

As Murdoch puts it: "In this way he will not only avoid liability to his client for breach of contract, but will also ensure the enforceability of the sole agency".

Where an agency agreement exists, each of the parties to it, i.e., both principal and agent, owes certain duties to the other.

The duties of the agent can be summarised as follows: he must act honestly in the interests of his client and should not accept any bribe, secret discount or commissions. As an example, estate agents can and do often receive discounts from the newspapers or journals in which they advertise. If the property-owner concerned is ultimately to re-imburse the agent's advertising costs the agent could only recover the gross amount and receive the benefit of the discount personally if the amount of that discount was first disclosed to his principal, who agreed that the agent should retain it.

The agent has a duty to carry out his client's lawful instructions.

What these are will, of course, depend on the terms of the agency contract, be it written or verbal. Certainly an agent cannot depart from these instructions, even if he genuinely believes that the action he wishes to take, and which goes beyond the terms of those instructions, would be in his client's best interests. One might here comment that for a property-owner simply to give an agent instructions to place a house on the market does not impose on that agent a duty to take any particular action, but as we have seen an agent accepting sole agency instructions does at the same time accept a duty to use his best endeavours to sell.

The agent in accepting instructions also accepts a duty to exercise reasonable care and skill in carrying them out.

An agent instructed to sell leasehold premises who failed to tell a prospective purchaser of the vendor's willingness to relax certain covenants, with the result that the premises were sold for less than they were worth was held to have failed to use reasonable care and skill. Similarly agents who made excessive valuations of property on which the vendor-clients relied and as a result suffered loss have also been held to have failed, and under-valuing similarly carries great risks (*Bell Hotels v. Motion*, 1935).

An important case was that of *Keppell v. Wheeler*, 1927, where an agent was found to have failed to sell at the best possible price by not informing his principal of a better offer. It is the agent's responsibility to report any better offer he might receive, notwithstanding the fact that a sale had been agreed "subject to contract". It is this duty of an agent to his principal that has led to agents being blamed for gazumping. Gazumping we will deal with later, but briefly, it is the name given to the practice of vendors, particularly in a buoyant market condition, abandoning a sale that has been agreed subject to contract in favour of a sale to another party at a higher price.

There is imposed upon the agent a general duty of frankness. He must not take any undisclosed commission or profit as a result of his appointment as an agent. Nor must he allow himself to be put in a position where his duty to his principal and his own personal interests conflict. He must not purchase his client's property himself, nor indeed sell his own property to his client without disclosing the full facts.

If, as a result of the agency, any secret commission or profit is received by the agent he is accountable to his client for it.

There is a general duty of confidentiality. An agent must not disclose to any third party any information or, indeed, show any documents that were given to him in his capacity as an agent unless he has first received his client's authority to do so.

Similarly, he cannot use any such information for his own benefit or for that of another client without his first client's consent.

Lastly, he cannot delegate the performance of his instructions without his client's approval. This is particularly important when an agent holding instructions to sell a property wishes, or thinks it advisable, to instruct sub-agents. It has been held that where a sub-agent is instructed without the vendor's specific authority and the sub-agent effected the sale, neither the sub-agent, nor indeed the agent himself, is entitled to any commission, for the agent has over-stepped his authority (*McCann & Co. v. Pow*, 1975). Here perhaps it should be noted that an agent given authority by his client to sign a contract on that client's behalf cannot delegate that authority.

In practical terms this means that an agent having accepted instructions has a duty to do his best to fulfil them. Certainly one appointed as a sole agent who took no action whatever could find himself in difficulties if, as a result of his inactivity, his client were to suffer loss, and this would clearly apply to one accepting sole selling rights.

We have already commented on the fact that while sole agency instructions are common in the northern parts of the country, in the south many vendors choose to instruct more than one agent to act independently. The relative merits of the two methods of operating will be discussed, but at this point it is of interest to note that any one of the agents so instructed would appear to have no responsibility to that vendor or client to take any action whatsoever.

We have to consider just what authority an agent is given. In the property market an agent is normally instructed to find a purchaser, tenant or lessee. This authority would allow him to take all steps necessary to carry out those instructions. It gives him the authority, for example, to describe the property and indeed to discuss with prospective purchasers or lessees all relevant matters, such as value, planning proposals and so on. It would not, however, give him authority to enter into a binding contract on behalf of his client, although circumstances could exist where he would indeed enjoy this authority. He could expressly have instructions to sell and provided these instructions were clear as to the terms on which he was authorised to do so, he could under those circumstances enter into a contract. In normal day-to-day practice such authority is very rarely ever given, although, as we shall see, it is enjoyed by an auctioneer.

It is clear that once having accepted instructions, whether as a sole agent or otherwise, the agent has responsibility to bring to his client's attention anything that could materially affect that client's position, and any information he receives as a result of being appointed an agent cannot be used for his own personal advantage or disclosed to a third party. We shall see, however, that he does albeit as an agent have a responsibility when dealing with others not to misrepresent, misdescribe or mislead. This latter responsibility is one that he has with his client. For example, if any agent is guilty of misrepresentation as a result of which a purchaser or lessee can be seen to have suffered loss, it is not normally to the agent that that purchaser or lessee will look for recompense; he will look to the client for whom the agent was acting. The agent may, however, be personally liable to the purchaser or lessee for fraud or negligence. The client in his turn could look to the agent, and if he has been negligent or failed to use due care, it is the agent who would ultimately foot the bill.

It is worth stressing at this point that the estate agent has a duty to his client, the vendor (he is a person acting for another). The fact that many people fail to appreciate this relationship is one of the reasons why to the "general public" as opposed to those who have regularly used estate agents, their image is bad. It is perhaps the very general use of the word "agent" that is at the root of the problem. A garage proprietor might call himself a Ford Main Agent, but in practice he buys cars from a manufacturer and sells them to make his profit. He could be described as an agent for that company because he represents it in that one particular location, but he does not sell as an agent. Having bought cars, he sells them and he is trading.

A travel agent does not in fact buy aircraft seats, although he may sell them. He is not trading. He is simply selling a commodity for an airline at a price and on terms dictated by that airline. He is a middle man and his responsibility to his airline client falls far short of that owed by an estate agent to his client. Here is one reason why estate agency should not be viewed as a purely commercial operation.

We have seen how an agency can be created, and we should look briefly as to how it can be terminated. The death or bankruptcy of the principal will automatically terminate any agencies he may have created. An agency can be determined by agreement between principal and agent, and this, as in the case of the creation of an agency, can be achieved either orally or in writing. An agent is normally appointed for a purpose, and the completion of that purpose would terminate the agency. Clearly an agent instructed to find a purchaser for a particular house will cease to act for the owner who instructed him once he has found a purchaser and the transaction has been completed. Either client or agent can repudiate the contract of agency by making it clear that he no longer is to be bound by its terms. In that an "agency", whether created verbally or in writing, is nevertheless created by way of a contract, termination by either party without the agreement of the other could be seen to be a breach of that contract and could lead to a claim for damages.

This last point could be important. In a multiple agency area a property-owner could instruct, say four agents, to act for him independently of each other. Indeed such an owner has no obligation to, and frequently would not, tell each of the agents who else was instructed. He may then receive an offer for his property through one of the agents and decide to accept it. He is under no obligation to tell the other agents involved of his action and unless he specifically terminates the appointment of the others, or they repudiate the agency they have been given, that agency subsists.

It could, and in multiple agency areas does frequently happen that one agent who has the property on his books but did not introduce the purchaser receives instructions to act for the would-be purchaser in the carrying out of a structural survey or possibly to advise as to value, or again he could be instructed by the building society from whom the purchaser is seeking a mortgage. He would be in breach of his agency contract if he acted for such a purchaser or building society without first obtaining the authority of the parties or with the vendor's consent terminating his agency.

We have noted that an agent has no authority to delegate. In the estate agency field, and in particular in the multiple agency areas, sub-agency is common. There are a number of reasons why an agent might feel it in his client's best interests, if indeed not in his own, to instruct sub-agents. He may have failed to find a suitable purchaser or lessee. He may indeed fear that if he does not appoint sub-agents his client may appoint other agents to act independently, or the property may be of a specialist nature where he feels that the involvement of an agent with more experience than he in that particular field will help to achieve his aim. Clearly anyone accepting such a sub-agency should be satisfied that the authority to appoint him has been given. His position from that point onwards now needs to be considered.

This is by no means as clear as it might be. Under normal circumstances the estate agent would obtain his client's authority either to appoint such sub-agents as he thinks fit, or to appoint specific individuals or firms. He would then issue the sub-agency instructions. There would be no contractual relationship between a sub-agent appointed in this way and the property owner or principal involved. It would be a contract between the main agent and his sub-agent. The former would be held liable for any loss resulting from the latter's negligence or default. It follows that the successful sub-agent would have no claim against the principal for his remuneration. As Murdoch puts it, "As far as the rights of the sub-agent are concerned it may be safely assumed, although there is no authority directly in point, that his claims for remuneration and indemnity must lie against the agent rather than the principal".

There are, however, grey areas. An agent having with his principal's authority appointed a sub-agent might as a matter of convenience encourage the principal or the sub-agent to deal directly with the other. Under these circumstances the possibility of a contract of agency being established directly between the principal and the sub-agent must exist.

Similarly there is doubt as to whether or not an agent who could show that he had used reasonable care in his selection of a sub-agent could avoid legal liability to his principal if that sub-agent defaulted.

For the main agent three rules appear to emerge: Never instruct a sub-agent without the specific authority of one's principal to do so. Use care in the selection of the sub-agent or sub-agents and, lastly, insist that all dealings with the principal are through you.

For the sub-agent it is clearly advisable in accepting instructions to ensure that the main agent has authority to give them, or that they are in a form that would enable him to look to that agent for his remuneration if he succeeded in his task.

If an agent has certain duties to his principal it follows that the latter has certain duties to the agent he appoints. The first of these is to pay the agent the agreed remuneration when that agent has successfully completed the task for which he was appointed, and with this goes a duty to do nothing which would prevent the agent from earning that remuneration in accordance with the agency contract.

Secondly, the principal has a duty to indemnify the agent against liabilities reasonably incurred by him in the proper carrying out of his instructions. Here again it is of vital importance that it should be clearly established between the parties at the outset just what these instructions do cover. In some parts of the country, and in particular the North, it is customary for agents to recover advertising and other out-of-pocket expenses. In the South the majority of agents expect to carry out some advertising at their own expense, principally in local newspapers. However well established local customs might be, the agent's ability to recover such expenses, in the event, for example, of a vendor withdrawing instructions, is very much in doubt if his right to do so is not specifically covered by the contract of agency.

The Entitlement of the Agent to Commission

It is appropriate to consider this question at this point, for the entitlement of the agent to commission depends upon the terms of the contract created between that agent and his principal. There is no general rule of law that governs the question of entitlement in every contract of agency, but for our purposes we could state a general rule that "the agent will not be entitled to his commission unless he has been the effective cause of bringing about the sale".

Difficulties normally arise when two or more agents are instructed to sell the same property. Under these circumstances a prospective purchaser may well be introduced to a property by agent 'A' but not proceed to purchase for one or more of many reasons. The price quoted may be beyond him. He may not at that moment be financially in a position to make an offer, or he may just decide to wait until something more suitable becomes available. At some later stage the house may be offered to him again, this time by agent 'B'.

Our prospective purchaser, having first been introduced to the property by agent A, may then decide, because the price asked is lower, because he has sold his own house, or because he has despaired of finding anything that suits him better, that the time has come to buy, and he negotiates and completes the sale through agent 'B'. Agents practising in the South will be only too familiar with this situation.

It may be that the agent introduces a property to a friend of his principal who was unaware of the fact that it was on the market, with the result that the transaction is negotiated direct between vendor and purchaser. In each case the test will be, whether or not the agent has been "effective" in bringing about the event that would entitle him to commission.

In the first case outlined above agent 'A', even if able to show that he was the first to introduce the property to the ultimate purchaser, would not be able to claim that that introduction had been effective and any claim by him for commission would be likely to fail.

In the second case the agent would need to show that, irrespective of the relationship between vendor and purchaser, it was his introduction of the property to the purchaser that was the effective cause of the ultimate sale.

An agent is normally instructed to bring about a specific event. An agent instructed to sell the freehold interest in a factory, who introduced a prospective purchaser only to find that subsequently that prospective purchaser had taken a lease, could well find it difficult to recover any commission.

Similarly, an agent who was instructed to sell and who brought the property to the attention of a Government department failed in a claim for commission when a year later the same department acquired the property at a substantially lower price but as a result of using compulsory purchase powers. The Court of Appeal clearly felt that the agent had not effectively brought about a voluntary sale as visualised when instructed, but had started "a train of causes which ultimately led to the defendant's property being taken away from him against his will".

As Murdoch puts it: "In order for an agent to claim commission it is necessary for him to show, not only that the event has occurred on which he is to be paid, but also that he is an effective cause of that event."

Again he says: "It is only in unusual circumstances that an agent will be entitled to commission on an accidental introduction."

It is clearly of the utmost importance that an agent should at the time he receives and confirms his instructions make it clear beyond all doubt what property and what interest in it he is to offer and precisely what he is to do to earn his commission.

In the great majority of cases there would be no difficulty in defining the property and the interest that is to be offered, but there will be occasions when care is needed. An owner of a shop, for example, might instruct his agent to sell the freehold interest, adding that if he cannot obtain an acceptable price, he might be prepared to consider letting it. The wise agent will ensure that the terms he agrees with that principal entitle him to commission if he is the effective cause either of a sale or of a letting.

It could well be that initial instructions are subsequently varied. It is important that the agent establishes, preferably in writing, the revised nature of his agency contract.

As to when an agent is entitled to his commission the law is confused, and many cases have been settled by the Courts. The subject is dealt with very fully by Murdoch, who sums up the situation when he says: "Claims of estate agents to be paid for services rendered have proved a remarkably fertile field of litigation."

It must be remembered that a sale negotiated by private treaty will normally go through three phases. First an agreement that is "subject to contract" and which is not binding on the parties. Second, an exchange of contracts, when the transaction does become binding, and lastly, completion of the act visualised by the contracts, normally the conveyance of the property to the purchaser and payment by the purchaser to the vendor.

Agents have, when taking and confirming instructions, used many phrases to define the circumstances under which commission will be payable to them. These have included:

Find a purchaser.

Find a party prepared to purchase.

Find a purchaser able and willing to complete.

Find a person ready, willing and able to purchase.

Find a party prepared to enter into a contract to purchase or

"when our purchaser shall sign a legally binding contract".

A detailed study of this "fertile field of litigation" is beyond the scope of this book, but the general principles established we should consider. Mr. Anthony Dinkin, who wrote the legal notes for the Royal Institution's "Practice Notes for Estate Agents", divided the commission cases into three groups. First, those whose terms required as a condition of becoming entitled to commission that the agent find a "purchaser," or where words were used that could be construed as meaning just that:

"find someone to buy";
"find a purchaser";
"introduce a purchaser";
"introduce a person willing to purchase"; and
"commission payable on a sale being effected".

Then those cases where entitlement to commission required a contract, such as

"introduce a party prepared to enter into a contract to purchase on the stated terms or on such other terms to which you may assent";
"commission payable if our purchaser shall sign a legally binding contract".

Last, those cases where entitlement was dependent on the agent introducing somebody "ready, willing and able" to purchase.

"If we find a person ready, willing and able to purchase"
"If we effect an introduction either directly or indirectly to a person ready, willing and able to purchase."

In general terms, if either of the first two types of formula has been used, a claim for commission is only likely to succeed if and when a binding contract has resulted from the agent's introduction. As examples, it was held that an agent who was entitled to payment on the introduction of "a party prepared to enter into a contract to purchase on the stated terms or on such other terms to which you may assent" was not entitled to commission until there was a binding and enforceable contract between the parties.

Where the requirement was that the purchaser "shall sign a legally binding contract", commission was payable when the contract was signed, notwithstanding the fact that the purchaser was subsequently unable to complete.

It is with the third group of formulae that difficulties are most likely to arise in practice, for the agent who believes himself to be entitled to have his commission paid and seeks to secure payment will have to do so notwithstanding that no sale or contract has come into existence. Mr. Dinkin suggests that the general rule in this type of case is that

"commission is payable when a person who is able to purchase is introduced and expresses readiness and willingness by an unqualified offer to purchase though such offer has not been accepted and could be withdrawn" (*Christie Owen & Davies v. Rapacioli*, 1974).

In this case the purchaser had engrossed and signed his part of the contract and had sent it to the vendor's solicitors with a cheque for the deposit, but the vendor withdrew when he received a better offer. As the Court said, "there was nothing more for the purchaser to do".

It is not, therefore, always necessary for a sale to be completed or a binding contract to exist before the agent could be entitled to payment. If he could show under these circumstances that the person he introduced was able to purchase and at all times expressed willingness and readiness to do so by making an unqualified offer to do so, there could be an entitlement even if there had been no formal acceptance of the offer and no binding contract had been created. There could, however, be difficulties, for it could be necessary for the offer to be within the terms the agent had been authorised to invite, and it might also be necessary for him to show that the purchaser could not only sign a contract but complete it. The experienced practitioner will know how difficult this might be to prove.

Where does the agent stand who, having introduced a person ready, willing and able to purchase, finds that the vendor has already entered into a contract with another purchaser? Again not an uncommon occurrence, particularly in a multiple agency area. The Court of Appeal recently considered such a case (*A.A. Dickson & Co. v. O'Leary*, 1980) and said Lord Denning, Master of the Rolls:

> "In the ordinary way commission is payable to the agent who is the first to find a purchaser who enters into a binding contract which both parties accept. If a binding contract is made before another agent has produced 'a person able, ready and willing to purchase' — or before any contract is made with that person — the first agent gets the commission, the second does not. It is a race as to which agent wins. He wins who first gets the binding contract".

This case has a direct bearing on the question as to whether or not a vendor can leave himself open where he has been dealing with more than one agent to pay more than one commission. The answer would appear to be no, for the Court's decision implies that commission would not be payable to an agent for the introduction of a "ready, willing and able" purchaser if before that introduction the vendor had entered into a binding contract to sell to a purchaser introduced by another agent.

It is little consolation to an agent in such circumstances that in another recent case His Honour Judge Laughton-Scott, Q.C., said

> "regard must be had not only to the great body of knowledge that the estate agent must amass in order to serve his clients at short notice, much of which is inevitably wasted, but also of the trust that he must create and retain with other members of his profession in order to gain an insight into the information available to them. It is clearly a hit-or-miss occupation, including many expensive misses".

Whether or not the situation His Honour recognises is in the interests of the public is a matter we consider elsewhere.

I stop short of giving firm advice as to the formula the agent should endeavour to use in normal circumstances, but speaking as an agent and not as a lawyer I tend to favour "the purchaser ready, willing and able" as the formula that appears to me to give the best chance of catching the vendor who would renegue. It is, however, important that the agent makes clear in precise terms the circumstances that are to entitle him to commission. A subsequent claim might fail if the words used were vague, uncertain or unreasonable. (*Jacques v. Lloyd D. George & Ptnrs*, 1968).

In concluding this chapter I must stress that it cannot do more than outline briefly the relationship between principal and agent in the estate agency context. The practitioner or student wishing to consider the subject in more depth is referred to "The Law of Estate Agency and Auctions" by J. R. Murdoch, LLB, of the University of Reading, published by The Estates Gazette, Ltd.

Six

Subject to Contract Procedure and Conveyancing

The requirements of a contract for the sale of land — The importance of "subject to contract" — Conditional and provisional contracts — Contracts subject to conditions — The mortgagee's involvement — The mechanics of a conveyancing transaction — The need to keep contact

It is vital that anyone involved in negotiating the sale of an interest in land should be aware of what does constitute a binding contract, of the significance of conditional contracts, and further, if he is to be able to follow the sale through to its successful completion, that he understands the steps to be taken by the solicitors to the two parties, both prior to exchange of contracts and between exchange and completion.

Use of the phrase "subject to contract" in all pre-contract correspondence will be stressed elsewhere. Here I want to consider the nature of the contract, what is required to form it, conditional contracts, and the sequence that leads to completion or to the conveyance in England, Wales and Northern Ireland. Scottish practice, as we will see, differs.

A contract for the sale of land is simply an agreement whereby one person agrees to convey by "the appropriate legal method" to another some land or some interest in land in consideration of a sum of money.

As Murdoch puts it, "It is only when the vendor and the purchaser, having completed their negotiations, enter into an unconditional contract that they may compel one another to complete the sale by an action for a specific performance. The contract is then said to be an enforceable contract."

The normal form of contract for the sale of land has to be a written memorandum, and Section 40 of the Law of Property Act 1925 stipulates that it should identify the property, the parties to the transaction and the price. In short it must provide sufficient proof of the agreed terms.

As we shall see, however, unless care is taken, such a contract could be created by correspondence and in certain other unusual circumstances.

An action for specific performance is in effect one party saying to the other through the court — "I have a contract with you under which you have agreed to do something; I now want it honoured".

There cannot, however, be an enforceable contract where the contract or the agreement is "conditional", where it is subject to some other requirement being satisfied; until that happens neither party could be compelled to complete.

It is for this reason that it is very important for the estate agent to appreciate when negotiating between parties that it is not the intention at that stage that an enforceable contract be entered into, and that this be made absolutely clear. Again, as we shall see, the use of the words "subject to contract" in all correspondence or indeed in a memorandum of intended sale and purchase is the normal way of making it clear, even if the parties have agreed on all the terms of the sale or the lease, that it is not their intention that an enforceable contract should be concluded until a formal contract or lease has been drawn up, approved, signed and exchanged between the parties. Until that happens neither party is bound and either is free to withdraw. It is this characteristic of "subject to contract procedure" that in the context of gazumping has led to much criticism and many suggestions as to how the procedure might be improved.

It is necessary to differentiate between conditional contracts, provisional contracts and contracts subject to conditions.

A conditional contract appears to me to be a contradictory term, for it is subject to the satisfaction of some other requirement.

The following expressions are frequently employed:
Subject to contract, which, as we have seen, imposes no obligations at all. Subject to title and contract. Subject to the preparation and approval of formal contract. Subject to the approval of a detailed contract to be entered into. Subject to a surveyor's report. Subject to formal contract to embody such reasonable provisions as our solicitors may approve, and in the case of a lease — subject to the terms of the lease all these could be said to be "conditional contracts", but in all cases either party could withdraw at any time prior to a formal exchange of contracts. If, however, the parties agreed terms of the sale in correspondence and included a document containing the words, "This is a provisional agreement until a fully legalised agreement is drawn up by a solicitor and embodying all the conditions herewith stated is signed", this would be a provisional contract pending a formal one and it would be enforceable (*Branca v. Cobarro*, 1947).

Contracts subject to conditions — as distinct from conditional contracts — can also constitute enforceable contracts. For example, contracts exchanged between the parties "subject to planning permission" would be enforceable once planning permission had been obtained. Contracts expressed to be "subject to the National Conditions of Sale 18th Edition 1959" and "subject to title being approved by our solicitors" and "subject to the property being found free from adverse entry on the local land charge and local registry searches" all have been held to be contracts subject to condition and enforceable once the condition is satisfied. The estate agent needs to use great care in the use of any such phrases and if in any doubt as to the wishes of his client the correspondence should also be clearly marked "subject to contract".

Before going on to consider the task of the solicitors once the transaction has been negotiated and agreed subject to contract, there is work to be done in those cases where a mortgage is required by a purchaser, in which the selling agent may or may not himself be involved. Even if the principle of an advance has been agreed, and we are concerned here mainly with advances from building societies and insurance companies, the proposed mortgagee will require a formal application form to be completed, giving details of the transaction and it will have to issue instructions to its surveyor/valuer. At the same time it may well want to verify the would-be borrower's financial status, either with his or her employers, or by perusing the accounts of a business in the case of a self-employed person, or in such a case it might be happy to have the borrower's stated earnings verified by his accountants. When it receives the surveyor's report, it has got to decide whether or not it will make a formal offer of an advance and if so on what terms. An offer of advance having been made and accepted, it will then need to instruct its solicitors in the matter.

The tasks that then face the solicitors acting for the two parties, or three if a mortgagee is involved, are set out in the schedule on the following pages.

All too often the estate agent, be he partner or negotiator, having negotiated the transaction, and informed the solicitors concerned of the terms agreed, turns his mind to other matters. His task, however, is by no means finished, for certainly prior to the exchange of contracts he has a responsibility to his vendor-client to see that that point is successfully reached. The vendor's solicitor and even less the purchaser's will not welcome constant checks on progress and implied criticism, and contact is perhaps better kept with the vendor and the purchaser. If this contact is to be meaningful, complete familiarity with the mechanics of conveyancing will be vital.

THE MECHANICS OF A CONVEYANCING TRANSACTION RELATING TO FREEHOLD LAND

A. Unregistered Land

	Vendor's Solicitor	*Purchaser's Solicitor*
1.	Obtain and peruse title deeds (or copies)	
2.	Draft and despatch contract with details of all encumbrances (restrictive covenants, easements etc.)	
3.		Peruse draft contract
4.		Raise enquiries before contract
5.		Make local search and search in Land Registry Index Map
6.	Consider and answer enquiries before contract	
7.		Consider answers to enquiries and return draft contract approved (amended as necessary)
8.	Fair copy contract and obtain client's signature	Ditto
9.		Despatch signed contract and deposit cheque (unless paid to Agents) on receipt of clear Local Search and Index Map search
10.	Date both contracts, agree completion date and despatch signed contract	

Contracts Exchanged

11.	Prepare and despatch Abstract of Title or more usually photocopies of all documents of title from root to date	
12.		Peruse Abstract or copy documents, raise and despatch requisitions on title
13.		Draft and despatch Conveyance
14.	Consider requisitions and despatch replies	
15.	Peruse draft Conveyance and return approved (amended as necessary)	
16.	Prepare completion statement and despatch	
17.		Engross Conveyance, obtain client's execution and despatch
18.		Make search at HM Land Charges Registry at Plymouth
19.		Obtain balance purchase money from client
20.	Obtain client's execution to Conveyance	
21.		Bespeak Bankers Draft and attend completion
22.	Hand over executed Conveyance and title deeds in exchange for Bankers Draft	Hand over Bankers Draft in exchange for Conveyance and title deeds

---

Sale Completed

23.		Submit Conveyance to Inland Revenue to be stamped "Particulars Delivered" or ad valorem. Rates: £15,001 — £20,000, $\frac{1}{2}$%; £20,001 — £25,000, 1%; £25,001 — £30,000, 1$\frac{1}{2}$%; £30,001 and above, 2%.
24.	Account to client for purchase money	

B. Registered Land

Vendor's Solicitor	*Purchaser's Solicitor*
1. Obtain and peruse Land or Charge Certificate	
2. Bespeak Office Copies of the Entries on the Register	
3. Draft and despatch contract with Office Copy Entries	
4.	Peruse draft contract
5.	Raise enquiries before contract
6.	Make local search
7. Consider and answer enquiries before contract	
8.	Return draft contract approved (amended as necessary)
9. Fair copy contract and obtain client's signature	Ditto
10.	Despatch signed contract and deposit cheque (unless paid to Agents) on receipt of clear local search
11. Date both contracts, agree completion date and despatch signed contract	
12. Send Authority to Inspect the Register	
13.	Raise and despatch requisitions on title
14.	Draft Transfer and despatch
15. Consider requisitions and despatch replies	
16. Peruse draft Transfer and return approved (amended as necessary)	
17. Prepare completion statement and despatch	
18.	Engross Transfer, obtain client's execution and despatch
19.	Make search at HM Land Registry and search at HM Land Charges Registry (limited to Bankruptcy)
20.	Obtain balance purchase money from client
21. Obtain client's execution to Transfer	
22.	Bespeak Bankers Draft and attend completion
23. Hand over executed Transfer and Land Certificate in exchange for Bankers Draft	Hand over Bankers Draft in exchange for executed Transfer and Land Certificate
24.	Submit Transfer for stamping (rates as above)
25. Account to client for purchase money	
26.	Forward Land Certificate, Transfer and appointed fee to HM Land Registry for registration and report to client when new Land Certificate issued in his name

C. Mortgages: Unregistered Land

Vendor's Solicitor

1. Obtain deeds from Mortgagee
2. When contracts exchanged and completion date fixed obtain redemption statement from Mortgagee
3. If possible obtain Mortgagee's receipt on Mortgage before completion and hand over to Purchaser at completion. If impossible send Mortgage to Mortgagee to be receipted and give Purchaser undertaking to forward to him within twenty-one days.
4. In any event remit amount shown on redemption statement to Mortgagee upon completion
    NOTE: A private Mortgagee will usually instruct his Solicitors not to part with the Deeds until completion; in this case the Mortgagee's Solicitor will supply an Abstract or copies to the Vendor's Solicitor.

Purchaser's Solicitor

1. Before exchange of contracts, ensure that new mortgage arranged and that funds will be available at proposed completion date. In case of Building Society, instructions to Solicitor should be received.
    NOTE: In certain cases when a Mortgage has been arranged but funds will not be available until after completion a Bank will provide bridging finance to enable completion to take place on the security of a Solicitor's undertaking.
2. After exchange of contracts, deduce title to Mortgagee's Solicitor who will draft Mortgage for approval.
3. Approve draft Mortgage and return to Mortgagee's Solicitor
4. Receive engrossed Mortgage Deed and obtain client's execution
5. Receive and agree completion statement which will specify deductions from advance including costs and stamp duty
6. Attend completion with Mortgagee's Solicitor, hand Mortgage to him and ensure that Bankers Draft for net advance handed to Vendor's Solicitor. Mortgagee's Solicitor will deal with remaining formalities.
    NOTE: The same Solicitor will often be instructed to act both for the Purchaser and a Building Society Mortgagee which greatly simplifies the above procedure.

D. Mortgages: Registered Land

The procedure is almost identical with that for Unregistered Land save that in place of a Mortgage Deed there is a Registered Charge form and after completion and registration the Land Registry will issue a Charge Certificate as opposed to a Land Certificate.

Seven

Sole and Multiple Agency

**Nature of both — Possible reasons for differing forms
of practice — Regional differences — Monopolies
Commission comments — Relative effectiveness —
Consumers' Association comments — Relevance of
market conditions — Relative considerations for
vendor and agent — The nature of competition —
Abortive work — Recovery of costs — The regional
pattern — The CALUS report — Advantages and
disadvantages**

I have already referred to sole and multiple agency when describing the
various types of agency that could be given in respect of sale or letting of
real property, but it is a subject that warrants greater study, for when
the Monopolies Commission made its investigations it found that estate
agency practice in Britain varied and, although the pattern was not
regular, north of a line drawn roughly from the Wash to the Bristol
Channel, sole agency was the generally accepted method of operating,
i.e., a vendor would only instruct one agent, or perhaps could only
instruct one agent, as others would decline to accept instructions where
one had already been appointed. If that vendor was dissatisfied he
would have to terminate that agency before making another
appointment. South of this line, multiple agency, more accurately
"mixed" agency, was the general rule, for although some vendors chose
to appoint a firm of estate agents to act as their sole agents in the
disposal of a property, many would instruct more than one and in some
cases several. This practice was generally accepted by the agents — not
only accepted as normal practice but accepted on the basis that only the
agent who ultimately succeeded would receive commission.

Before going on to compare the two methods of operating and the way
they bear upon the efficiency of the agent's operation and upon the
vendors and purchasers involved, it may be worth considering possible
reasons for this state of affairs.

The Monopolies Commission in its Report put forward one
possibility: "There is some ground for thinking that in this respect the
north and the south are at different points in an historical development
of the practice of estate agency ... the north has not reached this point

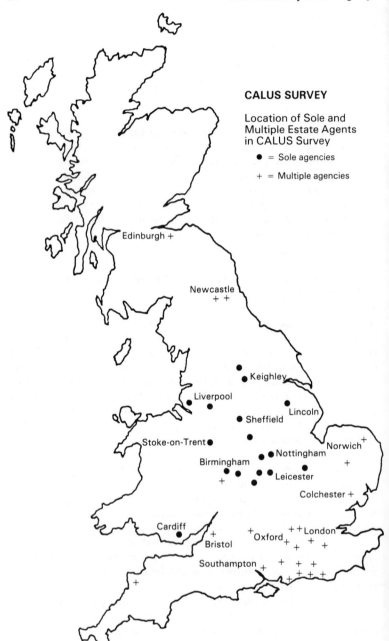

CALUS SURVEY

Location of Sole and
Multiple Estate Agents
in CALUS Survey

● = Sole agencies

+ = Multiple agencies

Edinburgh +

Newcastle
+ +

● Keighley

Liverpool
●

Sheffield ● Lincoln

Stoke-on-Trent ●

Norwich +

Nottingham
Birmingham ●
+ ● Leicester

Colchester +

Cardiff ●
+
Bristol

+ Oxford + + + London
+ + +

Southampton + + + +
+ + +

(multiple agency)." But this statement was made in 1969. Some years later the Centre for Advanced Land Use Studies carried out research, using, it is true, a very much smaller sample, but nevertheless a sample chosen that would reflect any regional difference in practice, and it published its findings in 1975. The location of the firms that took part in this survey and the nature of agency practice is shown on the Map facing this page. It is clear that over a period of some six years no significant change had taken place. This does not necessarily disprove the Commission's statement to the effect that the North and South might be at different points in the development of the practice of estate agency.

If the situation is changing, the rate of change is very slow indeed. In the late 'seventies the tendency to change was if anything directly contrary to the Commission's conjecture, for many agents in the South made a conscious and successful attempt to increase the percentage of instructions held on a sole agency basis.

Various explanations as to how the two differing forms of practice arose have been offered. It has been suggested that the explosion in home-ownership occurred earlier in the South and that it has been much more extensive.

It has also been suggested that Northern communities are more self-contained and house-buyers less likely to move from one area to another and at less frequent intervals, the high level of movement in the South providing a much wider market for the agents to exploit. The general level of house-values in the North has tended to be lower than that in the South and, significantly, commission rates also were historically lower. Not only might the market-place have been smaller but the rewards disproportionately less. These factors must have acted as a deterrent to the acceptance by agents of a multiple agency form of practice.

The fact that in the six years that followed the report no significant change took place may indeed have been in part a direct result of the Monopolies Commission's own findings, for it showed beyond any doubt that multiple agency practice generated abortive work and costs. The figures the Commission gave in their Report illustrate this dramatically. They showed the average commission per sale in the North to be about £44 and the average profit £7. But in the "multiple agency" South, the comparable figures were £91 and £8. A combination of lower house-prices and lower commission rates produced for the Northern agents only about half the income enjoyed by those in the South, but with very little difference in terms of net profit. The incidence of abortive work in the South was further underlined by the fact that whilst they sold only one house out of every five in respect of which they received instructions, the Northern agents sold three out of every four. It is difficult indeed not to draw the conclusion that both the public and the agents would be better served by the universal adoption of the sole agency system. That this conclusion is correct is borne out by research carried out by the Consumers' Association and published in "Which?" in November, 1969. They compared the time it took to sell their members' houses, first when only one agent had been instructed; and secondly when more than one agent was handling the sale. On the evidence they obtained they drew the conclusion that "This shows clearly that by instructing one agent only you have a far higher chance of a quick sale", and, as we noted earlier, they went on to say that "You make the situation worse for yourself the more agents you appoint. The reason for this may be that an agent is reluctant to spend money on promoting a sale if he knows that this money might be wasted, should another agent find a buyer first and so get the commission".

There is no doubt that the Commission's findings brought the attention of the estate agency world to the inadequacies, certainly in economic terms, of multiple agency practice and led many agents in the South to try to increase the percentage of instructions they held on a sole agency basis. They were helped in this by the abolition of scale fees following the Estate Agents Order, for they could no longer be accused of unfair trading by charging less to secure a sole agency. In doing so there is little doubt they increased their efficiency. It is open to question as to how much they were helped by the very buoyant market conditions of the very early 'seventies, which were to be repeated towards the end of the decade. Certainly, rapidly increasing house-prices gave them the incentive to reduce commission rates in an attempt to secure sole agency instructions and vendors, appreciating that the market was in their favour, were happier than they might otherwise have been to "go along".

There is no evidence that one could rely on to show what happened in the recession of 1973/74, when the market turned dramatically in favour of the purchasers. Indications are, however, that vendors, some becoming desperate, tended to revert to instructing more than one agent, but, and this is no more than an impression gained, the tendency towards sole agency practice was maintained, albeit at a very much slower rate.

One could now say there are grounds for believing that the movement is towards a more general acceptance of sole agency practice, rather than away from it.

It is not unreasonable to conclude that sole agency practice is not only more effective in terms of cost but that its general adoption in the South could lead not only to lower commission rates being charged, but a more efficient property market.

There are, however, other very important aspects to be considered, and these fall into clear areas. First the relationship between the agent, the vendor and the prospective purchaser and secondly, obviously linked with it, the operation of the market as a whole.

One must ask why a vendor would choose and indeed many would advise him, to instruct more than one agent. To get more than one opinion as to value would be a valid reason, although this would not necessarily dictate in the event instructing more than one of the agents approached. The answer must lie in the vendors' belief that by doing so he would increase his chances of effecting a sale.

Is this reason valid? The Consumers' Association research would indicate that it is not. Yet, on the face of it, to set two or more agents in direct competition with each other should in theory produce the quicker answer.

We earlier commented on the relationship between a vendor and a sole agent and the fact that somebody accepting a sole agency accepts with it a responsibility to use his best endeavours to carry out the instructions he has been given. An agent knowing that others have been or are to be instructed neither has, nor is likely to feel, the same sense of responsibility to the vendor. His primary concern will be to succeed before his rivals do and earn himself the commission. If he is efficient, he will move quickly. He might well produce a result acceptable to the vendor, but there must always be doubt as to whose interests were paramount.

A sole agent, knowing that he has no rival, may not feel the same sense of urgency, and if he receives an offer which he thinks is fair, but which he believes could be bettered given time, he has nothing to lose and something to gain by so advising the vendor. An agent who is one of several instructed, receiving such an offer, is bound to realise that if he advises the vendor to refuse it, because he believes it could be bettered, he is leaving the door open to his rivals. The temptation for him to try to conclude a sale quickly is obvious.

In a sole agency area an agent is clearly only going to succeed if he receives an adequate number of instructions. To draw these instructions he has not only to compete effectively in the image he gives to the public, but in the ultimate effectiveness of the service he gives, and the quality of that service must be his main concern.

It does not follow that in a multiple agency area an agent being one of several instructed would of necessity give a poorer standard of service; many give excellent service, but they are faced with different circumstances. An agent in these circumstances knows that everything he does and all the costs he incurs may well prove abortive, for despite his efforts one of his rivals might be the first to sell. The good agent will be aware, if he finds a prospective purchaser, that his duty is to the vendor and to negotiate the best possible terms on that vendor's behalf, but he will also know that his rival's sense of professional responsibility might not match up to his own.

A sole agent is unlikely to recommend acceptance of an offer if he doubts the purchaser's ability to proceed. He would be doing a disservice to his client and causing himself unnecessary problems. An agent being one of several instructed might react in the same way, but might he not also feel that if he could get a sale agreed "subject to contract" he might put the others off the scent and substantially increase his chances of being successful, if not with that particular purchaser then with the next one?

This line of argument could be summarised by concluding that the sole agent is more likely to compete successfully in terms of service and the multiple agent in terms of speed.

If this is correct then it is probable that a vendor would put more faith in the advice he received from a sole agent than he would in that from one whom he himself has put in to deliberate competition with others. This would support the argument that sole agency creates a more professional relationship between vendor and agent.

The movement towards sole agency practice in the South following the Monopolies Commission's Report would appear borne out by the fact that in 1965 in the North an average of 68 per cent of instructions led to sales and in the South an average of only 23 per cent did so. In the following ten years this gap had closed with rates of 71 per cent and 46 per cent respectively.

The fact that even in sole agency areas something approaching 30 per cent of the houses agents were instructed to sell were not ultimately sold by the agent concerned is in itself cause for concern. One must appreciate that a vendor's circumstances can change, perhaps the job he was hoping to take elsewhere did not materialise, or the house he was wishing to purchase was no longer available to him. Some no doubt succeeded in selling privately, for as we have noted the appointment of sole agents would not necessarily preclude them from doing so. Some no doubt became dissatisfied at the service they were receiving, terminated the sole agency they had given and appointed another agent. The fact remains that 70 per cent of vendors must be subsidising the abortive work caused by the other 30 per cent. This is mitigated to an extent, for the practice of recovering out-of-pocket expenses, such as advertising, is much more common in the sole agency areas, as the following Table reproduced from the CALUS Study shows.

From this Table it is clear that in a sole agency area, even where the agent fails to secure a sale following instructions, he will in the great majority of cases be able to recover his advertising costs and in very nearly half the cases certainly the majority of the costs he has had to

Sole and multiple agencies: proportion of agencies charging additional costs

Costs charged	Sole agencies All instructions	Multiple agencies	
		Sole instructions	Multiple instructions
		% of respondents	
All extra costs	44%	4%	10%
Advertising costs	39%	48%	40%
No extra costs	17%	48%	50%
Total*	100% (=18)	100% (=23)	100% (=20)

bear. His opposite number in a multiple agency area is in a far less happy position. Not only is he likely to sell less than half of the houses in respect of which he receives instructions; in 50 per cent of the cases he is unlikely to be able to recover any of his abortive costs.

Whatever the advantages of multiple agency might be, and we shall consider these, the evidence that it generates abortive work and is wasteful in terms of time and costs is conclusive.

The CALUS Report went on to suggest that "The disadvantageous position of multiple agencies is apparently further weakened by the fact that the average number of instructions received per office is lower than those received by the sole agencies — 320 as opposed to 445. This may reflect the greater levels of competition in multiple agency areas, resulting in a larger number of offices competing for available instructions".

It has been argued that there are far too many estate agents. If this is so it is a situation that would have been encouraged by multiple agency practice, for the vendor faced with having to appoint one firm only is much more likely to appoint one of the long-established and well-known firms in the area, than a firm that has only recently opened its office. The vendor able to instruct as many agents as he likes could well be tempted, having instructed two or three and met with no success, to instruct a newcomer.

There are other unsatisfactory aspects of multiple agency practice, which could be seen to be detrimental to the interests of vendor, purchaser and agent alike.

It can create confusion. The would-be purchaser on going the rounds will obtain particulars of the same house from a number of agents and not necessarily offered at the same price. Not infrequently a vendor, having failed to sell through the agents he first appointed, takes yet further advice, agrees with another agent to quote a lower figure and forgets to tell his original agents. Similarly a vendor, having accepted an offer through one agent, subject to contract, could either forget to, or deliberately decide not to, tell the other agents who hold his instructions. This could result in a purchaser, believing that he had found the home he wanted, seeing it advertised in the local paper or in another agent's window, and immediately there is distrust. It is in this context that multiple agency can be seen positively to encourage the practice of gazumping.

The advantages and disadvantages of the two methods of operating can be summarised.

The advantages of sole agency practice

a) It eliminates much abortive work, reduces costs and encourages agents to charge commission at lower rates.

b) It creates a better and more professional relationship between vendor and agent, in that it imposes on that agent an obligation to use his best endeavours to carry out his instructions and removes from him any temptation there may be to give anything other than the soundest possible advice.

c) It avoids confusion, not only for purchasers but for vendors, for the vendor, even if he has instructed his agent to appoint sub-agents, will only have the one agent to deal with, and purchasers, although they may not realise it, only one agent through whom they can effectively negotiate.

d) In buoyant market conditions it minimises the tendency on the part of vendors to "gazump".

e) It reduces the possibility of disputes as to who should receive commission, for it is not unknown in multiple agency areas for a would-be purchaser to view a house through one agent and subsequently submit an offer through another, giving to both agents the chance to claim to have made the effective introduction. There are, however, disadvantages.

Sole agency disadvantages

a) Although competition in the standard of service given to build up a reputation that will secure a higher number of sole agencies must remain keen, once these instructions have been obtained competition in terms of speed is eliminated. An agent receiving instructions, knowing that it is the vendor's intention to instruct others, would ensure that the details or particulars he prepares of the house will be sent to prospective purchasers just as quickly as possible. No time is likely to be lost in telephoning those most likely to purchase, and advertisements will appear in the earliest possible issue of the local newspaper. For the sole agent the temptation "to put off until tomorrow" is obvious.

b) Although the sole agent will, almost certainly, recognise his duty to obtain the maximum possible price for his client, that client only has the one agent's judgment to rely on as to when that price has been obtained.

c) Although the majority of prospective purchasers will contact the majority of agents in the area that is of interest to them, no one agent will be in contact with all and it must follow that the vendor having appointed a sole agent is likely to get less exposure for his property. In practical terms this may only be marginal, but the purchaser most likely to buy quickly and at the best possible price may be lost in that margin.

It follows from this that the vendor instructing more than one agent will obtain greater exposure. He will gain the ability to play one agent against another and purchasers against each other, and if this leads to gazumping, so be it, he is going to get a better price, and it does mean that having agreed a sale through one agent subject to contract he can, if he wishes, leave the others holding his instructions as an insurance against the first sale failing, or in the hope of perhaps a higher offer being forthcoming. As we have seen, if he did so, he could perhaps stop those agents advising or acting for a purchaser or his building society.

One significant advantage of multiple agency practice is often ignored. From the purchaser's point of view a visit to any one agent is likely to give him, if not a comprehensive list of the properties available in the area, at least a fuller one than he would probably get if sole agency was the generally accepted practice there.

Those who believe in competition at any price and in a "free market" will see little wrong in multiple agency practice, but the disadvantages are real and have been substantiated. If speed is the main criterion the attraction of setting a number of agents in competition with each other is obvious, but every agent is in business to make a profit; they will compete to be the first to effect a sale, but will this sale be on the best possible terms for the vendor?

In multiple agency areas the rate at which instructions are converted to sales is little more than half that in the sole agency areas. The agent faced with these odds is unlikely to devote the same time, effort or resources to his task, and we have seen, in considering the relationship between principal and agent, that a multiple agent assumes no specific responsibility and may do nothing on the vendor's behalf.

That multiple agency can lead to confusion, conflicts of interests, to gazumping and indeed to much of the criticism that is levelled at estate agents is beyond doubt.

The fact remains that the Consumers' Association research showed sole agency, despite the disadvantages we have considered, to be the most effective method of selling houses and certainly the majority of practising agents would agree with this point of view.

There is one other very important aspect of sole and multiple agency to be considered and we shall be doing so when we look into the possible future development of estate agency. If there is to be a much greater degree of co-ordination and co-operation between agents to avoid abortive work and give a more effective and efficient service to prospective purchasers, it is almost certain to be based either on "multiple listing" as practised in North America, which could be described as vendor-based, or on a system such as Leicester and District Estate Agents' Association's "Centre Point" project, which could be seen to be purchaser-based. Either would be difficult if not impossible to work effectively in a multiple agency situation.

Lamentably few attempts to bring about a greater degree of co-ordination and co-operation between agents have been made and I believe there are a number of reasons for this. The abolition of recognised scales of charges as a result of the Estate Agents Order is one, for it removed an obvious restraint on the general level of commission charges. Multiple agency is clearly another. It is difficult to see how methods can improve if the principle of sole agency is not first generally accepted.

Multiple listing and improved methods of operating, we shall be considering in some depth.

Eight

Alternative Methods of Sale

The choice, sale by private treaty, sale by auction, advantages and disadvantages — Sale by tender, advantages and disadvantages — Matters to be considered in choosing — Scottish practice — The Law Commission's conclusion

The Choice

In considering alternative methods of disposal we are concerned particularly with the sale, as opposed to the letting, of real property, be the interest freehold or leasehold, although some of the points raised will also be relevant to letting, particularly in the commercial market.

There are three methods of sale generally used in England and in Wales — sale by private treaty; sale by auction and sale by tender. Each has advantages and disadvantages, which must be considered in detail. Circumstances will sometimes dictate the method that should be adopted and much will depend on market conditions at the time the decision has to be made.

Sale by Private Treaty

Private treaty is the method most frequently used. The property is offered for sale, normally with a stated asking price, although not necessarily so, and would-be purchasers are given the opportunity to negotiate the terms of sale, "to treat" with the vendor or his agent. The use of the word "private" presumably is to indicate that under normal circumstances only the purchaser and the vendor and their agents are privy to the negotiations. The normal process of a sale by this method would be first the offering of the property, its inspection by the would-be purchaser, the negotiation of the terms of sale and purchase, the instructing of the vendor's solicitors to prepare a draft contract, the vetting of the property by the purchaser and if need be, his surveyor. The purchaser's arrangements for a mortgage, although possibly agreed in principle earlier, would be finalised at this stage — the signing by each of the approved forms of contract and their exchange between the parties, or more normally their solicitors and the vetting of the vendor's title by the purchaser's solicitors. Only at this stage does the agreement to sell and to purchase become binding on the parties.

The process has been described as "the subject to contract procedure" and has been the subject of much, largely ill-considered, criticism. A warning is necessary here, for while it is the normal intention of the parties to a sale by private treaty that it should not be binding on either of them until *all* terms have been finalised and contracts exchanged, it is possible for a binding contract to be established earlier and inadvertently. An exchange of letters between the parties or their agents agreeing to those aspects of the proposed transaction that Section 40 of the Law of Property Act 1925 requires to be specified in a contract for the sale of land could in practice establish such a contract unless it is made clear that it is not the intention of the parties to do so. It is for this reason that all correspondence passing between the parties or their agents prior to the exchange of formal contracts should clearly be stated to be "subject to contract". For this reason also agent's particulars describing a property to be sold by private treaty should clearly state that they are not intended to form part of any contract. This would normally be included in a general exclusion clause (or caveat) but the validity or value of such clauses, having regard to recent legislation, will need to be considered in more detail.

It is not impossible for a contract to be established purely on a verbal basis or again by what is known as "part performance", i.e., action taken by one of the parties with the knowledge of the other that could only be explained if both parties clearly regarded a contract to have been established. Such occurrences are very rare and a detailed consideration of them beyond the scope of this book.

The importance to the estate agent when selling by private treaty, of ensuring that all correspondence is clearly marked "subject to contract", cannot be too strongly emphasised.

It could well be that the agent having effected the introduction of the prospective purchaser will not be involved in some or any of the subsequent negotiations. If it is the intention of either of the parties that the "deal" should not be binding until formal contracts have been exchanged, it is important that they too should be aware of the risk and ensure that any communication between them is also expressly stated to be "subject to contract". An agent knowing that the parties intend to negotiate direct, or that they may do so, clearly has a duty to his vendor-client to ensure, in so far as he can, that he does not unwittingly commit himself.

There have been many criticisms of the "subject to contract" procedure as we know it, and many suggestions made as to how it could be improved. These have been considered elsewhere. It is, however, important, in considering the three alternative methods of sale, to look at the advantages of each.

Selling by private treaty has one major advantage over the other two.

The parties are free to negotiate in their own time and without final commitment; the exchange of formal contracts can be co-ordinated to coincide with an exchange in respect of the purchaser's previous house — or again with an exchange in respect of the vendor's new house; the date for completion can be arranged to the best advantage of both parties. The process is to a large degree flexible.

There is one very clear advantage from the purchaser's point of view — he can agree all the basic terms, such as the price, the date for completion and what fixtures and fittings are to be included, before he incurs costs that could prove abortive in the event of the sale not proceeding. These costs could include solicitor's charges, a valuation fee paid to a building society or a fee paid to an independent surveyor.

Another advantage to some purchasers would be the ability to agree basic terms, but with time to make other enquiries that might, to them, be of great importance. A purchaser may be acquiring a large house to convert into flats. He may be a doctor wishing to use part as a surgery, or his wife may wish to run a nursery school. The obtaining of planning consent for a change of use could, in such circumstances, be vital. In a sale by private treaty either of the parties could agree to delay the formal exchange of contracts pending a decision by the planning authority, or they could agree to exchange contracts that were conditional upon the required consent being granted.

Those who criticise the operation of the property market and the house market in particular, often fail to recognise that one or both of the parties may not wish to be committed from the outset, for example a vendor might be prepared to sell only if some other event occurs and a purchaser may well be in a similar position. The most common example is where a vendor is dependent on the purchase of an alternative home, or the purchaser on the sale of his present home. Both could negotiate openly and genuinely and the intention of both to sell and to buy be real, but the transaction unenforceable until both the parties wish a binding contract to exist between them.

It is important for many reasons that an agent does find out as much as he reasonably can as to the intentions and circumstances of every vendor and prospective purchaser, but in selecting and advising as to the most appropriate method of sale the intentions of the vendor and the circumstances that have led to the decision to sell are clearly vital considerations.

There are other advantages to selling by private treaty. It is comparatively inexpensive; advertising can be as intensive or as limited as the vendor might require; he might for a number of reasons wish his sale to attract little public attention. He may not wish the price obtained to be known. If his purchaser unduly protracts his pre-contract enquiries, or if he has reason to doubt his purchaser's intentions or ability to raise the necessary finance, he can continue to offer the house for sale and indeed "change horses" if he finds another would-be purchaser who can proceed immediately.

It is believed that 95 per cent of all real estate sold in England and Wales is sold by private treaty and the flexibility that the method gives is clearly the main reason for it. We shall be looking briefly at the operation of the market in Scotland, where selling by private treaty is rare.

The method does have disadvantages and we consider some of these.

It is customary to quote an asking price and inherent in doing so are two risks. First, particularly in a buoyant market or when the property is one likely to attract a great deal of competition, there is the risk of under-estimating both the extent of the likely demand and, as a result, the price likely to be realised. The result could be a loss to the vendor or a "private" auction leading to accusations of "gazumping" and to ill-feeling. Secondly is the risk, and it follows that this is greater in a difficult market, of being over-optimistic, with the result that one gets little response from early marketing efforts and is forced to reduce price. Clearly this could lead to unnecessary delay in finding a purchaser, but possibly worse, it could lead to the house becoming "stale" on the market and ultimately selling for less than might have been obtainable had the right price been asked initially.

The quoting of an asking price has been said to have the disadvantage that negotiations can only lead to the price moving downwards. This is, of course, a generalisation, for there are occasions when keen competition between prospective purchasers will force the price above that originally quoted. The fact remains that a price having been agreed between a vendor and his agent and publicly quoted is unlikely to be exceeded in the event.

For the vendor the timing of his sale can be another important consideration. He may have another house to move to, or a new appointment to take up. The flexibility selling by private treaty gives also creates doubt, for at any time up to the formal exchange of contracts, a purchaser can withdraw and a fresh start might have to be made.

Either of the other two methods of sale, auction or tender, seek not only to limit the sales effort to a specific period of time, but the effective exchange of contracts to a specific date. Clearly there is the risk that either of the alternative methods could prove abortive, but if the right criteria are followed in choosing the method of sale, this risk should be small.

Sale by auction

As we have noted, selling by auction dates from antiquity. It has been described as " sale by outspoken competition". If an auction sale is a competition, who are the competitors? Each and every person present wishing to purchase has to compete with those wishing to achieve the same end. They are competing against each other to secure at the best price they can an article, or in our context real property, that each wants to own. They are also, however, competing with the vendor, or the auctioneer acting on his behalf, for it is not only customary for real property to be sold subject to a "reserve" price, i.e., a price below which the auctioneer has no authority to sell, but in normal circumstances the vendor will reserve the right to bid for himself. His object and that of his auctioneer (in our context his estate agent) is to achieve the highest price possible.

It is probably because of the competitive nature of selling by auction that it has become established as a means of ensuring that "market value" is realised. In practice this is by no means always the result. Through lack of would-be purchasers, or reluctance on the part of purchasers to bid openly, a reserve price may not be reached and the auction sale prove abortive. Conversely, two would-be purchasers, both prepared for whatever reason to bid to a very high figure, might well produce a sale at a price well above that which could have been anticipated and well above the reserve price. There is, in my opinion, no evidence to suggest that the price resulting from a sale by auction is any more reliable as evidence of market value, than that obtained after private treaty negotiations. Indeed there are certain types of property where a decision to sell by auction could deter many otherwise possible purchasers, thus limiting and possibly adversely affecting the ultimate result, if not frustrating it.

If selling by auction is not the only means of ensuring that the best price is obtained, it is certainly accepted as the utmost one can do towards it. For this reason if for no other it should be carefully considered where fiduciary interests are involved. Sales by order of trustees, executors, mortgagees in possession and liquidators are examples. The good estate agent should not, however, let such interests dictate a course of action which, from his knowledge of the market he would, under other circumstances, consider to be unwise. Public auction is not suitable for the sale of every type of property and even if the property is suitable the advantage likely to be gained would not always justify the additional costs and possible delays involved.

We now look at the relative advantages and disadvantages of selling by auction.

First the advantages —

    (i) Competition between would-be purchasers is concentrated in time.

    (ii) As there *need* be no stated price, or even an indication of the price anticipated, bidding can only move the price upwards.

   (iii) If the reserve price has been reached the property will be "knocked down" to the highest bidder and a contract immediately established. Even if the reserve is not reached there is the possibility of agreeing a sale "in the room" when the keenness could still be there and the property sold on the auction contract.

   (iv) The sale takes place in public, purchasers therefore bid openly against each other. The risk of ill-feeling afterwards is virtually eliminated.

Then the disadvantages —

    (i) As competition is an important element of a successful auction sale, widespread and displayed advertising, albeit over a limited period, is normally essential. This combined with other abnormal costs such as printed brochures, posters, room hire, etc., tend to make it a more expensive method of sale than private treaty.

   (ii) Although "concentrated" in time it takes between eight to ten weeks and in exceptional circumstances longer, to carry out all preparatory work and to give the property adequate exposure. There is always the risk that market conditions could change, rendering the original decision unwise.

   (iii) Some possible purchasers may not be in a position to commit themselves by openly bidding, others may not be prepared to wait, and some just would not entertain buying "at auction".

   (iv) Although there may be several persons prepared to pay a price acceptable to the vendor, that vendor is deprived of choice as to who should acquire.

All these factors must be carefully considered by the auctioneer/estate agent unless his instructions override them. Trustees for example, particularly if they sense possible difficulties with any of the beneficiaries, may decide that it is essential for any sale to be by auction.

The most important factor is the amount of competition likely to be generated and its possible effect on the ultimate price. The Royal Institution's "Practice Notes for Estate Agents" stated that "There are occasions when it is difficult to assess the value of a property and sale by auction may then be considered as a method of establishing value". This certainly needs clarification. If it means that a property has so many attractive features and is likely to attract so much competition that it could fetch appreciably more than one would otherwise anticipate, and given that the maximum possible price is the aim, then auction clearly is the best method of sale to adopt. It is, for the reasons I have given earlier, questionable as to whether or not the process is one that establishes "value".

There are occasions, however, when property is difficult to value because the demand for it, if any, is likely to be very limited. Under these circumstances the element of competition is not likely to exist, the advantages of selling by auction are unlikely to be realised and the additional costs involved are likely to prove abortive.

Failure to sell at auction cannot be seen as establishing value except in the purely negative sense, but on rare occasions this negative evidence may be useful. Mortgagees in posession have a legal obligation to account to the mortgagor for any moneys received over and above the amount of the loan and the costs of disposal; they, for example, might well wish to sell by auction if only to satisfy themselves and the mortgagor that such a surplus cannot be achieved.

Even if the auctioneer/estate agent is satisfied that to sell by auction will generate competition, the likely effect of that competition on the price is still an important factor. To sell a semi-detached house on an estate of two hundred, eight of which are on the market at the time, by auction, might well generate competition, but only from those who would hope to buy at something less than would have to be paid for a similar house. Sale by auction is not likely to obtain a better price than could be obtained by private treaty. Such a house would, under normal circumstances, attract some purchasers from amongst those wanting high mortgages. They are unlikely to be prepared to pay building society valuation fees in the "hope" that they might be the successful bidder. They are more likely to agree to purchase a similar house "subject to contract" when their preliminary expenses are unlikely to be wasted. To sell such a house by auction would be to sell it under deliberately adverse conditions and whoever the vendor might be he should be advised accordingly. Trustees might require a statutory declaration before selling by private treaty to the effect that the price agreed is not likely to be bettered at auction. The estate agent with adequate market evidence available to him should have no difficulty in providing such a declaration.

When selling by auction with a reserve, the reserve price would normally be known only to the vendor, the auctioneer, his clerk and probably the vendor's solicitor, but it is possible to sell by auction with a declared reserve. A declared reserve is sometimes referred to as an "upset price". It is a device rarely used today, but it could be of value where the upset price would appear to be low and in itself likely to attract potential purchasers.

We shall be considering sales by auction more closely, but the significance of a reserve price should be stressed. It is the price below which the auctioneer has no authority to sell and up to which he would normally have authority to bid on the vendor's behalf. To sell without reserve would be to commit the auctioneer to accept the highest bid he received whatever that might be.

Private Auction

We have been considering sales by public auction. Private auctions are uncommon. The property concerned would not be offered to the general public, but to invitees only. It could be used as a means of resolving a conflict between would-be purchasers or where the vendor wishes to find a purchaser from a limited number regarded as suitable. A local authority wishing to let a site on building leases has been used as an illustration. Sale by tender, which we will now consider, would give the vendor the same power of choice with some other advantages and would normally be preferred.

Sale by Tender

Selling by tender has much in common with selling by public auction. Particulars are prepared with Conditions of Sale, and these would normally include a form of tender. The would-be purchaser is not of necessity, or usually, given any guide as to the price expected. He has to make his bid normally on the form provided by a certain date and time and the vendor or lessor need only formally accept to create a binding contract.

As with the case of a sale by auction the would-be purchaser or lessee has to make his enquiries before deciding on what figure to tender and having submitted his tender he is unlikely in normal circumstances, to withdraw it. The vendor selling by auction normally sells subject to a reserve price. A vendor selling by tender normally protects himself by reserving the right not to accept the highest or any of the tenders received. From the vendor's point of view it does, as in the case of a sale by auction, limit the sale in terms of time. It is a highly competitive method of sale. The would-be purchaser, who cannot see or sense, as he could in an auction room, the strength of the competition, has to make his mind up as to what the property is worth to him. To tender a figure anything less than the maximum he is prepared to pay runs the risk of disappointment.

It is an unpopular method of sale and it is perhaps the fact that a would-be purchaser has to tender without any knowledge of the strength of the competition he is up against, if any, that is the principal reason for this.

In the auction room he would know he only has to better the next highest bid by one jump. To secure a property by tender might well mean paying substantially more than the next highest bidder, or perhaps being the only bidder. It follows that this can be one of the principal advantages gained by the vendor.

As a method of sale, it has been used more frequently in the sale of building land than perhaps in the sale of any other type of real property and particularly in the boom years of the early 'seventies. Although market conditions in the late 'seventies were similar, it was less frequently used. One of its attractions was the ability to extract the highest possible price from a grossly over-heated market. It was for this reason that some development companies wishing to acquire land would take no part in a sale by tender, however attractive the project might be. The vendor and his agent should consider this factor in deciding to adopt this method. It may be the fact that to sell by tender is to deter some purchasers that has led to its less frequent use.

There are, however, some circumstances when a sale by tender has a great deal to commend it. A local authority, for example, wishing to dispose of a sensitive town centre site, may not wish the price to be the sole criterion by which a purchaser is chosen, as would be the case if they sold by public auction. The standard of design, the use or uses to which buildings are to be put, are matters which could be of equal if not greater concern to them, and they can, and often have invited interested purchasers to submit with their tenders information as to the uses visualised, sketch plans and sometimes even models to show the form of development proposed.

Tender has been used as a method of choosing tenants for prime shops, where, again, obtaining the maximum rent might not be the sole objective. The nature of the trade to be conducted and the financial standing of the would-be tenant could be more important.

Generally, therefore, it is a method of sale objectionable to some would-be purchasers but which gives the vendor the opportunity, having received the tenders, of considering them, rejecting them all if he wishes, or selecting one on the criteria most important to him.

A sale by tender does not have to be "public" in the sense that the vendor does not have publicly to invite all who would be interested to submit a tender. A local authority, again only as an example of the type of body who have used this method of sale, may well wish to dispose of a site that in its opinion should only be tackled by a development company of considerable standing and with experience of the type of development proposed. It may well select and invite only a limited number to consider the project and submit a tender. Particularly is this course likely to be followed if before submitting a tender a considerable amount of work and expense would be required on the part of the invitees.

Vendors and their agents having offered a property for sale by private treaty and being faced with more than one offer at the asking price, or involved in a "Dutch" auction with one bidder after another seeking to better an earlier bid, often well above the original asking price, may well decide to ask all involved to submit their highest offer by a given date. Unless such offers are called for in a form that the vendor could accept and thus create a contract, when it would become a sale by tender, one could describe the process as a sale by way of informal tender, a method, from the vendor's point of view, of selecting the prospective purchaser who should be given the opportunity in preference to others of proceeding with his purchase by way of private treaty, i.e., through the normal subject to contract procedure.

The handling of sales by these various methods will be described in detail in later chapters. It is sufficient here to stress that sale by private treaty is the method normally adopted in England and Wales. It has the great advantage of flexibility and it is the only method that should be considered by a vendor whose willingness to sell is conditional, for any reason, and similarly it is the only method of purchase that should be considered by a purchaser who has not had the opportunity to vet the property, to make his financial arrangements, or who for any other reason is prepared to commit himself only conditionally.

Sales by public auction should only be considered where either very considerable competition is anticipated, or there are special circumstances such as have been outlined which dictate this course. A sale by tender would be an alternative, and clearly indicated where the vendor would wish to select a purchaser on grounds other than price.

This is probably the appropriate point at which to discuss the normal methods of sale in Scotland.

In Scotland a sale by public auction is very rare and as a method of sale it tends to be regarded, as indeed it once was elsewhere in the British Isles, as the last resort — the method to be adopted when a property has proved unsaleable by other methods. Sales by private treaty do take place, but again they are rare. The great majority of sales of residential property are dealt with by a method very similar to a sale by tender.

A prospective purchaser, before making his offer, will have to take steps that, had he been purchasing elsewhere, he might have left until basic terms had been agreed subject to contract. If he wants to have a survey of the structure carried out, to arrange his finance or obtain estimates for works of alteration or extension, he will have to do so at this stage. He will also have to consult his solicitor, who would normally draft and submit the offer. This offer would be submitted by way of formal letter "adopted as holograph" this, again as in a sale by tender, may well have to be submitted by a given deadline or closing date. This offer may well be conditional. "It is customary for an offer to include conditions stipulating, apart from price and entry date, liability for mutual repairs, apportionment of rates and other burdens, compliance with planning conditions and obligations under title, that a valid title would be given and also a general description of the property."

The vendor may well have offered his property for sale subject to conditions, but an offer having been submitted and "adopted as holograph" if accepted in similar manner, becomes binding on both parties, subject only to any of the conditions specified being fulfilled.

The process of offer and acceptance is known as the "conclusion of missives" — the equivalent of an exchange of contracts.

In considering the practice of estate agency, the fact that methods normally adopted in Scotland differ from those elsewhere is of some significance. Many critics of the "subject to contract" procedure normal in England and Wales have advocated the adoption of the Scottish system as a solution to problems, such as gazumping. Strangely few, if any, have suggested much wider use of sales by public auction or tender as a solution. Certainly some seem to be under the impression that the Scottish system provides a fairer answer to both vendor and purchaser, but this is open to serious doubt.

First one should ask why the method normally adopted in Scotland should differ from that adopted elsewhere in Britain. It has been suggested that Scottish practice largely evolved and continues because of the solicitors' traditional role as estate agents. As we have seen elsewhere, in Great Britain, whilst the lawyers and the scriveners were at one time "the estate agents", they have long since lost the great majority of this work to those who have specialised in the profession of the land. Although estate agents as such deal almost exclusively with commercial, industrial and agricultural property in Scotland, the solicitors still dominate the residential market and indeed efforts by estate agents to displace them would appear to have done little more than make minor inroads into their control. It is argued that the Scottish solicitors "without valuation training and specialised knowledge" place property on the market subject to a reserve or upset price and then let it find its own level.

This appears to me to be most unlikely, for if the lawyers in practice carry out most of the estate agency work, they are likely to have as much knowledge of values and practical experience as the estate agents in England and Wales. I think there can be little doubt that the system evolved, as did sole and multiple agency practice in England, partly to suit the needs of those who operated the market — the lawyers, but in the main to reflect the nature of that market itself.

A contributing factor may well have been the relative simplicity of making title searches in Scotland, where a centralised register of property transactions is maintained. There could well be other factors;

owner-occupation accounts for a very much smaller percentage of the total housing stock in Scotland than it does elsewhere. It could well be that the rate of growth both in terms of total population and housing stock has been slower and that as a result of these factors the housing market in Scotland is not dissimilar from that in the South of England a century ago.

The system clearly shares the advantages and disadvantages of sales by public auction and tender elsewhere. The purchaser bids blind, as in the case of sale by tender. He has to "vet his purchase" and bear the costs of doing so, knowing that both the work involved and the costs could prove abortive and indeed face the fact that his offer is "open" until the time-limit set for acceptance either by him or the vendor has expired.

It is undoubtedly true that the overall adoption of such a system would prevent gazumping, but it is difficult to see what other advantages would be gained.

When Lord Hailsham, as Lord Chancellor, referred the gazumping question to the Law Commission, asking them to advise as to the possibility of legislation to improve matters, they sought the advice of the Scottish Law Commission, which was to the effect that whilst methods adopted in Scotland suited the Scottish market, they did not believe the methods would withstand the pressure of the market in the South of England. The Law Commission came to this conclusion:

> "The existing 'subject to contract' procedure for the sale of houses by private treaty, though it has drawbacks and is capable of being abused in certain circumstances, is based on a sound concept, namely, that the buyer should be free from binding commitment until he has had the opportunity of obtaining legal and other advice, arranging his finance and making the necessary inspections, searches and enquiries. Accordingly, we do not consider that the law should be changed to give legal effect to 'subject to contract' agreements or to impose criminal or civil liability on a person who withdraws from such an agreement."

Nine

Market Forces

**The economy — The broad picture — Regional and
local considerations — The need to be able to
interpret economic factors — The residential market
— Construction costs, their relevance — The boom
and slump of the early 'seventies — Interest rates —
Availability of mortgages — The cyclical market —
Increased money supply — Confidence as a factor —
Estate agents and house prices — Physical factors —
Town planning — Social and human factors — The
commercial market — The institutions**

When I first considered the task of writing this book, I obtained from
the Royal Institution of Chartered Surveyors their thoughts as to what
their final syllabus should cover in the field of estate agency, marketing
and management. Given that I am not here concerned with
management, I had to consider what was required in the estate
agency/marketing sense and I was faced with this very first paragraph —
"An analysis of the United Kingdom property market will be the prime
concern of the syllabus and all connected decision-making that has to be
made in estate agency as part of that market".

That there is a property market in the United Kindom is a simple
statement of fact and it might well be said that if there is a property
market it must be capable of analysis, but I believe the analysis could
only be made on a wide and sweeping basis. In short, if the country is
prosperous, if its gross national product is increasing, if its trading
balances are in surplus and if its people have confidence, then its
property market will be prospering, in that values will reflect the
national well-being, growth will dictate investment and investment, in
the property context, will mean development.

One could likewise make a sweeping statement to the effect that if
average earnings increase at the rate of 14 per cent per annum
compound, the ability of the people to invest in their own homes will do
likewise and one would see such an increase in the value of residential
property, in monetary if not in real terms.

One could further comment that in these circumstances the ability of
the people to save, whether in the strictly personal context, or by way of

their compulsory investment in pension funds, will also increase, and that, given a healthy economy, interest rates will be relatively low and funds necessary to finance the growth of the property market will be there.

In November, 1979, it is just as easy to make another sweeping comment to the effect that with inflation running at nearly 20 per cent, a Minimum Lending Rate of 17 per cent, a forecast decline in productivity, and the normal residential mortgage carrying interest at 15 per cent, the market is unlikely to be prosperous, investment will be at a very low level and at best we face a period of stagnation.

If there is such a thing as a "United Kingdom property market" and one must accept the existence of this strange and all-embracing animal, it is only at the Department of the Environment that records sufficiently comprehensive to make any sort of intelligent overall analysis might exist.

Let us briefly consider the nature of that property market. First, it is capable of being segmented by property-type, i.e., houses, shops, offices, factories, warehouses, other commercial property, agricultural property, woodlands, leisure-oriented property, mineral workings and so on.

Secondly, it is capable of being broken down by the nature of occupation or tenure — freehold, leasehold, short leasehold, and one could go on into reversionary interests and so on. In the widest sense of marketing, tenure is perhaps irrelevant, although it is certainly not irrelevant to the estate agent who has to deal with these interests, advise as to value and market them.

More significantly, the market is segmented geographically into regions, districts and localities.

Some regions decline, others prosper and to believe that any meaningful analysis can be made of "the national property market" that includes on the one hand Northern Ireland and Merseyside and on the other the City of London and the growth areas of the South-East is unrealistic, although one readily accepts that to the expert, segments within the overall cover of the national property market are within regions capable of separate analysis and comparison.

Taking this point even further, it is a matter of fact that office rentals in Southampton are, as I write this, certainly double those in Portsmouth, and yet both towns are in the same development area and would be covered by one regional analysis. Similarly, in my own county of West Sussex office rentals in Chichester are currently in the order of £3 to £4 a square foot. Seven miles away, and 12 minutes by road, in Bognor Regis there would be no takers at half this level.

Many factors vary from region to region and from district to district that will have a direct bearing on the property market within them. The availability of investment grants in the growth areas and a policy of severe planning and restraint on further growth in the South-East are obviously two such factors.

There are many other factors which would appear much less direct, but nevertheless have a bearing on market conditions. It has long been a mystery to me, resulting from very occasional visits to the North, that house-builders there seem to have been able to acquire land, provide the infra-structure, build houses, sell them and make a profit at a price that their South-eastern opposite numbers would claim to be totally impossible. It is hard to believe that the cost of materials from one region to another, or indeed the cost of labour, would create such enormous variations.

Amongst other factors are new motorways, new airports. For example, a third London airport in Buckinghamshire could send values at the top end of the house-market tumbling, but send commercial values rocketing. The effect of increased rail fares on commuter patterns must in turn have an effect on property values and these presumably are capable of analysis.

From all this it follows that some market criteria are purely local. House values are one. Even to say that on analysis house values in West Sussex are 30 per cent higher than those in Suffolk is meaningless, for in any one area they could vary by another 20 per cent between one village and the next, possibly as from one side of the road to another.

The commercial estate agent operating nationally and possibly specialising in only one sector of the market will be looking to different criteria on which to assess values and make marketing and development decisions than his residential opposite number. If he is interested in shops he will be concerned with population figures, whether they are rising or falling, and how pedestrian traffic moves within a town. If he is looking at the industrial scene he will be concerned with such matters as transportation, employment levels and so on. I do not think I and those who are helping me can do more than try to look at those factors that have a direct bearing on each of the main types of real property and even then without attempting to analyse the market in agricultural land, for in this area certainly my knowledge is so limited as to render any conclusion or even comment dangerous.

It is sufficient to say that in whatever field the estate agent is working, whether this be at one end specialising in shops throughout the United Kingdom or at the other working as a general practitioner in a small market town, dealing with everything that comes his way, it will be his task to understand not only the likely effect of the country's overall economic performance and its likely effect on his market, but to know and appreciate the significance of all those factors, planning policies and so on that will have a regional or strictly local bearing.

We will now look at those forces that could be said to dictate the state of the market at any one time. In doing so I do not wish in any way to detract from what I have just said about the segmentation of the market and its regional or local characteristics, but purely to give some thought to those factors that in each area of the market, and from region to region and area to area, are likely to have a bearing on the market for any one type of property or in any one place.

First, then, the residential market. Here I suggest we concern ourselves solely for the moment with the market in vacant possession residential property for sale and with it linking the market in land suitable for residential development. I am not attempting to put what I see as the factors that have a noticeable bearing on the residential market in any specific order, but the availability of money to the market is clearly a vital factor. It will of course reflect what has already been said about the overall state of the national economy. More directly it is the supply of new money that concerns us and this money could be real in one sense but not in another. Increased earnings even if they do no more than keep pace with inflation will inflate the house market and they may result in an increased flow of investment funds into the building societies. A town that is developing industrially will be attracting new labour, and in the context of that one town, this new labour will represent new money, for those who earn it will wish to acquire existing houses or to buy new ones and development will be given financial encouragement. If it does not get encouragement from the planning authority the value of existing housing stock will rise and rise in real terms.

Population changes not only in the sense of movement created by industrial development but by changes in the average household size and in age groups are also factors that could have a significant bearing on the future of the market.

Construction costs are generally regarded as a pre-determining factor. It is said "If building costs rise, so must house-values," but I believe that the last decade has shown this to be a dangerous assumption. Building costs, dictated as they are by the cost of materials and the cost of labour, cannot dictate to a market place. They can, however, dictate what is built and they can have a very direct bearing on land values. Given that a site is suitable in the eyes of the planning authority for one form of development or another, and that the land has a value, any increase in building costs without a corresponding increase in "market values" will initially serve only to drive the value of the land downwards, but it follows that there will come a point when the landowner will not sell, or where the land has a low or negative value and is incapable of development in the form visualised. This aspect of the market has been underlined by various Government planning circulars over recent years aimed at making better or more economic use of land, or put another way, aimed at bringing land to be developed with more and smaller units. What were the semi-detached three-bedroomed, two-reception room, kitchen and bathroomed houses of the 1930s selling at £795 on a £5 deposit if they were not "starter" homes? Planning authorities, and indeed the Secretary of State, now talk about "starter" homes as something new, something with two bedrooms, even only one, something with 500/600 sq. ft. as opposed to the post-war "semis" 800/900 sq ft.

One could argue that the nature of demand has changed, but has it? Would not today's young couple prefer the larger house? In practice a number of factors could be involved in this situation. In some areas the need to exercise planning restraint and to conserve good quality agricultural land or to protect visual amenity and what those already owning houses there see as being "the environment" are factors, but I suggest the dominant factor has been, given a period of years, that incomes and as a consequence house-values, did not keep up with building costs. This has the consequence I illustrated earlier of forcing land values down until in general terms land for residential development in 1975 and 1976 was worth only a fraction of what it had been four and five years earlier. It is, of course, true that the surge in property values in 1977 and 1978 allowed land values to recover. Here one could ask what factors brought about that surge, and I have heard many argue that it was indeed the ultimate effect of a period of rising building costs. Rather do I believe that these costs were only an incidental factor and that it was principally the supply of money that artificially held back the market, which then surged forward as interest rates dropped, money became cheaper and confidence was restored. I believe those who are brave enough to press ahead with residential development projects into the early 1980s, relying on house values to reflect the inflation rate and absorb increased construction costs, could be in for the same shock that their predecessors, or indeed they themselves, experienced in 1972/73. This view, perhaps, hopefully will prove to be wrong, but nevertheless it is the sort of view that the estate agent, if he is accurately to advise house-owners, and in particular developers — because a longer time-factor is involved — must be prepared to express, having appreciated those national and local factors that bear upon his market.

Before I say anything further I must stress that I qualified long before economics appeared in the examination syllabus. What follows are therefore simply the comments of a general practitioner and observer, and certainly no expertise is claimed.

The factors that could fairly be described as national and which have a bearing on the residential market can perhaps be broken down into

economic, financial, human, physical and seasonal, with one overriding and obvious factor summed up as "supply and demand".

The economic factors we have already touched on for the residential
market if looked at nationally must reflect the state of the nation's
economy; if there is no growth then new wealth is not created and in
real terms net spendable incomes cannot increase. The Price
Commission established that movement in house values can be more
directly related to net disposable incomes than to any other single
factor.

The 1977 Green Paper on Housing Policy gave the following number
of second-hand houses coming on to the market in each year available
for owner-occupation. In 1971, 685,000; in 1976, 710,000, and it
estimated that this would grow to 790,000 by 1981 and to 860,000 by
1986. These figures will be lower than the number of changes in
ownership, for some changes take place without properties coming on
to the market. It is difficult to see how in practice this growth can be
maintained without economic growth and with a rapidly increasing
level of unemployment. It is true that the Government's policy on the
sale of local authority housing to existing tenants might artificially help
to maintain this "broad picture of underlying growth" as it is described
by the Price Commission. If the state of the economy and the pressures
on it are such as to dictate an excessively high Minimum Lending Rate
this must in itself slow down growth, not only in the total number of
owner-occupied dwellings, but in the value of those that exist. It must
follow that if the growth in the number of houses is reflected in the
number of mortgages advanced each year, as the Commission believed,
growth will be stunted if, as an indirect result of the state of the
economy, the inflow of funds to the building societies is severely
restricted, and, as a direct consequence of this, building society loans
are either rationed or restricted in amount. These factors will act as
restraints against an increase in home-ownership, against increases in
house values and against the rate of new house building, particularly in
the private sector.

It could be argued that growth in these housing areas has, over the
last ten years, been greater than that in the economy, and the link
between them is more tenuous than I would tend to believe.

There are other factors, particularly of a financial nature, that have a
direct bearing on house values. The Green Paper emphasised the sense
of greater independence that home-ownership brings, a social or
personal factor, but clearly tax relief on mortgage interest on sums
borrowed up to £25,000 and option mortgage subsidies have distorted
the picture, but again, commenting on the long-term trend of house-
prices since 1960, the Green Paper stated that there "appears to be a
long-term tendency for house-prices to rise relative to the general price

level even if the effect of changes in the quality of houses sold is excluded". This may be a correct statement of long-term trend, but in the shorter term there are other factors at work. Over the period 1968-78 house-prices increased by 233 per cent and retail prices by only 187 per cent, but in the last five years of that period, between 1973 to 1978, house-prices rose by 52 per cent and retail prices by 110 per cent.

The cyclical nature of the market that we have already observed is obviously one of the reasons, but anyone who practised throughout this period will be aware that of the 52 per cent increase between 1973 and 1978 the greater part came in the last two years. They will also be aware that in the years 1970/1972 there had been an unprecedented rise in house-values and in particular in the value of land suitable for development.

What were the factors at work? There is little doubt that during the Heath administration, in the hope of generating greater investment in industry and higher levels of productivity, money supply was greatly increased, but the Institutions, the average house-owner, and in particular the clearing banks very often through their merchant banking subsidiaries, and the merchant banks, did not want to invest in this way (could it be they lacked confidence in British industry?). The money flowed into the property market and by no means only into the residential market; indeed one way in which this money was invested in British industry was by the building of new factories and warehouses, but not only factories and warehouses, also offices; who will forget the saga of "Centre Point", which seemed to symbolise the public antipathy to the property developer and perhaps also their concern at what was happening in the property market at large. If money supply was the direct cause of the "boom" there were other factors, albeit linked to this basic source, and the principal of these factors was confidence. The developer, and it matters not what sector of the market he was involved in, appeared to believe when considering a development project, that it did not matter if his site appraisal did not add up in the light of current values, he could rely on the market inevitably rising and he would be all right at the end of the day.

The house-purchaser, infected by this air of confidence and assuming that house values were about to take off, or were rising steeply, with money readily and relatively cheaply available to him, scrambled to get on the ladder. Existing house-owners, for the same reasons, sought to move up market and there was a period in all sectors of intense activity. As a result values rose at an unprecedented rate. Only relatively few sensed that it could not last. The bubble burst and the collapse brought down developers whose names were household words, Stern and Lyon amongst them, but with them many smaller development companies, leaving partially completed and abandoned sites for which ludicrous sums had been paid throughout Britain. It is my personal view that whilst money supply was the prime cause of the boom and the confidence that created it, the cause of the collapse was the other way round — confidence went and this confidence or lack of it was not so much directly related to the property market, but to the Government's inability to maintain growth. We therefore have two predominant factors underlying the market, related but not necessarily closely: the state of the economy and public confidence.

I turn again to the Price Commission's Report of August 1979. At paragraph 2.14 it said: "A question of particular public interest is whether the activities of estate agents have any effect on the general level of house-prices. In particular it has been suggested that the sharp increase in house-prices between 1972 and 1974 might have been exacerbated by agents who 'talked the market up', encouraged 'gazumping' and generally spread an atmosphere of speculation and panic".

I would question the years they quote, for I think most practising agents would agree that the heat was on in 1971 and that by 1973 it was all over.

The Commission decided to seek outside advice and in particular that of Professor D. Hendry of the London School of Economics.

Some of the conclusions reached are of interest in considering market factors and in particular the agent's role in the market place. For example: "In the short term, however, their (the agents') advice to clients may produce speculation which affects the speed with which prices adjust to their new stable equilibrium after a change, but the evidence suggests that this is mainly helping the market to adjust more quickly rather than engineering speculative booms and slumps".

Then again — "However, with sharp movements, it is easy to understand how it might be seen that estate agents were causing prices to move, by their advice to both buyers and sellers, when in fact they were only making the market work efficiently."

Acknowledging the boom/slump pattern of the market, (and here we are commenting on the house market alone) they concluded that "Prices tend towards equilibrium at which supply and demand are in balance".

Practising agents will be well aware that the periods when the market could be said to be in balance are relatively short-lived and for much of the time one either has a sellers' market with a totally inadequate supply and over-demand, or the converse. The research showed the factors which determine the equilibrium price as measures of real personal disposable income, interest rates in mortgage lending and the net increase in available houses.

For the house agent, therefore, we can conclude that the principal factors that bear on his market are the state of the economy, the confidence of the public in its stability, interest rates, the availability of mortgages, the relationship available mortgages have to incomes and, last and probably most significant, real personal disposable incomes.

Then we come to consider the physical factors that bear on the market, although in some respects environmental would be a better description. By far the most important is the gross distortion of the market place by Government interference under the heading of Town and Country Planning. It is not for me to argue here whether or not planning has proved constructive, destructive, necessary or unnecessary. When Dame Edith Sharp, after retirement from the Department of the Environment as the Arch Planner, saw fit to question whether anything had been achieved, there is little point in a lesser mortal asking the same question.

The distortion planning creates, however, is very much a relevant factor to anybody involved in the property market and in whatever section. This distortion, although applied by Government through local planning authorities, does in part reflect another distorting factor. The emphasis in recent years on public participation has brought planning ever nearer to people in their own homes and in their own environment and it is, although regrettable, natural that it is those who want to see no change who shout the loudest. One sees therefore in areas of high environmental value such as the South-East, where regional policy is one of general restraint, that this policy hardens when County Councils come to prepare Structure Plans and hardens even further when local planning authorities prepare their Local Plans. Indeed in many cases what was intended to be restraint becomes total embargo.

This will have its effect on the estate agent, for the restriction on the growth of the product with which he is concerned will force prices upwards, bring pressure for re-development within the built-up areas, affect movement in the market and possibly exclude some people from it, in particular young families and young and growing companies. I am not personally able to comment on planning as a factor in the major development areas — those practising within such areas would be better qualified than I. In general terms, however, planning, in that it either encourages growth or effectively restrains it, directly affects the supply of the product to the property market and must therefore affect values. It also affects the movement of people by the effect it has on job-mobility.

Another physical factor that many believe has a very real bearing on the market, is that of building costs, and I have already questioned just how relevant a factor it is in the housing market. A developer, and it matters not in this context whether he is building offices, factories, shops or houses, faced with rising construction costs must exert pressure on the market in an attempt to recover them by increased prices or rent. Under normal market circumstances this pressure is probably not significant, for increased building costs will almost certainly reflect and keep in line either with the increase in retail prices or incomes and thus become just part of the general movement in the market. There will, however, be and indeed there have been times when either building costs have risen far faster than these other factors and therefore faster than property values and there have been times when the property market has for other reasons held back, and mortgage famine in the house market we have already noted as an example. In these circumstances the developer/builder might, in an attempt to recover some of his costs, push hard to improve his return. If he is not going to be able significantly to affect the market, all he can do, and this too we have seen, is stop building.

The construction of a new motorway affecting mobility cannot only generate population movement and thus affect values, it can also affect them by its physical impact on specific houses or localities, and by causing the closing of schools. The stopping of bus or railway services would come into this category of physical factors affecting the market.

Then there are the personal factors likely to affect the market and of which the good estate agent should be aware. I have called them "personal" although perhaps "human" would be as good a description. They are far-ranging and some could vary from region to region, one locality to another or as between one village and another. Population trends — for example there has been an increase in the number of old persons that is likely to continue in the years ahead. Then there is the decrease in family size and the increased number of one-person families. We have already seen significant changes come about as a result of pressure from these sectors of the community. One recalls that even 20 years ago purpose-built flats were rare outside the main cities and many building societies would not advance on this sort of security. At that time, and indeed in the years that followed, the flats that were provided tended to be acquired by the elderly, or by the single. Now many are acquired by young married couples. Flat-living seems to have become accepted throughout most of the country and this is a pattern that is likely to continue.

None of the factors we have been considering can ever be looked at alone. For example, what leads to a young married couple buying a small two-bedroomed flat in the certain knowledge of great inconvenience if and when they have a family? Is it planning restraint forcing the price of houses beyond their pockets? Is it because they cannot afford to fund the mortgage they would need to buy a house? Is it because more flats are being provided following pressure from the Government to make better use of the land that is available, i.e., to increase density, or is it because they both will have to work in the early years that they choose to live in a flat and minimise maintenance work on both house and garden?

The agent working in the residential field has not only to be aware of the effect of the national economy and fiscal policy on his market, he must be aware of all the other trends — national, regional, local, social and personal — that could affect it. It could be argued that he need not worry about such things and that all he needs to do to prosper is to react to change when change occurs. This, as we shall see, will not be enough if he is going to deal effectively with building land and when advising development companies.

To a greater or lesser extent all these factors bear on the commercial market and it is perhaps unnecessary to consider them in this context in detail. Without growth in the economy one cannot go on building new factories and offices. The need to replace existing accommodation to suit new techniques or because of physical obsolescence, will continue, but this can be met only if there is sufficient profitability in industry to pay rents that reflect a realistic return on the capital involved. Again, from my own experience, if planning restraint against industrial growth has forced rental values for antiquated and inadequate premises to too high a level this will in itself act as a restraint on redevelopment. What encouragement is there for the owner of such a factory, able to obtain a rent of £2 a square foot, to demolish it and build anew at a current cost of say £14 a foot if he will only see another 50p a foot from that investment? I accept it is not necessarily as simple as that, for the new factory will be in a different investment category and rebuilding which might make little sense in rental terms might be justified in terms of capital value. The industrialist considering moving to a new area, or indeed the office-user contemplating decentralising will be concerned as to his ability in the new location to recruit the new labour and administrative staff that they will need. To this extent they will be concerned as to the age-structure of the community, the schooling, the general level of house-values, the likely availability of existing and proposed housing, and not least the attractiveness of the area to himself, his family and his fellow directors, the environmental and human factors.

Although the market factors that we have been considering will have a bearing on the house-builder and developer, it is essentially their effect on potential and existing owner-occupiers that concerns both the developer and the estate agent. When we look at essentially the same factors in the context of the commercial market we have to consider their effect on those who effectively fund that market. Accepting, as we have already noted, that some commercial property can only be regarded as suitable for owner-occupation, and given that some companies will always want to own their own freehold, this market is in the main funded and owned, and above all influenced, by the Institutions, for whom property is but one form of investment. The extent to which they are at any one time prepared to invest in the property market, the yields they will expect when they do so, and thus the nature of the property investments they are prepared to acquire, will all be considered by them in the context of the investment market as a whole and will be related to the performance and potential yield from forms of investment other than real property. It is certainly beyond the scope of this book to consider and review the investment market as a whole, or to make comparisons. It is, however, obvious that nearly all forms of investment will react to the economy and the money market. The Institutions in whom in one form or another the majority of our people have invested are not there to gamble recklessly with their money. Invariably, in regard to property, they are advised by surveyors who specialise in this market, who are conversant with their investment policy and with trends, not only in the property market but in the investment field as a whole. Having said that, underlying every investment the Institutions make in real property are the quality, advantages and disadvantages of the property itself, the immediate yield, the way it is likely to perform in terms of yield and capital value over a period of time, its likely life, its lettability in the event of vacancy and so on.

Ten

Valuation and Allied Matters

**The house agent and the commercial agent —
Valuation in the house market — Aspects of valuation
in the commercial market — The dual nature of the
investment — Commercial property as an investment
— Asset and income — The nature of the lease —
Yields — Prime defined — Factories, warehouses,
offices — Shops' limited interest in secondaries — The
need to reflect economic trends**

In producing a book dealing with estate agency as practised in this
country, and with practical considerations, the temptation has been to
stray away into those many "professional" areas of general practice
concerning property that have a bearing on the estate agency function.
The fact that I have made the house agency function my predominant
theme has been of some help in keeping me to my subject.

My reasons for choosing this theme were numerous. First it is the
field that most concerns the majority of general practitioners and it
follows should be of concern to the majority of today's students.
Secondly, the procedures to be followed in marketing residential
property are essentially the same as those to be followed in other fields,
although in the commercial market and in the business transfer field
there are other overriding considerations that will affect approach and
emphasis. Thirdly, I chose it because it is the one field that has been of
particular concern to the general public and thus to consumer
associations, the media and the Government.

It is easy mentally to divide the over-all market into two sectors, house
agency and commercial agency, but in doing so fail to appreciate the
scope that each covers.

Of the two, house agency would appear to be the more
straightforward, but it must be realised that this covers every thing from
the selling of small Victorian terraced artisan houses to the substantial
country estate. The agent faced with the former will probably only have
to look to a very small area to find his prospective purchaser. He may
not even need to look on a local basis, but merely on a neighbourhood
basis. At the other end of the scale, if the market for a fine country
house or a West End penthouse is to be explored in depth, it may have

to be on a national and possibly international basis. It must not be forgotten that there is a market in land, both for residential development and for commercial development. It follows that the agent whose practice is predominantly in the house market is the most likely to be active in the residential land market and vice versa.

Also, there are many house agents, particularly if the practice is an old one, who will also be involved with residential property management, and as a result will from time to time have investment properties to sell.

It is easy to see the commercial market dominated by the great national firms and concerned with major office buildings, factories, warehouses and prime shops. In practice the commercial market is as wide as, if not wider in its scope than, the residential one. For at the other end you have the small suite of offices in the country town and the shop on the corner of "Coronation Street". In towns and villages throughout the country there are office buildings, shops, factories, small filling stations, builders' yards and small businesses which it would be uneconomic for the leading commercially-oriented firms, to deal with, and where the market, as in the residential field, could well be a purely local one. Some commercial agency work is dealt with mainly by specialist firms, the sale of small businesses as going concerns and licensed property being perhaps the two most obvious examples, but a great deal of this commercial work has to be dealt with by the general practitioner.

If the general practitioner is to be able to cope effectively with all those types of property with which he could reasonably be asked to deal, he has got to have either in his own right, or readily available to him, a wide range of professional knowledge. A general practitioner dealing with potential residential building land cannot function effectively without a working knowledge of town planning law and procedures. Faced with the sale of investment cottages, he will need to know about the Rent and Housing Acts. In the commercial field he will need a working knowledge of the Landlord and Tenant Act 1954, also some knowledge of Town and Country Planning.

I cannot possibly hope in this book to give even a basic outline of all the knowledge that is required, but valuation is one field of activity normally regarded as "professional" in which it is absolutely vital that the estate agent, whether he is operating in the residential or commercial markets, or in both, must be competent.

In that I hope this book will come to be read not only by established members of the leading professional bodies and students aspiring to membership, but by those wishing to operate in the estate agency market who do not or cannot aspire to "qualify", I think it important that I should deal, albeit in very general terms, with valuations.

I look first at valuations in the context of the residential market.

Valuation in the house market

The average house negotiator is seldom if ever called upon to give an opinion as to value that cannot be arrived at by a simple comparison with other houses which he, or his office, have sold. This requires experience but little expertise. If a house is in a serious state of dilapidation, or lacks certain basic facilities such as a bathroom or central heating, he will need to know roughly what it would cost to repair or to provide those facilities and what improvement grants are available, if his opinion is to be reasonably accurate. He will make rough adjustments to his opinion for any adverse factors that are obvious to him.

An American realtor once said that there were only three matters important in determining the value of real estate — location, location and location, and as we shall see, particularly when we come to look at sections of the commercial market, there is a great deal of truth in this. The average house-owner, however, will assess the value of his own house on other criteria. If it is much bigger than its neighbours, with extra facilities, and he has been advised to insure for a substantially higher sum, he will rely on these factors to argue that his house is proportionately worth that much more, failing to realise that the nature of the property around him, or put another way the "location", sets the general level and that the factors to which he attributes great significance may have little more than a marginal bearing. "But I have just spent £4,000 on that extension, surely the house must be worth a great deal more than that" is the type of statement familiar to all negotiators. Unless they fully appreciate the significance of location, they will not be able to deal with that potential vendor sympathetically.

The estimated replacement cost can be a guide to current value, but it can be a misleading one. One can, if one knows the current level of building costs and has taken a gross floor area, assess what it would cost to replace the house, and then one could allow a depreciation factor for obsolescence or allow for the cost of modernisation, but the answer would not necessarily be relevant. A newly-decorated house may be depreciated, and not enhanced, in value if those decorations are garish, tasteless and would be abhorrent to the majority of purchasers.

All this is not to say that an analysis of basic value, i.e., an assessment of site-value, building costs, etc., is never relevant. With houses very recently built, replacement cost may well give a realistic guide to market value.

Mr. M. J. Vivian (the writer of "The Art of House Agency") expects his house negotiator to measure gross internal floor areas as he feels this enables him when necessary to give a second "armchair" opinion as to value. He presumably knows every square inch of his area well and in these circumstances he probably could advise.

Past records may not help, for in an inflationary market they rapidly become out-dated, but if increases in values have been carefully monitored by the office and the average percentage increase over the period is known, this could give a guide as to current value.

Values of identical houses could vary enormously, depending on factors such as the proximity of a local authority housing estate, proximity to a main road or a proposed main road, a noisy or obnoxious neighbour, town planning proposals and so on. The negotiator in the house market needs above all an intimate knowledge of his area, and this almost street by street, if not house by house. Also invaluable is knowledge of recent transactions, whether negotiated by him, by his firm, or by other agents and — this can be important — an awareness of what is happening and is likely to happen in his market. If he has a basic knowledge of structures, sufficient to identify serious problems, so much the better.

From this it is clear that there is no one method of valuing a house, and it is also clear that if the advice given to vendors is to be as accurate as possible it is likely to be based on evidence of current transactions. There must be arrangements made to ensure, within any one office, that every negotiator is kept fully aware of what is happening in the market place. The rapid passage of information is vital.

Closely related to the valuation of houses is the valuation of individual building plots. (The valuation of building land for larger development projects will be dealt with elsewhere.) The subject remains an emotive one, for a purchaser may wish to live in an area regardless of whether or not it is generally considered to be attractive and he may wish to build a house of higher calibre than those immediately surrounding it, for purely personal reasons, but the negotiator should be able to decide what sort of house the average purchaser will wish to put on that plot, what it is likely to cost, and from that arrive at a reasonably accurate assessment of the plot's value.

As we have seen, many factors contribute to the value of a house: situation, accommodation, style, suitability to the area, facilities such as access to shops, schools, public transport, current fashion, state of repair, decorative condition, availability of improvement grants, its suitability as a mortgage security, planning proposals for the area — the list is almost endless. In the end the house market remains an emotive one and the negotiator's decision as to value may also be emotive. Here lies a danger.

A negotiator can be attracted to a house because it is the sort of house he himself would like to live in and as a result he could over-value. He could look at another house and decide that it was a "horror" and down-value it, and at this point I would give to others the advice I received as a young valuer. "However horrible you think a house, however dreadful the district, remember somebody built it, others have bought and lived in it, all you have to do is find somebody else who wants to."

Earlier in this chapter, I commented that the residential estate agent is the more likely to have to deal with the sale of residential building land. This is generally a fair statement, but of course some of the larger areas of building land that become available and some of those in town centre situations, which possibly include a commercial element, are frequently dealt with by the larger firms and very often because of the need before any sale can take place to deal with the planning authority and obtain a planning consent. I think it is appropriate however to deal briefly with the valuing of residential development sites when considering valuations in the house market.

Circumstances will vary; sometimes one will be asked to express an opinion as to value where there is a planning consent for a specific number of houses and perhaps for specified types and sizes of houses. On other occasions there will only be an outline consent and the agent will need that knowledge of planning policy in his area that I consider vital, to decide what type of house the land is most suited for, and what density is likely to be approved, before he could consider the question of value. He must watch out for pitfalls — for land that can't readily be drained into the only sewer available because of its inadequate depth and where a pumping station would be required, for land that is boggy and will need to be drained, for the land that has been filled and where there will be a need for piled foundations, for Tree Preservation Orders, for the close proximity of non-conforming users that might affect value, or trees on adjoining land whose close proximity could affect the nature of the development to take place and so on.

The method of valuation normally applicable to development sites is the "residual method". This is simply, but not always that simple in fact, having decided or been told what can be built on the land, and having assessed the total value likely to be realised for the development at the end of the day, to subtract the costs of providing the infrastructure, building the houses, or flats, borrowing the necessary finance, paying the necessary professional fees and allowing for a profit, to arrive at the price the developer is likely to be willing to pay for the site.

I do not intend to go further into the residual method of valuation here, for the process is precisely the same as that one would follow in advising a development company client as to what to pay for land and I will deal with the matter in more detail when I consider the estate agent in the development field.

The residual method of valuing building land must always be treated with great caution, for from my experience it is only likely to produce a realistic value under very stable market conditions, and readers will realise that the economy of this country certainly over the last 20 years has seldom produced conditions of this kind. The same problem is faced by the agent advising a vendor as to what to expect or seek for his land as is faced by the agent advising a development company as to what to pay. He will have to "take a view," for many builders and developers will do just this.

Even if a builder is buying a site because he wants to develop it immediately, it will take him many months to have his detailed plans prepared, to obtain a detailed planning consent, to provide the necessary infrastructure works and to build his houses, all before the first unit is ready to be sold. If he sees a rising market and one which he believes is likely to continue to rise throughout this preparation and development period, and if, as is very nearly always the case, under such market conditions there is keen competition, he is going to make certain assumptions with regard to the likely increases in both house values and building costs, in deciding just how much he "dare" pay for the site.

Similarly, but perhaps more rarely in very difficult market conditions such as those experienced at the end of 1979 and in early 1980, with uncertainty as to what will happen to house-prices, with some commentators even suggesting a fall and with interest rates at a very high level, competition could be slight, for many will only buy land if it is absolutely vital to their building programme, and many will only buy if it appears cheap and if they could buy it at less than the residual valuation might show it to be worth.

A valuer should always be aware of current economic conditions, what effect they are likely to have on his markets, but in no field is this more important than in valuing sites for potential development.

Before leaving valuations in the residential market, we should consider briefly the valuation of residential investments. Traditionally, the method has been to assess or calculate gross rental income, to make allowance for the landlord's liabilities, which would normally include repairs, maintenance and insurance, but may also include payment of rates, to arrive at a net income, and then to capitalise it by adopting a multiplier or years' purchase figure, based on experience, and the valuer's judgment.

There are other matters that could show this traditional approach to be wildly inaccurate. The investor in cheap terraced housing investments is seldom looking just to rental income, he will be working on the assumption that over a period of time a number of his houses will become vacant and could be sold and his gain possibly subject only to Capital Gains Tax. It is sadly a fact of life, for which politicians are to blame, that a house occupied by a single aged tenant with no close relatives living in, is going to be worth a great deal more than an identical house occupied by a young family. Care needs to be taken to make sure that there are no outstanding repair notices, allowance must be made if a house is in a very poor state of repair and technically unfit for human habitation, possibly because of serious rising damp and so on. It may be that steps have not been taken to establish a fair rent and that the rent passing is well below what could be achieved. Again a word of caution: a semi-detached Victorian house let and occupied as one unit, could be worth considerably more than an identical house that has been divided and let as two flats, even if the overall rental income is higher, for if the purchaser is to stand any chance of getting possession of the latter and selling it on the open market with vacant possession, he has got to wait for two units of accommodation to fall vacant rather than one. It is for these reasons in recent years that I have found it more reliable to assess value by taking a percentage of the estimated vacant possession value. I hesitate to give any firm guidance, but, dependent upon the individual circumstances, anywhere between 30 per cent and 50 per cent would appear to be the bracket.

In talking about valuations, we have been considering only one aspect, i.e., what is the property likely to fetch on the open market. This is not necessarily the only value that can be attributed to it. If you were advising trustees, a bank or a building society as to the value that could be attributed to the property as security for a loan, you might well be justified in taking a more cautious approach, as any disposal could be under forced sale conditions.

Aspects of Valuation in the Commercial Market

The commercial market is created by demand for property from a variety of prospective purchasers or lessees, perhaps in marketing terms "consumers". These can be divided into four broad groups:

(1) Potential occupiers.
(2) Developers.
(3) Those seeking long-term investment.
(4) Those seeking short-term investment.

Certain properties may appeal to more than one or possibly to all of these categories of purchaser. A vendor or purchaser (and here one must remember that in the commercial market it is common practice for agents to act for would-be purchasers or occupiers), being advised by an estate agent has the right to expect that agent to be able to consider the property from the standpoint of each category of purchaser before giving advice, and it follows that the competent commercial agent must be fully aware of market conditions and the factors affecting each.

We have already noted that the commercial market is a very wide one and that it is generally recognised as including shops, offices, warehouses and factories, with some restricted specialised areas such as petrol filling stations, hotels, licensed premises, leisure facilities, and so on. These are of marginal importance to the property market as a whole.

The commercial property market differs in a number of very significant ways from the residential market. It is not an emotive market in which personal and social preferences can play such a part in determining ultimate value or the price ultimately paid, for these are not strictly the same thing. It is essentially "commercial". Those involved in it are profit-oriented — what the professional man can afford to pay for the freehold of his offices, or by way of rent, determined by the nature of his practice and its potential profit, and likewise a manufacturer will not purchase a factory at a price or pay a rent that at the end of the day would render it impossible for him to manufacture his product and market it to show an adequate return on the capital invested. The shopkeeper, whether a company such as Marks & Spencer or a sole trader, considering buying a neighbourhood shop, will ask the same questions — what population will my shop serve, how many of that population will pass the door, in what income and social groups are they? In the end, it will be the turnover which that shop is capable of producing that will determine its value.

The long-term investor contemplating the purchase of a major investment may not be concerned at the immediate yield it shows him, although if it is being bought into an existing portfolio the decision will be part of a plan of which the present overall yield will be one factor. He is more likely to be concerned with stability — and here the calibre of the lessee is clearly significant — and in long-term growth; in short how the investment will perform over a period when compared with other alternative forms open to him.

The motives of the short-term investor vary, but always the aim is profit.

As Paul Orchard-Lisle put it — "The parties to a commercial property transaction are motivated by profit. It matters not whether it is the purchaser or the vendor for whom the agent is acting, either way the agent needs to be sufficiently conversant with business generally to appreciate the significance of a given property transaction to the parties involved and it is the flair of the good commercial agent to be able to recognise a profit that potentially exists, and to point his client towards realising it."

We have seen that in the residential market the value of past records as an aid to valuation is questionable. But in the commercial market, because decisions made by industrialists, retailers and businessmen are made objectively, in the light of circumstances ruling at the time, records of past transactions and indeed of the properties themselves, are of much greater significance. This, of course, does not absolve the commercial estate agent from the need to be aware of trends in the market or in his particular section of the market, but a data-base to which to relate these trends will prove to be of very considerable value. We have already noted that in a practice wholly or largely devoted to commercial work, the agency function will be much more closely related to other aspects of the practice and in particular to valuation and management than would be the case in a mainly residential practice.

Nearly all major commercial estate agency practices have kept records, not only of the transactions in which they themselves were involved, but of those of which they were aware, for a great many years. In many cases their value has been seriously undermined by an absence of agreed methods of analysis, and inadequate information as to certain fundamentals which may have been apparent at the time of the transaction, but have got lost with the vagaries of memory. If one's records or data-bank are to be of real value, there needs to be agreement, first as to the way in which transactions should be analysed and, secondly, to ensure that all significant information is retained. A material advance in this direction would be made if all agents abode by the R.I.C.S. and I.S.V.A. Code of Measuring Practice (1979) and ideally all historic records considered to be of value should be adapted to this basis.

We seem to have digressed from the subject of valuation as concerning commercial agency, but in practice all that one has done is to stress the importance of a good data-bank that is capable of systematic analysis. No data-bank will, however, fulfil its functions unless it is kept consistently right up to date, and a simple set of house-rules should be sufficient to ensure that this happens. It is preferable that the partner or negotiator concerned with the transaction should personally contribute to the record system and not leave it to a third party. Completion of the analysis and the making of the record is best done at the time the terms are agreed and the solicitors instructed. They can be erased if the transaction does not proceed, but a considerable time might elapse between the agreement as to terms and completion of the transaction, and for future reference it is the date on which the parties agreed terms in principle that is most relevant.

When we were considering the growth of estate agency and commented on the vast increase in the number of homes now privately owned, we also noted the substantial reduction, as a result of political pressures and interference, in the number of privately owned rented homes. A few property investors, trusts and landed estates remain in the residential sector, but they are a dwindling number and as houses become vacant and are sold, their holding becomes less and less significant. In the residential field the major "investors" other than those who have decided to become owner/occupiers partly as a means of personal investment, are the local authorities and housing associations.

Exactly the converse has happened in the commercial field. The growth of the pension funds, insurance companies, unit trusts and property investment companies has been enormous and is likely to continue. One would express the hope that it is not in the future likely to be subject to political interference, for the rent-freeze in the early 'seventies had such far-reaching effects that it had hastily to be abandoned. Clearly the Institutions and other substantial investors in the commercial property market believe that it will, in the future, be allowed to develop freely, and that in doing so it will reflect the needs and support the activities of the industry and commerce on which we all depend.

Again I would appear to digress, but not so, for it is absolutely vital that the commercial estate agent who is advising clients as to value be aware of the requirements of the property investor, the yields that are currently sought and/or are acceptable and as to likely trends. Consider for a moment the estate agent advising the development company on the acquisition of land suitable for development as a small industrial estate, who knows that at the end of the day it is the intention of that company to let those factories and dispose of the investment it has created. Similarly consider the estate agent advising the board of a company planning to build a new factory to house its rapidly expanding business, but who at the end of the day will not want to hold it, but will be seeking to sell it and to lease it back.

It is in just such situations that one sees the role of the commercial agent and commercial property valuer as irrevocably linked. If either's role is more important than the other, it could be argued that it is the agent's, for he is the man involved in the market place, establishing the level of values. Again as Paul Orchard-Lisle said — "It is impossible to avoid linking commercial agency with valuation. Any valuer operating without an estate agency back-up cannot be as effective as one who is daily operating in the market place. The valuer therefore will be one of the principal users of the data-bank. He must not, however, lose sight of the fact that records only analyse what has happened and do not necessarily relate to the present or any future date. Valuation tables and a calculator will produce a theoretical value, but ultimately the value of a property is what it will change hands for in the open market between willing parties. If a firm is so structured that it has a separate valuation team it would be well advised at the end of any computation to check back to the agency team as to the appropriateness of the assumptions they have made and as to whether their computed answer is realistic in relation to the existing market place."

Because of the significance of investment to the commercial property market, it is perhaps appropriate before considering the general principles of valuation to consider the breakdown of commercial property into a number of investment groups. There is a market in almost any form of property investment, whether it be the freehold of one of London's major office buildings or a short leasehold interest in a third-rate shop, but for our purposes I think we can break the investment market down into four categories. These I suggest are similar to, but should not be confused with, the four varieties of consumer we looked at in opening this chapter and I will return to this point.

The categories into which we could break down the investment market are —

(1) Prime.
(2) Secondary.
(3) Tertiary.
(4) Owner-occupation.

The prime investment will be of interest to the Institutions, the pension funds and the insurance companies. This group would include shops in the best trading positions, good modern office buildings and factories where there are no obvious detrimental factors that could take a property out of this group. Simply to illustrate this proviso, a factory may be good and it may be brand new, but if, because it replaces an earlier building, it is situated in a predominantly residential district, difficult to find and gain access to, then it is not likely to fall into the "prime" group. A prime investment is likely to be occupied by a tenant of considerable calibre and it will be easy to manage. Multiple occupation could again take an otherwise prime building out of this classification. A prime investment will also be freehold or held on a long lease, with an unexpired term unlikely to be much less than 99 years and free from any serious restrictions or encumbrances.

Many of the institutional investors are also anxious to avoid holding too many of what they see as relatively small investments. For this reason anything with a capital value of less than £200,000, although it might be "prime" in every other respect, could well drop into the category of "secondary".

Secondary investments cover a wide range and I will admit to over-simplification for the sake of clarity in the groupings I have made. Dependent upon the supply and demand for prime investments, some of the institutional funds will move into the secondary market, but other investors will be investment companies, family trusts, trustees of some smaller self-administered pension funds and private investors. Older but modernised office buildings in main provincial centres, good shops on the fringe of the prime positions, older factories, leasehold properties that would have been prime were it not for the shorter number of years unexpired could all come into this group. By its very nature the secondary investment market is considered to be riskier than the prime, whether it be because the calibre of the tenants increases the risk of voids, or because when demand for investments is slack buyers will not be about and capital values will tend to fall, or because the capital value is not sufficiently great to attract the major investor. Certainly the secondary market suffered severely during the recession of 1973/74.

The line between this secondary market and the tertiary investment market is perhaps harder to define. There are those, again family trusts, private self-administered pension funds, individual private investors and speculators, who are prepared to buy into this field and the immediate or prime concern is likely to be a high yield.

I deliberately stressed that these investment groups should not be confused with the four categories of consumer suggested earlier, for now one comes to consider the owner/occupier. Many companies or bodies choose to be owner/occupiers, and here I run the risk of causing confusion, for owner/occupiers do not specifically form an "investment" group. Some of the major national retailing companies choose to hold their own freeholds as do the building societies and the banks. I have, however, classified owner/occupiers as one of my investment groups, for there are certain types of property that are not attractive to the investment market as such, but nevertheless have the one characteristic of all commercial property, i.e., the prospect, if not the actuality, of making profit from their occupation. The old, unsatisfactory factory suitable for a rough-and-ready process, the garage workshop, the village store, the house converted into or with planning consent to convert to offices could be examples. The person, company or firm wishing to occupy such premises for a commercial purpose may have great difficulty in finding an "investor" who will buy it and lease it to him. He will almost certainly have to raise his own finance and acquire and hold the freehold.

Stressing yet again that the grouping I have made is not only arbitrary but an over-simplification, I have used it to underline the fact that the calibre or potential calibre of the property as an investment is the first criterion to which a valuer must look in making any appraisal, and it follows that it is the first criterion to which the commercial estate agent must look in deciding how and where to market.

We should therefore consider commercial property as an investment in greater depth and I am indebted to Paul Orchard-Lisle for this section, for it is almost entirely based on his notes.

Commercial Property as an Investment

It is proposed here to deal first with commercial property as an institution investment, although much of what is said will also concern other investors and indeed owner occupiers.

It could be said that the institution buying a commercial property investment is buying two things. It is buying an asset and secondly it is buying income in the form of rent from a tenant or lessee. This is now the most common form of direct investment in property. At the same time the investor is looking for security, also in two forms. The property could be said to be its own security as an asset with an income-producing potential. Hence the concern of the institutions as to the nature of that asset, which we will later consider in more detail. The institution will, however, be looking for security as far as the rental income is concerned.

Rent is secured under contract in the form of a lease and, in the case of shops, factories, offices and warehouses in the United Kingdom, it has become customary for the lessee to be responsible for repairs, insurance and payment of rates. The landlord or lessor is thus left with a net income from which few if any deductions have to be made. The lease will state the rent that is to be paid, how and when it is to be paid, and it may provide for penalties for late payment.

It is now customary for leases to include provision not only for reviews of the rent at regular intervals, but for reviews that can only be in an upward direction and the lessor can take some comfort in the knowledge that in the event of the rent not being paid and action having to be taken for its recovery it does rank as a prior charge.

The leasehold system of tenure as we now know it has withstood the tests of both time and the courts and has proved to be flexible enough to adapt to changing circumstances, particularly during the last 25 years.

In short if the property is right, the lease properly drawn and the tenant's covenant to pay sound, rent can be regarded as "certain, stable and secure".

We earlier commented that the purchasing institution will be concerned with the yield from his investment and how this is likely to compare with the other forms available to him.

The real rental growth prospects of a property vary enormously from time to time and one is talking about growth prospects as opposed necessarily to the rent currently passing. Similarly, the opportunity costs and acquisition in terms of yield will vary. One therefore sees marked differences in prime yields from time to time and over the last eight years these have moved within the following brackets:

Commodity	*Maximum Rate*	*Minimum Rate*
Shops	$8\frac{1}{4}\%$	4%
Offices	$8\frac{1}{4}\%$	$3\frac{7}{8}\%$
Industrial/Warehousing	$9\frac{1}{4}\%$	$6\frac{1}{4}\%$

One of the characteristics of commercial property is that although, if it is well chosen in the first place, it is relatively easy to sell, it is not so in relation to most other forms of investment available to the institutions. In comparison, it is difficult to dispose of quickly without loss of some of its value and it is undoubtedly subject to the booms and slumps of the market. Because of this and the differentials in prime yields, its performance as an investment can only effectively be monitored over a period of time. It would, for example, be unwise to endeavour to do so on a monthly basis and probably to review at three-yearly intervals would be adequate and more reliable.

With the exception of the period from November, 1972, until March, 1975, commercial rents have been determined in a free market. Generally, therefore, it can be stated that rent flows from the direct economic value of the accommodation on the open market, and, again if the property has been wisely selected, the income will as we have seen directly relate to the economy as a whole. This is an attraction to the institutional purchaser, whose general requirements are similarly structured.

It is worth examining briefly how commercial property rents have performed against inflation in the last sixteen years, and a simple illustration is to look at the change in prime shop-rents over that period and compare it with the Retail Price Index. The former showed an increase of 485 per cent whilst the latter increased by 343 per cent. This, however, is perhaps too facile an interpretation particularly since, due to the intervals between reviews of rent, a property owner's rental increases come at fairly widely-spaced intervals. For example, property that was purchased in 1962 for £175,000 and then let on a fourteen-year lease at £10,000 per annum showed an initial yield of 5.5 per cent. When the lease expired in 1976 the property was re-let on a "modern" 21-year term with five-year rent reviews at the then open market value of £43,000 per annum, which was capitalised at the then open market rate of interest to give a capital value of £850,000. The growth in value from £175,000 to £850,000 over the fourteen-year period did not occur evenly but on a graph with an increasingly steep rising curve. To take the example a stage further, today the rental value is £53,000 per annum and assuming that there is no increase in rental value between now and the next review in 1981, at that time the property would be showing the purchaser an equated yield of 10.5 per cent per annum. If we then take the contrary view that the investment will continue to appreciate at the rate of rental increase shown historically over the years, by 1981 the new rental will be £73,000 per annum, which is a yield of 40 per cent on historic cost.

Property is, however, as we commented earlier, but one of the forms of investment open to a would-be buyer. The graph on page 132 reproduced with the courtesy of Messrs. Healey & Baker, shows property yields over the last nine years plotted against MLR as a comparison with the yield on $2\frac{1}{2}$ per cent consols as an indicator of the long-term interest rates. As before, the property yields given relate to prime properties and it is as well to define more fully what is meant by prime. To be a prime investment, in shopping for example, it has got to occupy the finest trading location in a major regional centre, be let on a rack rental basis to a major national retailer on a modern full repairing lease with frequent rent reviews, and the property must itself be of modern style, layout and construction. This definition has a myriad of component parts and the judgment of many of them is very subjective, which perhaps accounts for differing assessments of identical properties between surveyors. Clearly, as any of the component parts moves away from perfection so the valuer is entitled to adopt a "thicker" yield.

Initial yields, of course, react not only to the property itself but also to the alternative forms of property investment, the key to which is inevitably rental growth. Over the last fifteen years, growth in shopping rentals values has been at an equivalent compound rate of about 11 per cent. Thus a property acquired on a $4\frac{1}{2}$ per cent basis with a five-year rent review pattern can have an expectation of an overall equated yield of 15 per cent, representing a premium over the yield available on undated gilts of some 3 per cent. The necessity of such a premium is to reflect the disadvantage which property has against gilts in terms of marketability, properties' indivisibility and relative uncertainty.

There are variations between the various types of commercial property and perhaps it is as well to consider these briefly, as they are fundamental to the art of investment in real estate.

Factories and Warehouses

It is not true to assume that what goes for a warehouse, goes for a factory or vice versa.

As we have noted, institutional investors are looking for security both in the asset itself and in the rent that it yields. In broad terms, therefore, they have tended to shun specialised factory buildings, preferring those that could be put to alternative uses, particularly those that would be suitable for use as warehouses. Buildings specifically constructed to house a particular manufacturing process would tend to incorporate the specialist requirements of that industry, for example by having an abnormally high floor-to-ceiling height. Should such a building become vacant, the market for alternative occupational users may be limited. The building designed and constructed as a warehouse and reflecting the needs of a warehouse could appeal to any one of a number of alternative occupiers.

We earlier commented on the relevance of the motorway network and

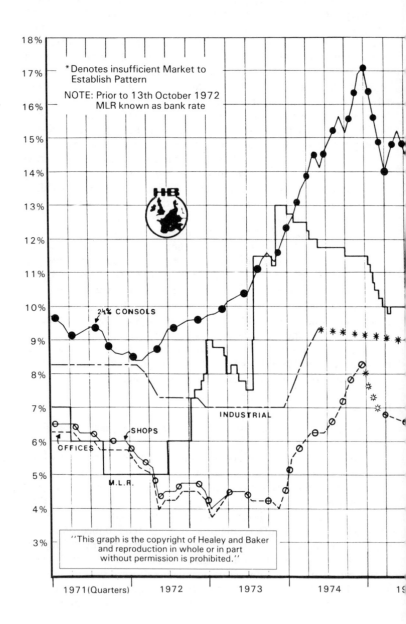

*Denotes insufficient Market to Establish Pattern

NOTE: Prior to 13th October 1972 MLR known as bank rate

2½% CONSOLS

INDUSTRIAL

SHOPS

OFFICES

M.L.R.

1971(Quarters)   1972   1973   1974

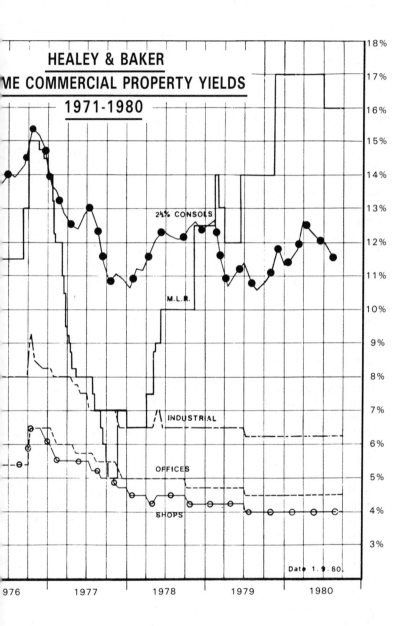

HEALEY & BAKER
ME COMMERCIAL PROPERTY YIELDS
1971-1980

2½% CONSOLS

M.L.R.

INDUSTRIAL

OFFICES

SHOPS

Date 1.9.80

the major airports in the industrial and warehousing scene. Certainly the greatest growth in rental values has been in areas close to the airports and in particular where these are connected to the national motorway system, and clearly if an investment is to be regarded as prime it must be readily accessible.

The design and specification of the warehouse building has been determined by modern mechanical handling equipment and computer-programmed stock control. The institutions and those acting for them are therefore seeking buildings of single-storey construction, with high, clear floor-to-ceiling space, to provide maximum capacity for stacking of goods and containers, with good floor-loading capacity, first-class external circulation areas to enable container lorries to manoeuvre without risk of damage. The provision of car-parking spaces for staff and visitors is also important.

It follows that changes in technical requirements and increase in demand for improvement in working conditions could bring about a significant increase in the rate of obsolescence, and this is something that both the agent and the valuer will be careful to bear in mind.

Generally, industrial rent-levels are not high and this may augur well for future growth. Certainly there were specific signs of further growth in the South during the latter part of 1979 and in early 1980.

Offices

The characteristics that make an office building of interest to the institutions and a "prime" investment are far harder to define. As Paul Orchard-Lisle puts it, "Offices are really no more than factories for clerical and managerial workers". When it comes to location, many of the same factors are relevant. It is a labour-intensive occupation of a building, so there has to be available a supply of clerical and managerial staff and we earlier commented on the relationship between this and the house market.

Public transport facilities must be good. There must be some car-parking, preferably on site, for senior members of staff, and reasonably close for others. Some companies would be anxious to be near a major airport. If entertaining is significant they would want to see reasonable lunching facilities in the area and many see shopping facilities within a few minutes as being important to attract the right type of female staff. In the City of London, for example, some occupiers, because of the nature of their task, would want to be close to certain institutions — the Bank of England, the Stock Exchange, Lloyds and so on. Some areas in the major towns become identified with particular types of office-occupier; solicitors are a typical example.

There is one characteristic of office development which in marginal situations might make it much more difficult to fund, for tenants tend only to agree to take a building when it has been completed, or is nearing completion, i.e., when it can be seen. There is clearly a considerable risk if there is not an obvious market or clear demand and the period between undertaking the venture and completion could be considerable. In this particular market the forces of supply and demand currently appear particularly sensitive and the institutions would be cautious about acquiring offices in a town where there was no clearly established market, and even where the building was pre-let, for they might see a danger that at the expiry of the lease or at a rent review date there will not be the evidence available to support the sort of rent needed if that investment is to perform as required. Forces of supply and demand certainly made themselves felt when in 1974 and 1975 the latter ceased to exist and rents fell sharply, perhaps underlining the point made earlier about the need to take a relatively long-term view when monitoring the performance of property investment.

There is, in this sector of the investment market also, the question of obsolescence, and institutions may well be concerned, when considering office buildings constructed in the late 1950s or early 1960s, at the potential costs of major refurbishment or even reconstruction becoming necessary as a result of labour demands.

In many areas there is currently an over-supply, with the result that rental levels are such that development is just not viable. To be regarded as "prime" an office building must therefore be modern, if not new, let preferably to one substantial occupier, have the essential physical characteristics we have referred to and be located in a town or city where there is at least equilibrium between demand and supply and where one can expect rental values to continue to reflect economic and inflationary trends.

Shops

In no other category of investment property are rental values so sensitive to location as in shops. For a shop to command the highest possible rent it must be able to attract the highest level of profitable trade. This in turn means the largest number of people from the most likely income groups. From the investor's point of view as well as that of the retailer the accommodation provided should be flexible, and from the point of view of the former, adaptable to any one of a number of trades.

On location, as Paul Orchard-Lisle says — "The root of it is the shopping desire line, which, simply, is the route shoppers take, from where they arrive to where they want to go. Their destinations are normally the main department stores, principal variety stores, markets and groupings of attractive shops equating to a major store. The starting points of the desire line are naturally the housing areas, bus stations, car parks and railway stations, but do not over-estimate car parks; as generators of pedestrian flow, most produce far less than one would expect".

Prime shops as an investment have two advantages when compared with other forms. First, not only is it customary for the lessee to spend a substantial sum fitting out his shop, but the need constantly to compete with his rivals dictates that he must maintain the building itself, the shop front and fittings to a very high standard and up-date where necessary. In doing so he removes much of the burden of obsolescence from the lessor. But perhaps more significantly, in a really first-class location and where rental value exceeds something in the order of £15,000 per annum, one will find possibly as much as 80 per cent of total value representing the value of the site itself. For this reason location is far more critical than it was in the case of factories or offices and it follows that the calibre of the building is less significant as a consideration.

Shops in really first-class locations seldom become available to the investment market, and for this reason the institutions will on occasions be prepared to purchase the very best of secondary shops, provided they can be satisfied that there is no risk of shopping patterns in the centre changing and the position deteriorating. They would, however, to get into a really prime site, be prepared to compromise when it comes to the standard of building or the standing of the lessee.

I am aware of having given the impression that the institutions are never interested in any investment other than the very best, let at full "rack" rentals. This is misleading. The pressures on the market vary from time to time and when demand far exceeds supply some of the institutions will move into secondary situations, but seldom very far. They are also interested in reversionary situations, provided the reversion is perhaps not more than 20 years off and if they do this, and have to accept a very low initial yield in order to do so, some will consider balancing this with the purchase of a short-term investment where the term equates approximately with the reversion and where the very much higher yield, after allowing for a sinking fund, will compensate for the initial low yield on the prime investment purchase.

It is beyond the scope of this book to go into those factors that would concern an institution and its professional advisers in building up a portfolio or in the management of that portfolio. What I have tried to do is to give the general practitioner some guide-lines so that he can identify those investments, or development situations, which are likely to be of interest to the institutions.

Eleven

Marketing

An American definition — The agent's role — Marketing a service — Marketing "the product" — The residential and commercial markets briefly discussed — The residential market — Marketing the agent's services — The need to attract the "product" — Setting up a practice — Considerations — Market appreciation — Assessing the competition — Location and nature of the office — Establishing an image — Communicating — The role of the window — Reception — Telephone discipline — Advertising

The American professors of Business Studies, Still and Cunliffe, define marketing as: "The business process by which products are matched with market, and through which transfers of ownership are effected".

The principal role of the estate agent, whether practising in the residential or commercial market, is to bring about the transfer of ownership of an interest in real property. The agent's task is, however, two-fold, for except where he is acting as an adviser to a developer, he is not handling a "product" in the normally accepted sense. He is not selling for a manufacturer. He is not acquiring at one price and selling at another. He does not have a product to sell in the sense that the insurance man will have available to him to market set policies with certain specific characteristics requiring specific rates of premium to achieve specific financial objectives.

The marketing role of the estate agent therefore comes to be considered under two separate headings. Before he can offer an interest in real property for sale, he has to receive instructions from another party. He first, therefore, has to market his own services; only when he has succeeded in this can he be said to have a "product" to market.

In considering the agent's marketing roles, it is necessary to remember his normal status as an "agent". He can advise, but many aspects of marketing will be outside his direct control. The decision as to what price to sell at will be his client's, who will normally also dictate timings. The vendor may well wish to exercise a degree of control over the way his agent sets about the marketing task and indeed may, in some circumstances, select or reject a purchaser or lessee.

It must also be remembered that unlike the normal salesman in the market place, the estate agent rarely takes the transaction to the point of contract. Sales by auction and tender are exceptions, but in the marketing context we must look at the estate agent whose role is to seek a purchaser or lessee, agree the terms on which the transaction is to take place, and who then has to leave it to others, solicitors, to finalise. This is not to say that the agent has no interest in that transaction once solicitors have been instructed. He has a duty to his client to follow the transaction through and give any help he can in seeing that it is successfully concluded. He also has a duty to report to his client any information that could influence that transaction — a higher offer being the obvious example.

There is a point of considerable significance here. There is in any sale by private treaty a built-in "cooling off" period; one that normally runs into weeks rather than days. The estate agent or the negotiator does not, therefore, have as his first aim the obtaining of a signature to a contract, but that of identifying a purchaser or lessee who is not likely to withdraw, who is able to finance the transaction, and who is prepared to agree terms acceptable to his client. It is this, particularly in the residential field, that dictates a soft as opposed to hard approach to selling.

It is necessary to consider residential and commercial markets separately, for there are many differences in their operation which directly affect the agent's approach to his marketing task. The would-be purchaser or lessee of an office building, factory or a warehouse is likely clearly to define his requirements before he commences his search. He is likely to know precisely how he intends to finance the transaction and his decision is likely to be made solely on commercial criteria. Similarly a manufacturer, having decided that his factory is too small, or that his supply of labour is inadequate, will have decided where to go and secured alternative premises before he markets the redundant factory and he is furthermore likely to take his agent's advice on value.

In the residential field, marketing is by no means as clear-cut. Many vendors will only sell if the price is right; some are in no hurry to sell, time is not important to them. Purchasers are influenced by many factors, by social status, educational facilities, the availability of public transport, by their income, by job prospects and, by no means least, personal taste.

This chapter is directed at the residential market.

First we have to consider how the estate agent establishes his business, or, expressed another way, how he sets out to market the service he wishes to offer.

The criteria to be considered are much the same for the person wishing to start up a business as for the established firm wishing to expand or indeed change direction.

The estate agent, as we have said, does not have a "product" to sell in the way that a manufacturer does; he offers a service to the property-owning public with an object in mind — that of securing instructions to sell property. As and when he succeeds and instructions are received, he can be said to be handling a product, and a view must be taken as to the nature of that product, for it could have a very direct bearing on decisions that are to be taken, i.e., the nature of the office, the nature of window display, the calibre of manager, the number of staff, the firm's style or public image, the advertising media to be used and the advertising budget.

It could well be that some factors are already known. A firm already established in a town may well have a very clear public image that could dictate the nature of business that they are likely to attract to a new location or branch office. It may be that the decision to re-locate or open a branch office has been made because existing premises are too small or because to open a branch office would provide the right opening for a valued member of staff, or possibly because the amount of advertising and promotional expenditure already being incurred is such that a branch office could be supported without a significant increase in some costs.

Given that it would be impracticable to cover the subject exhaustively, perhaps we could set a scene in an attempt to illustrate the marketing thought process that would govern the setting up of an estate agency business.

Imagine two young persons each with some years' experience deciding to form a partnership and to open in a town new to them — a town of say 65,000 people, one major and two minor established shopping areas. A county town, thus housing a County Council, a number of government and quasi-government offices, perhaps three or four major industrial and two or three major office users. Although they wish to establish a general practice, they have already appreciated that this will take time and that their first objective must be to establish a sound base as house agents. The matters that will concern them will include the following:

The Size and Nature of the Market

What total area of countryside does the town serve as an administrative centre? Of the total housing stock, what percentage is privately owned? Where are these privately-owned houses situated and in what broad price ranges are they? How many are in each; where are the "up market" and "down market" areas?

What assumptions can be made with regard to the frequency at which houses change hands? Is it going to be at or about the national level?

What effect on this factor could the town's role as an administrative centre generating a high level of staff movements have? What are the planning proposals for the area; what growth could be expected in the next ten years industrially and residentially? Are there any factors likely to bring about a significant change in the life of the town? Will a new motorway bring further prosperity or take present business away to a neighbouring town that will become more accessible?

There are other factors that could have a bearing on the type of "product" that the partnership will eventually sell. Which of the comprehensive schools has got the best reputation and is likely to attract children from the higher income groups? What effect on shopping patterns will a new super-store make?

Having built up a picture of the town and the area it serves, the young agents should with reasonable accuracy be able to assess the total amount of potential product, the amount of property likely to be sold in the average year, and the total income collectively available to the estate agents in the area.

A further picture needs to be built up. Who and where are the other agents? How many partners and negotiators have they each got? Who advertises in what media, how much is being spent and how does all this relate to the conclusions already reached as to the total size of the market and value of product?

We are still considering matters directly related to potential product. Have we the right financial resources to seek a town centre location and to practise throughout the area, or must we limit our sights? If so, which neighbourhood is of particular interest to us? If we choose the up-market area, would old loyalties prove hard to break down; would it be necessary to allow a much longer build-up period, or is there a much more obvious opening down market?

At the end of the day the product research may well have to be related to other factors — the availability of suitable premises, as to whether or not planning consent for a change of use from a shop to an office use is likely to be forthcoming, rental values and car-parking facilities.

Our two young estate agents are perhaps lucky, for in considering their product they are not, unless acting for or advising a developer, concerned as to its saleability. Houses find their own level in the market place. They would be most unwise, however, to set out on their course without first satisfying themselves that under normal circumstances product supply will be adequate. They must decide, if they are not going to try to cover the whole area and the whole range of housing, just what areas either geographically or in terms of price groups they are particularly interested in.

Their ultimate success or failure will depend on selling the service they have to offer to the owners of the product and in this context they must make a careful study of the firms already operating and draw conclusions as to their effectiveness or otherwise.

They must satisfy themselves as to their own ability, in terms of expertise, advertising power and premises, not only to draw sufficient instructions to succeed, but do so within a given time-span that will in itself depend on the finances available to them.

Setting up the office

It is quite impossible to be specific as to just what sort of building, in what sort of location, makes the ideal estate agent's office and it follows that one cannot be specific about internal layouts, window displays, or furnishings. Location might well be dictated by the attitude of the local planning authority to permitting what is an office use, in an established shopping street. Our two young estate agents may perhaps have found a run-down estate agency business, but with good premises, large display windows, and have decided that they could from that particular location make rapid inroads into the cheaper end of the house market in the town or neighbourhood, and have accepted that they are unlikely to attract instructions in respect of houses in the better suburbs or country houses outside the town.

On the other hand they may have decided to concentrate solely on the better end of the market and may have made a decision that they could do so from a listed Georgian building situated in the professional centre. They could in fact have already taken the first and perhaps principal decision with regard to their "firm's image", and the other decisions on such matters as advertising style, style of notepaper headings and even nature of staff could stem from it. One can therefore only generalise.

When considering premises one has to consider both aspects of marketing. Your premises have a role to play in drawing instructions to you, i.e., in creating your product, but they will also draw prospective purchasers. Unless one has made a decision to specialise in just one section of the market, one should aim at "the largest market place". In the average provincial town or centre this is likely to be close to the heart of a shopping centre. It is doubtful whether in economic terms estate agents can or indeed should compete with the major retailers, but accessibility both on foot and by car is important. If it proves impossible to find premises to make an impact on a large number of pedestrians passing one's window displays and one is forced to move further out, then perhaps prominence is of greater importance. A building that makes a visual impact will help to establish one's presence. In these circumstances, if the office can provide on-site parking for sales staff and the public, or if it immediately adjoins public parking facilities, so much the better.

It must be remembered that one's premises are only one means of presenting an image of one's firm and operation to the public. One's promotional advertising and window displays all form part of this operation, and it may be that if to get close to the shopping centre one's rental budget is exceeded this could possibly be compensated for by a reduction in the advertising budget. Conversely, if in order to obtain suitable premises one has to move well out of the centre, the initial advantage of a lower rental element in one's budgeted expenditure would soon get eaten up by the need for much heavier promotional advertising.

Public Image

It is a trite phrase, but of great significance. In any town, if you mention the name of one of the larger estate agents in the town the local business or professional man, indeed the average house owner, will immediately have an image in front of him. It might be that the firm mentioned is old-fashioned, slow but reliable, or it could be they are new, brash, cheap and untrustworthy.

If the image is unfavourable it could be for any one of many reasons. Perhaps the window display is always out of date. It may be because the firm are advertising that they charge a lower rate of commission than any of their rivals, for cheapness cannot necessarily be equated with a high standard of service or success. It may be because our hypothetical owner's wife 'phoned for details of a house for a friend and got a discourteous response, or that the enquiry was not followed up.

We here, however, are concerned with the firm's public image in the context of our two young estate agents starting a new practice. Again one cannot be specific, but three points could be stressed.

(1) The firm must have an objective or aim and the image must fit it.
(2) The image must be distinctive. Here a logo would help.
(3) It must be consistent. On the office fascia, in one's advertising, and on one's "For Sale" boards, and it must be promoted on all possible occasions.

Ideally, one's firm's image should immediately identify one's function. This presents difficulties to the general practice. All too frequently one sees firms described as "surveyors, auctioneers, valuers, estate agents, rating consultants, etc". This may be a correct recital of the services the firm can offer, but it will confuse the layman, and the other professionals who might have need of your services almost certainly already know what skills you possess. Many firms have tried to get over this particular difficulty by using as a logo a motif that clearly identifies with the estate agency function, such as one based on a house key or the shape of a house; others have sought to get over the problem by the use of such phrases as "The property professionals" or "We sell houses".

Many general practice firms, although dependent on estate agency for the larger part of their gross fee-income are loth (presumably because they fear it would create the wrong image) to emphasise the title "estate agents" and list it with their other titles in a minor way. Yet, strangely, they want the public to bring estate agency work to them. Some firms have sought to use different titles on the notepaper employed in their separate functions.

Our young estate agents, having made the decision that in order to get established they must concentrate on the residential estate agency market, would be well advised to make sure that their firm's image puts this across in no uncertain terms.

There has in recent years been a marked improvement in the image promoted by many firms, nearly always as a result of seeking the advice of design and public relations consultants. It is a highly specialised field.

There is, however, a lot more to one's public image than simply designing one's office fascia, notepaper, advertisement headings and general visual impact.

Estate agency is about people, both vendors and purchasers, and it is about people knowing you, the agent, and it is about contact and, hopefully, it is on-going. It is therefore important that both principals and senior staff are known in their town and in their areas. They should be encouraged to mix socially and take an interest in local commerce and local affairs and to meet people. Estate agency is essentially communicating. The vendor wants you to be able to communicate with prospective purchasers. The prospective purchaser expects you to communicate with them to understand his wishes, and to draw his attention to any house that might be of interest. They will both expect you to be well informed as to the state of the property market, as to planning proposals for the area, as to schools, as to the social life of the town and so on. Galsworthy left one in little doubt that Swithin Forsyte was a sociable man!

Communicating is, however, more than socialising. The vendor who comes to you before going to any other agent may do so because he knows you; it is more likely that he does so because he believes you are the most likely of the agents available to him to succeed. Within the limits of good taste and the rules of the professional bodies, to emphasise success is to generate success. Nothing can help the image of the firm more than "For Sale" and "Sold By" boards and regular reference in the property columns of the Press to the houses you have received instructions to sell, and in particular to those you have sold.

It is in this context that one's office display windows play an absolutely vital role. Most firms have come a long way since the fly-blown and fixed display image of the immediate post-war years, when dust and stagnation seemed the hallmarks of respectability and success. Most estate agents now seem to be aware of the role their windows can play as a point of contact and as a means of communicating. Many forget that house-owners in any one town tend to move around that town in fairly regular patterns. Some daily go to the same place of work, others shop regularly in the same shops. That potential vendor whom our two young estate agents will be relying on, when he comes to sell to supply part of their product, may pass their window every day, or two or three times a week, or perhaps only on Saturday afternoons. It is vital that that window be constantly changed, up to date and with some space devoted not only to advertising what is still for sale, but recording what has been sold. It should be alive, it should be lit after dark, it should be colourful and above all if it contains reading matter in addition to good large clear photographs, that reading matter should be readily readable by somebody standing on the pavement, not just thumped out on an old typewriter with a faded ribbon.

The window display should not only be informative but the form of display should be one that gives a sense of privacy to those inside the office, but still enables those standing outside on the pavement to see in and to feel invited in.

It is also important that the window display itself should promote the firm's logo, name and image. Too many forget that the man standing on the pavement looking in cannot read the fascia above his head.

There are two other points of contact, both vital in promoting the firm's image.

First, reception — the impression created when a member of the public enters your office for the first time. Office furnishings are a matter of personal taste, but they must be chosen, and indeed laid out, to create a welcoming feeling and give the impression of quiet efficiency. Shabbiness will not do this and ostentation could give the impression of slickness or sharp practice. It is important that the office be laid out so that a member of the public entering knows immediately where to go. Ideally the office should be staffed so that there is someone always free to receive. Politeness and interest are vital. All too often does one see a member of staff seated stubbornly in his chair when to stand up would create a totally different impression and immediately indicate an awareness of the caller and a willingness to help.

It may not always be possible for a potential vendor or purchaser to be interviewed immediately, and there should be somewhere where they can sit in comfort, out of the main stream of the activity in the office and with adequate up-to-date reading matter available, and that reading matter should include information about the firm and the services it can offer.

In establishing good communications the telephone is vital. It should never be forgotten that for many people it is their first contact with you and your firm and in all probability it will be with a junior member of staff. Telephone discipline is important and the training of telephonists needs to be taken seriously. The G.P.O. will nearly always help.

Arrangements must be made to ensure that anyone who will man the telephone exchange and first receive incoming calls does know exactly who in the office is responsible for what sort of work, so that calls can be passed on immediately. If anyone is out then the telephonist should know who is to receive his or her 'phone calls, and response to the calls must be immediate.

Telephone discipline must go further than just ensuring that incoming calls are well received. If a vendor or purchaser telephones to speak to a partner or member of staff, he has something to communicate and if that person is not immediately available there will be a sense of frustration. He or she will need to feel certain that if a message is left, it will be passed on immediately and accurately to the right person and then acted upon. If he wants the person to telephone him on his return, he must feel certain that this will happen. One has noticed from time to time when an office is really busy that there is a reluctance on the part of members of staff to receive calls from persons whom they cannot immediately identify. "It's not me, put it through to so and so". All telephone calls are important, but these perhaps more than any other. If a caller and the subject about which he or she wishes to speak can immediately be identified, the chances are that communications have already been satisfactorily established and a negotiator, for example, may be correct if he decides that what he is doing at that moment is more urgent and send the message that he "will ring back in 10 minutes". The caller who cannot be identified is trying to communicate with the firm. He may well be a potential vendor or purchaser and if his call is not immediately received, passed to the right person and effectively dealt with his business could go elsewhere.

Advertising — The Public Image

Continuing to discuss the firm's public image in the context of marketing the estate agency service, the advertising carried out by the firm is, of course, an essential part of promoting that image and marketing that service. This is quite apart from the role advertising can play in marketing an individual property. That we shall consider later and in that specific context.

The wide variety in the nature and size of estate agency practices makes it very difficult to lay down any specific rules as to where, when and in what form one should advertise. Much will depend on the nature of one's local paper and how frequently it is published, whether one is dealing solely at the lower end of the market, or regularly dealing with higher priced country houses, when advertising in national newspapers and journals should be considered; some will wish to advertise residential and commercial properties; others will be concerned only with the latter. Some will be spending their own money, but others their client's.

The points we have considered earlier in the wider context are, however, still relevant.

Every advertisement one inserts in newspapers, in glossy journals, specialised journals such as "Estates Gazette", on cinema screens, on railway hoardings, poster boards, etc, must —

(1) Have regard to what the firm is setting out to achieve, i.e., is it wishing to promote itself as a firm of estate agents or general practitioners? Is it aiming at the upper or lower end of the residential market? Is it concerned primarily with the commercial market?

(2) The advertisement must identify with the visual image the firm is setting out to create. It must follow the style in so far as it can of the office fascia, the letter-headings, the posters. It should contain the firm's logo.

(3) It must be exciting, for it is intended to draw the people to it.

(4) It must be informative.

In considering advertising in the context of promoting the firm's image and by doing so drawing instructions, three aspects are worth emphasising.

First the Price Commission's conclusion that the majority of vendors who used estate agents felt that however good the service they got, it was not good value for money, and further that the majority of those who chose not to use estate agents did so because of the cost involved.

One's promotional advertising should therefore be aimed at answering the criticism that we do not do enough to explain to the public the services we offer. To use advertising space to explain the agent's role and the reasons for using an agent could be well worthwhile. In doing so we should perhaps rely on the reasons the 75 per cent who chose to use agents gave for doing so — speed, convenience and "know how".

Second, although we are not dealing with the advertising of individual properties here, the style and content of one's advertisements are relevant not only to prospective purchasers, but to prospective vendors. When the time comes they will want their house presented in the best possible light and before giving anyone instructions they will be reading and comparing your advertisements with those of your rivals. Market conditions at the time will direct whether your advertisements should be aimed at potential vendors or purchasers but under average or normal conditions the securing of instructions must remain the first objective.

The third aspect I would emphasise is concentration, and with this I link my earlier comments with regard to the largest market place and the firm's aim. Not every agent in a town would, or could afford to seek to out-advertise his rivals to prove that he enjoys the largest share of the market, but he may be able to show that he is particularly active in one section of it, be it in price range or district. Similarly even the larger provincial firms seeking instructions in the upper price-ranges could not expect to keep pace with the larger London firms operating on a nation-wide basis and using the national press and journals such as "Country Life," but they could by concentrating on just one of the national papers and strongly identifying themselves with their own area reach and hold a section of that market.

The agent communicates in many other ways other than those referred to. He communicates by way of correspondence, by way of the property particulars he produces. Some of the larger firms produce weekly or monthly property newspapers and see them as an important means of communicating. It is not just important to communicate, it is also important that the quality of that communication be as high as possible, whether it be the content, the quality of and type of print-face used and the speed with which communication is made.

We have been considering the firm's public image and its office, but have emphasised the importance of communicating. Communicating is for the agent the very life-blood of his marketing function. The firm's public image is a means of establishing communications and the office is the communications centre. They must both be right if one is to succeed.

Twelve

Marketing — Further Considerations

**Definition — Study of marketing — The product
approach, the Institutional approach, the functional
approach, the decision-making approach —
Relevance to estate agency considered — Market
segmentation, its relevance to estate agency —
Residential, commercial, by area, by nature of
property — The market as a changing factor — The
indicators — The need for the agent to be involved —
Consumer behaviour and consumer demand — The
need to be aware and to interpret — Other marketing
functions — The role of the professional bodies in
marketing — Other marketing "institutions"**

Still and Cunliffe in "Essentials of Marketing" suggested various
headings for discussion. It is all too easy for estate agents to disregard
the "science" of marketing, even if they were to recognise it as such,
believing that their well-established methods cannot be bettered and
that they have nothing to learn from the way industry and commerce set
about marketing their "product". I intend now to consider the various
heads of discussion suggested by Still and Cunliffe and endeavour to
relate them to the property market.

The first of the headings was — "Definition". I opened the last
chapter with their definition of marketing and if one substitutes the
word "properties" for "products" and "purchasers" (or applicants) for
"markets" the definition would read: "Marketing is the business
process by which properties are matched with purchasers and through
which transfers of ownership are effected".

The second of Still and Cunliffe's headings was — "Study of
Marketing" and then they listed four approaches to marketing —

(1) The product or commodity approach. An approach to
    marketing that is centred on the commodity produced.
(2) The Institutional approach. An approach to marketing, for
    example, centred on the retailing organisation itself.
(3) The functional approach. One which analyses and concentrates
    on the steps to be taken in the marketing function.
(4) The decision making approach. One which centres on the
    decisions to be made in the marketing function or operation.

I suggest all of these can be directly related to estate agency. They are to a greater or lesser extent, dependent upon the marketing function that is to be carried out, inter-related.

In the normal commercial sense, a company may decide to centre its marketing effort on the product itself. One can think of many well-known products and brand names that would be instantly recognisable to nearly everybody, but where very few could name the manufacturing company. Detergents would be an example. An approach to marketing centred on the commodity need not necessarily ignore the institutional approach, for the standing of the company or firm, its organisation and its staffing are all relevant. It must have strength both in terms of finance and personnel to back up any product-oriented marketing campaign. The functional approach cannot be ignored, neither can decision making. Products have to be manufactured and decisions made as to quantity. They have to be stored, and decisions made as to the capacity required. They have to be distributed, and decisions made as to how this is best achieved, and finally they have to be sold, and decisions made on how, where and at what price.

We could now relate these approaches to estate agency. We have been considering the setting up of an estate agency practice, and its public image, and have stressed its most important function — that of communicating. We could describe an estate agency practice as an institution or firm set up to bring about transfers of ownership by effective communications.

In considering the organisation and public image we could be said to have been taking an institutional approach to marketing, but in doing so we laid particular emphasis on the fact that an estate agency business, before it could market anything (a product or commodity) had to draw instructions or seek that product. The product approach and the institutional approach are for the estate agent therefore irrevocably linked. Ways and means of attracting instructions, of improving the quality of instructions, whether it be by price, or, for example in the South, by increasing the percentage of instructions received on a sole agency basis, must always be the prime concern of the estate agent. The product approach could therefore be said to be the most important of the four, but it is the standing of the firm that in the end will determine whether or not the product approach is successful.

The commodity or product approach might at first sound irrelevant in the estate agency context. But I suggest that it is in practice just as relevant as it is to the sales director with responsibility for marketing a new brand of soap powder, a new motor car model, or any other mass produced item. It is true that only if the agent were instructed to handle the sale of a new estate of identical houses could his task appear to be similar. The fact, however, that the agent will have very few properties on his books that are similar in all respects does not detract from the importance of the commodity as a marketing consideration. Every house has its attributes, whether it be its style, its location, the accommodation it offers, its nearness to transport, its closeness to shops, a park nearby, accessibility to schools — the list is almost endless.

Similarly, commercial and industrial properties have certain characteristics that must be assessed and appreciated by the agent if he is to carry out an efficient marketing operation. It could be accessibility, the supply of labour, the size and shape of the premises, in the case of a shop, its proximity to major national multiples already established, or to car parks. In the case of warehouse premises, the height to eaves and access to motorways. It is one of the distinctive characteristics of the estate agent's marketing function that each individual property or "commodity" that he is instructed to sell or to let will have its own characteristics and it is these characteristics that will ultimately attract the purchaser or lessee, and it is these characteristics and the importance that the agent attributes to each of them that will dictate the way he presents that house, factory or warehouse. In short, how he markets his product.

The functional approach is also relevant — the steps to be taken in the marketing function. Many will argue that the good estate agent is born and not made, that flair is the strongest weapon in his armoury and that his task relies almost entirely on the personal relationship he can establish both with vendors and purchasers. But this has to be only part of the truth.

No estate agent working in either the residential or commercial market would deny the need for a thoroughly efficient back-up organisation, nor would they deny that there are certain quite specific functions that have got to be carried out if a property is to be presented not only in the most efficient and effective way, but to the largest possible market place. Given that the agent has already attracted the instructions, i.e., that he has already "sold" his firm and obtained the opportunity he was seeking, instructions have got to be taken, and in taking them he has got to do his best to ensure that they are realistic, that they set him an achievable aim. He has then got to go through a certain process that will arm his own staff with sufficient information competently to offer that property to prospective purchasers with whom they are already in contact, or who call at the office. He has then got to prepare the particulars, in one form or another, that can be sent to those enquiring from a distance and to a wider selection from those on his mailing list.

He has got to try to get the information he has taken to those who may not yet have been in touch with him or his firm, but who could be prospective purchasers. He has got to advertise, decide just where he is going to do this, what he is going to spend, and over what period. He will have other tasks. Some purchasers must be accompanied to the property concerned. He may have to handle the keys and be responsible for security. Appointments to view will have to be made, constant contact with the vendor will have to be maintained, as will contact with those who have viewed. Not only in the setting up of the office and its systems, but in the marketing of each individual property, there are specific functions that have to be carried out. Unless these functions are planned and carried out effectively, the marketing effort will be weakened.

Lastly the decision-making approach. In whatever market the estate agent is working, he is working towards two decisions — that to be made by his vendor or lessor client, to sell or to let, and that to be taken by his prospective purchaser or lessee, to purchase or take a lease.

In indicating earlier that estate agency is a "soft sale" as opposed to a "hard sale" one could be misleading. It assumes that either the would-be purchaser of a house or of a factory or shop will only agree to buy something that he likes and that the agent's task is simply to lead him to it. This in practice would be a gross over-simplification. Few prospective purchasers or lessees ever find exactly what they want, and in one respect or another they have in the event to accept a compromise. This, as we shall see in considering how the agent approaches the market and decides to whom to offer a property, presents difficulties.

Similarly a property owner may well have to compromise. He may be disappointed at the best offer his agent has been able to obtain for him. The timings may not be right and may involve him in borrowing from the bank to bridge the purchase of his new house. The good estate agent is one who can help the parties make compromises and reach agreement. To achieve this he will need to have a thorough knowledge of his market, to understand the wishes of both parties and to have obtained their confidence. He may need a degree of firmness to bring about a decision and could run the risk of being accused of "hard selling".

When we come to look in detail at the functions to be carried out by the agent and his relationship with vendors and purchasers, both before and during negotiations, we must remember that they are marketing matters and the more the agent can read and learn about marketing and apply the lessons learnt to his own task the more effectively is he likely to carry it out.

The next of the headings suggested by Still and Cunliffe is "Market Segmentation", which they divide broadly into the consumer market and the industrial market. For the estate agent the sub-division into residential and commercial is obvious, and the larger firms may find it necessary to segment further if the marketing effort is to be as effective as possible. In the residential market many firms in the larger cities need to separate the marketing of town houses from that of country houses. Some provincial firms with a number of offices have found it necessary to segment their areas, some have found it advisable to have separate departments dealing with building land, almost a thing of the past in some areas, and many have seen the marketing of new houses as a function that requires a somewhat different approach and one which could be carried out more effectively by a department specifically devoted to it. Many firms wholly committed to the commercial market or with a significant commercial practice have also segmented, with separate departments being responsible not only for different regions, but for different sections of the market, i.e., shops, offices, factories and warehouses.

"The Market as a Changing Factor" is the next suggested heading and it is one of particular significance to the estate agent, whether he operates in the residential or commercial field, or in both. The subject is one that has to be looked at in some depth. It is sufficient here to stress that there are many factors that dictate the state of the market at any one time and which can cause it to change. Supply and demand, the availability of funds, interest rates, planning policy, specific planning proposals, population trends and the inflation rate are just some of the most obvious. The estate agent, in whichever field he practises, is involved in a market that reflects not only the state of the national economy and the direction it is taking, but many regional and local trends and policies. If the agent is to operate effectively, either in the planning and management of his own practice, or in the conduct of his client's business, and if the advice he gives is to be soundly based he cannot stand aside. He must be involved, he must be well-informed and he must be able to interpret the information he obtains in terms of likely market trends.

The next heading, "Consumer Behaviour and Consumer Demand", is closely related to the factors we have just considered. The successful residential agent should understand what motivates both vendors and purchasers. He must be aware of changes in taste; of changes in social habits and of those factors that can bring about a change in the status of a residential area in the eyes of the purchasing public, be it for better or for worse. Similarly the commercial agent who is going to operate effectively must be aware of any changes, for example, in the retail shopping pattern, or in the requirements of the average industrialist or office user. He must be aware of proposed changes in the transport and highway facilities in any area and their likely effect on the market there. Similarly he must be aware of the current views and policies of the investing institutions.

"The Market as a Changing Factor" and "Consumer Behaviour and

Consumer Demand" are of particular significance to the agent operating in the development field. The ability to recognise changes in either area *when* they occur will not be good enough.

If the agent is to seek out viable development propositions, advise his clients as to value and as to the likely result of carrying out the development, he has got to be able to foresee change. Failure to anticipate a recession in the house market or a significant change in investment yields in the commercial property market could have serious consequences. Conversely the agent seeking to acquire land on behalf of developer clients who fails to anticipate an upsurge in values when most of his rivals have already done so will not acquire land and neither that agent nor his client will prosper, for they would have lost their "product".

Under the next heading, "Marketing Functions", come the sub-headings, "Planning and Developing the Product", "Buying", "Distribution and Storage" and auxiliary functions such as "Risk-Bearing", "Market Financing", "Market Information", "Advertising and Sales Promotion".

Perhaps a sceptic would say that these matters have little bearing on estate agency, but is this correct? Is not the agent who advises either a commercial or residential developer as to what land to buy, what to build, as to the size of unit, as to the likely selling price or rental value, planning and developing a product? He may not be doing it for himself as principal, but others will be relying on his advice and judgment and he at the end of the day will be expected to market the resulting product successfully.

Distribution and storage may be relevant to the manufacturer who has to get his product to the point of sale before it can be marketed, but it hardly sounds relevant to the practice of estage agency. If the function is, however, related back to the very important role of the agent in communicating, then it does become relevant. The distribution of information as to what property is available in the market, as to what it comprises, and on what terms it is available is a vital function. Further, the agent must have access to a store or "register" of property that is available. If he is to operate effectively in the market place he must be able to value, and few would claim to be able to do this without some reference to valuation records, and the storage of these records and easy and regular retrieval is very much a marketing function, and not dissimilar from the industrialist's storage of a manufactured product.

We started our consideration of marketing by stressing the agent's dual marketing function, i.e., that of first marketing the service he has to offer to secure the product, and secondly selling the product. These without doubt are his main functions, but there are auxiliary functions that could help him achieve them. Many firms in the residential field have separate mortgage and insurance broking departments, or somebody who specialises in this field. To be recognised as a firm who can give specialist advice and help in financing property purchase is clearly likely to attract not only prospective purchasers but add to the firm's standing in the eyes of potential vendors. Building society agencies could not only be of direct assistance to would-be purchasers but by attracting investors they bring members of the public regularly to one's offices; members of the public who are likely to be either potential vendors or purchasers.

The commercial agent who has the ability to assist developer clients by arranging the funding of development projects would probably regard this particular function as far too important to be described as "auxiliary", but as it clearly assists in securing property to sell or to let at the end of the day, it is a marketing function.

"Marketing Institutions", the next heading, appears irrelevant when considering marketing in estate agency terms. Certainly the professional bodies would not appear to regard themselves as marketing institutions, although they prescribe rules that their members must follow when operating in the market place, but the heading is one that deserves consideration and which could have a growing significance in the future. Many local associations not only, as we have seen, lay down codes of practice, but encourage co-operation between agents and in doing so play a marketing role.

One cannot, however, dismiss the professional bodies as having nothing to do with marketing. In their public relations they should be promoting the marketing function of their members. To an increasing extent they are doing this and this progress is welcome.

The Royal Institution recently published "Practice Notes for Estate Agents" and every year holds a week-end estate agency conference. The other two main bodies, being more closely identified with their estate agent members, clearly can and do promote their interests keenly.

Steps are being taken to examine potential members in marketing.

The Royal Institution and the Incorporated Society have set up a joint indemnity scheme to protect purchasers' deposits and both have co-operated with the Centre for Advanced Land Use Studies in presenting estate agency subjects. The Centre itself has instigated research into estate agency matters. Their report on Sole and Multiple Agency I have referred to and some of its data I have used.

All are therefore, whether they realise it or not, involved in marketing.

In this country we have seen in recent years the establishment of the National Network of Estate Agents, and Homes Relocation, Limited, both organisations established to enable member agents to give a better service to the public and in particular to those moving from one part of the country to another. The former now has over 600 offices in the United Kingdom involved. They are clearly a means of communication and clearly intended to be marketing institutions.

The control and organisation of estate agency in this country may appear piecemeal and disorganised when one considers the function played by the Real Estate Boards of North America, for example. Certainly neither the professional bodies nor local associations seek to conduct a marketing role that in any way compares with the multiple listing systems that are common practice on the other side of the Atlantic. These we will consider when we come to look at the future, but one can see the possibility of local associations in particular making use of modern data-processing methods to bring about a much closer degree of co-operation in the marketing efforts of their members and if they did so they would become significant as marketing institutions.

Thirteen

The Market Place

Attracting vendors and purchasers — The needs of the vendor — Relationships with vendor and purchaser — The ongoing nature of the estate agent's practice — Promotion of the firm — Communicating with the vendor — Qualities necessary to succeed — Reaching the market fringe — Canvassing for instructions — An American approach — The "do it yourself" vendor, can we reach him? — The partial service — Inefficiency of service to purchasers

It is essential, if estate agents are to become more market-oriented, that they first appreciate the size and nature of the market place they are in and the wishes and needs of those who populate it. It is all too easy for the residential estate agent, be he the partner responsible for the agency side of the business, or a negotiator, to assume that the product to be marketed is no more than the houses he has to offer at that particular moment and that his market place is populated only by those who have instructed him to sell and those who are on his registers as prospective purchasers.

I suggest that the thinking of many involved in the residential property market has gone no further than this.

In practice the market place is almost limitless. "Every man has his price," is a trite saying. There are a few who for sentimental or other reasons just would not or could not sell, but for the great majority of house-owners there is a price at which they would sell. Some owners have already gone one stage further: "This house has become too big for us, we ought to think of moving to something smaller." One can think of other situations — "If your mother comes to live with us, this house is going to be too small," and "If rail fares go up again, we must consider moving nearer to London." Statements made between husband and wife in the privacy of their own home; and yet a clear indication, if anyone had overheard, that they were in, or could become involved in, the property market, both as potential vendors and purchasers.

If we are to improve the firm's business, our marketing policy must be aimed in three directions.

First we must look at that share of the market being handled by our competitors, not with a view to supplanting them when they have already been appointed by a vendor, but by improving all those aspects of our business that could increase the number of initial instructions coming to us. In short, the market we have lost or might lose to others.

Secondly, we have to think of ways and means of activating the potential or latent market, of reaching those prospective vendors and purchasers who have not yet got to the point of approaching an agent with a view to selling or purchasing, including the owners of the large house under-occupied and the small house overcrowded, those about to retire, those who should move but have not considered doing so.

Lastly, we have to consider ways and means of drawing to us at least a proportion of the business being dealt with privately between the parties — the market that has eluded us.

Each of these fields raises a different question.

The first — what is it that our rivals are doing to attract vendors to them in preference to ourselves? And as a corollary, is there anything we are doing that is deterring those vendors?

The second — how do we set about identifying those who could be contemplating a move, and indeed those who could be considering purchasing for the first time, and as a corollary how do we, having identified them, stimulate them into action?

The third raises the question of why the vendors who are selling privately chose not to employ an agent, and in particular why did they not come to us?

If we consider these questions in depth and come to some conclusions and act on them, we would have gone a long way towards a complete review of our marketing policy.

The agent who is the first on whom a would-be purchaser calls when he decides to move or first arrives in the town, has the first chance of satisfying that purchaser's requirements. Whether or not he is the first agent will depend partly on the location of his office, and we must assume for the purposes of this study that he is established in what he considers to be the best position available to him. In attracting would-be purchasers there are two other important factors. First, our public image; secondly, the content of our advertisements, and it must be remembered that our window display is important not only as an element in our public image but as part of our overall advertising effort.

Would-be purchasers are attracted to the largest market place. If we have the right public image, if we can attract more instructions to ourselves than our rivals and if we can put this across clearly and invitingly, the applicants will come.

We are a service industry. We "sell" our services in the estate agency context on a contingency fee basis to vendors. We "provide" a service to purchasers. We should therefore look first to the needs of the vendor. What does he require of an estate agent? The assumed answer is a sale at the best possible price, as quickly as possible and with the least personal inconvenience. One could add at the cheapest possible cost, but there are reasons for believing this is seldom a significant factor to a vendor deciding what agent to approach. High professional standards and a good service are not compatible with price-cutting and many vendors recognise this.

In broad terms this assessment of a vendor's requirements may be correct, but many vendors' requirements go further and can be varied and complex.

The majority want to know what price they can reasonably expect to obtain, often weeks or months before the decision to put the house on the market is made. When they come to sell they may well seek more, but if they are considering moving up the market or taking a job elsewhere, they need to know what they can rely on from the sale of their own houses to finance the next purchase. Accuracy in valuation, which in itself dictates a very sound knowledge of one's market, is clearly required, as is a well-informed view as to the way the market is likely to move in the immediate future.

Vendors may want to know how to market their houses, or they may have particular problems — a deadline date for a move, when the need for speed would be paramount and could affect possible price. They may want to know what works of repair or decoration they should carry out before putting their houses on the market. They might want their sale handled in a particular way, i.e., with the greatest confidentiality. They might want advice with regard to the possibility of obtaining planning consent for further development or for a change of use and as to the effect the obtaining of such consents might have on the ultimate price realised. They may be trustees not living in the area, concerned as to how they should deal with the contents of the house and what arrangements could be made to show people over it. They may be moving away before the house can be sold and want to know just what the agent is prepared to do by way of keeping an eye on the house once they have gone and until the sale can be completed.

On many occasions they will want, before finally appointing an agent, to "vet" the firm or the individual concerned, or both, for above all they will want to feel, particularly if they are appointing a sole agent, that the firm is competent, trustworthy and likely to achieve the required aim.

I remain convinced that in addition to these factors, there is another very important one. The average owner would be reluctant to conduct his own negotiations and feel at a disadvantage if he had to meet and negotiate with his prospective purchaser face to face. He may also feel that a third party who "knows the ropes" would be better able to "vet" the status of that purchaser and once a sale has been agreed, to progress it, if need be in assisting that purchaser to find a mortgage, advising on the implications of a structural survey report, and so on.

To summarise, the average vendor in choosing his agent is looking for someone to carry out some or all of the following tasks for him.

(1) To advise with regard to value.

(2) To advise with regard to the method of sale and with regard to any particular problems with which he is faced, i.e., timings, works of decoration or repair.

(3) He is looking for someone he can rely on to carry out the marketing of his house efficiently.

(4) He is looking for someone whom he believes, once a prospective purchaser is in touch, will have the personality and ability to negotiate the best possible deal on his behalf.

(5) He is looking for someone whom he believes to be keen and tenacious enough to follow the progress of a sale that has been agreed subject to contract, in order to minimise the risk of it failing, and also to advise as to when a sale should be abandoned if the purchaser is being unreasonably dilatory or wishes to renegotiate the terms.

(6) Last, but by no means least, he is looking for access to a much wider market than he believes he himself could generate.

How does an agent set about ensuring that his firm has the image that will satisfy a potential vendor that it can cope effectively with all these functions and indeed is likely to be the most effective of the agents to whom that vendor could go?

Answering this question may involve repeating points that have been made earlier when considering the firm's public image, but at this point nothing will be lost, and possibly something gained, by some repetition. An important part of its public image is the reputation the firm has built up by the quality of service it has given in the past. It cannot be stressed too strongly that it is not only the quality of service to vendors, to one's clients, that counts, but the service one gives to prospective purchasers, for in the longer-term view they are tomorrow's vendors. The service and duty the agent owes to the vendor must take precedence, but in practice it is the standard of service given to both on which that agent will be judged and which will dictate his success or failure.

Even where a vendor is leaving the district as soon as his house is sold, if he thinks his agent was dilatory, talked him into selling at too low a price, or wasted time by negotiating sales to prospective purchasers who were not able to proceed, he may have time before he goes to pass on the impressions he has gained to his friends and his neighbours. Bad news tends to travel faster than good, but he is perhaps just as likely to tell his friends and his neighbours if he has received an outstanding service.

A purchaser, having found the right house, will on average come to re-sell it some six or seven years later. He is not likely to go back to the agent through whom he purchased if, at the time of his purchase, he was treated discourteously, if he had been sent over the preceding days or weeks particulars of houses that did not remotely meet the requirements he had earlier stated, if the negotiations were bungled, and, perhaps most important of all, if he gained the impression that the agent was on his side, and that the vendor from whom he was purchasing had a poor deal. He would choose the agent whom at the time he found most courteous, most efficient, most accurate in his attempts to meet his known requirements, and who drove a hard but fair bargain for his vendor-client.

The practice of estate agency is an on-going matter. The sale negotiated today will bring in a commission in a matter of weeks. If handled well it is likely to be one of several transactions carried out with one or other or both of the parties over the ensuing years. If handled badly, it is these transactions that will be lost.

Returning to our criteria, what in addition should an agent set out to do to ensure that he secures the maximum possible number of instructions? Above all the vendor wants his house sold and, normally, quickly. Our public image and reputation must be such that he believes that by instructing our firm, he will give himself the best possible chance of achieving just that. Success breeds success. It is in this context that "Sold by" boards are of most value, and why our windows should not just show what is available, but what is happening: "Under offer", "Sold subject to contract" and "Sold by" slips all help. The professional bodies frown on advertisements that announce the firm's successes, e.g., "We sold 1,000 houses last year, may we help you sell yours?" This would probably be regarded as being in bad taste. Similarly would a list of houses sold. One must question whether or not this is one field where the professional bodies unduly interfere with the agent's marketing role, for in almost every other field success is exploited to achieve growth. The vast sums spent by motor manufacturers in motor racing and rallying is an obvious example of seeking success, and exploiting it, in the interests of one's business, as well as that of the consumer.

It could be argued that if agents were encouraged to use such advertisements they could be dangerous, for they could become meaningless if every agent did likewise, and it could be self-defeating if one was not selling more houses than anybody else in the area.

There are, however, other ways and means. Press releases are one, and the good agent will be constantly seeking to ensure that his firm is referred to by the Property Correspondents of either the local or national newspapers as often as possible. Similarly articles written for the Press, or letters dealing with aspects of the property market that would be of direct interest to vendors are a way of drawing attention to oneself or one's firm and an indication that one is not only involved but takes one's task seriously, and with a sense of social responsibility.

Building a reputation for giving vendors a first-class service requires first, an intimate knowledge of one's market, so that one's original advice is likely to be accurate. Nothing is more damaging to the agent than advice given to a vendor that the price he wants to ask is too high, only in the event to achieve the vendor's price or even more, or to advocate an auction sale that proves abortive and costly.

The same bad impression is created if one presses a vendor to accept an offer and then it is very quickly exceeded. It may be recalled that this was one of the specific criticisms made by the Consumers' Association. Inaccurate advice in this area will lead to the complaint the Association's researchers received that some agents pressed vendors to sell at too low a price, just to achieve a sale.

One's service to a vendor has only started when one has taken his instructions and actually put the house on the market. When offers are forthcoming he is going to need advice and the soundness of that advice will have a considerable bearing on the reputation or lack of it the firm will have with that particular vendor. He will, during the course of negotiations, not only want advice, he will want to feel certain that his agent is doing his best to get him the best possible price and acting solely in his best interests.

There is one aspect of service to vendors where many agents fall down. This is a criticism that probably applies in the main to multiple agency areas, but not exclusively so. How many agents, particularly in a somewhat slackish market, when there are many houses "on the books", take instructions, prepare particulars, insert an advertisement and then just wait for things to happen? Nothing can be more disturbing to a vendor than silence. Nothing is more likely to cause him either to terminate a sole agency agreement, or, in a multiple agency area, instruct other agents. The agent must keep in touch. He must advise as to the result of his advertising and his circulation of particulars. He may feel that the results of the efforts he has made have proved his original advice as to value to be wrong, or that the price he was instructed to quote has proved too high. He must advise accordingly. It is of particular importance in the multiple agency areas to remember that if the price is too high it is not likely to be the first agent that effects the sale, but the agent who, by keeping in touch, first obtains instructions to reduce the price to a level at which the house is saleable. This is a field in which communication between agent and vendor is vital but where it is often lacking, perhaps because the agent has to instigate it. If he does nothing, nothing might happen and a possible sale be lost.

What else is vital in building the reputation we want and in creating the right impression? It is our approach to our task and that of our negotiators and staff. It is we collectively who represent the firm. How we talk to people and the impression we give as individuals plays an important part in the impression of the firm gained by those with whom we are dealing. It is not only the quality of the staff in the academic sense, or in terms of experience. It is above all our attitude to our task. If we are enthusiastic, those working with us will be. If we are confident, we will create confidence. If we, for example, in advising a vendor to accept an offer, give the impression that we have any doubt as to whether or not it is the best he is likely to obtain, he will not take it.

The Americans place great emphasis on the quality of staff. In the Real Estates Salesman's Handbook* there are two sections, entitled "Personal Qualities necessary to success" and "The importance of right mental attitude". In considering the personal qualities, the late William Hannon of Detroit listed 57 of them that he regarded as necessary to success in real estate selling. They would certainly serve as an excellent check-list for anyone whose task it was to interview potential negotiators.

He put the qualities under four headings — Physical (appearance and manner), Temperamental (attitudes, mental, imagination, memory and will), Moral (trustfulness, punctuality) and lastly Loyalty.

The late Stanley McMichael in his book "Selling Real Estate" listed 51 ways in which the real estate salesman could set out to improve himself — in mind, in character, in body and in contacts. The right approach to the task, the right attitude to people, enthusiasm and integrity are all important in one's staff and they are even more important to the partners or directors of the firm. It is they who should set the tone and give the lead in this most important aspect of the conduct of one's business.

Even if we have got everything else right and have attracted instructions from those who have made the decision to sell, we have not yet reached those on the "fringe" of the market, those who would sell if tempted, or those who have decided to sell privately. How do we communicate with them, other than through our normal advertising media?

Those larger firms who publish property newspapers clearly see these as a means of reaching out into this grey area. Most use "Wanted"

*National Institute of Real Estate Brokers of the National Association of Real Estate Boards, Chicago, Illinois, 1965.

advertisements setting out the requirements of a specific, but one hopes not fictitious, prospective purchaser, in the hope that it will draw instructions. Some firms will directly canvass or solicit instructions. This is permitted by the National Association of Estate Agents, but is still contrary to the Code of Conduct of the Royal Institution of Chartered Surveyors and to that of the Incorporated Society.

The National Association in permitting members to canvass for instructions does impose some limitations. They frown on canvassing with the intention of supplanting an agent already instructed and therefore make a rule that instructions should not be canvassed if the agent knows, or has reason to believe, that another agent holds instructions.

Most agents stop short of "door-knocking" and try to reach out to this grey area by canvassing in letter form or by telephone.

The rules against canvassing were not, I suggest, made solely to protect the interests of the established firms, although clearly a newcomer would find it that much harder to become established if he was barred from what many would see as a normal commercial approach to the procurement of business. There was a fear, and it still exists and is recognised by the National Association, that unrestricted canvassing could lead to harassment and the use of oppressive methods to secure instructions by those who see estate agency as solely a commercial operation and are determined to succeed at all costs.

In America canvassing is positively encouraged, as the following quotation from the Handbook shows. "By ringing door bells — there is no better way to get a real understanding of human nature, even though it is probably the hardest kind of work you ever will be asked to do." "Many of the best real estate salesmen continue to do some canvassing long after they have served their apprenticeship." "If you have calls for an apartment, a store building or a single residence in a certain area and none is listed in the office, a personal canvass will often unearth a listing. Telephone calls too are sometimes useful, especially in neighbourhoods where the population is constantly in a state of flux. Do not be too proud to ring door-bells. You may wear out some shoe leather but you will fatten your purse".

The British agent needs to consider his own position and what his approach should be. It does not, of course, follow that if the professional bodies were to relax their rules, canvassing would become a generally accepted feature of the practice of estate agency in Britain. One could well see some of the local associations, anxious to protect the interests of their members, to maintain good relationships between firms, and perhaps to an extent to protect the public from oppressive methods, openly or overtly continuing to enforce the no-canvassing rule that the majority of them currently have.

It does not follow that a practice that has clearly grown up over many years and is generally accepted in another country, and a more commercially oriented society, would be acceptable to the British property-owning public. The firm that decided to send its negotiators round ringing door-bells might well find owners regarding this as an invasion of their privacy and the reputation of that firm might be damaged beyond repair.

On the other hand, if one does have a specific enquiry, whether it be for "an apartment, a store building or a single residence in a certain area" and one cannot help that prospective purchaser because one has nothing to offer, what could possibly be wrong with a carefully worded letter, setting out the position, sent to owners of property that could be of interest? Many, and I am one of them, regard the rules, whether they be of professional bodies or local associations, that restrict canvassing of this sort as being unnecessary.

Certainly the agent who makes no attempt to reach the "fringe" market cannot be said to be operating effectively or constructively. He is doing what comes to him to do and no more.

Last, on the obtaining of instructions, we should consider how we might reach those who decide to sell their houses privately — that 30 per cent, or is it more?

In considering how we could obtain their confidence and get instructions from them, we should ask ourselves the reasons why vendors decide to dispense with the services of an agent and as to whether or not the practice of doing so is more prevalent in one market than another. We have considered the factors that might lead to a vendor deciding to approach an agent and it follows that the vendor who decides otherwise feels that he does not want the help of an agent in some or any of them. Perhaps he does not need advice as to value, for his house is like every other in the road and he knows what his neighbour got and what Mrs. Jones is asking for No. 24. Perhaps he works in local government and is moving elsewhere and he knows of somebody in the office, perhaps even his successor, who would like his house. Perhaps he feels that his wife is better qualified to sell his house than any agent could possibly be (and he may be right). He may be the self-confident type, who rather than leave negotiations to a spotty youth from Messrs. Bricks and Mortar, would like to meet his purchaser, look him straight in the eye and carry on with the conviction that he was going to do the best possible deal. Perhaps he would like to employ an agent, but feels that the benefits he is likely to obtain from doing so are marginal and are just not worth what he is going to be charged. (The Price Commission report clearly indicates this to be the dominant reason.) In all these things he could be right.

What changes in the practice of estate agency would be necessary if this type of vendor is to be brought into the net?

The most obvious factor to look to would be the level of commission charged. Are commission rates in this country too high? In practice they are lower than almost anywhere else in the world. If property owners in France, Germany, America, Canada and Spain are prepared to pay anything between 4 per cent and 10 per cent for an agent's services, what could the British agent hope to achieve by charging less than at the present time when normal rates in Britain vary between $1\frac{1}{2}$ per cent and $2\frac{1}{2}$ per cent, other than, of course, bankruptcy?

This matter will be carefully considered in a later chapter when we look at the future, but I believe there are ways and means of improving the way estate agency is practised that could lead, certainly in the lower price ranges where the majority of the business is being lost, to lower levels of commission being charged without, necessarily, loss of profitability.

I take the view that, as the professional bodies' Witnesses before the Monopolies Commission foresaw, the Estate Agents Order abolishing scales of charges will prove a deterrent to more efficient methods and not an encouragement.

A few agents have attempted to get into what might be called the unconvinced section of the market by offering part services at a specific cost, i.e., advice as to value for one price, preparation of particulars for another, placing an advertisement in the window for another and so on. It is too early perhaps to tell whether this approach will appeal to those who would otherwise have stayed away from the agents. Clearly it will attract some, but it certainly has not caught on widely. It clearly has attractions both from the agent's point of view, for to be involved in part only is better than not being involved at all, and from the point of view of the property-owning public, who need only employ an agent to carry out that part of the sale function that they do not feel confident to do on their own. It is a matter to which the professional bodies and local associations should give serious thought, but it is my personal view that the solution, if there is one, does not lie in this direction for it ignores some of the main reasons why the majority of vendors do choose to use agents.

It is not, of course, only in the lower price ranges that private sales are arranged. The cocktail party sale, the sale as between friends, as between relatives and as between business associates will continue to take place, but in the higher price ranges there would appear to be a much greater likelihood of the estate agency being involved. Vendors and purchasers in this section of the market rely more on professional advice than would those dealing with the standard semi-detached or terraced estate house.

Some owners, having agreed to sell privately, or identified a private purchaser, will leave the detailed negotiations to an agent. Others will seek advice as to value. Purchasers, in particular, will normally seek advice on structural condition and more often than not link this with valuation advice. It is, as we have seen, lower down the price scale that one finds the majority of vendors who see no need for professional help. If the agent wants a larger share of this market, a re-appraisal of the way he operates and charges will have to be made. Greater promotion of the variety of services the agent can offer and his willingness to give a partial service may well be one way forward into the market that at present eludes us.

I have heard it argued by a marketing expert that the British agents do not charge enough by way of commission when selling the higher-priced property. It is thought that owners in this field are more likely to be involved in one of the professions, or in commerce, that they are used to relying on professional advice, would more readily recognise the benefits of employing an expert and are prepared to pay for that expertise. The fact that commission is charged by the majority of the big London house agents at rates higher than those charged in the Provinces would support this theory, but conversely it was argued that the rates of commission currently charged, when applied at the lower end of the market had a very much greater impact on vendors and deterred them from seeking professional help. Consumer research would appear to bear this out.

Perhaps agents do not give enough thought to the nature of the service required of them and as to whether or not methods could be improved in terms of efficiency and related costs. Could it be that more variety in the way property is marketed could help? These questions will receive attention later.

We have been considering the market place as regards potential vendors, but no consideration would be complete without looking at the position of the purchasers. One of the criticisms of the way agents currently operate is that no purchaser can be satisfied that he has a comprehensive list of houses that might be of interest to him until he has contacted every agent in the area of his choice. The day before writing this I heard someone in my own village pub asking where he could park a car in Chichester to get at all the agents by the shortest possible route. This is a wholly unsatisfactory state of affairs and it shows, on the part of the agents collectively, at the best inefficiency and at the worst irresponsibility. Given the will there are ways in which it could be changed.

In discussing not only the market place, but sole and multiple agency and the criticisms that have been levelled at estate agents, one has been talking purely about the residential market and one could well appear to be unduly critical of oneself, one's own chosen profession and those who practise in it. There are obvious ways in which the operation of the house market-place could be improved, but those who are unduly critical and those who advocate change might well consider the way estate agency has developed in this country and the present standing of estate agents as shown by the consumer research that has been carried out and ask themselves the question as to whether or not it is the agents who dictate how the market works, or whether the market reflects the wishes and demands of the people it serves. It could be that however much better co-ordinated the marketing effort became, whatever electronic aids we use to speed up its processes and make it more efficient, however much less we could charge for the service, the man who gets a sense of achievement out of selling his own house and ignoring the experts will continue to do so. However strong the arguments against multiple agency might be, are there not some vendors who are going to continue to demand the exposure obtained by instructing several agents at the same time, even if at the end of the day they have to pay more for the privilege of doing so?

Some changes in the operation of the market are undoubtedly necessary and will come about, but they must be approached with caution by the agents, their professional bodies and associations. Despite the hue and cry of the early 'seventies on the subject of gazumping, (and I exclude Scotland from this), the Law Commission, having considered the problem in depth, concluded that there was no way in which legislation could bring about a change that would not unacceptably detract from the purchaser's right to vet his purchase. We have seen the National Property Register come and go. We have seen local authorities decide that they can provide an estate agency service. We have seen the "cut price" agents and we have seen the property supermarkets. They all failed because in one way or another they did not meet the requirements of vendors and purchasers. Any attempt to improve methods or bring order out of what some see as relative chaos must have regard to those requirements if progress is to be made.

Fourteen

The Organisation of the Office and its Procedures

The office — Reception — Requirements of a receptionist — Layout of the office — Communications within the office — Responsibility of partners — Allocation of staff duties and responsibilities — Responsibility to vendors — Back-up staff — The property register — Information required — Negotiator confidence — Types of register — The computerised register — The property bulletin — Updating — The applicant register — Information required and its function — Importance of revision — Use of revision letters — Filing and past records — The property file, its relevance to marketing — The central index, board records, key records, advertising records — The multiple office firm — Office areas — Inter-office disciplines — The day-book.

One of the difficulties I have been faced with in writing this book is the need for the sake of clarity to analyse and separate the various functions the estate agent carries out. The organisation of his office and the procedures to be followed within it are just as relevant to his marketing function as, for example, taking instructions from a vendor, writing particulars, circulating them and advertising. In this chapter I intend to deal with "the nuts and bolts" of the estate agency practice, the organisation and the procedures that will be needed in a firm if it is to carry out its marketing function efficiently. I have to try to avoid being too specific or dictatorial and ask for apologies to be accepted if I am either. I recognise that there are more ways than one of doing most things. Some readers will no doubt disagree with what I have to say, for example, about the maintenance and nature of property registers within an office. I can only set out one person's view as to how things might be done and leave others to add and subtract as they think appropriate to their own needs.

Another of the difficulties that has faced me has been the ever-present tendency to drift away from the main theme. In my opening chapters I was critical of bodies such as the Consumers' Association and the Monopolies Commission for having looked only at house agency, when in the great majority of general practice firms this is just one function among many. Yet in the course of writing I found I had to discipline myself to do, to all intents and purposes, just that — to concentrate mainly on house agency.

In considering the organisation of an estate agency office and the procedures that might be followed within it I have tried to confine myself simply to its estate agency function, though realising that in many offices other functions are carried out and that the organisation of the general practice office and the laying down of its procedures will have to reflect its tasks. I have not, for example, tried in any detail to deal with the very close liaison and the procedures that I think should be laid down to ensure effective inter-change of information between those carrying out the estate agency function, be it residential or commercial, and those carrying out valuations. As a result some readers are bound to feel that I have dealt with some questions inadequately and totally omitted some that they would have regarded as essential.

The Office

I face yet another and immediate difficulty. If I am writing about the practice of estate agency I cannot fail to make some comments as to how I believe an estate agency office ought to be laid out and its staff deployed within it. Yet I am very conscious from personal experience that much will depend on the building itself, on its size, its shape, its location, the nature of the market in which the practice is operating and so on. Within my own practice we have to cope with everything from 30 feet of modern plate glass to a "listed" Georgian building where even the window glazing bars are sacrosanct and the central hallway is shared with a firm of solicitors who sit above us and whose building society agency notices are even closer to ours than the respective head offices of those societies are to each other in their native Yorkshire. I can therefore only generalise.

First impressions are important. Openness tends to be welcoming — enclosure tends to be daunting. I commented earlier on window displays, on the need for those looking from the outside to feel invited in. Someone arriving inside the office should continue to feel invited there, and there should be a sense of having been welcomed. One feeling they must not have, once they get inside the door, is "Where do I go from here?" or "Whom do I talk to?". If the office is very small there may be no problem, but the office may be a large one. It may be serving as the reception area to a practice with a large commercial department, a large management department, as well as a residential agency side. It may be right to separate callers, even before they are formally received, by clear notices and directions: "Residential Department Reception," with a directional arrow if necessary.

Ideally, a receptionist must always be available. If her time is shared between reception and the telephone exchange — a common enough combination — then there must be somebody else briefed and ready to receive any caller immediately. This will be particularly important in a small office that could not afford one person wholly dedicated to reception work and will need from time to time to rely on the receptionist to interview a potential purchaser, or to make viewing arrangements.

The way in which callers are received and directed should be laid down and too little attention is often given to this aspect. All too often one hears, even in one's own offices, the opening comment — "Good morning, can I help you?" to which there is only one logical answer "Yes" for your caller would not be there if he or she did not think you could. "Good morning, how can I help you?" leads the way open to — "I am looking for a house" or "I would like to sell my house".

The next stage in the small office might be easy, for there may be only one negotiator in. But in the larger office the receptionist will need to know precisely to whom the enquirer should be referred. It is as important at the front office reception desk as it was on the telephone.

There are certain matters of which the receptionist should have a sound knowledge.

(a) He or she must be fully conversant with the organisation of the firm and of that one particular office and the respective responsibilities of the partners and senior staff, so that the moment the nature of an enquiry is known the person can be directed to the right department or person.

(b) The receptionist must be capable of taking messages and getting them to the right place and above all recording them intelligently. He or she must not only be aware of the office's own procedures, but will need to know something of the various stages in the sale and letting of property, the difference between vendors and purchasers, clients and applicants.

(c) He or she should have a knowledge of the geography of the area and in particular of the town itself — where the principal shops are, where the car-parks are, of bus services, and where local authority offices are.

Readers will no doubt be able to add considerably to this short list, but strictly in the estate agency context, a receptionist should have a knowledge of the general type and price range of properties dealt with by the office and if there is any possibility that the caller cannot be immediately seen by a negotiator, should, for example, be able to identify advertisements that have appeared in the press and have access to negotiators' particulars, and in the small office should be able to interview if a negotiator is not available.

Some regard it as important that a receptionist should record names, addresses and telephone numbers of all callers. This, however, could only prove to be annoying if they are to be asked for exactly the same information a few seconds later by the partner or negotiator who is to see them. Many callers, particularly prospective purchasers perhaps only making a tentative enquiry, fearing a deluge of paper over the next few months, would be reluctant to give an address or telephone number at this stage and an embarrassing hiatus could be caused. It is essential, however, that a procedure be laid down to ensure that the information is recorded before an unknown but possible house-purchaser crosses the road to a competitor.

Turning next to the layout of the office as a whole, the tendency in recent years has been towards large open-planned offices. It is perhaps good to see people at their work, but only if they are busy and their desks are tidy.

Assuming that the estate agent has a choice as to how he lays his office out, and he may not be that privileged, much will depend on the nature of the market in which he is operating, but openness should not in my opinion be achieved at the cost of all privacy.

The older person with a lovely country house to sell may feel they have not been properly received or treated if they are interviewed in a large open space where they sense rather than know that other people can hear them. They will expect to be seen by a partner, or a manager, in the privacy of his own office. But similarly the young couple hoping to buy for the first time and far from certain whether or not they can get the mortgage they want, may well feel embarrassed talking about their respective incomes, their plans for a family or lack of them in a goldfish bowl.

Again, it can only be my personal view, but I feel there must be an area, be it an office, or an area created by partitions, where a would-be vendor or purchaser can be taken and interviewed in an atmosphere of privacy.

Particular problems can arise when an office is on more than one floor. Ideally any caller to an office should be taken to the person they are to see and introduced, but you clearly cannot have a receptionist or other member of staff running up and down stairs all day, nor will a lift solve the problem if a caller arrives on the second floor not knowing which way to go. In these circumstances a receptionist or secretary must be available either at the top of the stairs, or by the lift-door, to receive, escort and introduce.

By the very nature of estate agency, there will be callers wishing to see particular partners or members of staff who are not in and there must be a set drill to deal with them courteously and helpfully. This may have to be the receptionist's task. It may be the individual's secretary or his assistant. Whoever it is must know when the wanted person will be available, the reason for the call must be ascertained, as should the likely whereabouts of the caller at the time the partner or member of staff concerned is expected to return, and the message must reach that person immediately he does return.

To use the word communicating again is immediately to cause one to think of telephones and the post, but good communications are absolutely vital within the office itself. This we shall shortly be considering.

The receiving of callers, whether it be by the receptionist in the front office, or by the senior partner into his own office, is an opportunity to communicate well or badly. One could communicate welcome or hostility, interest or boredom, patience or the lack of it, "too busy" or "I have plenty of time to help," efficiency or inefficiency, and finally courtesy or discourtesy.

The organisation of staff and responsibilities

All too often in the past have the partners, even in large well-established general practices, taken little part in the residential agency function. They have seen the task as either too menial for their "chartered" status and felt themselves more profitably, or perhaps more "professionally" employed in commercial work, valuations, town and country planning, rating, management and so on.

Recalling how estate agency developed it may be that this professional aloofness which one can still see in some firms today, retarded the growth of some of the older well-established firms into the estate agency market, and opened the door to others. Nobody in fact would claim that it was necessary, in order to practise estate agency, to have a degree in Estate Management, or indeed be a Chartered Surveyor, but it is essential that where a firm has an estate agency department of any significance, the responsibility for it, for its organisation, its conduct and day-to-day management should lie with a partner or indeed partners, if its size justified more than one. R.I.C.S. "Practice Notes" suggested what such a partner's principal responsibilities should be — selection and training of staff, control over the office and, in the larger firm, inter-office procedures, control of the advertising budget and advertising content, the opening and distribution of mail, dealing with complaints, the allocation of responsibilities and daily tasks, discipline, supervision of correspondence, checking progress of all current negotiations and ensuring that vendors are kept informed and advised at all stages in any transaction.

It would not be difficult to add to this list. In his book, "The Art of

House Agency", M. J. Vivian devoted a chapter to what he called "The Systematic Office". In doing so he underlined one essential characteristic of an estate agency office. Systems must be established and one of the partner's responsibilities must be to ensure they are meticulously adhered to. This, of course, could be said of any office, but it is of very great importance to the estate agent.

Negotiators necessarily will be out taking instructions, or taking prospective purchasers to view property, new houses come on to the market and others get sold, prices change, viewing arrangements change, and it is vital that all involved in the selling process are kept informed. Again we come back to communications, within the office itself.

This chapter sets out to describe and discuss the organisation of an estate agency office and the systems that may be found in it, but it cannot be regarded as exhaustive; there are no doubt many offices in Britain organised on different lines and using systems that differ from those that will be suggested here, but which nevertheless are efficient. In this context it is what the organisation and systems set out to achieve that is more important than the actual methods used. In particular many of the larger firms in the commercial sector, but now also some in the residential sector, have computerised many aspects of their practice, including some of the systems or processes that are dealt with in this chapter. The use of computers in the practice of estate agency will be referred to later.

Some small agents might regard the computer as totally irrelevant, its cost likely to be totally disproportionate to what could be achieved, but computers come in many forms and there are other simpler and less costly means of data-processing that could be relevant to the small practice, particularly at a time when staffing costs are proving an ever bigger problem to the average agent.

No agent, however small, can be totally unaware of what modern techniques could accomplish or the possibility of linking with others to take advantage of them. This deliberate digression leads me to another qualification. Of necessity this chapter must relate to the majority of practitioners. The fact that some firms have gone much further and are using more sophisticated methods and systems is acknowledged. However sophisticated those methods and systems might be, however, they cannot depart far from the general principles that will be outlined.

Allocation of staff duties and responsibilities

We have already considered responsibility for receiving callers, either at the office or by telephone, both in the context of the firm's public image and the marketing of its services. It is important that every member of the estate agency team knows precisely what his or her duties and responsibilities are.

In the larger office one would have a team of negotiators. They are likely to differ in age, experience, manner, social background and personality and all are relevant in considering what tasks they should primarily be responsible for. The larger office dealing in the residential market is likely to cover a wide range of property types and it follows that it will be dealing with vendors from different age groups, different business or professional backgrounds and — a matter relevant to the question of communicating — different social backgrounds.

When a potential vendor contacts the office, whether by telephone or by calling, it is desirable but not essential that the call is taken, or he is seen by that member of the estate agency team with whom he is most likely to establish a good rapport. It is, however, absolutely essential that whoever goes to that vendor's house, or in the commercial field it may be his factory, to take instructions is that member of the team with whom he will be able to establish such a rapport and in whom he is likely to have the most confidence.

How the partner responsible for the practice sets about ensuring this will depend on a number of factors. We here can only consider one or two possible criteria.

It may be that he could effectively break his market down into two or perhaps three price groups and make one of his team primarily, because it is unlikely that any rigid allocation would work in practice, responsible for each group.

There are exceptions to almost every rule, but generally the highest priced property will be owned by the older vendors or those holding senior positions in industry, commerce or the professions, and it is probable that a partner or the most senior and experienced of the team would have responsibility to take their instructions and to be responsible for the conduct of the sales in this section. It follows that the majority of the young vendors will be found in the lower price ranges and the younger member of the team, possibly having children of the same age as the vendors, possibly even at the same school, possibly sharing some leisure interests, would be a much more effective communicator than the older person.

The partner or manager responsible may, however, decide that for his particular practice it would be more effective to break his area into districts and make a member of his team, again primarily but not exclusively, responsible for that district. In that each district is likely to have a predominance of one level of housing as opposed to another, the age and experience of members of the team might still be relevant in deciding who should be responsible for each district. The size of the area covered by the practice and indeed the size of the practice itself might be such as to render any such allocation of responsibility irrelevant. Indeed both arrangements have their drawbacks.

Any allocation by district has the advantage that the member of the team responsible for that district will have a far more intimate knowledge of it, its values and its inhabitants than he would have if he tried to cover the whole area, but that member of the team will be at a disadvantage if, as inevitably will sometimes happen, he has to deal with property in a district other than his own. Many partners and managers would argue that this disadvantage outweighs any advantage gained and that it would be better for each member of the team to operate throughout the area. If this is the correct solution for one particular practice, and one feels it probably is for the majority, the partner or manager has still got to make a decision as to which member of his team is going to be responsible for taking instructions from a particular vendor.

If responsibilities are allocated in any of the ways suggested or indeed by use of totally different criteria, it is important that the back-up staff — the receptionist, telephonist and secretaries — are aware of the general pattern established and are in a position to get any enquirer to the right person, or the most suitable person available without delay.

One thing is vital. However well organised or "haphazard" the allocation of responsibility, there must be one member of the team responsible to each vendor, responsible for co-ordinating the sales effort for him, responsible for keeping in touch with him and responsible for the advice given to him. There will be occasions when other members of the team will have to communicate with that vendor, either to make arrangements for someone to view, or possibly, if the member of the team directly responsible is not available, submitting an offer to him, but the person responsible must be informed of what has happened immediately he is available. If a vendor does not know whom to ask for, or even worse, if he gets conflicting advice from two members of the team, there has been a serious breakdown in communications.

It follows that, ideally, back-up staff should be directly responsible to one or more of the team, keeping their diaries, knowing their whereabouts, knowing when they will be returning, dealing with as many of their enquiries as possible and dealing with their correspondence, in short constituting an *"alter ego"*.

The allocation of other secretarial and back-up responsibilities is beyond the scope of this book. It is sufficient to comment that however simple or complicated the systems are, they are likely to break down if responsibility for ensuring that they are adhered to is given to no one person.

There are two further duties vital to the efficiency of the sales team, for which individuals must be made responsible. First the window — it must be the duty of a member of the team, or it could be a member of the back-up staff, to ensure that this is constantly changed and kept up to date and further that each member of the team is aware of just what properties are shown in the window. A simple diagram reproducing the lay-out of the window, with the addresses of the properties and the prices quoted written in, photo-copied and kept by each member of the team on his or her desk, would enable that person immediately to answer an enquiry, without having to scramble out from behind a desk, possibly disturbing the enquirer and going outside the office before being able to give an authoritative answer to a simple question.

Similarly somebody should be responsible for ensuring that each member either has a copy of all advertisements inserted, or an abbreviated list, so that any telephone enquiry, for example, could be dealt with immediately and efficiently.

The Property Register

To the estate agency team this is the most vital record of all. It is simply a register of all property of one type, i.e., either residential or commercial, that the office has to offer. It is the negotiator's bible, for it should tell him all he needs to know to operate efficiently and effectively in his world — the property market place.

It must be remembered that in most offices there will be occasions when prospective purchasers are initially interviewed by someone who has not seen all or perhaps any of the houses available. Again, there will be occasions when a negotiator or indeed a member of the back-up staff has to answer an enquiry about a property he or she has not seen. In these circumstances the member of staff, or it may be a partner, must be able to rely on the property register, and in two respects.

First, and above all, there must be absolute confidence in its accuracy and secondly, it must give sufficient basic information to enable a prospective purchaser to decide whether or not any particular property is likely to be of interest. It is accepted that full particulars of each house should be readily available, but it is unlikely, particularly at a time when a lot of property is on the market, that it will be practical for each member of the negotiating team to have them to hand at the desk. If constant getting up and down to go to the drawer or cabinet containing the particulars is to be avoided, the information given by the register must be sufficient for that negotiator with the prospective purchaser to prepare a list of those houses most likely to be suitable.

This information should include:

(a) A photograph, actual or reproduced.

(b) The principal characteristics of the house, whether it is detached or semi-detached, its accommodation, approximate age, size of garden, garage, etc. It should also give principal room-sizes.

(c) It must quote the asking price, or if the property is to be sold by auction or by tender, the date of the auction or the date by which tenders have to be submitted. In these cases it should also give an estimated price bracket.

(d) It must enable the negotiator without leaving the desk to make arrangements for the would-be purchaser to inspect, so it must give the name, address and/or telephone number of the vendor, instructing solicitor, or in the case where instructions are held only as a sub-agent, the name and address of the head agent.

(e) There will be, in some cases, other information that could be particularly important to a prospective purchaser. The property may need complete redecoration; it may need re-wiring or its boiler might be useless. It could be that the vendor cannot give possession immediately. Any one of these factors could for example rule the house out for the prospective purchaser who must move in a month.

(f) It is not essential, but it may well help the negotiator if the register card or slip gives directions as to how to find the house, although this information should be on the particulars.

Although some would consider it dangerous, I believe that if someone is to offer a house he has not seen to a prospective purchaser with confidence, or be able from a given list of properties to direct a prospective purchaser's attention to those most likely to be of interest, it is important that the register gives more than just the basic information already suggested. The state of decoration, the quality and state of fittings, how the asking price relates to value in the opinion of the person who took the instructions are all matters of which the negotiator should be aware. It may be felt sufficient just to give an indication as to what the negotiator who first took instructions thought that particular house's saleability to be, by putting it into say one of three categories — (A) highly saleable; (B) difficult to sell as offered; (C) most unlikely to sell as offered.

Given, however, that a house requiring complete modernisation or in appalling decorative state would be highly saleable at the right price, just to categorise in this simple way does not, in my opinion, give a negotiator sufficient information to inspire confidence.

If we took the following factors — value (V), suitability of house to locality (L), apparent state of structure (S), standard of Fittings (F), decorations (D) and then marked 1 to 5 the attractiveness of the property from a prospective purchaser's point of view, with 3 being the "average" or "fair", a house coded as follows — V3/L5/S3/F2/D1 — could be seen to be fair value at the price asked, to have no apparent structural problems, to be poorly fitted, in a poor decorative state and therefore requiring modernisation, but to be in a very good locality for a house of its type. Whereas a house coded V1/L2/S4/F4/D5 could be seen to be poor value at the price asked, to be apparently a very good structure, with good modern fittings in a very good decorative condition but too good for its locality. There could be many variations on such a theme. It is just one way of communicating and passing information amongst members of the sales team.

What is important is to remember that any negotiator offering a house to a prospective purchaser, who has not personally seen it, is at a disadvantage, and the more information he has available to him the more confident he will be, and the less will be the risk of the purchaser being sent to see something totally unsuitable and losing respect for the individual and the firm or both.

One has seen many forms of property register in use and certainly I do not feel prepared here to make a firm recommendation. I would simply comment on some that I have seen and what appear to me to be their most obvious advantages or disadvantages.

By far the most common would appear to be individual sheets in a loose-leaf binder or on cards secured in trays. These could be described as "fixed" registers. They have the advantage that the register cards cannot easily get mislaid and they can easily be maintained in price order. The loose-leaf binder had an advantage that the fixed trays do not have, in that, given that each negotiator has his own register, he would, if taking prospective purchasers out to inspect houses, be able to take his register with him. One clear disadvantage of any register contained in trays and in a cabinet, is that one cannot readily involve the prospective purchaser in his own initial search. The loose-leaf binder, provided it does not contain confidential information, or provided that information is coded, could be handed across the desk to the prospective purchaser who can look at what should be an illustrated sheet and express a view — a view that should tell the negotiator something of that purchaser's likes, dislikes and requirements. The one disadvantage here is that whilst the purchaser has the register the negotiator has not and cannot continue his search.

A register of individual cards would overcome this, for the negotiator could hand one card over to let the purchaser look at the photograph and read the brief particulars, and continue searching the register himself for other possibilities. Any "loose" register has the disadvantage that cards can get out of order or even mislaid. If loose registers are to be used it is essential that one fixed master register is maintained and is used as a control against which negotiators can check their personal registers.

I have seen individual sets of particulars in a loose-leaf binder used to form a register. This avoids the production of register slips, but this system has, I believe, serious limitations.

First, particulars take time to produce and ideally a property should be on the "register" just as soon as its basic characteristics are known. If a vendor telephoned instructions towards the end of the day, it might not be possible for a formal inspection to be made and particulars taken until the following day. In such circumstances a good negotiator will obtain basic details of property-type and accommodation, if not price. The fact that that property is becoming available and what it basically consists of could be recorded on his register and those of his colleagues that night. Registers based on the full particulars would not be available until later the following day. In the interval the right buyer could be lost.

Secondly, particulars are likely to be similar in size to the binder itself and a negotiator using that register can see details of only one property at a time. Where slips or cards are used they can be overlapped, enabling the negotiator rapidly to run down his page and quickly identify those properties most likely to suit.

I do not intend here to deal with the drafting of particulars, which I regard as very much part of the marketing function and one not directly related to an office system, but in my own firm we devised a standard form of particulars which serves also as a record of instructions and aide-mémoire. The three categories are those referred to earlier. (See illustrations, pages 181, 183 and 184).

It was intended to achieve two things. First that, where practical, particulars were kept to a length that could be contained on one side of an A4 sheet avoiding unnecessary wastage in time, paper, money and verbal padding. Secondly, it was devised so that the top half of the form could be completed by the negotiator immediately he had finished his inspection of the house, and in practice gave the information needed for the front of the register card, other information such as the vendor's name, telephone number, viewing arrangements and confidential codes, information needed only by the negotiator himself going on the reverse. In practice, and provided there is no undue loss of time involved, we print both particulars and register cards at the same time. I illustrate in diagramatic form what I believe a negotiator's register slip should contain. Others will be able to adapt and no doubt improve.

Many larger firms operating in the commercial market have their registers on computers and, as we have noted, a few in the residential market have now done likewise. There is little doubt that many more firms will be using computers to maintain their property registers and to assist in many other functions. Their application we shall now consider briefly.

As a store for one's property register the computer has obvious advantages. It can be up-dated in seconds and a list of the properties most likely to be of interest, whether it be, for example, four-bedroomed detached houses in a given district, or factories with a floor area of between 5,000 and 7,000 sq. ft., can almost instantaneously be

DIRECTIONS

PHOTOGRAPH

TYPE AND BRIEF DESCRIPTION

ACCOMMODATION WITH SIZES

SPECIAL FEATURES

ADDRESS

PRICE/AUCTION DATE

ACCOMMODATION.   BEDS [ ]   RECEPTION [ ]   BATH [ ]   GARAGE [ ]

Front

INSTRUCTIONS RECEIVED FROM

TELEPHONE NUMBER
OR ADDRESS

INSTRUCTIONS TAKEN BY   DATE

| V | | L | | S | | F | | D | |

Agency Sole [ ]

Multiple [ ]

Sub [ ]

OCCUPATION DATE

VIEWING ARRANGEMENTS

SPECIAL COMMENTS

Back

displayed on a visual display unit, the list printed out, or a further selection made and fuller particulars of individual properties printed out.

The effectiveness of a computerised register in the commercial property market is beyond doubt, but there are dangers in the use of any data-processing system to store one's residential property register. It can be too selective, for it is precise. Purchasers on the other hand, whilst selective, are seldom absolutely clear (accurate) as to just what they want and often end up purchasing something that differs materially from what they went out to seek.

The negotiator with flair, able quickly to scan the whole of his register, stands a better chance of making the unusual "match" than one relying on a limited selection of the property available extracted mechanically or electronically. I have heard many use this argument in support of the belief that computers cannot effectively be used in the residential estate agency process. It is a false argument, for a computer could rapidly print out the whole of a property register. The negotiator can scan the whole on his visual display unit and select more narrowly from there, using his flair if need be and print out in full the details he wants.

There is, however, the danger that given the ability to select with great accuracy and speed, the negotiator, under pressure, will do so and lose the ability to use either his own knowledge of the properties concerned or his own instincts as a salesman.

To illustrate this point, a negotiator visually scanning his register for a four-bedroomed detached house might well pick out one that meets the purchaser's requirement in every other respect, but which has three bedrooms because he knows a fourth could be added over the garage. A computer asked for a list of four-bedroomed houses will not identify that house, *unless* the negotiator who took the instructions on the three-bedroomed house in the first place, appreciated that a fourth bedroom could be added and fed this information into the computer. In short, there are obvious dangers to the use of computers in an emotive and flexible market, but if these dangers are appreciated and the computer is used intelligently, the property register is one of its obvious applications.

The computerised property register does, at the present time, have one severe drawback, although again applicable mainly to the residential market — the computer itself cannot illustrate. It might be argued that illustration is not vital to the negotiator who knows the properties he has on his register, but it is of indirect help, for it gives the prospective purchaser a means of communicating to that negotiator his likes or his dislikes.

DIRECTIONS
(keep it brief)

Photo Space—Side. L.R/Centre

Vendor

Property details (to be recorded even if not used in write up)

Tel. Nos.   (work)   (home)

Age

Viewing

Plot size

Solicitor

Fittings Available/Included

Board

Reason for sale

Other information

Sole Agents ?

Date Instructed

Category   A   B   or   C

(Address)

(Price)

(advert)

ACCOMMODATION

_____

_____

_____

_____

_____

_____

_____

_____

_____

_____

OUTBUILDINGS

_____

GROUNDS

_____

_____

_____

SERVICES   R.V. £

VIEWING

VACANT POSSESSION (only if something specific to say)

The Office Bulletin

The need for accuracy if negotiators are to have confidence in their registers has been stressed and this leads one directly to considering the role of the property bulletin, a means of circulating information within an office or between offices. It should not be confused with what many firms refer to as the "Day Book", for in my opinion it should be concerned with nothing other than the estate agency function. Further, if an office has departments dealing with both commercial and residential property, there should be separate bulletins for each. Only in the small firm which deals with both, and where individual negotiators deal with both, should the possibility of combining them be considered.

Responsibility for keeping the bulletin up to date must be given to one person. It must be readily accessible to all negotiators; for this reason the reception desk might be the best place to keep it and the receptionist the best person to maintain it, for there it would be readily seen by negotiators as they come and go. It should record:

(a) new properties in respect of which instructions have been received, with brief details and the asking price and, if it is to be sold by auction or tender, the relevant date.

(b) It should record all property sold by that office subject to contract, with the name of the purchaser, and here many might consider it of value to know the town from which that purchaser is coming, particularly if it is a neighbouring town where the firm itself might have an office and where a sale might indicate an opportunity to obtain instructions from the purchaser for the sale of the property he is leaving. It should also record any houses in respect of which sub-agency instructions are held and where sales subject to contract have been notified by the head agent.

(c) It must record all sales where contracts have been exchanged or houses which should be removed from the register for any other reason.

(d) It should record all price-alterations and any alterations in viewing arrangements and

(e) any other information that affects the property register.

The bulletin should be produced daily and copies circulated first thing every morning so that those who have to take action on the information it contains can do so. Registers must be up-dated; ideally each negotiator will have and will maintain his own. The window will need to be up-dated. Where houses have been sold, the particulars will need to be removed. Price-changes will lead to particulars being altered or further particulars being "run off".

A suggested form of bulletin is illustrated. Where it is to be circulated to those responsible for the various tasks that have to be carried out

PROPERTIES PUT ON BOOKS : ADDRESS		

PRICE ALTERATIONS	OLD PRICE	NE PRI

FALLEN THROUGH·RE-OFFER	SOLD S/C
BULLETIN FROM	DATE

	CAT.	COMM	BEDS	REC.	BATH	GGE.	GDN	PRICE

EMOVED	REASON

	PURCHASER	TOWN ORIGIN	BY	IN CONJ.	PRICE
	SEEN BY				

there could be space provided where each person involved, once his or her task has been completed, can initial it and pass it on.

In the larger office such a circulating drill will prove to be too slow, and copies of the bulletin should be provided to each person concerned. If the partner or manager responsible for the estate agency function in that office is anxious to keep tight control, he should ask for each copy of the bulletin to be returned to him, initialled, by a given time each day, so that he knows all necessary amendments have been made and action taken.

Many larger firms may have a number of offices close enough to each other for a regular inter-change of properties and would-be purchasers to take place. It is vital that any property bulletin should be sent to them at the time it is circulated within the office of origin, so that they too can up-date their records. Until such time as we have a vastly improved postal service, such firms may be able to arrange circulation not only of bulletins but of particulars, memorandum and so on by messenger.

It cannot be stressed strongly enough that the immediate up-dating of property registers is vital and if no other way is open, then the contents of the office bulletin should be telephoned to any other office likely to be concerned that night or first thing the following morning and this telephone conversation should take place between the persons whose responsibility the property bulletin is in each office; copies should then be sent simply to confirm.

Where the property register is held on a computer, all changes should be fed in immediately if this is possible, but as an absolute minimum in daily batches. If and when individual negotiators have their own terminals and visual display units, they will have immediate access to the register that should be right up to date, but for the majority of firms who use computers a drill will need to be established to ensure that information is passed from the computer to negotiators and back-up staff for such tasks as window up-dating.

The Applicants' Register

Every estate agency office will maintain in some form or another a register of prospective purchasers. At one end of the scale this may be no more than names and addresses and requirements, written in longhand on card, or in a notebook or loose-leaf binder. At the other end, it may be a register filed on a computer.

The interviewing of prospective purchasers is a marketing function and we will deal with it as such. Here it is only necessary to comment on the basic principles that should underlie the applicants' register and the role it plays in the office system. It is necessary in anything other than the smallest office that the register and the information it records be in a prescribed form.

Each negotiator will want to differentiate between the probables and the possibles and have immediately available to him his list of "hot" applicants. The details of all applicants' requirements, "hot" or "cold", should be readily available to any one of the negotiating or back-up staff.

Irrespective of the form in which it is kept, i.e., whether it be on cards or on a computer, it is the applicants' register that will decide to whom property particulars, when they are prepared, will be sent.

If a computer or other data-processing equipment is to be used to match prospective purchasers with houses available, standard forms of setting out the characteristics of the houses and the requirements of the purchasers will be essential. I suggest that it is equally vital where this matching process has got to be done by a member of staff who possibly has seen neither the house nor the purchasers. The use of standard forms will increase speed and accuracy in the matching process. Inaccuracy in the circulation of particulars is one of the principal criticisms made of estate agents.

The efficient agent will try to maintain contact with as many of his prospective purchasers as possible and the applicants' register must facilitate this.

The matching of houses to prospective purchasers and dissemination of information are very much a marketing process and considerable research and thought has got to go into the way applicants' requirements are recorded if that process is to be carried out with sufficient accuracy not to annoy prospective purchasers and yet with enough flexibility to make at least the vast majority of likely matches.

It is appropriate that we consider the actual content of particulars and all the information that needs to be recorded on the applicants' register when we deal with the marketing function. It is sufficient here to stress the role the applicants' register plays and the basic information that should be recorded, and later to consider the register in more detail.

The applicants' register is primarily there to enable negotiators to communicate with prospective purchasers and this is done in two principal ways.

(1) Indirectly, by the matching of recorded requirements to available houses and circulating particulars of the houses likely to be of interest. If this is to be done effectively the applicant's card must record a name and address, accommodation required, localities acceptable, the maximum price the purchaser can afford, and any other "basic" requirement of that applicant. A basic requirement can be positive, i.e., "My husband has a bad heart and the main bedroom must be on the ground floor", or "We are keen gardeners and must have a large garden". It could also be negative — "We currently live on a main road and are moving to get away from the noise and we will not live on a busy road again". I stress the use of the word "basic" as meaning a

requirement of that particular purchaser that is to him or her absolutely vital. It is where such a stated requirement is ignored in circulating particulars that annoyance is caused. At the other end of the scale, care has to be taken in recording "preferences", for they can be meaningless. "I would prefer a detached house" also means "I will buy a semi-detached if I have to". Too much regard to "preferences" will lead to lost "matches".

(2) The applicants' register is there to enable negotiators to communicate with and keep in touch with applicants by post and telephone. A telephone call may be routine, intended to show interest in that applicant and to check on the progress of their search. It may be urgent, it may be that a house has just come on the market that the negotiator believes would suit and he wants that applicant to know of its availability immediately, or negotiations may have reached a critical stage, creating a need to communicate instantly. It is not sufficient just to have the home telephone number of the applicant if both he and his wife are out during normal working hours. If possible the card should record a home telephone number and a telephone number at which either the husband or wife could be reached at work and the times when they are most likely to be available.

Lastly, the card should be dated and the name or initials of the negotiator who first put the applicant's requirements on to the register clearly given.

The way the applicants' register is kept or the information is stored is important. If the matching process is carried out at a central point, either within an office or within a firm, whether it be by computer or otherwise, clearly each applicant's requirements must be recorded and stored at the central point, but each negotiator must also have ready access to the recorded requirements of the applicants that he or she first saw or spoke to personally. These should be on his or her desk and, as earlier noted, divided between probables and possibles so that immediate contact can be made with the most likely purchasers immediately a house comes on to the market.

In the larger office a complete or central register should be maintained, probably in price groups, in strict alphabetical order, so that any negotiator can check immediately whether an enquirer is already on the register and if so to have the card available during his discussions and for up-dating.

On any applicants' register there is a danger of duplication. A prospective purchaser could over a matter of a few weeks see more than one negotiator and each, possibly unaware of the other's involvement, record that applicant's requirements. As a result that applicant receives two copies of the particulars of any house that might be suitable, which is not only wasteful but gives the impression of inefficiency and further, if an applicant finds a suitable house, or for any other reason withdraws from the market place, there is the risk that only one card will be withdrawn and he will go on receiving particulars — again wasteful. Collating to avoid duplication is simple if a computer is used, but on any other system it requires manual checking.

There is another risk here for the firm with a number of offices. An applicant may be interested in more than one office area. In such a case the office at which he first calls should send details of his or her requirements to any other office that might be able to satisfy them. Again it is important, to avoid duplication, that at the originating office a note is made that the requirements were passed to another office, and at the receiving office a note made of the office from which the requirements came, so that if either sells a house to that applicant, or is informed by him that he has been suited elsewhere, both cards are removed from the register and not just one. This "interchange note" will also be important when an applicant changes his requirements, for the other office will need notifying immediately.

In considering the property register I stressed how important it was that it be "accurate" and that all involved in the estate agency team had confidence in it. In the context of the applicants' register I use the word "alive" as opposed to accurate, although it should be both. Some applicants or prospective purchasers will take months if not years to find the house of their choice, for they are in no hurry. A couple retiring in two years' time would be an example. Others remain "alive" only for a matter of days or at the most a few weeks. Unless care is taken and regular checks made, one's register of applicants will rapidly become largely "dead" and unmanageable in size, and if it is used regularly to circulate particulars or property newspapers it will become immensely wasteful in terms of stationery, postage and time. The majority of agents use regular pre-paid reply cards or letters to revise their registers, removing that applicant's name and requirements within a stated time if no positive response is achieved. The frequency with which such letters are sent out is a matter for the individual office and much will depend on market circumstances. One can only give some guide. In the lower price-ranges most applicants, if one has not heard from them within the last month and does not know them to be "alive", can be assumed "dead", and it is in the higher price ranges where most of the applicants who are prepared to take months or years to find the right house are to be found.

If one's register is to be really alive it is important that every contact with the prospective purchaser is noted and dated. Nothing could be more irritating or give a worse impression than an applicant receiving a pre-paid "Are you still looking?" letter, if he in fact spoke to somebody in that office only two days before and gave up-dated requirements or made arrangements to look at a house.

Whatever interval is chosen as appropriate for a regular review to be carried out, and this will differ between the various price groups and from area to area and in varying market conditions, it is vital that that interval be applied to the date of the latest contact and not to the date of the original enquiry.

That such procedures are necessary is regretted, for ideally one would like to think that one's negotiators were in regular touch by letter or telephone with all prospective purchasers and therefore knew just who was alive and active, and had already removed those that they knew were not. Under average market conditions and for the great majority of estate agency offices this is a practical impossibility, and it is for this reason that I earlier underlined the importance of each negotiator having readily available to him the requirements of his "hot" applicants, known in most of my offices and as I know in other firms, as "hottie lists", and does do everything possible to keep in touch with these. Most offices will, therefore, have two groups of applicants — the hot lists and the pool, but it must never be forgotten that the applicants in the pool can suddenly become very hot indeed. For example, a telephone call from an applicant with whom one has perhaps had no personal contact since the initial enquiry to the effect that "I have now sold my house and I must find something within the next six weeks" immediately brings him into the hot category and any such change in circumstance must be noted and produce immediate action.

Lastly, in considering the applicants' register as part of the system as opposed to part of the marketing function, if an applicant's recorded requirements are removed because they have failed to reply to a revision letter, that record or card should not immediately be destroyed, for many perfectly genuine applicants fail to reply within the time-limit given. Their cards should be kept on one side for a further period in case they make further contact. The nature of the market will dictate for how long.

There is one other type of applicant that has to be considered. He is the person known normally to one of the partners or staff who "Would move if I found just the right thing, but I am not really looking".

The tendency is for this type of prospective purchaser to be kept only "in the mind", but this will be the mind of perhaps one individual who may be forgetful or just not there at the right moment: "Out of sight is out of mind." This type of applicant will be amazed if he finds himself simply on a matching list. I believe they should be put on the register but with a referral back to the member of the firm concerned, so that he or she can decide if contact should be made, and in what form.

If the firm is one that produces a periodic property newspaper these applicants should be sent copies on a regular basis, to show that their possible interest has been noted and in the hope that it might activate them.

Different criteria will apply to the maintenance of a commercial property applicants' register. The firm or department dealing exclusively with commercial property will develop its own disciplines, but some smaller firms' individual negotiators will be dealing with both residential and commercial. The requirements of the commercial applicant are likely to be much more clearly stated and to be less flexible. A firm of accountants wanting larger offices, or a small industrialist wanting a larger factory, will only be satisfied and will only become a "dead" applicant when they have found what they want. Revision letters could only annoy. Contact in this field should be kept either by letter or by telephone, and preferably the latter. Again care will be needed if one is not to irritate busy people. They are only likely to want to hear from you when you have something positive to offer them and they are much more likely than the average house-buyer to let you know if they find suitable accommodation elsewhere.

Filing and Past Records

Again I have to be careful not to be too specific, for although filing is in any office a fact of life, just what should be filed is certainly to a degree a matter of opinion. What records should be kept will vary enormously from one market to another and the value of past records will again be a matter of opinion.

I look first at the house-market. One's initial instructions will come either by telephone, when they may be no more than an invitation to call and agreement as to the time the initial inspection is to take place, or they could be detailed, with specific instructions as to price, as to viewing arrangements, as to who are the solicitors who are to act, as to the date when possession could be given, etc. In such a case a detailed note should be taken by whoever received those telephone instructions and a file should be started. In any event as soon as the instructions have been formally taken there will need to be draft particulars and other basic information essential to the conduct of any negotiations that might result from the property being offered on the market. From then on there should be on that file or on the register card or slip of that particular property, which in itself will ultimately be filed, a note of every contact, with its date, not only every contact with the vendor, which might be by way of a personal visit, telephone call or a letter, but, if it is possible, a note of every person to whom the particulars were sent, of every applicant who viewed and of every enquiry by telephone or letter made following circulation of particulars or advertising.

In particular it is important that a note be made on the file of any specific advice given to the vendor, of any significant information obtained from him; for example, he may have indicated a willingness to accept a lower price than he was earlier hoping for, or given revised instructions with regard to viewing. The file should tell any negotiator who has not earlier been involved with that particular house precisely where matters stand, and enable him to talk authoritatively to the vendor if need be. On to that file will go all correspondence directly related to the sale of that particular house. Once a purchaser has been found and a sale completed, it is, however, questionable as to just how much of the information contained on the file need be kept. A copy of the particulars could assist if at any time in the future one was instructed to sell the house again, but if used they have got to be very carefully up-dated, for the majority of owners, having acquired a house, will make some alterations. Even the price paid for the house is likely to prove of little long-term interest in the valuation sense. It could be argued that once the sale is completed the file could be destroyed, but there is a public relations opportunity that would be lost if this were done. If some five years later the then owner of that house gives the firm instructions to re-sell it, he can be nothing but impressed if the negotiator who arrives to take instructions has not only a copy of the earlier particulars, but knows when he bought it, can immediately identify improvements made and knows whom he bought it from. With rapidly escalating prices, he is not likely to be so impressed by a reminder of what he paid for it!

Any record of what type of house was involved, what it contained, when it was sold and to whom, could prove a great value in the marketing sense. It is marketing information that could be of use in the smallest office, but which could be even more relevant in the years to come to the larger office equipped with a computer.

Given that the agent who knows his market will know approximately how frequently the average house changes hands and given, for this purpose, that it is approximately every six years, he could search his records, possibly a laborious task manually, but one taking only seconds if one's records are computerised, ascertain precisely what houses he sold six years beforehand and to whom they were sold, and he could make contact.

In the simplest form, if he has a prospective purchaser very anxious to live in a particular street, he can without any records write to the owners of the houses in that street, and here I do not discuss what is professionally acceptable and what is not, but how much more effective that approach to vendors will be if the letters are personally addressed and recognise any earlier involvement.

I suggest that the minimum records that should be kept, and whether this is kept on a card-index, individual files or on a computer, makes to my mind little difference, is the address of the property, its type, accommodation, the date when it was last sold, to whom, and at what price. Even this information will, however, be valueless unless it can be very easily retrieved, and a central index containing a card for every property with which the office has dealt in district/village/street order is probably the simplest way to ensure that retrieval is easy.

Given that the records are kept on some form of central index, manual or computerised, on to the record for that particular property can go any other dealings that the firm has had with it. It need not necessarily be the record of a sale, it could be the record of a building society valuation carried out, structural survey made, a valuation for rating or fire insurance purposes, or a planning application for a change of use. Some of these occurrences will, of course, require the keeping of permanent records, and this is not a matter relevant to the consideration of estate agency, but the central index could easily cross-reference to any individual or departmental filing system.

In the commercial field the information recorded will probably need to be in much greater detail and here there is for me a danger of getting involved in the subject of property management, for dates when leases expire, and dates of rent reviews are information that could all be of great value to the commercial property agent, who is likely to be much more involved in the professional aspects of his market and in management than his "house agent" opposite number.

Many firms produce property newspapers and many produce an annual property market review. Some produce occasional bulletins dealing with specific problems; these would tend to apply more on the commercial than the residential side. What better use could be made of one's record system than to ensure that such productions are sent to those relevant persons or companies with whom one has had dealings? It will not only keep the name of one's firm in front of them, but will give them an impression not only of efficiency, but of continuing interest in them.

Board Records

We have already noted the relevance of "For Sale", "Sold By", "Let By", "Acquired For Clients By" boards as a means of promoting the firm's image, apart from their relevance in reference to the property concerned.

A firm that uses boards extensively will have a considerable amount of capital involved and the expense of maintaining boards, erecting them, taking them down, and from time to time checking not only their state, but their safety, will not be inconsiderable. They need therefore to be carefully controlled.

In addition to boards of this nature, many firms will have advertising hoardings on railway stations, in shopping centres and on hoarding sites.

A board record book is needed and the following information should be recorded:

(a) A numbered list of all boards, with a note of their sizes and any special wording that may be on them.
(b) The date the board was made, possibly the materials of which it is made, when it was last repainted, when it was last inspected and by whom.
(c) The location of each board and when it was erected.
(d) Where the board is kept when not in use and
(e) if relevant, which of the firm's board contractors is responsible for that particular board.

Much the same sort of information will be needed in respect of any permanent hoardings, but some additional information may be required, for example as to whom the space is rented from, the rent payable, and the terms on which it is leased.

The wording used on any such hoarding or display advertisement should also be recorded.

Hoardings used for display of auction posters or other promotional posters need particular care, for they can rapidly get shabby and out of date.

All staff should be board-conscious and when travelling around their area should be on the look-out for any boards that have been improperly or carelessly erected, for any that might have become damaged or dangerous, for any that are clearly out of date or looking shabby and should report back.

It is absolutely essential that one particular person should be made responsible for maintaining board records and for carrying out regular checks.

Key Records

The keeping of keys brings with it particular responsibilities. The R.I.C.S. "Practice Notes" suggest that an agent holding keys could be doing so as a gratuitous bailee. If an agent wants to hold keys or is asked to do so, he would be well advised to obtain clear instructions as to the capacity in which he holds them and as to what his responsibilities are to be, and in particular as to whether or not he is authorised to release them at his own discretion to members of the public. An owner handing keys to an agent could well assume that the agent was assuming responsibility for security, regular checks at the property, that the plumbing systems are drained off if frost is threatened, and so on. There is a need for great caution. Squatters present a danger and in 1968 the City of London Police found it necessary to draw agents' attention to the fact that keys were being borrowed and copied, and the copies used at a later date to effect entry.

Clearly, careful records are essential — and "Practice Notes" recommends the following:

(a) The use of permanent (metal or plastic) discs for all keys in two colours, say black for unfurnished property where the agent has authority to release keys to persons unaccompanied, and red for furnished premises or premises where the owner's specific instructions are that the key is not to be allowed out of the office unless the person to whom it is given is accompanied by a member of staff.

(b) That keys then be identified by number only i.e. Red 25.

(c) That a key book be kept in loose-leaf form, with one page for each key, with its colour clearly indicated; and that for security purposes this book should be always kept in the office safe when the office is closed.

(d) One person should be made responsible for maintaining the key book. Every key taken by a member of staff or a member of the public should be signed for. If a key is to be given to a member of the public, a note of the name and address must be taken, and preferably some form of identification requested. No "red" key should be let out to an unaccompanied person without the express authority of a partner. The approximate time of return should also be noted.

(e) The key book should contain a note that the keys are handed out for inspection purposes only and the borrower's attention should be drawn to this before they sign for the key.

(f) The key label should have on the reverse side the agent's name and address and a space for a stamp.

One would make one or two additional comments. First, however well and carefully organised one's key system is, there is always the risk that a key might not be returned by a prospective purchaser and not in the event prove easy to recover, or that it could be mislaid, not necessarily by a prospective purchaser but possibly by a member of one's own staff. If this occurs the vendor should be informed immediately and instructions obtained to change the locks. If copies are made they must similarly be accounted for.

Advertising Records

I deal with these under Office Systems, but they are in practice very much part of the marketing function. There are three different aspects to be considered.

First, the advertisement record essential to the efficient running of the office. We have already commented on this when considering communications, but there should be available to every negotiator a note of what was last, or currently is, being advertised in any paper or journal, or in the window, so that the property to which any enquirer is referring can immediately be identified.

Secondly, a record should be kept on each property file or card of every advertisement of that particular property inserted, a note of the paper, the journal, the date and, if advertising costs are recoverable, of the cost. Even if advertising costs are not recoverable the partner responsible for the marketing function of that office, or the office manager, should know just what has been spent. The precise amount may not be known until an account is received, in which case an estimated amount should be recorded.

Thirdly, a record should be kept of any replies that can be specifically related to any particular advertisement. Only in this way will one be able to assess the effectiveness of the media one is using in reaching prospective purchasers. It is accepted, of course, that this, for the estate agent, will not always be his sole criterion, for to an extent every advertisement inserted plays a part in building the public image and some advertisements will be designed with this as their main function; applicant response might be of no great significance.

The Multiple Office Firm

I think it is appropriate, when dealing with office procedures, to refer to certain procedures that will need to be adopted by multiple office firms, although these are also relevant in the marketing sense.

We are concerned here particularly with firms with a number of offices sufficiently close to each other to have over-lapping areas and a need, if the firm's marketing function is to be carried out effectively, to have a very close degree of co-operation. This will only prove to be possible if the procedures are clearly set out and understood by all concerned.

Circumstances will vary from firm to firm and possibly even between one office and another. Again we are dealing in the main with the house-agency problem, but it is one that is also faced by some firms in the commercial sector.

First, the partner responsible for the estate agency function, or indeed the partners responsible, for there may well be more than one, must decide over what area each office can expect to draw instructions, and allocate these areas on a map, ensuring that the firm's overall area is covered. There are bound to be areas common between offices, and copies of the map should be provided to every office to avoid any misunderstanding as to just what their area includes, as to what parts of it are common, and with what other offices.

If instructions are received to sell a house in an area covered solely by one office, it will be that office's sole responsibility to take those instructions and to make all relevant marketing decisions, including, if they think it appropriate, the passing of register slips and particulars to neighbouring offices.

Where an office receives instructions in a common area, it is our own policy that the other office or offices involved are immediately notified, and if the calibre of the property justifies it, their staff are invited to join in the initial inspection.

The office or inter-office bulletin could be used to circulate information. These bulletins should go to all neighbouring offices and, as we have commented earlier, they should contain details of all properties in respect of which instructions are received, those sold subject to contract, those where contracts have been exchanged, those to be removed for any other reason, price alterations and any variations of instructions in respect of viewing, completion date and so on. In many firms having a number of offices professional services would be centralised in one or more of them. The use of the inter-office bulletin will minimise the risk of another office or the professional centre accepting instructions to act for the purchaser or lessee, or for a building society or insurance company, in respect of property that another office may have sold, and where to carry out those instructions would be to create a conflict of interests.

We have already, in discussing the applicants' register, considered the circulation of information with regard to prospective purchasers as between offices, and we shall be looking at this more closely when we come to consider in detail the various marketing functions, and in particular the dissemination of information.

If co-operation between offices is to be at the highest possible level, very careful thought has got to be given as to how staff are motivated. Many years ago I understand, in one of the larger West End firms where individual negotiators looked after their own vendors and indeed purchasers, if such a negotiator let one of his colleagues offer one of his properties to one of that colleague's applicants and a sale resulted, the negotiator acting for the vendor would only be credited with having earned a third of the commission, whilst had he decided to give sub-agency instructions to local agents he would have been credited with a half share. This sort of anomaly has got to be avoided at all costs. Ideally, to encourage co-operation between neighbouring offices, the negotiator, however he is remunerated, should not be the loser as a result of letting a neighbouring office offer a property he has been instructed to sell, or indeed passing a very good prospective purchaser to that office. My own firm in practice have not experienced any difficulties in this direction as far as the house market is concerned; such difficulties as we have encountered have been between the straightforward house agency offices and those at which special agency functions, such as commercial agency and business transfer, are centralised.

Day Books

I believe many firms still keep a Day Book and find it of value — a Day Book into which every visitor, every telephone call, is entered. I personally question their value, although they may be more relevant in the professional office where some fees may be assessed on time spent, than in the estate agency context.

Strictly in the agency context, I believe it to be vital that every partner or negotiator does have a girl or assistant *"alter ego"*, who should be the link between that person and any callers.

There are other matters that we might consider under the heading of office procedures; how we co-ordinate the efforts of the sales department; how we direct the efforts of negotiators and how we record their work, but I think these are all more appropriately considered elsewhere.

Fifteen

Marketing Functions — The Product

On taking instructions — Immediate response — The
initial visit — The quality of the product — Method of
sale — Practical considerations: auction, tender,
inviting offers, For sale by auction at a later date —
The nature of the agency — The need for a policy on
sole agency — Expenses, regional variations — Need
to agree overall basis of charging — Fixtures and
fittings — Viewing arrangements — The vendor's
authority to sell — Sub-agents — Development
potential — Leasehold property — Confirming
instructions — Standard letters — Property
particulars — What should be included — The use of
photographs — The role of particulars in marketing
— Special considerations in multiple agency areas —
Commercial property particulars — Planning uses —
Importance of location — Special property
considerations — The relevance of tenure — Building
land and properties with development potential —
Planning considerations

On taking Instructions

Instructions will come to an office in one of many ways. The vendor
may call in, or he may telephone. The instructions may come from
solicitors, from the Executor and Trustee Department of one of the
banks. They may come in by letter. They may even come in through a
third party — a friend of the vendor's, a local bank manager, and so on.
The amount of information that will be available to the office at this
stage will vary. If one has had the opportunity of speaking to the vendor
direct, one may have been able to obtain sufficient information on
which to start marketing. For example, telephoning the applicants who
are most likely to be immediately interested: "We have just received
instructions to sell 24, Acacia Avenue; we won't be seeing it until later
this afternoon, but it has the following. . .We haven't got a price yet"
(or "the vendor is looking for a price in the order of £30,000") "and we
believe it could be of interest to you. Would you like us to make an

appointment for you to see it?" This sort of immediate reaction could be of particular value in a multiple agency area, where you may know, or there is at least the possibility, that the vendor has given, or will be giving, instructions to others.

What is important and must be stressed is that in whatever form those initial instructions are received, the fact that they have been received has got to be recorded. It would not be the first time such a thing had ever happened if a busy negotiator received telephone instructions and either failed to act at all, or acted so belatedly that the opportunity to sell was lost.

An immediate entry on the office bulletin, however sketchy the information, and it might be no more than the address, would be one way of dealing with this, but it has a disadvantage. In the world of the future, it may be that the negotiator will be able to feed this basic information straight to the computer without leaving his desk. But lacking such a sophisticated aid, if he has to leave his desk to make the record, there is always the risk, if he is under pressure, that his telephone is again ringing, or somebody is waiting to see him, and he will not record the instructions then and there. If negotiators are well disciplined in keeping diaries, this is where this data should be recorded as it is received.

Another alternative would be a book of tear-off slips with a carbon, possibly using a pro forma such as shown here giving the basic

---

Instructions From   By telephone/call/letter

Name.....................................   on behalf of.............................

Address................................   Address Of Property To Be Sold

....

....

Tel......................................   ....

      Type...

      Accommodation/bed. Recep. Kit. Bath. Garage.

      Approximate Price...

      Arrangements To Inspect..................................

      Instructions Received

      By..

      Date..

information necessary for that property to be recorded and the instructions acted on.

If such slips were used, the top copies can, at a convenient moment, be passed to the partner responsible or the office manager, so that he is aware that the instructions have been received and involve himself if he thinks it necessary. He may indeed insist on knowing within minutes, for many persons responsible for an agency department would, for the reasons we considered earlier, want to direct just who should go to the house personally to take the instructions.

Both R.I.C.S. "Practice Notes" and M. J. Vivian in the "Art of House Agency" stressed the importance of this initial visit. The former said that the instructions should be dealt with initially by an experienced person, who will thereafter be responsible for supervising the general conduct of the sale and follow it through to completion. It is acknowledged that sometimes somebody in a junior capacity may have to take these initial instructions, and it is recommended that the person who is to be ultimately responsible should follow them up as quickly as possible. Mr. Vivian conjectures that the poor image of the average house agent must to a measure "be due to the appearance, dress, manner and attitude of the average ambassador sent by the firm to inspect...first impressions are so important and this exercise is the beginning of a special relationship with the client".

If one considers this initial inspection in the context of the various approaches to marketing, its importance is underlined. In the majority of cases the firm's representative, be he partner, manager or negotiator, will meet the vendor, and the outcome of that meeting will dictate the quality of the product the firm will have to sell.

The advice with regard to method of sale and with regard to value, the decisions to be made (ideally jointly by the vendor and the agent, often after carefully considered advice, preferably backed up by recent evidence of comparable transactions) are all important in the marketing sense. If the wrong conclusions are reached, the vendor will be disappointed and frustrated, possibly driven to another firm, and the agent runs the risk of abortive work and expenditure.

Confidence is the key word. Whoever goes to take instructions must be somebody who in age, manner and experience is going to instil confidence in that vendor. If this can be done, even if the initial instructions are not in precisely the form — in particular as regards asking price — that the agent would have wished, if the vendor has confidence in him there is every likelihood that after early abortive efforts to arouse interest in the property, that agent's subsequent advice will be taken. It is for this reason that I believe the decision as to who should take instructions must rest with the partner or manager in charge of the department.

I can recommend no set procedure for taking instructions. Much will depend on the information the agent already has and as to whether or not the vendor is present. There are two stages in the taking of instructions. First, the inspection of the property and the actual taking of the physical particulars and, secondly, the advice that is given either at the house or later by letter or at a meeting. We will consider these in reverse order, for by far the most vital matters in progress to a successful sale are the conclusions one draws having inspected the property, the advice one gives based on those conclusions, and the precise nature of the instructions one actually obtains.

An instructions pro forma should be taken and completed whenever one takes instructions and this should achieve two things. First that the person concerned does consider all matters that are likely to be of importance, and ask all relevant questions, and secondly that anyone in the office who subsequently has to deal with that property or the vendor will have sufficient background knowledge to work on.

The first thing to be established is the reason for sale. This will sometimes be known from the information given at initial contact, or will be volunteered by the vendor. Arriving at it sometimes needs tact but its importance cannot be over-stated, for it has a bearing on most of the matters we shall now be considering.

Then advice has to be given and a decision reached as to the method of sale to be adopted. We have already considered the relative merits of sale by private treaty, by auction or by tender. The negotiator concerned may have already decided, following his inspection, that the house is one that could generate a great deal of interest in the market, that it is one where the best results are likely to be obtained if prospective purchasers are put into open competition and without a specific price being quoted from the start. But, if a sale by auction is to be contemplated, certain other factors must be considered. It is not, for example, a suitable method for sale if the vendor is not prepared to be committed in terms of time. He must be prepared to give possession at a specific date, probably some three months ahead. It is, as we have seen, a more expensive method of selling under normal circumstances than private treaty. The method should not be recommended if the price the vendor has in mind is one the agent believes will not be achieved, however strong the competition. If there are compelling reasons why this method of sale should be adopted, these are likely to be known before the inspection is ever made. To set off on the auction path knowing that the vendor is unlikely to agree to a realistic reserve is to run the risk of the sale proving abortive, client's additional expenditure wasted and the firm's image tarnished. The negotiator must be aware of just what it is likely to cost to mount the auction and this will vary greatly on the quality of the property to be offered, this will dictate the quality of the particulars, the degree of advertising and the media to be used, and it is in these items that the bulk of the additional expense lies.

Some vendors will automatically be opposed to the idea of selling by public auction and given that the negotiator is absolutely sure of his ground and knows that the advice to sell by this method is right, this opposition has got to be overcome.

The reasons most frequently given by vendors for not wishing to sell by auction are as follows. Expenses — these would vary so greatly, dependent upon the calibre of the house, that the agent or negotiator must be prepared to assess what will be required and give an approximate cost. The negotiator has got to explain to that vendor why he believes that the competition likely to be generated is such that this cost can be seen as relatively insignificant when compared with the possible benefits likely to result from two, three or more would-be purchasers bidding against each other.

Then there is often opposition from vendors who believe that selling by auction is a last resort, a method to be adopted only when a property has failed to sell by the "normal" method. If the firm of agents concerned has indeed adopted sale by auction as a last resort, the opposition on this ground will be very hard to counter. If the firm has behind it a recent record of very successful auction sales, convincing a vendor should not be difficult. It will be seen that the firm's policy towards the use of this method of sale could be vital in securing instructions to adopt it.

Some vendors, rather than being attracted by one of the advantages we earlier noted of selling by auction, namely that the sales effort is likely, and certainly intended, to be limited in time, will still be daunted by the amount of time it will take to mount the sale and complete the transaction, assuming it be successful. One of the counters to this argument is that there is nothing to prevent a vendor selling earlier if an attractive offer is received and that once the auction particulars have been prepared, and given that they include a memorandum of sale, any prospective purchaser wishing to acquire before the sale can be asked to sign the memorandum and the normal process of a sale by private treaty be avoided.

We have noted that selling by tender is a method very seldom if ever used in the house market. It is a method that will occasionally need to be considered when instructions are received to dispose of building land and some commercial property. The advantages and disadvantages we have already considered. They do not need much elaboration in the context of taking instructions. If one is dealing with a private individual, for example with a private house-owner who has obtained planning consent for substantial development, the considerations and the arguments related to them are very similar to those we have just considered in the context of selling by auction. I stress two points: under normal circumstances the vendor will not be committed to accept the highest or any tender that is received, and that it is the only method available that would ensure that those actually submitting tenders do so at the maximum figure they are prepared to pay, rather than at a figure that represents a bid just one jump ahead of the next highest, as would happen in the auction room. With only few exceptions selling or leasing by tender is likely to be relevant only where the vendor is a Government department, local authority, property undertaking, an institution, trust or company specialising in commercial property. They are likely to have reasons of their own for wishing to sell by this method. More often than not, this will be the ability to select the purchaser or lessee on criteria other than simply price.

Before going on to consider those other matters on which instructions have got to be obtained if one is to sell by private treaty, we should consider two methods of offering a property on the market without committing oneself or one's client to a price. These represent alternatives to selling by public auction and retain some if only a few of the benefits. They were frequently adopted in the higher price ranges of the house-market during the buoyant conditions of 1977-79. They can be considered together, for they are very similar.

One is to offer a house as being for sale by auction at a later date unless previously sold, and the other is simply to invite offers in the region of a quoted figure.

Although I personally do not like the use of either method, for I think they are vague, confusing to purchasers and give the impression of being evasive, there are circumstances where their adoption could be considered. To offer a house for sale by public auction at a later date unless previously sold, could be wise if the house is one where auction would under other circumstances have been appropriate, but when the vendor is not in a position to commit himself to a possession date, or where he has not yet exchanged contracts in respect of the house he is buying. It is a method of informing the market that the house is available in the hope that an early purchaser can be found who would be prepared to fit in with the vendor's circumstances. If adopted it makes it simple, the moment the vendor's situation has crystallised, to adopt an auction date and proceed with an auction in the normal way.

To invite offers whether they be in the region of a given figure or not has less to commend it. If no guide figure has been given, purchasers are still going to ask "What sort of price am I going to have to bid?" and like it or not the agent has got to give some sort of guide. If it has been adopted as a method of sale because, as is often the case, the agent feels that to quote the price the vendor wants, (which he may or may not agree with), would be to deter purchasers, it is likely to prove abortive in the event. If it has any merit it is in the fact that it could generate interest, bring in offers and enable negotiations with prospective purchasers to continue until the highest possible price has been reached, without the vendor or the agent being, albeit only morally, committed to a specific asking price. If keen competition for a house where a price has been quoted takes the bidding above that price, there is likely to be ill-feeling and somebody is likely to end up accusing the vendor, the agent or both of gazumping.

Although I personally believe that these methods should be avoided if at all possible, they are worthy of consideration when one believes one is going to generate considerable competition, or where one is uncertain as to price and for one reason or another a formal sale by auction is at the time out of the question.

The Nature of the Agency to be Given

In many areas this is a matter that will not need to be considered unless the issue is between sole selling rights or sole agency, but in a multiple agency area it must be the next point to be considered and discussed with the vendor.

The rate of commission to be charged could well depend on the nature of the agency given and it will also have a very considerable bearing on such matters as the nature of the particulars, the advertising to be carried out and recoverable expenses. There is no need here to consider again the merits of sole agency, but it is important that the firm concerned have a very definite policy with regard to sole and multiple agency and what it is prepared to do by way of reduced rates of commission, advertising expenses and so on to obtain a sole agency. The negotiator taking instructions must be able to discuss these points with the vendor authoritatively.

Evidence would show that agents acting in the sole agency areas in the Midlands and the North are in many places able to charge somewhat lower rates of commission than their Southern opposite numbers, and in areas where values are generally lower without any significant drop in profit. If this is so, then in theory if not in practice a Southern agent should be prepared to charge less where he sells while holding sole agency instructions. How much less is a matter for each firm to decide. Much will depend on the nature of its market. The agent practising in a wealthy rural area, with a relatively high average value per house unit, will certainly have more room in which to manoeuvre than the agent practising in the poorer suburbs of one of the larger cities.

It is the establishment of a policy that is known and understood by the negotiators that matters.

Having considered both the nature of the agency to be held and the method of sale to be adopted, we come to consider expenses, although this subject will undoubtedly have arisen in reaching the earlier decisions.

I am aware that in some parts of the country it is the accepted custom for agents to recover expenses over and above the commission payable. The Price Commission found that over half the firms in the North did not charge an all-inclusive fee, but made a separate extra charge for advertising expenses. Nearly 20 per cent also charged for other direct expenses, such as a "For Sale" board, photographs, and printing of brochures. In the South, 85 per cent of agents charged an all-inclusive fee and in Greater London this increased to 92 per cent of agents. It is important when taking instructions to tell the vendor, and agree with him, on just what basis commission is to be charged, and what extra charges will be made and what they are likely to amount to.

Although clearly the majority of agents in the South charge on an all-inclusive basis, many do use their willingness to bear advertising costs, particularly when the national press and journals are concerned, and the printing of special brochures, as bait to secure a sole agency, but just what is to be done by that agent and the basis of overall charging must in any case be agreed at this early stage. In particular must it be made clear to the vendor what he will be charged if no sale takes place. In the South it is rare indeed for any charge to be made, although it is my belief that agents could in many cases agree to be reimbursed at least some of any abortive costs, if they were not so afraid of discouraging business.

Elsewhere there are so many variations in practice that they go beyond the scope of the book. Although the point is not strictly relevant to the taking of instructions, if the agent agrees to carry out specific advertising, whether or not the costs are to be separately recovered, and whether or not it is a comprehensive campaign, for example to back up a sale by auction or by tender, details of what has been agreed and the dates on which advertisements are to appear should be confirmed to the vendor, so that he may see them if he wishes.

Questions concerning furnishings, fixtures and fittings have to be considered, and many sales have foundered because these matters were not conscientiously considered at the time instructions were taken, or if they were, the particulars of sale did not make the position absolutely clear.

Many vendors will want to include, or to sell to their purchaser separately, curtains and carpets, but there are many other items which, if the negotiator does not raise the matter, the vendor might assume a right to take and the purchaser might assume he has purchased. The list could be almost endless. In my experience arguments have arisen about light fittings, cookers, bathroom cabinets, moveable kitchen cabinets, fire grates, curtain tracks, garden ornaments, garden sheds, growing shrubs and coal. I well remember selling a house, in current terms probably worth £75,000, to a local person renowned for watching his pennies for a Scotsman who certainly watched his. The coal in the bin was duly measured, its weight assessed and it was paid for. Weeks later the purchaser found that the bottom of the pile was nothing but dust. A civil action was only averted by negotiations more complex and longer to conclude than those that brought about the sale of the house in the first place. Fuel, oil and television aerials are other items that must not be overlooked.

Although many vendors will make clear what they wish to include and what they are specifically excluding, the list may not be comprehensive and the agent must, when making his inspection, look for any item that could be contentious or in doubt. In general terms this means almost any fitting that could be removed without damaging the structure, and he must query them on his way round.

Viewing arrangements must be agreed with the vendor. Times when viewing will be convenient, whether or not the agent is to hold a key, what authority he has to show prospective purchasers over the property if he cannot contact the vendor; whether or not it will be in order for purchasers to view unaccompanied, and so on.

The vendor's authority to sell is a matter that perhaps rarely will need to be considered but on those occasions when it does it will require considerable tact. Instructions may come from a husband without any indication that the house is owned jointly with his wife, and that their marriage is in difficulties, or that they have already separated. One has known occasions where sales have been agreed and solicitors instructed, only to find, to everybody's embarrassment and gross inconvenience, that an estranged partner has effectively put a stop on it. I have known instructions for sale to be given by a son on behalf of his mother, without authority, to pay her nursing-home bills. I have known instructions to have been given by a son whose interest in the house was only that of a residuary beneficiary, without any authority from the Trustees and without any reference to his father, the life-tenant.

The negotiator who believes that circumstances of this sort might exist may not feel able, or feel it appropriate, to challenge the vendor's authority. During the course of taking the instructions he should ask the vendor who his solicitors are and where the Deeds are, and indeed if he understands that the vendor has to sell, whether or not it is in order for the solicitors to be instructed immediately to prepare a draft contract. This will obviously improve the chances of a speedy transaction, but the negotiator who knows who his client's solicitors are has somebody he can refer to if he doubts that vendor's apparent authority.

Once instructions have been taken, the agent will need to have access to the vendor, to report progress, to seek further instructions if the initial sales effort has proved unsuccessful, and to report offers. He will therefore need not only the vendor's home telephone number, but ideally, a telephone number where he can be reached at work; and if he is going away for any period, where he can be found. If the vendor is going to be inaccessible for any period, possibly touring abroad, that agent should either have authority to agree a sale subject to contract and have a minimum figure at which he can use that authority, or he should advise the vendor to give that authority to somebody else; it could be his wife, a member of his family or his solicitor. A purchaser with a choice of two houses and not feeling strongly one way or the other may well go in the wrong direction if he is not given an immediate response to an offer.

The vendor's intentions or wishes with regard to moving also need discussing and could be very important at a later stage when discussing the suitability of a number of houses with a prospective purchaser. On what date can the vendor give possession? Will he in fact move at all before he has found something else? Would he be prepared to move into a furnished house if need be and can the firm help him in doing this?

There are other points on which the negotiator may need instructions. If the house justifies it, may he employ a professional photographer, and who will pay? If curtains, carpets or any other fixtures and fittings are to be offered to a prospective purchaser at valuation, who is to arrange that valuation and with whom? Can a "For Sale" board be erected? Is the firm to have authority to appoint sub-agents? Indeed a negotiator may well have agreed to do this after a specific period, particularly if he has received sole agency instructions. If authority is given to appoint sub-agents, is the identity of those agents to be left to the discretion of the agent, if not, who is to be sub-instructed and on what terms?

I would comment here that in those areas that I know where the appointment of sub-agents is a regular occurrence, it is customary, where the sub-agent sells, for the commission originally agreed by the head agent to be split 50/50. This always strikes me as being unfair to the head agent, who is likely to have spent a lot more time taking the instructions and dealing with the vendor and to have spent more money in advertising. If when he is taking the instructions he also seeks authority to instruct sub-agents, he may be wise to try to agree a somewhat higher commission rate in the event of the sub-agent selling. Where, as a sole agent, he has agreed a 2 per cent rate, if he can agree $2\frac{1}{4}$ per cent if one of the sub-agents sells, he will have done something to recompense him for the extra work.

If the house is to be left vacant, whether furnished or unfurnished, the negotiator should, when he takes instructions, satisfy himself with regard to such matters as garden maintenance, security, draining down the plumbing and heating systems, and as to whether or not services are to be switched off.

As we noted earlier when considering whether or not estate agency was a purely commercial operation or a professional one, the negotiator must be alert to the development potential. The ability simply to extend a house may well affect its saleability. To apply for planning consent to erect a house in the garden, enabling the property to be sold in two lots, might produce a substantially higher overall price for the vendor. Where a house stands in extensive grounds, or is situated close to the centre of a town where the principle of flat development has been established, it may be that the best possible price would be obtained by getting planning consent to demolish and redevelop.

Development does not necessarily involve either works of demolition, building or reconstruction. It could take the form of a change of use from that of a house to offices, or to a nursing home, or of the division of the house into two or more units. If a negotiator senses development potential, he should seek instructions to discuss his ideas with the planning authority and if need be, to submit a planning application.

If development potential exists, whether by way of redevelopment or a change of use, a negotiator will need to satisfy himself that the form of development he has in mind will not be barred by a restrictive covenant. He will therefore need access to the Deeds, or authority to consult the vendor's solicitor to satisfy himself that no such covenants are involved, or, if they are, that they are so out of date that the risk of anybody trying to enforce them could be insured against, or that, if the financial reward would justify the delay, the Lands Tribunal is likely to remove or amend them.

We have been considering the taking of instructions related to the private freehold dwelling house, but one will come across leasehold interests. Particularly will this apply in some of the larger cities, some of the larger country estates and indeed in many high-density residential developments. In these circumstances a negotiator will need access to the lease to establish just what restrictions there are; for example, pets are forbidden in many blocks of flats, and the hanging out of washing on many private estates and high density housing developments. Covenants can be positive as well as negative and there could well be an obligation to contribute towards the maintenance of common parts, towards the running of lifts, employment of porters and so on. The negotiator must be aware of these matters and of the responsibilities of the lessee, know what arrangements are made for common maintenance, how the the maintenance charges are assessed and what they currently amount to.

The use of the check list already referred to will avoid any important matter being overlooked.

Finally the instructions must be confirmed to the vendor in writing. It may not be necessary to cover every point that has been discussed, but this confirming letter must set out the basis of charging agreed, the event upon which commission will become payable, the nature of the agency given and for how long; it should seek to confirm any authority given to appoint sub-agents, and if authority has been given to the agent to accept an offer at or above a certain figure subject to contract, this must be clearly stated.

What "needs" as opposed to what "could" be put in such a letter will depend to an extent on the circumstances and I cannot be specific. The negotiator must use his own discretion as to what over and above the principal instructions given are points of sufficient importance to need confirmation. If the sale is to be by auction or by tender then I think the basic arrangements for sale, including timings, should be set out and if an extensive advertising campaign has been agreed, then a schedule of the advertisements to appear, with dates and approximate costings, should be included with the letter and, ideally, although I accept there will be occasions when to do so might be inappropriate, a copy of the particulars or draft particulars should be sent to the vendor, with the request that he notify one immediately if they are inaccurate in any statement of fact.

Such a letter of confirmation may be of little value if it is not acknowledged by the vendor. I would like to be adamant on this point, but realise that many agents would feel they were pressing too hard in demanding a formal response, or indeed might even be giving the impression that they mistrusted the vendor. A formal acknowledgment is nevertheless advisable and I suggest that one could send an extra copy of the confirming letter to the vendor, simply with a statement at the bottom to the effect that "I/we confirm that the instructions as set out in this letter are agreed by me/us" and then a space for signature. A stamped, addressed envelope will encourage a response, and if the negotiator knows, as hopefully he will, the solicitors who will be acting for the vendor, a copy of the confirming letter could be sent to them with a covering letter.

I know many agents do use standard forms of letter for many purposes and their use will be encouraged if automatic typewriters or word processors are available. There are in my opinion dangers in their use. They can be impersonal, they can seldom cover every circumstance. The confirming letter you write to a vendor you do not know personally, or had never met before you made the inspection, and the letter you write to his solicitors if you again have no personal contact, would make very strange and possibly unfriendly reading to the vendor and his solicitor if they are both personal friends of yours.

What one is seeking to do, not only in actually taking instructions, but in confirming those instructions, is to make one's agency brief as clear and as precise as possible and to avoid any doubt as between principal and agent as to what is intended. For example, if, sensing development potential, it was agreed between the negotiator and the vendor that the former would make enquiries of the planning authority and without further instructions submit a planning application, it must be made clear as to whether or not this is to be done as part of the agency service and the costs intended to be covered by the agreed commission, or be the subject of a separate charge, as I believe it should be.

Much of what one has said about taking instructions, although said in the residential context, would be applicable in the commercial market, but there are other considerations there that we will be looking at.

On the taking of particulars

One faces the difficulty yet again of wanting to be specific as to just what particulars or details a negotiator should take of a house, or indeed any other property, when he makes his inspection, but one knows that one cannot be so. If one uses a particular pro forma such as that shown on page 183, the intention of which was to try to ensure that where possible particulars were kept to one side of an A4 sheet, one is dictating a degree of brevity and indeed generalisation in description that some agents would feel inappropriate. Some would feel it right that a prospective purchaser be told just how many power and lighting points there were in each room, others would feel that particulars set out in this detail would read too much like an electrician's catalogue or specification, and would consider "Well equipped with power and light points" adequate.

One of the objects of that particular pro forma was to enable a negotiator to draft most of the particulars as he went round the house, leaving him only to sit in his car to write in the directions and general description, so that they could be typed immediately on his return to the office. This might be considered suitable for the average house, but I would be the first to agree that the larger house and the one with a number of special features needs different treatment. In such a case, as much detail as possible needs to be noted and from these details the particulars will be drafted carefully and in the peace of one's office, probably after hours.

However brief or long and detailed one's particulars are going to be, the need for accuracy is vital, for misdescription or misrepresentation can lead to legal action. This is particularly important if one is preparing particulars to be included in an auction brochure, or in tender documents, which at a later stage are likely, and are intended to, form part of a contract.

The basic information from which the particulars will be prepared could include some or all of the information referred to under various headings below. It may be of value when talking later to a prospective purchaser to have all of it, but it will be up to the negotiator to decide how muct he would wish to incorporate in the particulars. His main object must not be necessarily fully to describe the house, but to assist the purchaser from a distance to decide whether or not it is likely to be of interest. At the same time he must present the house, without being misleading, in the best light but with accuracy as to fact.

In practice I believe that the average house can be adequately described in the space provided on the pro forma illustrated, and I believe most purchasers appreciate not only clarity but brevity.

Description

The type, style and setting of the house, its period, its age if known, and any historic details that could interest a would-be purchaser. If a house has no historical links, it may be that it was designed by a well-known local architect, or constructed by a builder of good local repute.

Construction

The materials used in the construction of main walls and roof, whether the latter is boarded and felted, if either are insulated. Other information it might be useful to have on file would include the question of whether there is a damp-proof course, and of what type, but when a house without a d.p.c. is the exception rather than the rule to say one exists does nothing to attract a purchaser.

Accommodation

Many agents used to describe the accommodation within a house, starting on the top floor and working downwards; a few still do and it seems to me totally illogical. I believe it right to describe accommodation in the order in which the agent would want the prospective purchaser to move round the house and therefore starting at the front door. Mr. M. J. Vivian suggests that a sketch-plan might be of assistance, but I would question this. Room measurements should be taken in feet or metres or both. Measurement of rooms of irregular shape can be averaged, or any significant extensions by way of a bay-window measured separately. One is setting out to tell a purchaser with reasonable accuracy the size and approximate shape of the room. Details of fixtures and fittings that are to be included, radiators, power points and any special feature, such as a flagstone floor or oak-block floor, or oak panelling, should be noted, together with details of cupboards and kitchen and bathroom fittings.

Outbuildings

The size and nature of garaging is of interest to most prospective purchasers and should be detailed. Notes of any services, such as electric power and light, availability of water wash-down areas, additional car-parking areas or space for additional garaging that could be provided should also be noted. Brief details only would be required of any additional outbuildings, unless they were of particular significance. A barn or stable that would, subject to planning consent, convert to a granny annexe or studio block could be of particular interest to some would-be purchasers and a fuller description and measurements may well be needed.

Services

Care will be needed when it comes to taking details of the services provided. It is easy to assume that electricity and water supplies come from mains, but private generators and water supplied from private sources are not unheard of. A house may once have been gas-lit and gas-heated, but some owners have been known through fear of fire or explosion to disconnect and seal off. The fact that there is a mains sewer in the public highway to which the property fronts does not entitle one automatically to assume that the house drains into it. It is within my own experience to find one built in the early part of the century before the road was "made up" or the sewer laid, which originally drained to a cesspool. Sometime in the early 'twenties all the other owners in the road connected to a new main sewer, but the then owner of this house possibly could not afford to do so. In 1975 it still drained to its original cesspool. This was not discovered until after completion, and the agent paid the costs of connection.

If drainage is not to a mains sewer it may be to a cesspool or septic tank and care must be taken to differentiate between the two. The former is meant to be nothing more than a below-ground impervious receptacle to take foul sewage and it will need regular emptying by the local authority. Many owners have minimised this problem where ground drainage conditions are good, and one knows of many cesspools which as a result only have to be emptied infrequently or have never been emptied. It is dangerous to assume that no need to empty indicates a septic tank. A septic tank system is normally of two chambers. Sewage is received in the first, the second forms a filter chamber into which the liquid element is allowed to flow; there it is filtered and from this chamber it is drained either into a neighbouring water course, or into a series of open-jointed land drains that allow the effluent to drain away naturally into the ground. It would be unwise to describe any drainage system as being to a septic tank, unless this has been visually checked.

Additional land

Houses with additional land need care and the extent of ownership should be checked on the ground with the vendor. If the negotiator knows before leaving the office to make his inspection that additional land is included or could be made available, he would be well advised to take the relevant Ordnance Survey Sheet with him. If not, on his return he should take an extract or extracts from the Ordnance Survey Sheet, outline the boundaries as he understands them and when confirming instructions ask for the vendor to confirm that the extent of the land is accurately shown, or alternatively ask his solicitor to check it against the Deeds.

General Comments on Particulars

In practice the negotiator will know the policy of his firm with regard to the preparation of particulars and will know, dependent upon the type of house, just how much information he will need to take at the initial inspection, but again a check-list would be helpful, unless a pro forma on which the particulars will actually be drafted is to be used.

The role of particulars being to inform and attract prospective purchasers, nothing can be more informative than a photograph. Those whose offices have the means of reproducing photographs on stencil or plate will require a polaroid photograph, but in addition most will also require a conventional (35mm) negative from which enlargements can be made, if, for example with a larger country house, an abnormal sized photograph is to be used on the particulars, and from which photographs for the window can be produced.

A thoroughly bad photograph, of course, could deter a prospective purchaser from looking at a house that might well have been of interest to him. Photographs need care and thought.

One firm I know, albeit with some 12 offices, within a relatively tight area, use full-time professional photographers. My own firm by enlisting the help of the professional photographers whom we use for interior work and work of a specialist nature, as instructors, have been able to achieve what I believe is a reasonable standard of photography by the negotiators themselves. It may be that the view of a house that the negotiator believes to show it to the best advantage is in shadow and there is no alternative other than to make a return visit to take the photograph at the right time and this could be the opportunity of letting another member of the sales team see the house. This may prove to be a luxury where speed is absolutely vital as can often be the case in a multiple agency area. In these circumstances a negotiator will have to decide whether the best photograph he can take is adequate, or whether he prepares initial particulars that are unillustrated but with as good a visual description as possible.

Having said that I could not be specific as to what details should or must be taken at the initial inspection, I find it even harder to give a clear lead, when it comes to the actual content of the particulars and their drafting. I have seen firms, particularly amongst those practising in the cheaper urban areas, succeed with unillustrated particulars and with the simplest and most basic of descriptions: "24, Acacia Avenue, a modern freehold semi-detached house containing. . ."

I have also seen another gain control of the market, in what was an up-market seaside area, partly by the use of long and very detailed particulars, sometimes taking three pages when their rivals had only taken one, with the setting out, spacing and type face all carefully considered, illustrated with two if not three photographs at a time when these had to be individually produced and stuck on and at what must have been considerable cost. It was one of the lessons I learned in marketing, for the person concerned clearly saw a market that he believed to be inadequately served, and went out to create the public image that enabled him to dominate it.

The Role of Particulars in Marketing

This leads me to ask just what role our particulars play in the sale of real estate and again I do this mainly in the residential context, although some of my comments will apply to the commercial market.

Many agents see their particulars as a means of communicating with the prospective purchasers on their applicants' register. This is correct, but do they sell houses? From my own experience the percentage of sales that could be directly attributed to circulating particulars or to the "send out" has been very small and certainly the negotiator who relied on it to produce his contacts, rather than approaching the most likely purchasers direct and personally, would fail. I believe our particulars should play three roles.

First they are an advertisement for our firm and a major part of the image we project, in particular to would-be purchasers, many of whom will be future vendors.

Given that under normal market conditions or anything like them, the negotiator could not possibly hope to keep in personal touch with every prospective purchaser he has seen or has heard from, the particulars form a vital means of communicating with those who have not, to date, been identified as "hot". They are sent to them in the hope that they will react and either make further enquiries or telephone to make arrangements to view. They are a means of advertising, but in that the advertising is directed to individuals or companies who in one way or another have already made contact with the firm, it is a very direct means.

For many years my own firm have circulated particulars for eight neighbouring offices from one centre. At one time we sensed that negotiators were relying far too much on the "system" rather than on personal contact. They clearly saw the circulating system as a means of selling houses and to emphasise what we believed to be its correct role, we named the department responsible, D.M.A. "Direct Mail Advertising" and I was interested to note that Mr. Vivian adopts a similar phrase.

Last but not least the particulars of a house are intended to help the negotiator and the would-be purchaser with whom he is dealing. To the negotiator and particularly those who have not themselves seen the property, they will give more detailed information than a register slip. Further if at one time the number of properties on the market is such that it would be impracticable to send particulars of everything likely to be of interest to a prospective purchaser enquiring from a distance, they will enable a negotiator to make the selection most likely to generate interest and bring a response. For a purchaser, particulars will give the means of establishing a short-list, accepting that in buoyant market conditions this is likely to be unnecessary. When making his inspection it will provide him with immediate access to basic information such as room sizes and, having inspected, if he is still interested, a permanent record of that property's features.

It follows that one's particulars should be in a form that will enable them to carry out these three functions in the most effective way.

I emphasised their importance in the public image sense, as a means of impressing prospective purchasers as tomorrow's vendors, but today's vendors must not be forgotten. I believe a copy of the particulars should normally be sent to the vendor, not only as a check on accuracy and as protection against the risk of misrepresentation, but because they should be good enough to impress him. The majority of vendors are likely in any event to see a copy, even if they are not sent by the agent, for they will almost undoubtedly be carried by purchasers when they come to inspect. Vendors talk, and anybody contemplating the sale of a house, knowing that one or more of his friends have theirs on the market, is likely to enquire as to their experience with the agents of their choice.

Quite apart from any role particulars might play in actually selling a house, they play a vital role in advertising one's firm and as an indication of the way it sets about its task. Within reason, therefore, their quality should be as high as sensible budgeting will permit. They are a means of attracting the product and a valuable "aid" in selling it.

The agent practising in a multiple agency area may see himself at a disadvantage, if others are to be instructed, (and they may have been instructed on the same day). He may feel that the risk of losing a sale does not justify the care and in particular the time a really good set of particulars will take to produce.

He will rightly feel that those particulars should be in the post that night if he is to maximise his chances of succeeding. But there are a number of ways in which he can deal with this problem. He should, in any event, be contacting all his "hot" applicants by telephone, and if this is not possible, some by short personal letter, sent first-class post, but he could also prepare preliminary particulars, following them up with the full particulars as soon as they are ready or retaining these for use in the office. If he adopts this course then the "preliminary particulars" should be clearly marked as such and if he wished to avoid the relatively high cost of sending the full particulars out to everybody, he could put a footnote on the preliminary particulars to the effect that, if they proved of interest, full illustrated particulars would be sent on request. If he is lucky enough to be the first of the agents that the vendor instructs, he has the opportunity to stress the importance of a really good set of particulars and the time it will take to produce them as a means of securing a sole agency, even if it is only for a week. To this end when he interviews a potential vendor in his office or goes to take instructions he should have available to him particulars of other houses which he feels show the quality the firm can produce and ideally these particulars should be of houses similar to that of the vendor.

Many would disagree with my view that there are very few houses indeed where the particulars should be unillustrated. I recognise the natural reluctance to illustrate particulars where a negotiator feels the house concerned is a really ugly one, does not look worth the asking price, or indeed where it is just a typical modern terraced box, but not to illustrate is to fail to communicate information that is available; what the house looks like. I also believe the photograph helps a prospective purchaser reading one's particulars to build up a very much clearer picture of what the house is like overall. To those who hesitate to illustrate whenever possible, I would point out that if a house is to be sold, sooner or later somebody has got to see it; why not therefore let your purchasers see an illustration at the earliest possible moment? If you illustrate some but not all, the prospective purchaser may well assume on getting unillustrated particulars that the house was in some way inferior and put it aside or on to a secondary list.

When using a photograph on particulars there is one simple rule that should be followed. Any house would normally be photographed at an angle and the photograph should be so placed that the house illustrated looks into the particulars rather than outwards into space. This of course will only apply where, as on the standard format we try to adhere to, the photograph is set off-centre.

What else should one's particulars contain? I believe directions as to how to find the house vital. The negotiator cannot always accompany and certainly he cannot prevent the would-be purchaser going to look at the house from the outside, so he should be told how to get there.

I think it important to give every assistance one can to one's prospective purchaser and I therefore think it essential that early on in one's particulars, and in a prominent position, one includes a brief summary, setting out the house's main characteristics, its accommodation and price.

This summary could well be used on one's register card or slip. It could also be the draft of one's normal newspaper advertisement.

The applicant receiving particulars may by the same post receive particulars from other agents. He or she will want to sort out the most likely prospects as quickly as possible and if the post contained particulars of the same house from more than one agent, they are likely to keep the particulars that they find present the house in the best light and which were the simplest to read and absorb, rejecting the other. It is for this reason that I put emphasis on illustration, on the brief summary and on price.

The layout of one's particulars must be clear and well spaced with well-defined headings. Nothing is more daunting than a closely typed foolscap sheet where you have to search to find even the house's most salient features.

I think an attempt should be made, whether the pro forma we have used is adopted or not, to keep one's particulars on one page where this is possible. It is easier for the purchaser to read, it involves a degree of discipline which helps to eradicate superfluous matter. It will avoid the use of two stencils or plates and it will save time and money. On the other hand if there is any rule that should be followed in preparing particulars, it is that they should do full justice to the house and if this can only be achieved by breaking one's own rules, so be it.

I find I cannot even be dogmatic as to the degree of description. This again must be dictated by the quality of the house, and the better it is, the more important it will be to stress points of detail, but, remember, particulars must always be readable and the more detail one includes the harder they become to read and absorb.

I earlier commented on the advisability of using collective phrases such as "Well equipped with electric power and lighting points" to avoid endless repetition.

When a few years ago I was to speak to students at Reading on the preparation of particulars, I got together a collection of particulars prepared by agents from all over the country and to underline the value of using collective descriptions I will quote critically from one set of particulars. In their preamble appeared "full oil-fired central heating" but then in the description of every room appeared central heating radiator, but when it came to the dining room, "Attractive curved windows with pelmets" (would the reference to pelmets get somebody to look at the house who would not otherwise have done so?) and it went on to say "Curved central heating radiator matches curved window" and later in describing services appeared the words "Thermostatically-controlled oil central heating unit". The opening phrase; full oil-fired central heating was, I suggest, all that needed to be said.

A decision has to be made as to the use of imperial or metric measurement in giving room sizes or site area. The golden rule must be again to communicate as clearly as one can and since the majority of people still think in terms of feet rather than metres and of acres rather than hectares, imperial measurements should be used. Ideally and if there is space then metric equivalents should be given in brackets. Even in the commercial property world where one might have expected more, and where many firms have made a conscientious attempt to "go metric" one seldom hears office or factory space described verbally in anything other than square feet.

When one has set out the accommodation, one would then describe the outbuildings, then the garden or grounds, then deal with services, give the rateable value, ideally the rate in the £ or the rates payable, but caution is needed here, for this information can become out-of-date. State clearly either that vacant possession will be given on completion, which most would interpret as meaning there was no particular difficulty as to when completion could take place, or state that completion will not be before a given date.

Nearly every house has a feature that will sell it; it may be its style and appearance; it may be that its rooms are particularly well-proportioned; its garden may be much larger than is normal for a house of its type; it may be that the house is capable of modernisation and improvement. Even one modern terraced house can have advantages over another. It may be that it is close to good local shops, or that it is very close to schools, or that it is on a bus stop. Whatever feature you wish to stress, make sure you do so early on and in the brief summary.

In those cases where, for whatever reason, it has proved impossible to illustrate the use of a word-picture, a description of the type of house, and particularly what it looks like will help the reader to form an overall picture of the house in his mind and decide whether or not it is likely to be of interest. A few words of warning. Many agents incorporate, normally at the foot of their particulars, lengthy caveats to the effect that although care has been taken in preparing them no guarantee is given as to accuracy, that the agents are not responsible for any misrepresentation or misdescription and so on. The value of such caveats is at best doubtful and we shall later be considering the relevant consumer-protection law as it could affect the estate agent.

It is, however, essential to make it clear that one's particulars are not intended — if that is the case, for it would not apply to auction particulars for example — to form part of a contract. Some agents specifically state "Subject to contract" in a prominent position on the particulars themselves. A simple caveat is probably all that is needed and I would suggest — "These particulars are believed to be correct but their accuracy is not guaranteed and they do not form any part of any contract".

One has made the point that the particulars are not intended to form part of any contract and by a warning as to their accuracy one may well deter frivolous attempts to extract compensation for any minor error or misdescription.

To avoid the risk of misdescription or misrepresentation, phrases such as well-built, or soundly-built should not be used, and care should be taken in describing central heating systems. The National House Building Council defines three levels of central heating.

(a) **Full central heating**
When the external temperature is 30 deg. F and the room is ventilated at the rate shown, internal temperatures achieved in respective locations shall be those indicated, as follows:—

Location	Ventilation	Temperature
Living room, dining room and other 'reception' rooms	2 airchanges/hr.	62 deg. – 66 deg.
Bedrooms	1½ airchanges/hr.	50 deg. – 55 deg.
Kitchens	2,000 cu. ft./hr.	55 deg. – 60 deg.
Halls, corridors, staircases and circulation space	1 a–c/hr.	50 deg. – 55 deg.
W.C.'s and bathrooms	2 a–c/hr.	50 deg. – 55 deg.*

*These temperatures may be achieved by infiltration from other areas without provision of heating units in the area concerned.

(b) **Partial central heating**
It shall be clearly stated which areas of accommodation are served by the heating system and whether the system is designed to provide full or background heating. Where spaces are indicated to be fully heated, then the temperatures achieved shall be in accordance with the table in sub-clause (a).

(c) **Background heating**
Where background heating is provided, it shall be clearly indicated which areas are served and in these areas temperatures shall be achieved as indicated in the following table (with the ventilation rates as indicated in the table in sub-clause (a)):—

Living room, dining room and other "reception" rooms	55 deg.
Other areas	50 deg.

To work out whether or not these standards are met requires detailed calculations of such matters as room-size, window areas, boiler capacity, etc., and clearly it would be impracticable to expect one's negotiators to determine whether or not the description of full central heating is justified.

No clear direction can be given as to the use of the term "full central heating" and enquiries both of lawyers and the two leading professional bodies have failed to produce any guide. As I write this my own firm are party to a dispute in which one of the issues at stake is whether or not "central heating" as a description could fairly be taken to mean full central heating. It is my view that it can mean no more than it says, that the house is heated from a central point. If in doubt I suggest one does not use the word "full". If there are not radiators in every room then the word "partial" must be used and in this event one would have to say where the radiators were in dealing with the accommodation.

Watch for the house that is of unconventional construction. Some very modern houses are timber-framed with brick or stone cladding giving the appearance of entirely conventional construction. Between the wars some houses were built entirely of blocks, sometimes of concrete, sometimes only of breeze and then rendered and painted. It is all too easy, particularly if the wall thicknesses are right, to assume that they are of cavity brick construction.

If one is making statements as to development potential, "capable of being extended", "suitable for conversion into flats", etc., these must be qualified by "subject to planning consent".

The rule must be that if one is in any doubt as to the accuracy of a statement that one would like to make, it must either be left out or qualified.

All that one has said with regard to the preparation of particulars would apply when preparing particulars for a sale by auction, although this particular task will be looked at when we consider selling by auction in more detail.

Presentation of Particulars

Many firms are now using some sort of folder or hold-all in which to present particulars to prospective purchasers. A prospective purchaser is likely to have written by the same post to other agents and if he has called in your office he is likely to have called on some of your competitors, or he will be doing so. Just to hand over say 12 pieces of paper, however well prepared, is to run the risk of their being put in a heap with the others he will receive. To present them in a folder that puts across your firm's name and image is tidier, and when he comes to consider the particulars at leisure will create a bigger impact. Into the folder one could put other material; a street map, mortgage repayment tables and notes on house purchase, such as the RICS's "Buying and Selling a House".

Commercial Property Particulars

In preparing particulars of commercial property our aim is basically the same as it was in the residential field — to present both the property we are offering and our own firm in the most effective way possible. There is, however, a change of emphasis. A house is an emotive thing and its occupation is personal. We considered earlier the motivation of house purchasers.

In the commercial market the property is bought either for occupation or investment. If it is for occupation then with very few exceptions the ultimate aim of the occupier, be it a major multiple retail company, a small shop keeper, a firm of solicitors or accountants, a medical practice, manufacturer or somebody wishing to store and distribute goods, the aim is to make a profit and the suitability of the accommodation to that function is the main criterion.

In this market vendors are more likely to accept advice as to the price or rent to be quoted than in the residential field. Your purchaser, whether an individual, the estates manager of a large company, chairman of a board of directors, or a pension fund manager will know what he is looking for, and what criteria he has to meet.

In the context of the firm's image commercial particulars are likely to impress if they show confidence and awareness. Dressing-up will not do this. The would-be purchaser or lessee wants to be told simply and as quickly as possible the facts on which he can make a decision as to whether the property offered is worth further investigation, or is useless to him.

Our aim therefore is to set out the essential characteristics as concisely as we can and I suggest that these come under five main headings:

Use

Here we are concerned not only with the established planning use of the accommodation, but with any alternative use that might be acceptable in planning terms, and permitted in the case of leasehold premises under the terms of the lease.

The uses one is likely to encounter are shops, offices, light and general industry, warehousing and storage. There are, of course, in planning terms, other special uses such as petrol filling stations, motor repair workshops, builders' yards and so on. If they come to be marketed one would either be looking at a very narrow and specialised market beyond the scope of this book, or one would have sought a planning consent, or agreement in principle with the planning authority as to what wider uses the premises might be suitable for. We will consider each use briefly.

Offices — appears clear and straight forward, but into this category could come some High Street shops or similar premises. Premises where banks, building societies and estate agents have established their use, are regarded as offices in the planning sense and in that the majority of planning authorities try to resist the growth of such uses in their main shopping centres, there is considerable demand and sometimes there is a premium value, (particularly to building societies) attributable to premises previously occupied by a bank or an estate agent. The use of a building by a medical or dental practice as consulting rooms, cannot safely be assumed to have established a general office user; they fall into a special use-class.

Light Industry

In planning terms a light industrial use is generally regarded as a manufacturing processs which is not by reason of noise or smell incompatible with being in a residential area and the difference between it and general industry is normally determined on those two factors. It does not follow, therefore, that the factory either built with planning consent for light industry or where the use established is clearly a light industrial one can be used for all types of manufacturing processes.

It has become the practice in recent years when building factories to build in a form, and in particular with a height to eaves, that would enable those buildings to be occupied for more than one alternative purpose. The suitability of a building to a wide variety of users is one of the factors that can affect its value as an investment. Again it cannot be assumed that a building constructed with a planning consent for warehousing and storage purposes, or where such a use has become established, can, however suitable the building might physically be for an industrial process, be used for such a purpose without planning consent. Industry is much more labour-intensive than warehousing or storage. For this reason some planning authorities, particularly in the South-east, trying to restrict house-building, seek to limit pressure on the housing market by limiting industrial development. Thus they might seek to prevent a change of use from warehousing and storage to light industry.

Shops

These come into perhaps a more clearly defined planning use-class. Although when marketing a shop, particularly in a prime or good secondary position, the established use is clearly a retail one, the agent will need to know the planning policy towards the banks, building societies and estate agents, if he is to know where to market it.

The essential first step to marketing commercial property could therefore be a planning one. Establishing by way of planning application, or by discussion with the planning authority within what use-class they regard a particular building as being, and what uses they will or are likely to permit could be an essential preliminary. Only then will one know precisely how to deal with the question of use in one's particulars.

Location

This is of great importance to both occupier and investor. The office user will in particular be concerned as to the availability of secretarial staff, possibly because of the nearness of a shopping centre — this is known to be one factor that can affect the recruitment in particular of female labour — and the investor will want to be satisfied that the offices are located in a position where if he is faced with a void at the end of the lease they are likely to re-let with ease and where values will show a reasonable rate of growth. The availability of public transport and public car-parks are factors that could also affect the attractiveness, and therefore the value, of office space.

The industrialist is also, of course, concerned with the labour market in the area, and with accessability not only for his labour force but for the suppliers of his raw materials and those who have to distribute his products.

Warehousing and storage accommodation especially needs to be readily accessible, particularly to motorways, and closeness to a major airport is a factor that has greatly affected demand and therefore value in recent years. This can be expected to continue.

It follows from this that in preparing one's particulars, and having regard to the use or potential uses of the property, one must stress the advantages of the area and/or the precise location, and the inclusion of maps will help achieve this. In the case of industrial and warehousing premises, one would aim to show the location in relation to principal traffic routes. In the case of offices one would try to show the location in relation to principal office users in the town itself, public transport, car parks and shops; and in the case of shops, assuming one is dealing with prime or good secondary position, one would want to show on a street plan where the principal national multiples are located, and, ideally, where the principal car parks are. This will enable a prospective purchaser or lessee to make an immediate assessment of the likely volume of pedestrian traffic and potential trade.

The office user and the industrialist are both going to be concerned with the size of the labour market, and the retail trader by the number of likely customers; population statistics for the town and immediate area are likely to help.

Accommodation

All potential commercial users are likely to have a known requirement when it comes to floor area, but there are special considerations.

The office user may well want the public to have very easy access to his accommodation and require ground-floor premises, or at least premises that include a ground-floor area. The number of floors, availability of a lift and whether the premises are air-conditioned are factors likely to be relevant. The industrialist and warehouse user will probably only be interested in ground-floor accommodation. He will certainly expect to be told if the accommodation is on more than one floor. He might be concerned with the height to eaves, as to whether the building is insulated in any way and therefore the nature of its construction; the extent of any outside storage areas; parking facilities; the office content; the heating arrangements; whether or not there is a sprinkler system; and in particular will they want to know that the accommodation is suitable for their own particular function; so again a site plan and floor plan would be valuable.

A retail user would be interested in frontage, in overall floor area, in the shape of the accommodation, as to whether or not there is a rear access and as to what storage or preparation areas are available. Yet again in addition to a street plan showing the location of the major multiples, a floor plan would be of considerable assistance in the making of the initial decision as to whether or not the premises are likely to be of interest.

Tenure

To the commercial estate agent this can be a very wide subject. He may be acting for a development company having constructed, or being in the course of constructing, an office building, but where the ultimate aim is to dispose of the created investment to a pension fund. In a wider sense of tenure, he is going to be concerned not only with the rent to be obtained if his aim is to be achieved, but with the nature of the lease and the calibre of the lessee. These are important marketing considerations, but not strictly relevant when considering the production of particulars. Nevertheless the commercial estate agent dealing either with a leasehold interest or a freehold that is subject to a lease or leases must satisfy himself as to the nature of the lease or leases. Mr. Orchard-Lisle comments that "In commercial work it is normal and reasonable to rely on the client providing accurate information as to tenure". Nevertheless if a property is leasehold, or if it is freehold subject to leases, the agent would be well advised to ask for a copy of the lease involved before he commits himself to any particular course of action. He will need to check how long the lease has to run, how frequently rent reviews are to take place, the date of the next review, and the construction of any rent review clause. He will need to be aware of any restrictive covenants, for these may dictate to whom those particulars can be sent, and he will need to know the respective obligations of the lessor and lessee. To illustrate the need for care, it is not uncommon when dealing with shops to find a restrictive covenant or covenants that effectively limit the use of the premises to one specific trade, or which bar the use of the premises to certain specified trades.

It may not be desirable or necessary to include all the information that is gathered in these preliminary stages in one's sale particulars, but they will need to be recorded on the file and certainly the prospective purchaser or lessee will need to know the basic terms of the lease that he is acquiring or being offered and he will assume, if particulars are sent to him, that he could occupy the property and not find at a later stage that his use is barred by a restrictive covenant.

As with residential property, the inspection of commercial property is a matter that needs considerable care if one's particulars are to be accurate and informative and a standard check list or inspection pro forma will avoid the risk of essential facts being overlooked.

It is just as important for the commercial negotiator as for the residential one to be aware of and accurately appreciate the relevance of any further development potential that might exist, and highway and planning proposals.

I can recall acquiring for clients a shop in a prime position where the agent's particulars described the existing building, which was a shambles, adequately, stressed its frontage, but made no reference to site depth by plan or measurement. In practice the developable site area was capable of being increased by 70 per cent, still leaving the rear loading area to be served by a new service road, the construction of which was about to be started, but which was not referred to in the agent's particulars. This notwithstanding the fact that the service road proposal was shown on the Town Map, and the shop itself within about 100 yards of the planning office.

The agent was presumably satisfied having regard to the rent passing that the purchase price showed a realistic yield and was fair. A very valuable reversion was overlooked for the sake of a 100-yard walk and perhaps 15 minutes with the planning authority.

In commercial agency work plans are more important than photographs, and the physical characteristics of a building in terms of construction and floor-area more important than visual appearance, but one is still trying to communicate to the best of one's ability, and photographs should therefore be used.

A glowing description, a sweeping drive-in, roses over the porch, and inglenook fireplaces and beamed ceilings might impress your would be house-purchaser, but in the commercial market unnecessary rhetoric would only irritate. One's particulars need to be concise, factual and informative and should put the prospective purchaser or lessee in a position where all he need do is to ask for an appointment to view.

Building land and properties with known development potential

I am still here concerned with the preparation of particulars, and not with the process of identifying land or buildings with development potential, establishing that potential and obtaining planning consent. I am therefore assuming that that process has been gone through and that planning consent has been obtained in a form that will realise the full development potential of a particular site or building. I am not, perhaps, here concerned with the single building plot with consent for one dwelling. In such a case one is essentially selling to a potential house-owner and the same considerations apply as to the sale of a private dwelling-house, except that one's particulars should give brief details of the planning consent, and the form of development approved. (It might for example be limited to a single-storey dwelling.) The planning consent reference number should be given and any onerous conditions set out, particularly with regard to timing. It would be helpful to give the name and address of the Planning Authority.

I am here concerned with the preparation of particulars of those development sites that would be of interest to the small builder or major development company.

I am not going to try to differentiate between the residential and commercial markets, clearly the factors with regard to area and location that we considered relevant in considering the preparation of particulars of houses and commercial property would also apply to land suitable for their development.

The matters that will in addition concern the prospective purchaser of development land are first, the nature of the development proposed and its extent: "Seven acres of freehold building land with outline planning consent for 100 houses"; or "Freehold site with outline planning consent for 10,000 sq. ft. of office accommodation". Having decided from this whether the site is of interest, its location in relation to the town and its shape will be of interest. This will dictate including in the particulars a location plan and a larger scale plan, probably an extract from the Ordnance Survey Sheet.

The prospective purchaser will need to know precisely what the planning authority have approved and subject to what conditions, also when the consent was given, and what time-limitations were imposed. This will tell him how long he has got to prepare and submit detailed plans before an outline consent — in the majority of cases that is all it will be — lapses. Ideally the particulars should include a copy of the planning consent, but at a minimum the particulars should state the name and address of the Planning Authority, their reference number, the form of development approved, and set out in full any conditions attaching to the consent.

The developer will need to know whether there are any access problems and the standing of the road or roads to which the site has frontages should be stated, i.e., whether it is a public or a private highway and if the latter, what rights over it pass with the land. He will want to know where the services are located and whether immediate access to them is available. To give the invert levels of existing sewers might be helpful.

He will want to make his own enquiries of the local authority and the public utility companies. The local authority's name and address has probably already been given as the planning authority; this may not necessarily be the case where the consent was granted by a County Council, so the name, address and telephone number of both will need to be stated. Similarly the developer will need the names, addresses and telephone numbers of the local electricity board, the gas board, the water authority and local telephone manager. Other matters that could be relevant are the existence of any agreement under Section 52 of the Town and Country Planning Act 1971 that might, for example, seek to phase the development or limit it in the case of office or industrial development to occupation only to firms already located in the planning district. He will need to know of any Tree Preservation Orders. If there are any buildings existing on site he will need to know if they are "Listed".

The fact that today's purchaser is tomorrow's potential vendor has a more immediate and important significance when one is handling developable land. The impression one creates as the vendor's agent could well determine whether or not when that developer comes to market his product your own firm is used.

Many developers would find it helpful to be given a guide as to current house values, or office or factory rental values in the area, whether or not there is a particular shortage in one sector of the market as opposed to another, as to the level of demand, and as to whether or not other developments in the area could directly or indirectly affect the development he is considering. For example, a development company considering a site with planning consent for a substantial office building is likely to be interested not only in the availability of secretarial staff, as we have earlier noted, but in the availability of houses likely to appeal to his potential tenant's executives. Much of this information, which would be gratuitous, would be better given in a covering letter than in the particulars themselves, which need, as in the case of commercial property, to be concise and factual.

Sixteen

Marketing Functions — The Applicants' Register

The applicant's register as a means of communication — The ideal — The register, relevance to the vendor, the purchaser, the agent — Flexibility — Analysis of past transactions — Price grouping — Probables and possibles — Selecting areas — A back up to the personal role — The need to keep the register alive and active — Up-dating revision.

An absolutely vital part of the estate agent's armoury is the applicants' register. It is the means by which he communicates with those who in one way or another have indicated to him an interest in buying property in his area. I use the word "register" because it is within the profession the generally accepted description and for this reason I will continue to use it, but I think it is dangerous, for a register, certainly to me, implies something that is of a permanent or static nature and this is exactly what the estate agents' register of prospective purchasers should never be. One of his principal tasks must be to ensure that it is alive, not just breathing, but active and a really vital part of the matching process he has to carry out.

When speaking in the Oxford Union to the last Conference of the Chartered Auctioneers' and Estate Agents' Institute in 1970 on the subject of residential estate agency, I said that the ideal unit in the residential estate agency business was — "a first-class negotiator with an equally good 'alter ego' working in a well sited office in a town where he knows everybody, with sufficient time to deal personally with every vendor and every applicant with whom he has had contact".

It is an ideal beyond reach, particularly in regard to knowing each applicant personally. The applicant, or prospective purchaser, will have made contact with the office in one of many ways. He may have visited the office to make his enquiry, he may have written, he may have telephoned, he may have seen a partner, he may have seen one of several negotiators, he may have seen one of the back-up staff.

The applicants' register is concerned with how we subsequently communicate with him, but again we are back to the subject of communications within the office. We have seen that one of the criticisms levelled at estate agents is that the particulars they send out all too often do not correspond, in the applicant's view, with what he told that firm he was looking for. Where this happens it is clearly, a failure somewhere along the line to communicate. It may well be that the applicant did not communicate his requirements clearly, but that in turn could be a failure on the part of the firm's representative whom he saw, to whom he spoke on the telephone, or who dealt with his written enquiry. Every negotiator will have a ready answer to this particular criticism, normally that "The average purchaser doesn't know what he wants." But in practice the failure is much more likely to be on the part of the agent than on the part of the applicant. I do not want here to get involved with the interviewing process, but rather to make the point that if the right questions are asked and recorded in a set form that is understood by all in the office, that particular purchaser's wishes should be capable of accurate interpretation by any member of the sales team, or indeed by any mechanical or electronic sorting process, be this very simple or a computer.

The ideal unit I described visualised a situation where the negotiator had himself interviewed every personal applicant, could remember precisely what their requirements were, their expressed likes and dislikes, and would therefore be able immediately to say to whom any one particular house was likely to be of interest. To a limited extent this can happen, for we earlier commented that every negotiator should have his or her personal list of "hot" applicants, people that he has seen, whom he has in all probability shown round houses, whose requirements he really feels he knows, and with whom he will immediately make personal contact the moment a possible house becomes available. No estate agent can ever hope, however, under normal market conditions, to service every potential purchaser who has been in touch with him in this way. The requirements have to be passed into the "system". In the smaller office it may well be perfectly adequate for the applicant's requirements to be written in longhand on a card and subsequently kept in alphabetical order. But even in the smallest office there will be two persons and "the girl" may have seen the applicant when "the negotiator" was out. Even at this level it is advisable that requirements be recorded in a set order and form albeit with such personal comments as the interviewer may think appropriate, for when it comes to deciding who should be contacted by telephone, who should receive the personal letter, who should be sent particulars, somebody, either the negotiator or the girl, has got to interpret somebody else's impressions as to what that applicant was seeking and it is in this interpretation that the difficulties occur. The problem does not alter from the office manned with two persons working in longhand and manually to the office with twenty, using modern data-processing methods.

Great care and a lot of thought is therefore needed, not only as to the information that is obtained from the applicant, but as to how this is recorded. We shall be looking, when we consider marketing in detail, at those factors which motivate would-be purchasers. For the purpose of our applicants' register, requirements can be seen to come under five main headings:— price, location, type, accommodation and special requirements.

What one is aiming to achieve in recording an applicant's requirements may be looked at from the point of view of all three persons involved.

a) The vendor — he has instructed his agent to find a buyer for his house and he will want his house brought to the attention of as many people as possible to whom it might be of interest, and as quickly as possible, and he will not appreciate appointments to view that are not kept because purchasers do not like the outside of the house, or purchasers who take up his time when the house is clearly not likely to be of any interest to them.

b) The purchaser — he will want to know that the agent will communicate with him by telephone call, by letter or by sending a copy of particulars, when he believes that he has a house that could be of interest to him. He will not appreciate set after set of particulars of houses that in his view in no way match the requirements he gave to that agent.

c) The agent — he wants to bring about the sale. To this extent he must make sure that he does communicate with everyone known to him to whom that house might be of interest, but he will want to do so as economically as possible, both in terms of time and money. If negotiators telephone applicants or write personal letters to them and the house is totally unsuitable, time and money are wasted. An indiscriminate circulation of particulars is also wasteful in terms of time, stationery and postage.

How does the agent, who is the link man, attempt to reconcile these three somewhat different viewpoints? First, and this is related more to how he uses his applicants' register rather than how he compiles it, he has got correctly to interpret the wishes of the vendor. He may be instructed to offer a house for sale at £49,500, which he believes to be worth little more than £40,000, but he should also know whether that vendor has got to sell, or whether he will only sell if he gets his price or something very close to it and is in no hurry. If he believes that that vendor will, if he is not lucky, have to sell at little over £40,000 this will influence his decision as to whom to communicate with. He has also, of course, to appreciate just what it is he is selling; a three-bedroomed house is one thing, a three-bedroomed house that could be readily adapted or extended to provide four, is another. The semi-detached house being one of a pair on an estate of 50 identical houses is "semi-detached", but the wing of a Georgian house, or the semi-detached country cottage with a lovely garden may be of interest to some of those who said that they were looking for a detached house — character could over-rule type. These are marketing considerations but should have a bearing on the way in which the applicants' register is compiled.

He has also got to decide in his own mind just what type of house and in what district the applicant is likely finally to live. It may be that the applicant in his letter set out requirements impossible to achieve, or was interviewed by somebody not really conversant with the market place who failed to recognise that the requirements of that applicant were unlikely to be achieved at the maximum figure he had given. That applicant, if he has got to buy, is going finally to accept a compromise, and somehow the applicants' register has got to be compiled in a form that will enable him to receive information concerning that likely compromise. The alternative is that he may receive no communication at all.

In the house market, except possibly in the very high price-ranges, price is inevitably the first criterion and it is for this reason that every agent's property register that I have seen has been in price order and every applicants' register kept in price groups. The price grouping of the applicants' register is important, for it means that when it comes to communicating with applicants the negotiator will first turn to the price group that he believes to be appropriate. For example, in the case of the house worth £40,000 or a bit more with an asking price of £49,500 the negotiator will know instinctively that his buyer is likely to be somebody who gave a maximum price not much over £40,000 rather than one who gave a maximum price of say £55,000. How many practising agents who read this believe they really know the relationship between the maximum price given to them by the average applicant and the price that average applicant ultimately pays? Until in my own office we carried out an analysis I for one believed that the average applicant, assuming that the agent would subsequently send him details of houses where the asking price was substantially in excess of the maximum price he gave, would under rather than overstate the maximum price he was prepared to pay, and end up paying more. The analysis in fact proved the converse.

From this point I must relate the applicants' register to my own area and my own personal views to an extent that I would like to have avoided. I have, however, no alternative for, as often stressed, residential estate agency is a very localised matter and only with considerable experience and detailed knowledge of an area could effective criteria be laid down as to how an applicants' register might be compiled. I only hope that what I say and illustrate will be readily capable of interpretaton and application in other areas, be they urban or rural.

First I consider price groupings. One may feel able, not quite arbitrarily, but relying on one's personal experience and instinct, to decide what price groupings are appropriate in one's own area, but if one has the information available, or is prepared to undertake the task, one could analyse, as we did, and compare applicants' quoted maximum prices against prices actually paid by them and at various price levels. Our own analysis was carried out too long ago to be relevant to day, so the diagram I produce over page is intended to be illustrative of a process only.

I have taken three typical maximum asking prices, £15,000, £45,000 and £55,000, and against the £15,000 datum I have plotted what 31 hypothetical purchasers giving this as their maximum price in fact paid, and it will be seen from the dotted probability lines that out of 31 purchasers in this group 28 ended up paying between £12,000 and £18,000. If the gap were narrowed to one of say £14,000 to £16,000, of the 31, 12 bought outside the bracket.

Using the £45,000 datum line and a bracket of between £40,000 and £50,000 with sales again marked with crosses, 4 buyers out of 31 bought outside the bracket.

Using the £55,000 datum line, I have shown a wider variation in prices paid, which in real terms is what we found and have illustrated. Taking a price bracket of £50,000 to £60,000, 9 are shown as having paid a price outside the bracket and 5 below it.

Some would regard this type of analysis as unnecessarily complex, others as too simple. In practice one would not of, course, find one's applicants all falling neatly into groups giving the same maximum price, and over the period of a year changing property values could distort the picture, but I put it forward for two reasons.

First to illustrate just one way of separating the probables from the possibles among the applicants and trying to balance the risk of losing sales against that of thoroughly irritating some applicants, secondly to illustrate the danger of precise price groups. To have submitted the house with an asking price of £49,000 that was worth it only to those in the £40/50,000 price group would be, on my example, to have missed five possible purchasers from the £50/60,000 group, who might well have purchased. The negotiator, or office where a manual system is used, will be able to direct that the particulars should go to those whose maximum price was stated to be £45/55,000 where his probables lie. Those using data-processing methods could program in this "over-lap" between groups, but this could lead to a duplication of records where the equipment does not have a collating capacity. This from our own earlier experience was often the explanation why the applicant who

ANALYSIS OF STATED

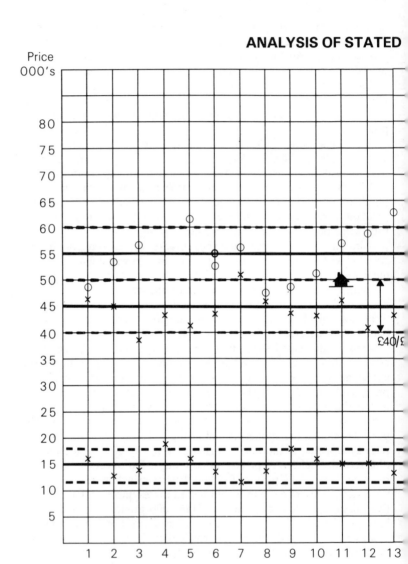

Price
000's

⌐ AGAINST PRICE PAID

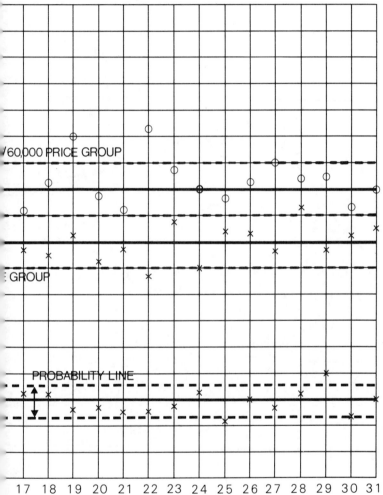

✓60,000 PRICE GROUP

GROUP

PROBABILITY LINE

17 18 19 20 21 22 23 24 25 26 27 28 29 30 31

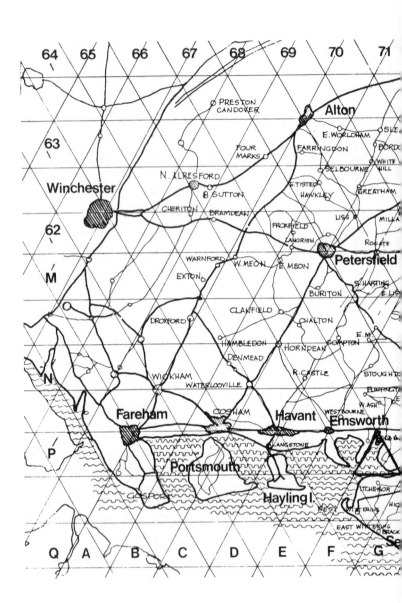

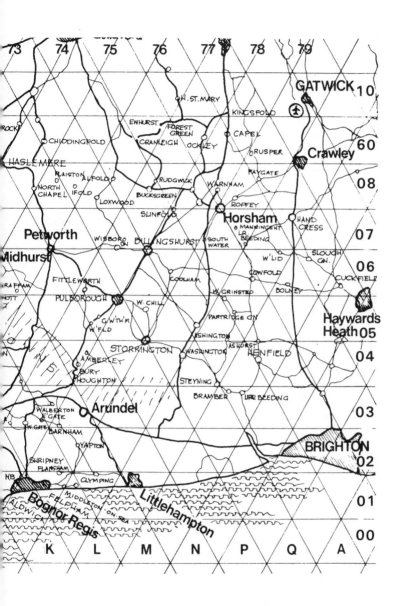

informed us that he was suited, and was dutifully removed from the system, continued to receive particulars.

The application of any data-processing system to deal with an applicant's stated requirements concerning locality is perhaps the most difficult aspect of programming. To illustrate the method we used, and it was many years ago, so techniques may well have improved, I illustrate a map showing the Chichester area of West Sussex. This enabled us by the use of a lenticular grid to get the "sort" down to triangular areas of three miles and by distorting the map we were able to isolate certain specific localities or villages. For example, Reference F/02/66 enabled us to pinpoint the village of Old Bosham, for analysis had shown "Old Bosham only" not only to be a specific requirement of a significant number of applicants, but one which if ignored caused more annoyance than almost any other. Similarly Reference F/03/68 would isolate the best residential area of Chichester itself, again a specific requirement for some. Clearly this grid pattern would not suit every location, but the principle I hope is clear and could I think be applied to other areas both urban and rural.

Accommodation does, I think, speak for itself as indeed does type of house sought. The information on the applicants' register should be factual or, put another way, inflexible. The flexibility will depend on the skill of the negotiator in interviewing the applicant, and interpreting his wishes, and later in deciding to what price groups a house should be submitted.

Finally, however sophisticated the matching process, there must be the ability to isolate an applicant when the negotiator concerned wishes personally to "vet" any particulars before they are submitted. It may be a personal friend, perhaps in no hurry to move, but who has said "Please only send me details of those houses which you personally think would be of real interest to me."

Although we will, when we look at the future, be considering the use of computers in estate agency, their application to the matching of the property register and the applicants' register is perhaps one of the most obvious and it was certainly the one that attracted the companies who first interested themselves in computerised agency, such as the National Property Register.

Nothing that I have said with regard to the matching process and the applicants' register must detract from what I see as the ideal — the personal contact between negotiator and applicant maintained. It is for this reason that I have stressed the need for each negotiator to have his "hot" list. The general applicants' register where all requirements are recorded is a second-best answer. It recognises that it will not be possible for negotiators to keep in personal contact with every applicant, and recognises the fact that many applicants perhaps only vaguely contemplating a move would not justify the time and expense involved in trying to do so. There will be occasions when a negotiator out viewing houses with an applicant or taking instructions just will not have time that day to telephone those on his own hot list to tell them about the house his firm is instructed to sell that day, and where the particulars were taken by a colleague. He should know, however, the following morning what particulars were sent and he will then be able to make his personal contact.

This leads me to what I see as a difficulty, that is how in the larger busy office one tells negotiators which of their personal applicants has been sent particulars and of what house or houses. There is no set drill. In the office using a manual system, it may well be that the negotiator will go through and ensure that those on his hot list to whom the house would appear suitable were sent particulars. It would also be possible for the girl doing the selection to write up on each applicant's card the particulars sent and for each negotiator quickly to run through the cards he initiated to see which if any should be personally followed up. Those with a computer could have the great advantage of being able to let each negotiator have a print-out each day of these applicants that he saw and the property of which they have been sent particulars.

How are we to ensure that one's applicants' register is kept alive and active? We start wth each negotiator's hot list. These will be live and active if regular communications are maintained and the negotiator should know of any change in requirements, such as a decision, perhaps because they have not found what is suitable, to pay £10,000 more if they have to. There should be no problem here if the negotiators are conscientious.

The next point I would make is the importance of up-dating. Although the negotiators will have their hot lists, all applicants will be in the main applicants' register and it must be remembered that the register will be comprised not only of hot applicants but others, for amongst the others will be applicants who have become hot without a negotiator being aware of this. They may have been casual seekers when they first enquired, but a change of circumstances may have rendered their need a pressing one. I do not intend to lay down how this should be done, but in a number of ways the office may learn that that applicant's circumstances have changed to the extent that he must from then on be regarded as "hot". It may be a letter telling of changed circumstances, it may be a telephone call and it may not be the negotiator he originally saw who receives that call; it may be one of the girls. It may be that he telephones for an appointment to view. It may be that a vendor telephones to say that he visited the house over the week-end and was he interested? Somehow the fact that the contact has been made has got to be passed "through the register" and that applicant promoted to somebody's hot list. It may be the negotiator who originally saw him. It may be the one who had the last contact.

Then there could be those applicants, and there could be many of them, who having made the original contact and having received particulars, one has heard nothing from. To do nothing will be to clog your register with a lot of potential purchasers who probably are nothing of the sort. They may have bought elsewhere, their initial enquiry may have been a casual whim, the husband may not have got the job he was hoping to get, and so on. Wherever possible and this will probably mean where the applicants are local, these should be followed up at regular intervals by telephone and if it is confirmed that they are still seeking, their cards must be up-dated, but this will still leave many with whom, for reasons of time and cost, such direct contact cannot be made. A standard revision letter asking if he is still seeking a property in the area, with a pre-paid reply form, warning that applicant that unless one hears from him he will be taken off the register, and inviting him to let you have any revised requirements or comments, may be the only way of making contact. Some will not remove applicants from the register after the first letter, or if they do will send a second letter informing them that they have been removed and again inviting them on the pre-paid reply to let you know if in fact they wish to stay on, or if at a later date they want particulars sent to ring you.

This is not perfect; some will not bother to reply, some will intend to and will not do it and others will believe they have, but in fact have not. One estate agent writing on this subject said he even sent with his revision letter that applicant's actual addressing card, so that he automatically would know that unless it was returned no further particulars would be sent.

One is tempted to say at what intervals revision letters should be sent, but so much must depend on the state of the market at the time, and in what section of the market that office is working, or that applicant looking. In even average market conditions it is my experience that the applicant looking for the standard terraced or semi-detached house will approach his purchase in the way he would approach almost any other commodity, and if you have not sold him something within the first week or two, he is almost certain to have bought elsewhere. It may not be necessary to keep that sort of applicant on the books for more than a month. At the other end of the scale, those contemplating retiring and many of those looking in the higher price-ranges, are prepared to take months to find what they are after, and it is this type of purchaser that ideally should not be removed without personal contact.

The partner responsible for the department, or the manager, must make it his personal responsibility to ensure that the register is kept alive and active in this way. A computer would clearly do a great deal to help, for it could tell each negotiator those applicants of his from whom nothing has been heard for say a month, with their telephone number and with a list of the properties sent since the last contact was made. But I believe there is still a danger of the register becoming, if not dead then impersonal. However efficient the computer might be, its standing in this particular context is no more important than that of the more humble manual applicants' register. Again it must be the partner or manager's responsibility to ensure not only that the right information gets to negotiators but that they act on it and keep personal contact whenever this is feasible.

We live in times of change. Mr. Hugh Cubitt writing on "The Organisation of Branch Offices" said this —

"Certain highly integrated firms operate a common register throughout, sometimes computerised. This requires absolute centralisation and introduces the problem of communications between branches and the office housing the computer — a problem made particularly acute by the present state of the postal services".

This was not written early in 1980 as one might believe. Amazingly, it was written in "The Chartered Auctioneer and Estate Agent" of February, 1970.

Nothing in my view removes the need for an applicants' register so far as this consists of hot lists, whether these are maintained on the negotiator's desk or each negotiator has access to his own through a visual display unit, but costs, not only of postage, but of printing and stationery, and the appalling state of the postal service, are causing some firms to re-think. At least one major firm, well known to me, has stopped all circularisation in the normal sense; only the hot applicants receive this service. The others receive a weekly property news sheet listing all properties new to the market since the last issue, up-dating prices and so on. This may be the way ahead for many, but it would require careful thought, for it moves away from the personal service. Unless the average applicant on one's register is receiving more than one set of particulars a week it may not in fact result in the saving expected and there will be just as much time-lapse in the post, and I think it could result in one's register being less alive and active than it should be.

Marketing Functions — Advertising

Creating market activity — Significance of advertising in marketing — The partners' responsibility — The local press, national papers, journals — Choice of media — Concentration of effort — Content and form — Points of emphasis — Accessibility — Differing market conditions — "Wanted" advertisements — Panel advertising — Sponsorships — Charities — Press releases — The press as a means of communicating

We earlier considered advertising, but principally in the context of promoting the firm's image. The other aim of one's advertising, although the two are irrevocably linked, is that of marketing one's product. This aim is not limited to selling specific houses, for one's ability to market one's product in the wider sense will depend to an extent on the amount of activity your advertising generates amongst would-be house purchasers, and vendors. One is aiming, therefore, to do two things; first to expose in the best possible light the properties one wants to advertise and, secondly, to do it in a way that will generate maximum activity. To illustrate this point. There may be a tendency if in one week you receive instructions to sell ten houses, six of which are very similar in type, accommodation and price, to advertise all ten, because they are "new", whereas one could include in that advertisement only one of the similar houses, and the one that sounded most attractive, but advertising also other houses which perhaps had been on the market for some time, but were in different price ranges, with the obvious chance of creating activity across the whole of one's market range, and not predominantly in one sector of it. I accept that the expectation of vendors cannot be ignored and that a balance has to be kept.

We have seen when looking at budgeting that the average firm is spending something in the order of 10 per cent of its gross fee income on advertising. One accepts that all one's advertising must have some "spin-off" value to the firm's functions other than estate agency, but accepting that, and at the same time accepting that for the average firm estate agency income is little more than half the total, it is probable that the average firm is spending something in the order of 13 per cent to 16 per cent of its estate agency income in advertising that can be directly related to estate agency work. In that this approaches half of what the average firm is reputed to spend on wages and salaries, it is both in terms of cost and indeed in terms of effectiveness in property marketing the second most significant aspect of the estate agency practice. Everyone would accept that staffing levels, the appointment of staff, the level of remuneration, staff relationships and welfare are considered to be the responsibilities of the partners, and probably not just of the partner responsible for the estate agency function, but of the partners collectively. One questions whether to a greater or lesser extent this could be said of responsibility for advertising. Many firms do, of course, give it a very high level of importance, with the partners deciding on budgets, media, frequency and so on. Some larger firms, and indeed I know of one or two that would come in the description of average-sized firms, employ public relations/advertising experts to advise on policy and to use whatever budget he or she is given to the best effect, but all too often, looking at the content of local newspaper advertisements it is obvious that the task is left to those at a lower level. This is not to say they cannot word a perfectly good advertisement, indeed if one's negotiators have, as they must, responsibility for drafting particulars, why should they not draft advertisements?

I am more concerned here with policy and co-ordination. A standard pattern of advertisement could perhaps ensure that four advertisements written by four different negotiators at least followed a common pattern and did not appear when published to be inconsistent or scrappy, but advertisements drafted week in and week out by the same four individuals to the same common pattern will soon make one's advertisements in that particular medium appear somewhat drab and uninteresting.

I believe that the partner responsible for the estate agency function must, within any overall policy and budget that may have been set by the partnership as a whole, dictate the media to be used and the amounts to be spent. He must ensure that vendors' wishes are followed, that the aim to create maximum activity is not lost, he must therefore decide what is to be advertised, in what style, whether illustrated of unillustrated, and he must personally check all advertisements before going to press. This may sound a tall order, but I do not believe anything less is acceptable.

The choice of media will be the partners' responsibility. Those not involved with the type of property that would dictate the use of national advertising media and operating in a well defined area with only one established local newspaper will find little difficulty, but advertising can take many forms. We have already considered the office window, our boards, advertising hoardings and our circulation of particulars, which are all forms of advertising, even if not charged in our accounts under this particular heading. We have now to consider the following:

The local press. In most rural areas there will be a local paper, but there may also be a county paper, daily evening newspaper, based on a large urban centre, which has influence throughout a wider area and there may be one of the free distribution advertising papers. Simply to illustrate the problem, and conscious of the need to generalise rather than personalise, in the part of West Sussex where I practise, with an office in Chichester, we have a weekly paper, "The Chichester Observer" published on a Friday. We have a county paper "The West Sussex Gazette," published on Thursday. We have a free distribution newspaper, "The Promoter", and an important and influential daily evening paper, "The Portsmouth Evening News", with a wide circulation within our own area. The branch offices outside that immediate area have similar problems of choice of their own. In that our offices were established over a period of many years, some are stronger than others, and it is natural for the weak to look for advertising support from the stronger. Great care is needed if one's advertising is to make maximum impact and dissipation be avoided.

The national newspapers. Many will have no need to advertise in these. Others, for example those dealing predominantly with the higher-priced market within Greater London, will have to use them, but many Provincial firms also have a need to do so, particularly when dealing with the upper end of the market, when they are in practice competing with the firms that operate nationally, but not necessarily only in this context. The small country cottage might appeal to many living far outside the immediate district. Again we find a problem that must be common to many. The offices in rural areas have a much greater need to advertise nationally than those in the larger urban centres, yet all are looking for some benefit from the role national advertising plays in promoting the image.

The Journals. Then there are the journals. "Country Life" for country houses, but why not "Horse and Hound" for houses in riding country, or for that matter "Yachting World" if the house happens to be in a well known sailing centre?

Last but not least are the advertising newspapers, often neglected but very often effective in certain sections of the market and not only the local ones — "Daltons Weekly" and "Exchange and Mart".

Although I have identified the problem locally, I am well aware that firms throughout the country face similar problems and similar choices. The danger of dissipating one's effort and one's investment is obvious. The interests of offices vary; the office in a major urban centre with a strong local daily paper with high advertising rates will be reluctant to give support to the firm's national advertising effort if it sees no immediate and direct advantage to it.

All this is to underline not just the problems but in particular the need for management to set specific policies and budgets, and having done so, to monitor them and keep control.

Mr. G. R. Robertson, then Group Classified Advertisement Manager to Thomson Newspapers Ltd., opened an article on property advertising in newspapers, written in 1968, with this paragraph:

> "An advertisement is a salesman in print. A salesman's work consists of finding customers for his firm's products and an advertisement's job is also to attract buyers. Property advertising is no different, for it seeks to find the right buyer and, at the same time, it should make readers aware of the existence of a particular agent. The majority of property advertisements appear in the classified columns of the newspapers, grouped together so that readers can read all of them with the minimum of effort. Classified advertisements are unique in that they are usually sought by a reader who has made up his mind to buy and who is searching for his particular choice, whereas all other forms of advertising try to attract the attention of the reader."

I would relate this back to what was said earlier about "the largest market place". It leads to the first question the agent has to ask himself. Given instructions to sell a house what type of person is likely to buy it, where is he likely to come from and to what medium is he going to look to help him in his search? One is in practice looking for the largest market place, and if this philosophy is right, as it must be, and Mr. Robertson is right that the reader will seek the advertisements that are grouped together, then I suggest that it must also follow that the estate agent, having identified the one medium that will give him the widest market place, and accepting that this will not necessarily be the same for each and every property that he has to sell, should concentrate on that medium and strongly resist any temptation to fragment his overall advertising effort. Fragmentation could take two forms. In the context of weekly newspapers it could, for example, take the form of putting half one's planned advertisements for the week into the local and established newspaper and the other half into the free distribution newspaper. A temptation which as this type of publication becomes more common many will feel, but to give in would be contrary to the philosophy of "the largest market place" and possibly also Mr. Robertson's advice unless, and this is unlikely, the free distribution advertising paper becomes recognised as the "right" medium for houses. The agent is aiming his market in two directions, to existing house-owners who may or may not be contemplating a move and to those contemplating the purchase of a house. The former will be already resident in the area, but the latter may not.

Given a choice of newspapers, or media, the agent must ask himself which is most likely to be read by these two groups of people. One important factor could be those who are interested in buying houses in the area but currently living elsewhere. They may well arrange to receive regular copies of the local newspaper, but will never receive the free distribution paper.

The question of concentration can be particularly relevant to the agent operating in an area where the recognised local paper is not only a daily one, but one which in terms of advertising space is expensive. In the majority of cases such papers will concentrate property advertising into one, two or possibly three days a week, but even so the agent will be left with the question as to how best to reach the readers he wants and to impress potential vendors. To spread the advertisements over all available issues will be to maintain continuity and many advertising experts would argue in favour of this. On the other hand it may, if rival firms are adopting the alternative policy of concentrating the majority if not all of their advertisements into one issue only, run the risk of appearing small, with little to offer.

I do not pretend to give an answer. This is likely to be indicated by the rival firms, for in the context of one's public image, it is vital that one's advertising, if it cannot outstrip one's rivals, at least reflects one's proper standing in the local market place.

Those who feel a need to advertise nationally or in regional papers to reach a much wider spread of readership have perhaps an easier choice to make.

On the one hand there are papers such as "The Times", "The Observer" and "The Daily Telegraph" and their Sunday editions, but, on the other, journals such as "Country Life". The former, relatively much more expensive, might be seen as the most direct means of marketing the product, the house or houses that you wish to sell. Advertisements can appear within days of copy being sent and they are likely to be read on the day of publication, although some of the leading Sunday papers may be read over the following few days. Once read, these papers are thrown away. A journal such as "Country Life" on the other hand appears weekly but "copy" has to be provided well before publication, with some chance that a buyer might have been found for that house before the advertisement appears, but it does reach a particular type of reader and is left about and read over a considerable period. Not only is it left about in homes but in professional waiting rooms and it is read not only in Britain but by British citizens living abroad, and certainly we have received a number of enquiries from remote corners of the earth through advertising in this particular medium.

Use of such media is perhaps more important in image building than it is in direct selling, but it has a particular value in the latter context if one has the time available and wished to mount an advertising programme for one particular property over a period — for example when one is selling by auction.

I do not overlook the fact that many agents in London and in the other major cities of the country may have a different problem, for their "local" paper may in practice be a national daily, morning or evening paper or a regional. Nor do I overlook the fact that there are other national daily papers carrying a significant volume of property advertising, whose use may be appropriate to agents other than those practising in the major cities. I do not feel qualified to comment on their use, but the basic questions remain unaltered. What am I trying to achieve with my advertising? Whom do I want to reach? and what medium is going to help me most? Lastly, in the context of my overall budget, is this going to be cost-effective?

We next have to consider the content and form of our advertisements, and here I find a wide divergence of opinion, not only between practising agents, but between those in the advertising world. At one end of the scale there are those who argue that the more you say about a house in your advertisement the more likely it is to attract interest. Mr. Robertson seems to be of this view, for he said —

> "As a house is probably the most expensive item that a person purchases, he is certainly anxious to know as much about it as possible before he goes to view it. There is a saying concerning advertising which is 'the more you tell the more you sell'. Sometimes it is not possible to say everything, but if one is trying to describe something to the right buyer his interest must be aroused. He should be partially 'sold' on the house before he even sees it!".

Others would argue that the more you advertise, in terms of volume of houses, the more likely are you to generate interest, not perhaps so much in one house in particular, as interest and activity of a general nature.

Mr. Robertson said "People want to know as much as possible about what is for sale *before* they come forward", and similarly there is no doubt that the vendor of a nice house who sees it amply if not very fully described, well illustrated and clearly with a lot of thought given to presentation, is going to be impressed. But again the other side of the argument is that potential vendors would also be impressed by the large number of houses that you have to offer and come to you believing that you represent the largest market place, or at least part of it. Similarly prospective purchasers would believe the same and also come to you.

I believe there is room for both schools of thought and that there is room for a great deal of flexibility and variety. A list of houses giving very brief summaries only of accommodation and price might by the very number of them impress, but they will not necessarily make interesting reading. One cannot lay down hard and fast principles. The agent whose market place is a suburb where houses differ little in price range or type, if he is to arouse the maximum amount of interest and impress vendors at the same time has got a very different problem from that of the agent in a country office with a wide variety of house-types to offer, many of them in the upper price ranges and differing greatly in character and the accommodation they provide.

In a seaside town that I think one could fairly describe as suburban in character we have found that a large number of short but to-the-point advertisements that can be torn out with an enquiry pro forma, with boxes where prospective purchasers can tick the advertisements of particular interest to them, is effective in generating general interest, specific enquiries, and in impressing vendors. At the same time we feel that this approach would be entirely wrong in what one might describe as the "county" market.

There are, however, certain guidelines. First within the overall space that one feels one wants to devote to advertising a particular house, one has got to be as informative as possible. Clearly a good photograph, although expensive in terms of space, will in itself give a great deal of information, particularly as to type, style and character. In deciding content we must bear in mind those factors that we know are the most important to would-be purchasers and all who have commented have put financial factors first. If a price is being asked, and there will be occasions when this is not the case, it must feature prominently. Research, Mr. Robertson said, showed that to quote the price was the key factor in the effectiveness of advertisements. "If a price is not quoted it is calculated that at least 50 per cent of potential purchasers will not even trouble to make enquiries".

Every house will possess one or more characteristics that the agent believes will sell it.

Mr. Robertson comments on this point — "The particular feature which makes one person buy a house will also attract the next buyer when it is sold again". The feature or features may be obvious — a very large living room, a south aspect with a view, it may be the playroom or the studio, but in some cases there will be no very obvious feature and to try to make a modern terraced house sound particularly interesting can be difficult. Purchasers are, however, looking for different things — a large garden will be of interest to some, the fact that a small patio garden has been completely paved will, conversely, appeal to others. Some hate painting and decorating and some are in a hurry to move in: the house that has been recently redecorated throughout will be of interest to them.

Likewise there are some who enjoy "doing it yourself" and believe they will be buying a bargain if they buy a house that gives ample scope for modernisation or simply complete redecoration.

As we have said, a photograph can describe much, but if one cannot be used, or one's budget limits the number that can be used, then the house must be as clearly described as possible, for the type and style of house, together with locality, we know to be of particular interest to purchasers. Remembering always that we are trying to be informative, it may be possible, certainly for the sole agent, actually to give the address. Others may feel able to name the road if this is likely to be a feature of particular interest.

Accommodation is another determining factor but beware of adjectives that are capable of wide interpretation. The words "large" and "small" if applied to rooms or gardens mean different things to different people, dependent on social group, income group and what they have been used to. It will not always be possible, and indeed would make dull reading, for measurements to be incorporated in advertisements, but if the living room of a semi-detached house is unusually large, it would take little more space and be more informative to give the measurements. To say that a detached three-bedroomed house has a large garden does not underline or really stress this fact as a feature. To say that it has an "unusually large garden" will lead the reader to believe that when he comes to view he is going to find that for a house of its type the garden is exceptionally large. If he is a keen gardener he is more likely to be attracted by the advertisement and, equally important, if he views will not be disappointed, provided, of course, that the statement was true.

Similarly the phrase "well fitted kitchen" could mean anything, from a kitchen that has all the "basic" requirements to one that is really lavishly equipped with high-quality cupboards and equipment. Be as specific as possible. To say that a house is on a bus route, says something, but the person to whom this will be an essential feature is likely to know where the main bus routes run, to say, therefore, that it is on the No. 31 bus route, 15 minutes from town centre, will be much more helpful.

The list of those features that one might find and that might be of particular interest and which would need stressing in any advertisement is almost endless, but when one comes to draft advertisements, space never is.

There are, other general factors we should consider.

First accessibility. The person whose interest is aroused by an advertisement is likely to want to see that house at the earliest possible opportunity and agents generally, although there are some good exceptions, all too frequently are less than helpful in this direction. "View by appointment only" is daunting. If your relationship with the vendor and the nature of your agency is such that you could without undue risk of the information being abused by your competitors give the vendors' name and telephone number, then do so. If not, give your own. Many people could only view either in the evenings or at weekends, so to say "For evening or week-end viewing, telephone Mr. Smith at ....." will not only give the interested purchaser the feeling that the house is readily available to him to inspect, but will give the impression that the vendor and the agent are anxious to sell.

The way one's advertisements are presented is important, as is choice of words. The denser the reading matter the harder it is to read, the less immediately interesting, and above all the harder it will be to emphasise the particular feature you have chosen. Again, space will be a limitation, but the more white paper there is, the better will the advertisement appear. The choice of words is a personal one, but I well remember in early days being sharply criticised for using the word "lounge". My then senior partner was of the view that "lounge" was a vulgar 20th-century word that should only be used to describe vulgar 20th-century rooms. Other rooms were, dependent upon the type and style of house, sitting rooms, living rooms or drawing rooms!

Mr. Vivian suggests, as one way of creating variety, not only just wording one's advertisements bearing in mind the known reasons why people move house but actually directing them to specific groups: "About to get married"? then "This highly mortgageable ....." Then one might address oneself to those with a growing family; those getting promotion; those about to retire; those who must have a bungalow; those whose gardens have become too big to manage and so on. Caution is, however, needed for no one house is likely to be of interest to only one type of buyer. The modest four-bedroomed house may well be of interest to the young couple with a growing family, but it might also be of interest to a very much older couple, used perhaps to a very much larger house, but whose children have grown up and left home, but whom they hope will visit regularly.

Two further comments from Mr. Robertson — "A concentrated series over a short period is more effective than an advertisement which appears over a number of scattered and random dates". "An advertiser is usually more interested in the quality of replies received than by the quantity and a good advertisement with a good description aims directly at the most likely purchasers".

So far we have been thinking in the context of newspapers and journals, but the greater freedom now given to members of the two leading professional bodies, and always enjoyed by others, has led to some experiments with other media. One firm known to me sought advice from an advertising and public relations consultant with a specific view to increasing their market share. They were advised to go for cinema advertising as likely to prove cost-effective and this advice appears to have been based on the then data given by the Nationwide Building Society Bulletins to the effect that 70 per cent of purchasers were aged 35 or under, and the fact that a similar percentage of film goers were this age or less. I qualify this by stressing that the type of advertisement visualised was one that would promote the firm's image as estate agents, rather than the advertising of specific properties.

We ourselves tried television advertising, believing that the disposition of our offices within one relatively inexpensive television region would make it cost-effective, but we were guilty of the classic mistake. We tried to get across the whole range of services that we could offer. We did not concentrate but dissipated our effort and because we did this we had no means of monitoring results. To this day we shall never know what if any effect it had.

One thing however, is certain, whatever medium you use will be bought by and read or screened to many who have no intention of owning their own homes, or who will never be able to do so and to many who have no intention of moving. The degree to which this is so will vary from medium to medium. But coming back to Mr. Robertson's opening comments —

> "Classified advertisements ... are usually sought by a reader who has made up his mind to buy ..."

Any departure from usual channels carries with it the risk of dissipating effort and one's budget.

The cyclical nature of the house market was underlined by the Price Commission Report, but it is something of which all agents are only too well aware. There are times when the market is flooded with houses, serious purchasers are few and far between, and times when the converse applies. Most agents would acknowledge that under the former conditions there is a tendency for costs to rise as the work-load increases, but for income to fall. These conditions also bring on the agent the greatest pressure to advertise, either pressure he feels himself because of the large number of unsold houses on his books, or pressure exerted by individual vendors. It is a time when advertising houses for sale is likely to be the least fruitful in creating activity and generating sales.

It follows that in very buoyant market conditions when few houses are available and those that are, with few exceptions sell almost immediately profits are high but the need for advertising specifically to sell houses almost if not completely vanishes.

Under these buoyant conditions when houses are scarce and buyers plentiful, why should we not change the whole emphasis of our advertising? From observation of agents' advertisements over very many years it seems that few have ever really made a concentrated attempt in these circumstances specifically to advertise to attract vendors. The most the majority have attempted are a few singularly brief and uninspired "Wanted" advertisements tacked on to the end of their normal display of houses for sale, many of which are probably sold or are under offer in any event. How many agents could really claim under such conditions to have sought retainers from prospective purchasers? The role of the estate agent to seek and acquire on behalf of prospective purchasers is very much a feature of the commercial market, widely recognised and widely used. Why should this be acceptable in one market and not in another? It may be that the agent's role in the house market as the one who acts for the vendor is more widely recognised than many believe and that many purchasers, faced with the suggestion that they might retain the agent to seek and find, and become responsible for his fees if he succeeds, would believe it was being in some way unethical. Certainly we have not really seriously attempted this, and this may be because we ourselves see it as an unusual approach and there is always a fear that the unusual will be seen as the unethical.

Again I would ask, accepting that many would feel they could not seek retainers from prospective house purchasers in the sense that the purchasers would pay them the normal commission, or something approaching it, if they succeeded, how many have tried to seek even a modest fee or contribution towards expenses to undertake advertising on behalf of that applicant, to approach other agents, or to carry out a specific canvass in those areas which might be of particular interest to him? Under these market conditions this seems to me to be something that ought to be feasible and worthwhile — a service which, given the will, the agent could sell to some frustrated purchasers. The full retainer is infinitely to be preferred, for it would enable any advertisements and any letters specifically approaching vendors to make it abundantly clear that if a sale is effected through your introduction you are not seeking any commission from the vendor concerned.

If "Wanted" advertisements are to be used, and we are here considering advertising and not canvassing, or, what I think would be a much better description, searching the market, they will need as much thought and care as property advertisements.

Continuing for the moment on a critical note, will "Mr. S. urgently needs to find ... usual commission required" really carry any weight? If it produces an instruction and you cannot produce Mr. S., it will certainly lose you credibility. Advertisements of this sort may appear to be catch-pennies and there is little doubt that this is just what many of them are.

Such an advertisement as the following, however, will appear genuine and is likely to produce a response:

"Mr. S., a keen gardener taking up an appointment in Chichester on September 1st, urgently needs a four-bedroomed house with a large garden, Parklands or Summersdale area preferred, but others considered if on good bus service to get children to school. Prepared to consider a price of between £35/40,000. Please contact Mr. Smith of ... Tel- ... Usual commission required".

I have a "Wanted" advertisement illustrated with a house, having the caption, "Mr. S. of High Wycombe was unsuccessful in acquiring this house at about £35,000 and is urgently seeking something similar on the outskirts of Guildford etc".

Apart from the sort of advertising we have been discussing, which would absorb the greater part of any agent's advertising budget, the partner or manager responsible will come under regular pressure from organisations that produce local guides, theatre programmes, professional and trade directories, and magazines directed at the house-purchasing public. Saying 'No' to resolute space salesmen is never easy, but to say "Yes" could be to dissipate one's effort. The basic questions remain. Whom do I want to reach? What is the message I want to get across? Will this particular medium or form of advertising help me to achieve both? If not, the answer must be "No".

Sponsorship I find more difficult, particularly if this is related to some essentially local event, for this can achieve more than just getting across the name of one's firm and what it does. To sponsor a charitable event, if it is going to get adequate publicity and exposure, is to identify the firm with a worthwhile local cause and could help appreciably to build one's public image as a firm concerned, not just with earning money out of an area, but being responsibly involved in it. Similarly, in a sport-oriented society, to sponsor sporting events, particularly those likely to be of interest to possible vendors and purchasers in one's area could help build the image. We, ourselves, have been prepared to sponsor holes at various pro/am golf meetings, one event at a significant local tennis tournament, and so on. The result of such advertising can never be monitored, but we were left in little doubt that our involvement was appreciated by the organisers, by the members of the clubs concerned and by many of the spectators. We felt the effort had been well worthwhile.

Requests for direct financial help from charities can be a constant source of mild or even acute embarrassment if significant clients are involved. We have a principle, which, like so many, cannot be followed in every case, that support for national charities must be a matter for individual partners, whose interests and sympathies can vary greatly. Locally we identify a limited number of charitable causes which we are prepared in a limited way to support. The Friends of the two Cathedrals in our area and the Friends of local hospitals, for example, get regular support. Others we try not to say "No" to, taking the view that involvement in the local community is an essential part of public relations.

There are certain other things which we touched on briefly in considering our public image. Press Releases are important, and a very good liaison needs to exist with the property editors or columnists of the local press and indeed, where applicable, the national press, to ensure that any house of real interest that one is instructed to sell is featured with the firm's name in editorials and similarly any sale of significance reported, provided the consent of both parties has been obtained. Partners should be aware of the opportunities presented from time to time to write articles or letters to editors, to comment on property affairs, also to talk to local clubs or groups. This again will help emphasise the firm's responsible involvement in the community.

Annual market reports are likely to be of interest to readers and will give them a sense of awareness as to what is going on and of keeping themselves well informed. Those who have purchased houses from the firm, and its commercial contacts, will have special reasons to follow developments in the property market with interest.

Within the rules of good taste, for anything else could be counter-productive, the aim of one's advertising must never be forgotten. It is to put across on every possible occasion that you are, or certainly are part of and very active in the largest market place, and sensitive to the needs of all those involved in it.

Eighteen

Marketing Functions — Selling

The art of selling — The responsibility of the
individual — Qualities needed of a negotiator —
American emphasis on personality — The salesman's
use of time — What motivates house-purchasers —
The psychology of house-buying — Reasons for
buying, reasons for moving — The house as an
investment — Motives inter-related — The negotiator
and prospective purchasers — The initial interview —
Moving up market and down — The vital minutes —
The status of the purchaser — Interview, accompany,
maintain contact — Stages in selling — Attracting
interest, narrowing the field of interest — The hard
and soft sell considered — Closing the sale — Sale
subject to contract — Need to develop one's own
approach and techniques — The role of the vendor —
Presenting the house — Importance of knowledge of
the property — From receipt of offer to completion —
Gazumping — Deposits — Two or more offers —
Agent's action on completion

There are many in the estate profession who have deplored the lack of
training in "marketing" and this book is to an extent the result of this
apparent shortcoming. Yet in considering marketing we have seen that
many of the tasks that estate agents have traditionally carried out, and
the way they approach them, can readily be related to recognised
marketing techniques. I suggest that the majority of the critics do not
have in mind the whole of the marketing process but simply that, very
important but nevertheless limited, marketing function of selling the
product. How to sell real property or how to increase the negotiator's
ability to sell are the questions they want answered.

"Salesmen are born and not made" is often the answer given and it
must to an extent be true; nevertheless there are recognised techniques
and attitudes that apply to salesmanship, whether it be of baked beans,
houses, factories or any other commodity, and are capable of being
taught. It is not sufficient in the estate agency context for managers or
negotiators to accept the present level of achievement.

Many, I know, are hoping that this book will deal exhaustively with marketing in the selling sense and will be disappointed that I do not intend that it should. Many books have already been published on the subject although few related to estate agency. I think it far more important to set a general scene and to highlight those aspects of real estate marketing that differ from normal "product" marketing, so that those who wish to study "selling" can relate the work and experience of others specifically to their own field. This book would fall well short of its aim, however, if it failed to consider not only the art of selling but what attributes to look for and develop in negotiators.

What comes across strongly to me from all that I have read on the subject is not only the importance of personality or efficiency but the responsibility of individuals for their own approach and attitudes, physical appearance, keeping themselves informed and for improving themselves not simply as salespersons but in every relevant respect.

Characteristics of the good negotiator

We earlier mentioned the 57 qualities listed by the late William W. Hannon of Detroit as necessary for success in real estate selling and we shall consider some of these. Henry E. Hoagland, in considering the qualities needed for success, used a quotation interestingly related to those qualities needed by a woman.

"A warm likeable personality, and a boundless interest in people. A marked capacity for self direction and self management. The ability to take rebuffs, even the bad manners of strangers, philosophically; to take all disappointments in her stride. The patience and foresight necessary to work very hard for months, perhaps two or three years, before the monetary rewards begin to manifest themselves. The ability to study, and acquire a comprehensive grasp of her field, and to go on studying all through the years. A high degree of analytical ability. Finally a capacity for sustained effort and the good health necessary to maintain it".

That very well known, forthright and successful Yorkshire surveyor and estate agent, John Smallwood, whom I have the pleasure of knowing, when writing on the occasion of his retirement said this: "The other day I came across the ten commandments which I jotted down many years ago for the benefit of articled pupils, and I believe that these are equally relevant even in today's differing society:

1. Start early to organise your mind and thought and plan the events of your working day.
2. Aim to do whatever job is offered better than you believe anyone else could, then you might do it as well.
3. Always do what you believe to be morally right without regard to the financial consequences or the opinions of your clients.

4. Never consider any job too small to be worthy of your attention.
5. As and when a mistake is made, admit it. Everybody makes mistakes once, but there is no excuse for making the same mistake twice.
6. Late starters tend to spend the rest of the day trying to catch up.
7. It is offensive to drink alcohol during working hours and to inflict your smoking habits on either clients or customers.
8. Pay all your bills promptly. You can never expect others to do what you are not prepared to.
9. If you do not know how to tackle a job then don't be afraid to ask someone who does.
10. If you get into trouble then make sure it is for something you have done, rather than for something you have not."

He was not referring specifically to the agency role but the similarity with the writings of American realtors is striking.

We now consider some of those 57 qualities which William W. Hannon considered necessary to success in real estate selling and which came into four groups, physical, temperamental, mental and moral.

The physical qualities could themselves be broken down into groups; first "attitudes" — the qualities of being spirited, alert, aggressive and energetic, and then "appearances" — neatness, voice, health, and cleanliness. The last three he listed were "clean teeth, odourless breath and clean finger nails". The qualities listed under the heading of "temperamental" included ambition, enthusiasm, initiative, tenacity, the ability to converse easily, but also to listen, optimism, courage and perseverance.

Under "mental" came a strong will, good memory, imagination, the ability to concentrate, originality, patience and resourcefulness. Under "moral" came loyalty, punctuality, truthfulness, friendliness, faith in oneself, in one's firm, and thrift.

It is the strength of the emphasis that he and other writers place on physical, personal, mental and moral attitudes that would perhaps surprise many British estate agents, who certainly give the appearance of being more concerned that their staff are taught selling systems, that they are efficient and that they perform, if not well, at least adequately. Some British firms, however, are becoming conscious of the importance of the individual, sending partners, managers and negotiating staff on courses designed to improve personal attitudes, rather than technical efficiency.

I recall the day I was commissioned into the Royal Artillery in 1948. As a cadet my Battery Commander had shown great concern at the way those in his charge would dress when they finally emerged as young officers, insisting on approving the tailors to whom they went for their uniforms, and attending fittings. On "Pass-Out Day" he talked to us about those qualities necessary if we were to function efficiently and well as officers. I remember my amazement when he quoted from Shakespeare "Costly thy raiment as thy purse can buy, but not express'd in fancy; rich, not gaudy: for the apparel oft proclaims the man".

I was equally surprised to find the same quotation in "The Real Estate Salesman's Handbook" which quoted from the speech at greater length and ended..."this above all: to thine own self be true, and it must follow, as the night the day, thou canst not then be false to any man".

Although elsewhere we shall be considering overseas practice, in particular that in North America, and comparing certain aspects of it with our own, one thing comes across strongly. Across the Atlantic real estate salesmen tend to operate as individuals working for a broker but with a large degree of independence, and dependent for their remuneration largely, if not entirely, on their own success. This perhaps explains the importance given to personal characteristics and attitudes, their relationship with success and the need to build personal contacts for the future. Although the Americans do not under-estimate the importance of the salesman's loyalty to the firm with which he is operating we may have a lot to learn from the importance they attribute to the individual.

The other point that comes across strongly is the need to plan time. We discuss this elsewhere when considering the responsibility of management, but it is the individual's responsibility to plan his day, his week and his career. Effective planning and use of time is a vital element in salesmanship. It must be planned or budgeted and must be accounted for. If it is not planned, there is the danger that it will be frittered away and this is a resource wasted. Moreover if it is not planned there is a danger of attempting too much in a given period and as a result operating ineffectively or inefficiently. John Wesley said "Though I am always in haste I am never in a hurry. I never undertake more than I can handle with calmness and spirit".

Having considered briefly the characteristics one is likely to find in the good negotiator we can go on to consider how he actually operates when endeavouring to sell his "product", how he deals with prospective purchasers and his approach to this aspect of his job.

He will need an understanding of the reasons why people want to purchase property. These may be obvious in the Commercial market but not as obvious in the residential market, which is our particular concern. Various studies have been carried out into the motivation of house-purchase. One put motivations in the following order — status, care of family, security, recreational pleasure and comfort.

Research carried out by the Department of Social Psychology at the University of Surrey differentiated between buying a house, posing the question "Why buy your home?" and moving house. Responses to the first question fell into seven broad categories.

Reasons for Buying.	Number of Reasons falling into Category as a Percentage of Total Number of Reasons.
1. Financial	41%
2. Socio-emotional	21%
3. No alternative considered	10%
4. Freedom — independence	7.5%
5. Ownership per se	7.5%
6. Quality and choice of house	7%
7. Part of an on-going plan	6%

The reasons given for moving differ considerably:—

Reasons for moving.	Number of Reasons falling into Category as a Percentage of Total Number of Reasons.
1. Environmental	49%
2. Financial	23%
3. Personal	20%
4. Special	8%

They commented:—

"The distinction between moving and buying is a crucial one, which is frequently omitted from studies. This is because researchers accept the popular wisdom that home-ownership is inevitable. Yet as can be seen . . . it is partly because of attitudes towards and beliefs in home-ownership that the social policies encouraging it have been instituted. The reasons given by purchasers for buying indicate that the values of home-ownership are considered across a broad front and have a quite different structure to them from the reasons for their particular choice. Although it may be the case that houses are bought for financial reasons, the particular house selected is less likely to be considered for its economic potential."

This may be seen to be stating the obvious, or it may be seen as irrevelant to any consideration of selling in the house market, simply because the negotiator dealing with an applicant is dealing with somebody already motivated to purchase and presumably able within a given financial restraint to do so. There is a point made of very considerable significance here. I think the majority involved in residential agency work believe financial motivation to be the dominating factor in the market place. To an extent they are right, for the Research shows it to be the largest single reason for house purchase *per se*. Certainly the first-time buyer will be financially motivated, both in a positive and negative sense. In the positive sense in that he will be seeking the long-term financial benefits that he believes will accrue from home-ownership; in the negative sense because in the short term his resources will be severely limited. Financial considerations motivate but they also act as a restraint.

In the majority of transactions in which the estate agent will be involved during his career, he will be dealing not with the first-time purchaser, but with those moving house, when environmental considerations dominate and financial considerations drop into a very poor second place. In most estate agents' offices one will find property registers kept in strict price order and in all probability the applicants' register will be similarly kept and all too often do I suspect the negotiator's first question to a prospective purchaser is related to price, when in many cases this is only a secondary consideration. If the negotiator is to interview applicants intelligently and in a way that is going to create confidence he must understand both in general and local terms what motivates the majority of would-be purchasers.

Let us look again at why people buy houses and as financial motivation seems to be predominant in this sector let us look at that first.

We have seen in considering housing in Britain in the general sense, and in particular the decline in the private rented sector, that all but a few have available to them a straight choice between home-ownership on the one hand and on the other homes rented from local authorities, housing associations, their employers and so on. For the great majority of these the choice is even more straightforward. You buy or you rent from the local authority and accept all the restraints that come with the rent-book. Many would reject the latter out of hand and elect to struggle on in temporary and probably unsatisfactory rented accommodation until they could afford to purchase.

Many see no alternative to house purchase. Those who have grown up in families that have owned their homes are unlikely to consider, notwithstanding the financial difficulties home-ownership will bring, any alternative, believing in particular that their status would be adversely affected. As we have seen status is a significant motivator. I digress, for we are considering the financial reasons for house-purchase.

Before doing so it is worth stressing the obvious, that no one house purchaser will ever be motivated by one factor only, but by a combination of several. The good negotiator in interviewing a prospective purchaser will be seeking to identify all those factors that are motivating him, and to get them into the right order of priority.

We shall consider elsewhere the operation of the building societies, the financing of house-purchase, the tax relief that is available on mortgage interest on loans of up to £25,000, and here we need only comment that though the ready availability of mortgage money in average market conditions and the tax concessions available are clearly motivating factors in house-purchase, there are others.

There is still a widely held belief that to pay rent is "money down the drain". One has been involved in many discussions on the advantages and disadvantages of home-ownership and although I have often heard comparisons made between the level of mortgage repayments on the one hand and the rent that would be payable on the other, I have seldom heard anybody take into account the interest that could be earned from the capital invested in the house, perhaps because for the majority of first-time buyers, the amount of capital "put down" is relatively small. There is probably another reason, for "investment" is clearly one of the financial motives for house-purchase and it may be that the majority see the capital initially invested as something totally apart from the monthly mortgage-repayment-versus-rent argument.

Investment is the principal underlying financial motive, for the belief, albeit sometimes unfounded, that property never loses its value is widely held, and the advantages of investing in one's own home have been sharply underlined over the last fifty years, and over the last few years in particular, by inflation. Care for one's family and security are undoubtedly closely linked with the investment motive.

Of the social and emotional motives pride of ownership is clearly one, though it must be clearly linked with others, and in particular security. Pride of ownership does not apply only in the house market, nor in the house market does it apply to one sector more than another. The young couple buying their first house, or for that matter their first new Ford Fiesta, are likely to be no less proud than the successful tycoon buying his first mansion or his first Rolls Royce. It is a significant factor for the negotiator, for dealing with his prospective purchaser, he will want to try to form a view as to what would give that purchaser the greatest sense of pride. If he can build up a picture of the would-be purchaser's likes and dislikes, his hobbies, his life-style and his ambitions, he is going to increase his chances of directing that purchaser to the house that he would be proud to own.

Going back to the view of house-purchase as an investment, it is doubtless looked upon not as a single investment transaction but as an on-going one, and not just in the financial sense. As mortgage repayments and inflation increase the owner's equity in his house, he will get a sense of achievement and satisfaction in the thought that his original investment has paid off and is continuing to do so. I believe that the majority of home-owners also see their houses as an investment in another sense, an investment they themselves can improve, whether by way of adding a new porch, double glazing, building a rockery or even putting in a swimming pool. It is an investment which they can add to and derive even more pleasure from, and at the end of the day have something significantly better than they originally purchased.

A tenant could, or course, carry out improvements and derive pleasure from them, but the sense of investment is not likely to be there.

House-ownership carries with it responsibilities, and in particular that for maintenance. The tenant may indeed have similar responsibilities in this direction, but he is not likely to find carrying out his obligations so rewarding. Many home-owners derive positive enjoyment from house maintenance and improvement, and from gardening, and this enjoyment of recreational pleasure and comfort is enhanced by the underlying sense of ownership.

There is, I suggest, for many a close relationship between home-ownership and family life, a relationship that, regrettably, can be bad as well as good. Many marriages break down in the early years either indirectly or mainly as a result of the pressures put upon them by the financial commitment involved in endeavouring to own one's own home, often, for example, preventing the start of a family or forcing the wife out to work. It is a sad reflection on society's inability to deal adequately with the housing problem.

On the positive side many a young husband will see house-purchase as the most important step he can take to secure his marriage and to provide a base for his future family which they in later years will identify as "home", and from which they will also derive a sense of security.

Freedom and independence also play their part in the motives for house-purchase — freedom to decorate, and to alter but more than this it is freedom in the sense of not having a landlord who could interfere or to whom one would feel a sense of responsibility, the building society being too far removed to create a feeling of restraint. "It is not so much that we will do things to the house, but it is the feeling that we can if we want to".

It is also freedom to move. The investment in the house can be realised and the proceeds invested elsewhere. It is freedom to move jobs, it is freedom to move up market, freedom on retirement to choose whether or not to sell, invest in something smaller and free some capital. This could be very closely related to "quality and choice of environment". Given that in most cases there will be some financial restraint, the house purchaser is free to choose the home which in his opinion would best suit his family's style of living, and be most convenient in regard to closeness to shops, schools, public transport and so on.

The last of the reasons Surrey University give us as to why people buy, is "part of an on-going plan". This again relates to investment, but in a sense that will not apply to all those who purchase. Many buying their first house, with limited job prospects or little ambition to climb up the social ladder, will remain there for the rest of their lives. Some will see it as the family home until the children have gone, when they will be free to sell, buy a bungalow by the sea and retire. Even this prospect could be seen as an on-going plan.

But many will have prospects. They may be in jobs where they can expect or hope for promotion, or in businesses which they hope will prosper. Some will anticipate inheritance. They are likely to see their first purchase, and possibly their second and third, as just steps up the ladder, looking forward to a further move in a few years' time. A negotiator identifying a purchaser in this category will realise that ambition, and know that as a consequence capital gain is the factor most likely to motivate him. He might not be so concerned about the environment a particular locality would provide if it could be demonstrated to him that it was a locality that was improving and that over the next few years values were likely to increase at a rate significantly above the average.

In his dealings with would-be purchasers the negotiator must also concern himself with the question of why people move. It will be recalled that a common criticism of estate agents referred to their sometimes sending applicants particulars of houses that in no way met their requirements as stated, and indeed sending purchasers to houses that were totally unsuitable. If an improvement is to be made it must start with the initial interview between the negotiator and the prospective purchaser. The reasons for the proposed move must be elucidated, and reflected in all communications. It may be that what a particular purchaser is setting out to achieve is, or is likely to prove, unobtainable within the price restraint given.

The bad negotiator faced with this problem might accept this fact, get rid of the applicant as quickly as reasonable decency permitted, and do little more. The good negotiator, with time and patience may identify not only the would-be purchaser's principal motive for wanting to move, but other motives related to it, and be able to lead that purchaser to a section of his market place where some if not all of the desires will be in whole or in part satisfied. It is here that the good negotiator's skills are of greatest advantage to him and here, given that most purchasers accept a degree of compromise, that the less obvious sales are made or lost. Negotiators must not only be aware of what motivates people to move house, they must also develop interviewing skills that will enable them to find the right compromise.

Among reasons why people move one may be a change of job that dictates a move to another town, but the family may well want to achieve other objectives at the same time. The Department of Psychology at Surrey researched the matter, but many of the reasons they identified will be familiar to the average estate agent or negotiator and we need not consider them in depth. I think it sufficient for our purpose simply to identify the principal reasons.

First, what might be called environmental reasons, which the Department broke down into four main sub-groups. Of these the first concerned the house itself, the need for additional accommodation, the wish for a house that was easier to run, an entertaining commitment leading to the need for a separate dining room, more parking space, another bathroom, a playroom, a larger garden and so on. The negotiator's task will be to establish just how specific the requirement is. (We recall the problem of the would-be purchaser who would "prefer" as opposed to "must have".) The need for a larger house may conceal the fact that the purchaser is seeking to achieve something else at the same time, a move from an estate of largely similar houses to a house with more character, one that he feels will better express his own character and standing, or the wish to move to a locality where there will be more people "like us". The underlying reason for wanting to move may well be one that they find difficult to put into words.

Some may be forced to consider a move for reasons the Department put under the heading of "environmental nuisance" — increased traffic noise, adjoining development, change in the character of a locality. One can readily think of areas on the outskirts of our towns which twenty years ago could have been described as rural or semi-rural but have been submerged in the urban sprawl and areas that have changed because the balance between privately owned housing and local authority housing has changed. Those wishing to move for this sort of reason might find it hard to explain to a young stranger in an estate agent's office just what it is they are trying to move away from and therefore just what it is they are trying to find. It is the negotiator's task to try and establish the aim and satisfy it.

"Location" was the Department of Psychology's third heading and one can think of many reasons why local circumstances should prompt a move. It might be that increased rail fares dictate a move nearer to the place of work. It might be the need to get close to a particular school. It might be that age and immobility demand a move nearer to shops, or children growing up and needing access to public transport. Some of the requirements that fall into this group are specific and a would-be purchaser will not appreciate being sent particulars about, or being sent to look at, houses which do not meet their requirements which they saw as having been clearly defined.

Very close to location is the fourth of the Department's sub-headings — Area. "People also indicate that they move in order to live in a more attractive area" they say. This could be a move from an urban to a rural setting, from an inland situation to the coast. The majority of purchasers wishing to move want to achieve a change in their environment and it follows that they want to leave the environment they are in. Consequently, if the negotiator is fully to understand their motivation it will help to know what it is they want to move away from. The type of house they are presently living in, the sort of area in which it is located, the problems currently faced in getting to and from work, and getting children to school are matters which will provide clues to the negotiator. We earlier noted that of the reasons given for moving financial reasons represented a relatively small percentage; perhaps the majority see financial circumstances not as the reason for moving, but as the means to make it possible. They may have felt their present house to be too small, the changes in their locality unacceptable, or the immediate area too urban and oppressive, and have been unable to contemplate a change. The Department found that "economic reasons for moving seem chiefly to be concerned with up-grading". Increased earnings, the ability perhaps to take an increased mortgage and still obtain tax relief, or an inheritance could all make what was little more than a hope, a practical reality. Given that the first-time purchaser is aged 25 to 30 and retires at 65 and lives a further 10 or 12 years, if one has regard to the frequency at which the average house changes hands, it is understandable that the majority of moves that are financially motivated are "upwards". Yet one senses that in the late 'seventies there was a significant increase in the number wanting to move to retrench, to reduce outgoings, to lose a large garden, to need to run only one car, to reduce heating bills and so on. The sort of change to which the negotiator must be sensitive.

Those moving down market for financial reasons present a problem needing careful handling by the negotiator. Nobody lightly gives up status, or admits financial "cramp" to a stranger and however logical the reasons for moving this type of purchaser may want to conceal them. The negotiator, if his approach to the problem is to be sensitive and ultimately effective, must assess the situation.

There are also those who wish or have to move, for purely personal reasons. Perhaps a widowed mother or aged parents whom they want to house, perhaps illness has caused a need for living on a single floor, perhaps old age or arthritis has made the garden impossible to cope with, perhaps the parents wish to live nearer grown up children, or to re-settle following divorce or bereavement.

The fourth group of reasons for moving identified by the Department came under the heading of "Social", those that "have to do with social and recreational activities and status" — "the 'keeping up with Joneses' syndrome". They broke this group down further into

(i)   The social comparison process

    (ii) The social composition of the neighbourhood, that may be unconducive and

    (iii) Privacy

As a practising estate agent I stop short of isolating the social reasons for moving from the others considered, environmental, financial and personal. In my experience social considerations underlie the others and underlie nearly all movement in the house-market. Mankind is not so far removed from the herd instinct. People are happier amongst those with whom they share common interests, common standards, similar levels of income and similar interests. They want to live where they are likely to be happiest and in making their choice no one single factor of those we have been considering will in itself be decisive, it will be a combination of two or more.

In considering the marketing of houses we emphasised the importance of the initial inspection of the house and the nature of the instructions one obtained from the vendor. At the opposite end of the spectrum is the prospective purchaser, sitting at a negotiator's desk for the first time. The quality of service that purchaser is given and whether or not he ultimately buys a house from that firm will depend on that negotiator's ability to extract in a very short time the information he needs, his ability accurately to assess that purchaser's requirements and how they are most likely to be met, and either then or subsequently find the compromise in a specific house. In the marketing process those minutes are vital.

In concluding its report on why people move and buy houses the Department dealt with the "forced move". Apart from those who want to retrench, there are those who have to; there are husbands who recognise the need to and wives who do not. There are the widowed and divorced faced with having to accept a very different style of living. There are those having to move at the dictate of their employment, perhaps from one of the lower priced areas of the country to one of the highest priced and who are reluctant to accept that the same money will buy only a very inferior house.

Their approach to house-hunting is likely to be very different, reticent, unco-operative and critical. The negotiator will need great patience. I well remember a learned judge who retired from service overseas, looking for a house. He insisted on dealing with the then senior partner who, after countless meetings, and after the judge and his wife had inspected over 100 houses and nearly two and a half years later, struck him from the applicants' register. Six weeks later the judge bought a house — from our rivals across the road. It was a test of endurance — our patience on the one hand, the judge's determination on the other to get just what he wanted, despite his mounting hotel bill. We lost our patience and the sale.

The Status of a Purchaser

When considering the applicants' register and organisation within the office we differentiated between those prospective purchasers or "applicants" who were "hot" — the probables as opposed to the possibles. If the negotiator is, with reasonable accuracy, to differentiate between the two, he has got to establish the status of the applicant as a prospective purchaser. This is not necessarily a once and for all task. It is one that can be tackled at the initial interview, but one must never forget that the status of an applicant can change at any time from somebody who might be interested to somebody who has a very real need, and must buy, and conversely from one who is in a position to buy, "because he has sold his own house", to one who might possibly be interested, but can no longer actually buy, because his sale has fallen through.

What does one mean by status? When considering an applicant we are not so much concerned here with motives in buying or trying to buy, or with what he states to be his requirements. We are concerned with his ability to purchase. We are concerned with the time-span in which he is likely to be able to purchase; the urgency of his need, whether or not he has a house to sell elsewhere, if he has, what his plans are, whether he must sell before he purchases, or is prepared and able to put up bridging finance.

I have avoided until now giving advice as to how interviews should be conducted and I have done so deliberately, not to avoid giving away trade secrets, but because there are a number of different approaches, which, dependant on the personality of the negotiator, could be equally successful. I think it important to avoid, certainly early in the interview, any direct question related to status, such as "Will it be a cash purchase?" One must avoid making the applicant feel that he is being "sized up".

The Estate Agent as Salesman

Cliff W. Krueger, in his book "Successful Real Estate Selling" published in 1960, in his very opening paragraph stated that "The public wants to be sold", and he defines selling as "Sharing and reinforcing the enthusiasm of the prospect". This is not far removed from what I have said about the agent's role in helping a purchaser reach a compromise, although, as one might expect, from someone who had only practised in the United States, it was more purchaser than vendor-biased.

Mr Krueger went on to give four definitions of selling, which he believed applied specifically to real estate work.

First, he said, "Selling is timing" and "No real estate sale moves of its own accord, it is moved by the diligence and perseverence of the broker. Buyers and sellers left to themselves would, and do, flounder indefinitely without reaching a definite conclusion". Perhaps here he has hit upon one of the reasons why the great majority of those wishing to dispose of real estate do seek the assistance of an agent.

Developing his point that a real estate salesman needs a good sense of timing if he is to take the sale to a satisfactory conclusion, Krueger says he must know when the vendor is ready to sell and the purchaser to buy. People, he says, will buy at one time, but weeks or days or even hours later they will not. He stressed that failure to buy at the right moment could be for the purchaser to miss a great opportunity, and similarly, for the vendor who fails to sell, the loss of an opportunity that may not quickly recur or recur on the same terms. "The broker", he says, "with experience, understanding of human nature and a sense of timing, is able to discern those moments and instances when a sale can be made and at that time he pushes doubly hard to accomplish it". His second definition is that "selling is planning" and "all successful business executives regardless of their line of endeavour, find that they can accomplish much more by carefully planning their time. All successful salesmen find that they can sell much more effectively by planning the sale carefully from start to finish".

Under this heading he says much that would be equally applicable to a sale of real estate in this country and we will deal with it when we come to consider responsibilities, motivation, the planning of negotiators' time and other aspects of the estate agent in operation.

Mr Krueger's third definition is "Selling is telling the truth attractively" and there are one or two comments he makes under this heading that estate agents here might well consider carefully.

"Not only our statements and representations but our own personality and presentation must bear the stamp of truth throughout. The slightest action or word which loses for us the prospect's confidence may ultimately lose the sale".

He then relates the importance of being truthful directly to the real estate market, in a way that many of the critics of estate agents in this country would appreciate:

"Being truthful is a pretty challenging ideal in a business which historically has been characterised by misrepresentation, 'stretching' the fact, half-truths and the little white lie. The modern salesman must adhere to a standard of truth which may be far above that of his predecessors or even of his current competitors. In a business as vital and all-encompassing as real estate, telling the truth is essential".

"Exaggeration is the foe of truth. Exaggeration may be lying. Exaggeration destroys confidence. Exaggeration splits the buyer and the salesman".

The last of his definitions is perhaps more nebulous, "Selling is walking down a path of agreement". The points he tries to make under this heading are to me far from clear, but basically they are to the effect that "the sale begins and ends with a yes. The only thing that disrupts or interrupts it is a no".

Both the American "Real Estate Salesman's Handbook" and "Real Estate Practice in Australia" quote Sheldon's Sales formula: Attention — interest — desire — action. (A.I.D.A). It is said that every sale, however instantaneous it may appear, or however long drawn-out, will go through these four steps. The estate agents' task can be related to them. What has been said about one's public image, the office, the window and advertising could have come under the heading of drawing "attention". One's particulars are clearly intended to "interest". The four stages should be borne in mind as we now consider the estate agent as a salesman and interviewing a new applicant.

The applicant's reaction to an interview could be to think that if he gives the right answers interest will be taken, if he does not that the notes the negotiator is taking will go into the waste-paper basket. He will be tempted to give the answers the negotiator wants to hear, and he may not tell the truth; either way some confidence will be lost, because he will know he has been put in a position where he felt it necessary to mislead, or because he believed that the true picture would have caused the negotiator himself to lose interest.

Often the interview will not be entirely in the hands of the negotiator. The purchaser who really knows what he wants will set out to dictate the form the interview will take and it will be the negotiator's task tactfully to regain control and then to adhere as closely as he can to what should be a pre-set, but flexible, interviewing formula. My own personal comments are these:

Initially one must adopt an approach that indicates a belief that that purchaser is in every respect genuine and give him an opportunity of saying what he is seeking, avoiding until it is absolutely necessary to introduce the subject — price, commenting generally about the availability of property in the area, about the area in general, and about price levels, trying to establish what style of house would be of interest; what family the applicant has, what ages the children are, what his interests are. The reason for moving may be volunteered, if it is not, then a question as to the timing of a possible move, might well give useful information. The applicant may volunteer that he is not retiring until the spring, or that the need is urgent, because he takes up his new appointment on 1st September.

Whilst much of Mr Krueger has to say is of interest, it needs to be approached with caution by the British estate agent, for throughout his book he not only sees the estate agent as a broker but specifically refers to him as such: "The broker is essentially a middle man between the parties". It cannot be too strongly stressed that this is not a view shared by the leading professional bodies here, nor does it accurately describe the estate agent's position under the law. It is this erroneous view that has led to much unjustified criticism, and those practising estate agency in Britain should take every possible opportunity to stress to the public that they are agents for one of the parties only; normally the vendor, but occasionally, if retained and paid by the purchaser, as agent for him.

There comes a moment when the negotiator, trying to obtain as much information as he can without asking questions that could appear too personal or inquisitive, feels that he must get something more concrete as to the background from which the applicant is wishing to move. In these circumstances to delay asking for the applicant's address until fairly late in the interview can be helpful. Having been given the address, the question "Have you put your house there on the market yet?" would come more naturally than would "Is your own house on the market?", asked out of the blue.

Perhaps I am being too precise, but I suggest that to ask "How do prices there compare with those being asked here for the same sort of house?" could lead easily into a general discussion of the steps the applicant has taken, or is intending to take, to sell his present home, and this could give one the opportunity to make an introduction if one is a member of one of the two national link-ups, to an associated firm, or it could elicit the name of the agent who has been instructed, giving the opportunity subsequently to check out on asking price and saleability.

The negotiator's time is not always limitless, but help and advice on matters not directly related to the possible new house itself will show a genuine interest and instil confidence — schools, hobbies, local amenities are all suitable subjects. However desirable it may be to assess the status of an applicant at the first interview, the matter must never be pressed. It is clearly helpful to do so at the earliest possible stage, but it only becomes of great importance and possibly imperative when that purchaser is interested in a specific house and having given him all the help you can, your task becomes that of protecting the interests of your vendor-client.

The interviewing of an applicant should not be regarded as concluded when the first meeting ends — it should be a continuing process. All too often today one finds negotiators reluctant to accompany applicants when they go to view houses, unless they have to. The habit of "accompanying" seems surprisingly to have lost its attraction to some negotiators but I regard it as absolutely vital and something a negotiator should seek to do whenever he has the opportunity, or whenever he can persuade the applicant that it would be helpful. The applicant's reactions to the locality, and individual houses can give very valuable information to the negotiator, who in his turn, from his knowledge of the area and recent transactions, could do much to establish in the applicant's mind where he wants to live, what type of house he wants and in what area he can afford to purchase. I accept that many applicants prefer to find their own way, to look at the outside of houses first, but this all too often means their going to see other agents on the way. Where one's efforts to accompany have failed, or when it has been impossible to do so, that applicant should be contacted again as quickly as possible and his reactions obtained. If information as to other houses that might be of interest, or which have just come on to the market could be given on that occasion, so much the better.

The negotiator's task is to interview, accompany, and maintain contact, but too often one senses that the first is too hurried, the second not pressed or possibly even avoided, and the last left to the circulating system.

As I said in the context of the applicants' register, that register is necessary because it will, under normal market circumstances, prove impossible to maintain physical or verbal contact with every applicant. It is the role of the register to keep contact in the hope that the applicant will himself contact the firm or the individual negotiator. When the applicant is in the office, that contact has been made, and every opportunity must be taken of it. But not every applicant, of course, makes first contact by calling at the office. Some do it by telephone or by post and one's ability to respond is much more limited. The quality of the response is, however, important, and the content of the letter that accompanies any particulars sent needs carefully considering. If, as often will be the case, the particulars sent include those of houses that do not meet that applicant's requirements closely, this should be acknowledged, possibly by drawing attention to those that do and saying that the others have been included to give a more general picture of the market in the area. Anything that can be said that will indicate, and this is not impossible in standard letter form, that a personal interest has been taken will be of help.

Stages in Selling

If the negotiator knows he has only three houses that are really likely to be of interest and another seven that could be said in one way or another to meet the purchaser's requirements, he has two courses open to him. He could say "I have only three houses that would suit you" and present the particulars. The purchaser's reaction is likely to be one of disappointment. In his disappointment that he has so little to choose from, he is likely to see reasons to reject the three and to leave that negotiator's office as quickly as possible to call on the agents across the road. On the other hand that negotiator could first present the particulars that are the least likely to interest, qualifying them perhaps as he does so: "This house has the large garden you want, but I think your wife would find it too far from the shops". Presenting this wider selection of houses, he can help direct the purchaser's interest to the three real possibilities. That purchaser, if attracted by these, will feel that he himself has made progress in narrowing his field of choice. He will wish to see the houses that he himself has identified. When he says: "I would like to see these three, would it be possible this afternoon?" he has taken the first decision in the selection process.

It is at this point that the negotiator can make the appointments and let the prospective purchaser go on his way, or he can decide to try and accompany himself, or if that is not possible, get one of his colleagues to do so. If he accompanies or not, he may influence the order in which the houses are seen. This could further help in narrowing down interest. Where in the viewing order should he put the house which he believes is likely to prove to be of the most interest? First or last, or where I believe it would have psychologically the most impact — in the middle? If the purchaser has seen two or three houses that fall short of his requirements and rejected them, when he sees the one that does not, he will feel a sense of relief: "I could live here". This could be underlined if he goes on to see one or two more that again fall short.

In viewing houses and before reaching the point of desiring, the purchaser has got to go through the process of selection, reacting to each house that he sees, of deciding what features he likes and what he does not, how one compares with another. There may be questions that he would like to ask on the spot. It is here that the negotiator who does not accompany loses a vital opportunity — an opportunity to observe reactions, to draw attention to particular features of the house or to the attractions of the area, an opportunity on the way to point out other houses and to comment on values, all this aimed at narrowing down interest to the point where one house in particular is desired. The negotiator who is with the purchaser at that time will be able to assess just how strong that desire is. If he is not with him and that purchaser calls later in the day, or the following morning, to open negotiations, that purchaser will have had time to consider how to start the negotiations. However strong the desire to purchase a particular house, it may be concealed.

The real estate salesman in America takes the selling process to the point where the purchaser signs a contract, albeit in some circumstances conditional. The negotiator in this country is seldom in this position. He can only take a sale to the point where the parties agree "subject to contract" that one will sell and one will buy. The lawyers will have their work to do and many difficulties could arise and have to be dealt with before that sale could be "closed". The adverse survey report, the failure to get a mortgage of the amount required, the vendor finding that the house he hoped to buy has been sold elsewhere, an increase in interest rates, the illness of one of the parties — the list is endless. The negotiator, having agreed a sale subject to contract, cannot possibly be said to have closed it. He may have completed the desire stage of the selling process, but the closing stage is too often left to somebody else, the vendor's solicitor, who may or may not tell the negotiator or enlist his help if anything goes wrong and further negotiating is required. The negotiator who does not accompany his purchaser could have been said to be out of touch during a vital part of the selling process, and so is the negotiator who, having instructed solicitors, leaves the matter there.

He will be out of touch at the most critical phase of the process — a long cooling off period, when unforeseen difficulties can occur, and when either party could have second thoughts. The good negotiator will not let this happen, but will, as unobtrusively as possible, for constant questioning could be seen as harassment and in itself give rise to doubts, try to keep in touch with the parties.

The average house sale is for the ordinary man in the street the largest single transaction of his life. Few, except those with very limited resources and limited borrowing powers and therefore very little choice, are likely to approach house purchase as they would the purchase of a car. They will constantly be balancing the factors we earlier considered, and the selection process will be very personal. It may be that the American real estate salesman, having gone down the path and reached the point where he believes his "prospect" is ready to take action may successfully be able to use some pressure to bring that action about. There will be occasions when his opposite number here will be able to do likewise and when it may be in the interests of the purchaser that he does so, but he will not have a contract in his hand. If he has used too much pressure, if he has convinced the purchaser that he desires a house that falls well short of what he was seeking, that purchaser will have ample time to reflect on his decision and withdraw. Further if that purchaser feels he was pushed too hard, he may avoid that negotiator when seeking a better answer.

I have found no definition of "hard selling." I assume it to mean aggressive, forceful and pushing, selling that is effected over a very short period, during which pressure is maintained at a high level to bring about a deal that when closed cannot be avoided. But the residential negotiator needs understanding, knowledge, a willingness to help, and patience, to bring about not a deal but but an agreement between two parties, an agreement that each will want to honour. We recall Mr. Krueger's apt description of real estate selling as "walking down the path of agreement." If the estate agent's task has to be either "hard" or "soft" selling, then it has to be the latter.

There may be some significance in the fact that in both North America and Australia those who sell real property are known as salesmen, or sales persons, but here as negotiators. It is perhaps indicative of the different ways in which the markets operate. Contrary, in fact, to practice. "Salesman" would more aptly describe the agent who is instructed to sell for his principal — the British agent's role, and "negotiator" more accurately the role of the broker.

One is tempted to lay down golden rules, to say what is the right approach and what the wrong, This is impossible — much will depend on personalities. One negotiator may be able to use an approach which for another would be disastrous. Each negotiator will develop his own approach to his task and his own techniques, adapting and improving those with which he succeeds, and abandoning those which he can identify as having led to failure.

Further thoughts on selling

The role of the vendor in the selling process should not be forgotten, for it is not only the negotiator who wants to effect a sale, the vendor wants to sell and can help in the process. Every second-hand car salesman will ensure that cars he has to sell look as near new as they possibly can, he will not leave his overalls, newspapers, cigarette packets, etc., on the seats, but all too often vendors do not consider presenting their own houses in the best possible light. Tidiness gives a sense of space. Doors left open can give a sense of space and make a landing or passage-way pleasant, but when shut cause a sense of crampedness, darkness and claustrophobia. Cooking smells can detract from the impression, a neglected garden will look twice as hard to maintain as one that is neat and tidy. The over-talkative vendor might distract the would-be purchaser, who could leave without appreciating some features of the house that might have been important to him in his selection process. The would-be purchaser approaching a house and entering it for the first time will feel either attracted, indifferent or repelled. Everything must be done to attract. Many purchasers will feel inhibited by the very presence of the vendor and his family. The negotiator will often need considerable tact if the house is to be presented in the best possible light. If he himself is showing the purchasers round, he can emphasise particular points. The house might look particularly attractive from one corner of the garden. There may be a view from the main bedroom but not from the living room, or the living room itself may be the most attractive feature of the house. If he can halt at such places to discuss other aspects of the house he will attract attention to those features.

However desirable it is that a negotiator should accompany prospective purchasers, it must not be forgotten that for the married couple and for the family, the choice of home is a very personal matter. As they go round a house they will be trying to relate to it as individuals, as a couple or a family. They may say a great deal and give rise to false hope for the negotiator; They may say nothing; they may be reticent, embarrassed at being in somebody else's home and want the negotiator to take the lead, to protect them, while they invade somebody else's privacy. Others will feel thoroughly irritated if the negotiator intrudes. If the house is of interest, they may want to relate to it quietly together; the negotiator must step back, engage himself in conversation with the vendor or somehow make himself unobtrusive. The good negotiator will know how to react and when; the bad one will not.

We commented on knowledge of the property as being one of the factors necessary to the negotiator and discussed how it could be communicated in the office. The negotiator showing a prospective purchaser round a house he has not seen is, whatever he may have been told, at a distinct disadvantage. He cannot draw attention to particular features. If he is asked questions, he may not be able to answer and confidence will be lost. In many a large office this is a problem. It will be one of the tasks of the person responsible for marketing to ensure that as many of the negotiators as possible do have an opportunity of inspecting. I am told that in the States the realtor who listed a property will often organise an open day, a day when all other realtors who are members of the Board offering that property for sale, have an opportunity to see it. No negotiator here should be satisfied if he has not himself seen every house he is expected to offer. Accepting that it may not always be possible to achieve this, it is an objective that should never be lost sight of.

From receipt of offer to completion

At the stage when an offer has been made, if it has not been done earlier, the relationship between vendor and agent should be explained to the prospective purchaser. We now deal with the negotiator's reaction to the receipt of an offer and I put the matters that he should then consider, in no particular order.

The amount of the offer — how does it relate to asking price, the vendor's known wishes, the vendor's circumstances and as to value? We realise the importance of avoiding if possible a rejection or negative answer, but at the same time the vendor's interests must be protected. The approach of individual negotiators could differ and yet be equally effective. Much will depend on market conditions. A purchaser offering a price close to that asked should in a buoyant market be warned of the danger of somebody offering the asking price. An offer below the asking price but at a level which the negotiator recognises as being at or close to real value should be more sympathetically received than one which the negotiator knows he will recommend the vendor to refuse. He must not at this stage run the risk of deterring a purchaser clearly willing to pay a price which in his opinion the vendor should consider seriously.

If the offer is one which he knows he cannot recommend the vendor to accept, the negotiator should acknowledge it graciously, but leave the would-be purchaser in no doubt as to his expert opinion. He may be sufficiently aware of the vendor's views, circumstances and reasons for sale to feel that he could express that vendor's opinion, but if he is in any doubt great care needs to be taken.

The negotiator must then seek to establish the strength of that offer. Is it subject to survey? Is a mortgage required? Has the purchaser already arranged his mortgage? If he has, is the house likely to stand up to valuation and survey? If he has not, the same question arises, but also does the purchaser's borrowing "status" match up to the amount he will need? Has the purchaser sold his own house; if not, has he arranged bridging finance? When does he want possession and how does this fit into the vendor's plans?

The extent to which the negotiator should go into these matters could depend on the amount of the offer. If the offer is clearly too low, and one the vendor is unlikely to accept, the negotiator might weaken his position if he asks searching questions. The more he can establish about the purchaser and the strength of the offer, the better, but only the negotiator at that moment can assess how searching his questions may be if he is not to weaken his position as the vendor's agent.

The negotiator has one more task, he has got to form an opinion as to where the offer stands in the mind of the would-be purchaser. Is it a "try on"? Is it a genuine attempt to negotiate, however far below the asking price? Has the purchaser stretched himself to the limit in making it? Is it an offer close to the asking price for a purchaser near to his limit with perhaps only a little room in which to move? The negotiator cannot consider that offer in isolation. He has got to relate it to his market place, to how long a house has been on the market, the way prices are moving, the number of people who have viewed it, the likelihood of another offer being forthcoming. If the offer is subject to survey and he knows the report will make bad reading, he could sound out that purchaser as to what he expects the survey to reveal. "It is an old house and it is bound to have many of the problems that old houses do suffer from, are you prepared for a result that will reflect this and have you allowed anything for the costs of putting right defects?"

This underlines the need for the negotiator to have seen the house for this type of question could not be asked without knowledge.

Having thus done what he can to assess the strength of the offer he has received, the negotiator must submit it to the vendor as quickly as possible and give that vendor as much of the information he has obtained as he thinks relevant, and he should advise. Is the offer a fair one but likely to be bettered if refused, either by that purchaser, or another? Is the offer so good and apparently so sound that the vendor should accept it without hesitation? Is it one that should be refused without qualification or one that should be refused with a counter-offer being made? Is the offer subject to conditions, what are they and how should they affect the vendor's response?

At this stage the vendor and his agent may be *ad idem,* but it may be that there are three conflicting views — what the vendor wants, what the negotiator, knowing the house and the market, believes to be in the vendor's best interests, and what the purchaser is trying to achieve. There is only one golden rule, and it is in this context that the description given to the real estate salesman here in Britain of "negotiator" is relevant, he has got to keep open lines of communicaton unless he is absolutely satisfied that there is no hope of reaching an agreement that he can advise his client to accept.

Gazumping

When the vendor is minded to accept an offer and enter into an agreement subject to contract the negotiator has another task — that of assessing the vendor's attitude to that agreement. He will have already done all he can to assess that of the purchaser. Vendors in a fiduciary capacity, trustees, mortgagees in possession, the Court of Protection may be bound to consider any higher offer that might subsequently be received, but others may feel that they would like to be able to do so, or simply that they would do so. It is from this point that so much of the ill-feeling and criticism summed up in the word "gazumping" arises. The moral position in my opinion is clear, if the vendor and his agent have no reason to doubt the sincerity of the purchaser, that purchaser is entitled to a reasonable period in which to "vet" his purchase and honour his word, but this is not the law. The agent cannot be certain that he has been told the truth by the purchaser, and indeed the purchaser himself may have earlier been misled. The agent cannot dictate to the vendor, but he does have a clear duty to both; that of minimising the risk of serious misunderstanding. If, for example, he has reason to doubt the purchaser's ability or will to proceed, he should advise the vendor not to withdraw the house from the market and the purchaser should be told that the house will continue to be offered until such time as contracts are exchanged, or that the vendor reserves the right to consider any other offer that might be received because it is either higher or unqualified. If the vendor is one who must consider any higher offer, this must be explained to the purchaser at the time his offer is accepted.

In short the negotiator should do all he can to ensure that both parties understand the nature of the agreement between them, the conditions that attach to the offer and its acceptance, and any reservations made.

The public concern at "gazumping" is well known but the Law Commission's view as to why any change would be undesirable is not well known. The good negotiator can do a great deal, not necessarily to reduce the risk of gazumping or of the purchaser reneguing, but to make each party aware of the nature of the agreement between them and lessening the risk of bitterness if the agreement fails.

Until recently it was customary in most parts of the country for a deposit to be paid at this stage and 10 per cent of the agreed purchase price used to be the norm. Much significance was attributed by both parties to the deposit, the purchaser believing that it gave him some "hold" over the property and the vendor believing that it showed at least an earnestness on the part of the purchaser to proceed. The deposit was normally held by the agent as a stakeholder. Things have changed, deposits paid to the agent now tend to be less than 10 per cent, very often purely nominal sums, with the full deposit being payable, on exchange of contracts, to the vendor's solicitor. A change resented by some agents.

We have not considered accounting matters, but we should deal briefly with the holding of deposits. It was customary and still is sometimes the case that the agent holds a deposit as stakeholder. Whether in fact this is the true definition of his capacity prior to the exchange of contracts is open to doubt, but certainly on the exchange of contracts a stakeholder cannot release that deposit until the event against which it is held occurs and he has authority from both parties to release it.

This pattern has again changed and very often a deposit is held as agent for the vendor, in which case it can be released to that vendor. Under normal circumstances, where a deposit is paid subject to contract, the purchaser who withdraws has a right to reclaim it, although again some vendors, and in particular some developers, will have reserved the right to retain a proportion of it to cover abortive costs. It is sufficient to state that if a deposit is received by the agent, he must issue a receipt that makes it clear in what capacity he holds it, i.e., as stakeholder, or as agent for the vendor, and if it is a deposit payable prior to the exchange of contracts, that it is received and held by that agent "subject to contract".

Two or more Offers

The estate agent, having put a house on the market at a stated price, might receive more than one offer to purchase at the price asked, or, having received an offer at the price asked, and having told another interested prospective purchaser that such an offer has been received, may receive one yet higher. The importance, under these circumstances, of assessing the relative strength of each offer by the criteria we have already referred to is obvious and the advice given to the vendor will depend on that assessment. The agent or negotiator must remember that whatever his own views are, the decision as to the course he should follow is properly that of his vendor client. But the agent has to advise. Yet again there are no golden rules; for that advice and its quality must depend on the negotiator's ability to assess the strength of the would-be purchasers, not only in terms of their ability to proceed, but in the genuineness of their intent. The Royal Institution's "Practice Notes" says this on the subject:—

"It is recommended that the first to submit an offer is advised when another offer is received, and be given the opportunity to increase his offer. If he is willing to do this but is not prepared to increase his offer to the asking price, it should be explained to him that the other would-be purchaser will be invited to make a further offer, and that if this is greater or at the asking price it could be accepted.

"If it is clear to the agent that a private auction is developing, then it is recommended that the would-be purchasers be given a specific date and time in which to reconsider the matter and submit their highest and final offer. If the vendor wishes to impose any conditions upon his acceptance i.e., as to completion date, this should be made clear. It is also recommended that the would-be purchasers be informed that the successful bidder will be given a specific period in which to exchange contracts. When a higher offer is received after one has been accepted, the agent should inform the purchaser that an earlier offer has been accepted subject to contract. He should then, before taking any further action, report the higher offer to the vendor and seek his instructions.

"Unless there is any particular reason why the higher offer should not be accepted . . . then it is felt that the first to submit an offer should be given at least the opportunity of matching the higher offer.

"Although the practice of sending out two contracts is deprecated both by the Institution and the Law Society, it is a course that a vendor client might wish to adopt. Under these circumstances the agent can do no more than make the position clear to the would-be purchasers and do everything in his power to ensure that each is given a fair chance".

This quotation highlights one of the difficulties the agent faces in carrying out his task, for unlike the salesman who can "close" his deal, he is, when selling by private treaty, acting for his vendor client in a market place where agreements are reached to which neither party is bound, in which offers, i.e., to sell at a certain price, are not binding. This familiar situation begs an important question and one that is clearly of enormous public interest. Just what is the agent's role, not in legal terms, for that is clear, but in practice? Is he simply the agent for the vendor, or does he have some wider responsibility, as his critics would appear to assume? The public outcry at "guzumping" was aimed at the vendors and, it follows, at their agents. Nobody considered that the more insidious form of gazumping by purchasers in difficult market circumstances — the purchaser who, for example, having strung the vendor along, at the end of the day said "I can only proceed if you drop your price by £5,000."

The public clearly see a need for some sort of moral standard, albeit biased in favour of "the consumer". Where does the agent stand? His duties to his vendor client are clear. The purchaser has little protection by the law, but I suggest that the agent has another duty to which he must always have regard — his duty to himself as a professional man in the community. It is on the way he carries out this duty that his continued success will depend. He cannot dictate to either party in a transaction how they should behave, but he can influence. Although he has a clear responsibility to his principal, his general approach to all with whom he is involved can set the standard by which in the long term he and his firm will be judged.

We have been considering principally the "over-bid" — the situation where there are two bidders at the same price, or where one has bid the asking price and another has topped it — but what should the agent's or negotiator's reaction be, given that a price has been agreed between the parties, when the purchaser reduces the amount of his offer? There could be many reasons for this happening. It could be an adverse survey report; it could be that the building society has offered less than was asked for; it could be that the purchaser has come to believe that the price he bid is too high. If the reason is an adverse survey report, he should try to find out what defects it revealed, and again we must touch on knowledge, for he should be able to relate these to the house concerned and decide whether or not the comments are fair, whether or not the estimate of the costs of putting defects right is reasonably accurate; as to whether conclusions drawn are right. Unless the agent can do this he cannot give proper advice to the vendor. If the reason for a reduced offer is related to value and a building society offer based on a valuation figure less than the price agreed, he has got to decide whether or not the building society valuer was right and he can only do so in the context of the market place as he sees it.

If he advises the vendor to reject the reduced offer, will he be able in practice to find a buyer at a higher figure? He has got to consider the vendor's circumstances; to reject the reduced offer may well lose weeks that could be inconvenient to the vendor and possibly very costly. He will be influenced by the advice he has given the vendor. If the reduced offer is for a sum less than that which he told the vendor he could reasonably expect, he is in difficulties. If he advises acceptance there is the risk that the vendor would believe him to be seeking to effect a sale for his own benefit. The vendor having agreed a price will be reluctant to see it reduced. Advice to a vendor to accept a lower offer must be supported by carefully considered reasoning. The agent must beware, for having found somebody willing to buy that particular house, albeit at a price less than that originally offered, there will be a reluctance to abandon that purchaser, a temptation to abandon one's role as the vendor's agent and to act as a broker to bring about a "deal". The vendor's interests are paramount, his need for the agent's advice at this juncture is possibly greater than at any other time. That advice when given must be backed up with as much fact and considered opinion as possible.

The need for the agent to be involved and to keep in touch with the progress of the sale after its terms have been agreed and the solicitors instructed we discussed as part of the sales process. If all goes well the agent will have no need to take action, but if he has any reason to believe that the sale might founder, he must become involved, for it may be in the vendor's interests that that sale be abandoned, or if not abandoned that the property be re-offered in the open market in the hope of finding an alternative purchaser. In either case it will be necessary for the negotiator to involve the would-be purchaser, to explain his concern and to tell him of the action that is proposed, giving him every chance to honour his agreement.

Last we consider the agent's action on completion of the sale. We have considered the holding of deposits, although there are many areas in Britain where agents neither by custom hold deposits nor would seek to do so. Where a deposit is held, it is customary for the agent, when accounting to the vendor's solicitors, to deduct the commission and expenses due to him, but he has no right to do so unless this has been prior agreed. He should on exchange of contracts render an account, and if he so wishes then seek authority when releasing the deposit to retain what is due to him. Completion is, however, more than the receipt of a commission. It is the final stage in the sale's process. A property has changed hands and two parties were involved — the vendor who entrusted the sale to the agent and the purchaser that agent found. For both of them the event is significant. All too often does the agent take his commission without recognising those who were involved. A letter thanking the vendor for entrusting his business to you and a letter, card or even flowers welcoming the purchasers will identify the agent with the change that has taken place in their lives.

Nineteen

Marketing Functions — Responsibilities and Motivation

Allocation of responsibilities — Need for an objective — Relating the objective to the market — Possible criteria — The need for team work — Motivating the team — Targets in a fluctuating market, control of the marketing function, control of the product, sales effort, time and other resources — Responsibility for communications — Adjusting the aim — Staff training — Responsibility for training and motivation considered.

If the standard of real estate marketing in this country falls well below what could be achieved, and certainly from some of the criticisms we looked at earlier, it would seem that this could be the case, then it is to the partners, the directors and the managers of firms that we first look to bring about an improvement. If they themselves are not involved or concerned they cannot expect a salesman or negotiator to be. It is therefore vital that a partner, or partners and possibly selected other persons are given a specific responsibility for marketing or for certain aspects of the marketing function. It is their task that we shall look at first.

A clearly defined aim or objective must be stated, and it must be credible. Only when the aim has been established can the method of achieving it be considered in depth.

Earlier we looked at the thought processes two young men setting out in practice might go through in deciding just where to practise and in what sector of the market. The partner of an existing and possibly well established firm responsible for marketing should do a similar exercise and ask himself similar questions, such as the following:

What section of the market do I aim to cover comprehensively, am I achieving this, and of what further section could I have a greater share?

Do I really know my market place?

How many are there?

What price-ranges are they in?

In each area what is the average age of the inhabitants?

What is the average size of household?

(A successful man nearing retirement is probably living in one of the up-market areas in a house that is too large for him and his wife now the children have gone. He is a potential early vendor and possible purchaser of something smaller)

How do I reach him?

Can I safely assume that houses change hands in my area at about the national average of once every six to seven years, or is there any particular reason why I should assume that either over the whole area or in certain parts there is a higher or lower rate of change?

If I do this, how many houses change hands every year?

How many of those are sold privately?

If the research carried out by the Price Commission is correct it is about 30 per cent. Does that apply to my area?

How many does that mean are sold through agents?

What is the average price of a house in my area?

What does that represent by way of fee income at the average rate charged by us and our main competitors?

How many competitors have I got?

How many partners and negotiators have each of them got deployed on the residential sales side?

How many have I got?

How do our positions in the town compare?

If I accept my own estimate of the houses sold through the agents each year and the total commission income derived from these sales, accepting my estimate of the relative strengths of our own firm and the opposition, what is the fee income of these firms and mine?

How do these estimates of income compare with the relative weight of advertising expenditure? This I should be able to get at quickly.

How do we measure up even to our fair share of the agents' market? Are we below it? Or above it?

How much would it mean to my firm if I could increase my share of the market by 15 per cent?

Furthermore what, given the assumptions I have already made, is the potential income to be earned from the sales that are currently being achieved privately?

If I could attract even 10 per cent of that market, how much would that mean?

Would this be a realistic aim for me to set myself?

If it is — how am I going to achieve it, and how am I going to motivate the staff to help me do it?

I have clearly got to do more than simply give them an aim. They have got to believe in it and be enthusiastic about achieving it. Certainly I am going to have to be convinced if I am to get my partners' financial support.

It is impossible in a book of this nature to be specific as to the criteria against which a marketing aim should be set.

One could consider commission income and set a new target, but there is a danger here, for a 20 per cent increase in property values, assuming the firm concerned is charging on an *ad valorem* basis, could produce a 20 per cent increase in commission income without the firm necessarily attracting a higher number of instructions or effecting a larger number of transactions, and in all probability the increased income would be largely absorbed by increased expenditure. If one is to set a target related simply to commission income one would have at the outset to estimate and provide for an increase in property values before adding the percentage increase that represents one's aim.

It may be more realistic to set that aim against the number of transactions achieved during the preceding year. Given equal competence and efficiency, the number of sales likely to be achieved by one firm as opposed to another will relate in the main to the number of instructions received. It would therefore not be unrealistic to set an aim related to the number of instructions. The number of applicants on one's register is not so significant, and should be disregarded. To set a target in this direction could be a secondary aim and it will underline to all concerned in the office the importance of an attractive, colourful window display and the importance of making one's advertisements interesting, informative and inviting.

There are other aspects that ought to be considered. What percentage of the instructions received are converted into sales? This could be particularly relevant in a multiple agency area. Ways and means of attracting a larger number of sole agencies ought to be considered as one way of achieving one's aim.

It may be that in the past most of the firm's income and residential estate agency work has come from one section of the market, for firms, as we have commented earlier, do tend to identify with one sector of the market or miss out on one sector. In particular some of the larger firms have been identified especially with the middle and upper price ranges and have created themselves an image that has largely excluded them from the market in the cheaper ranges. If this is the case then in setting one's aim one should consider ways and means of attracting work that one has not previously enjoyed, and one would have to question whether this could be achieved without loss in one's customary market. It does not follow that there should be only one target set, one's aim might be to achieve progress in a number of directions, but care is needed to leave the aim absolutely clear. One thing is vital. Having set an aim it must be communicated to all who are to help achieve it. They have got to be motivated and made enthusiastic. We shall be considering remuneration of staff later, for financial incentive is clearly one way of motivating. Each individual in the sale force has to be encouraged but there is a possible snag here. To give each individual an aim and reward him individually could put negotiators in competition with each other, resulting in poorer team work, and be self-defeating. It is important in this context that back-up staff, secretaries, telephonists and receptionists are not forgotten. In one way or another they must benefit from the success of the team of which they form an essential part. In my opinion team-work, certainly in the residential market, is vital. One way that one might motivate a team is to set one's target and relate it to the number of negotiators. "To achieve this I estimate we will need to increase the number of instructions processed per negotiator from 100 to 110 and the number of transactions achieved per negotiator from 60 to 70"

We shall be considering questions concerning team-work amongst one's sales force in more detail later. For the moment one would stress that if a target has been set for the ensuing year and the team is to be kept enthusiastic throughout that period it will help if one can keep them constantly reminded of what they are trying to achieve. A graph readily available showing what was achieved in the preceding year, preferably month by month, in terms of instructions and sales negotiated, showing the target one is aiming at and setting out by the month what has been achieved towards it would be a help.

We have stressed the need for any aim to be credible if all concerned are to be motivated by it, but in considering market forces we saw that the market can vary greatly in response to factors over which the agent himself has no control. In boom times instructions will tend to fall away and in times of recession they will flood in, distorting the workload of the sales team, which will be forced to spend most of its time on taking instructions when in practice it is the sales effort that needs the time, the thought and the energy. Such fluctuation in market conditions will make nonsense of one's aims or targets. however carefully set, and could seriously affect the morale of the team. This does not remove the need for targets, but it does mean that those responsible for management must have other ways of ensuring that the team operates to the best possible effect. These we may for convenience give the heading, "Control of the marketing function", and we could break it down into:

    i) Control of the product.
    ii) Control of the sales effort.
    iii) Control of time.
    iv) Control of resources.

Some of these aspects of marketing have been considered under other headings but no harm will be done in referring to them again briefly, but specifically under the heading of "Control of the marketing function" and assuming adverse market conditions.

First control of the product. We earlier discussed the quality of the product in the context of taking instructions; under adverse market conditions the number of instructions one received could well absorb most of the team's time and result in a register too large to service adequately, and if one attempted to operate as one would in normal market conditions — preparing and illustrating particulars, circulating and advertising every one — it could result in costs vastly exceeding the budget. Close control would be needed if this were to be avoided and the maximum potential achieved from the register.

It would be the manager's responsibility to decide priorities — which instructions were to be fully serviced — where a reduced service only was possible and in extreme cases which instructions were to be declined. Several factors would bear on this decision, the state of the market, the type of house in demand, the number of houses of the same type already available, the intentions of the vendor (his flexibility as to price) being amongst them.

Control of the sales effort involves the control required of the sales team to ensure the right balance between service to vendors on the one hand and to purchasers on the other. The manager has the responsibility to direct the team in the servicing of both vendors and purchasers to provide the maximum possible sales potential; to dictate priorities; to co-ordinate the work of individuals within the team; and maintain enthusiasm.

Good communications are an essential element in the control and co-ordination of the sales effort and a major responsibility for management. The manager must not only ensure that he communicates well with staff but that individual members of the team keep him fully informed and communicate well between one another. The daily conference early in the morning or at the end of the working day is one way of achieving this.

For the manager of the sales team the control of the collective time of his team is perhaps his most important concern. With an enthusiastic team it will not be strictly limited, but neither will it be limitless. Certainly there is a limit to the number of hours any one individual can work if he or she is to be fully effective. Decisions on opening hours, weekend and "out of hours" work are obviously matters in which management must balance increased sales potential against increased costs and maintaining the team's morale. Not perhaps as obvious, but of vital importance, is the tactful direction and supervision of the time each member of the team can give.

In giving a personal service making the best use of time is perhaps the most important factor but other resources for the management in achieving maximum efficiency include getting their best efforts from the back-up staff, the use of the telephone, the advertising budget, the window and the cars. There can be wastage if some of these are allowed to get out of control.

For the reasons we have discussed, aims or targets can become unachievable or unrealistic. They may have been simply wrong, the result of poor judgment. They must never be lightly abondoned, but management must be prepared to set new targets if the originals have become meaningless. They may in practice become counter-productive. A person or team faced with an unattainable goal could lose heart and as a result work well below potential.

If there is a golden rule in this matter it must be "never *totally* abandon an aim unless absolutely convinced it was wrong from the start". To do so will appear as weakness on the part of management and in itself lead to loss of morale. If one sets a target for a year, one retains a certain amount of flexibility if one runs into a very sticky patch. Many practitioners will recall years that have started disastrously and ended satisfactorily, and vice versa. One could call the team together explain why in one's opinion the market has become difficult, whether because of interest rates, mortgage availability, or political uncertainty. One should say that in the circumstances it might prove difficult to achieve the target, express the hope, or, better still, explain the reasons why, one believes that conditions will improve and the target be reached by the end of the year, and then set a more modest target for the next three months, or even monthly targets. Maintaining one's aim but hopefully keeping the team motivated by an immediate target that is credible.

Staff training

In opening this book I was critical of the profession as a whole for what in my early days was a lack of planned training in "estate agency". There has been some improvement and this improvement one hopes will continue. The responsibility for training does not, as many would appear to believe, rest entirely with the professional bodies, the universities or the colleges. I know of very few firms who have set out to provide considered, planned and regular training for their sales team and negotiators, and yet it is they who would directly receive the benefit from doing so.

If this book does anything to encourage in-house training and to provide material for it I believe it will have achieved something worthwhile. It cannot, however, cover every area in which training could be given, nor can any reading matter replace direct personal instruction and the questions and answers that flow from it. I would make some suggestions and give some ideas.

In every firm one person should be made responsible for "in-house" training. (Even the one man in a "one man band" office has a responsibility to those with whom he deals to attain and maintain a reasonable standard of competence). The person responsible for "in-house" training in a firm must be one with enthusiasm and a good communicator; a syllabus must be set and a time-table made and adhered to. Outside help must be enlisted whenever possible. The person for whom a young man or woman works every day may not, and indeed is unlikely to be, the best instructor; he may have already passed on all he can, bad habits with the good. Many life assurance companies will instruct on mortgages and life assurance, and have staff trained to do just this with carefully prepared visual aids. It should not prove difficult to find an expert photographer to help on his subject or a lawyer to talk on the law of agency, contract and conveyancing. Many firms will already have somebody who could give instruction in building construction and the faults one is most likely to encounter, or again outside help could be found. Many will have other ideas. One cannot denude a firm during the working day of the whole of its sales force; training may have to take place out of hours or be given to groups at different times, but, given the will, it could be done.

We once organised two sessions at each of which instruction was given on the preparation of particulars by a partner and a professional photographer. With the co-operation of two vendors, each group inspected and "took instructions" on houses that were difficult to present well, and each individual had to prepare illustrated particulars of both. These were submitted anonymously and judged by a panel consisting of the photographer, the senior partner and an advertising expert, with worthwhile prizes to the winners. It was a great success. All concerned enjoyed it and the average standard of particulars and photography improved noticeably. The fact that we have not, as yet, repeated it is indicative of the apathy with which I believe staff training is regarded in far too many firms.

Remuneration is for all of us a prime motivation and I believe that "incentive" reward is a valuable part of every negotiator's overall remuneration. I hesitate to say much on the subject, aware that views differ greatly, that practice might vary from one area to another and that one is competing for staff in a limited market place where local practice may influence, if not dictate, the pattern. For example, if other firms in the area provide staff cars and allow them to be run "on the firm" the firm that insists on staff providing their own transport, being given only an allowance for business mileage, will have to pay a substantially, and possibly disproportionately higher, basic salary if it is to compete.

I know of no firm in this country that, in the accepted sense, rewards solely by way of commission. One or two have been known to pay senior staff on a percentage of turn-over basis, but the majority, in widely differing ratios, pay by way of a basic salary and commission. A few pay "flat" salaries and look to other ways of motivating the competitive spirit.

I repeat two personal views. First that the incentive element should not be such that it would create undue anxiety for the employee that could lead to oppressive "over-sell" tactics, and, secondly, that any incentive element should encourage the team spirit and not detract from it.

Having said that, I see nothing wrong with the bonus given occasionally for a job particularly well done, a significant improvement in performance or performance well above the firm's average. Bonuses not clearly related to individual or team effort and given on a regular basis tend to become "the norm". As such they do little to motivate and when, perhaps in a bad year, they are not paid or are reduced, resentment can be caused.

I hope we shall never reach the stage where negotiators are paid solely or mainly on commission and on an individual basis. This question does not only bear on morale and effectiveness, but on the very nature of estate agency as practised in this country. If the incentive reward is disproportionately high, there will be an understandable move away from the agency approach into "broking".

Twenty

Marketing Functions — Budgeting and Expenditure Control

Time apportionment — Degree of control — Forecasting commission income — Significance of "subject to contract" sales — Analysis of instructions received and sales effected — Assessing performance — Relevance of data in decision-making — Profitability: the Price Commission's findings — Breakdown of expenditure — Setting a budget and forecasting — Target-setting — Seasonal and cyclical variations

Time and cost apportionment is a field where as a "general practitioner" trying to write specifically about the practice of estate agency I find myself in some difficulty. Although I believe that in a large general practice office involved in a variety of professional and commercial work as well as house agency, an attempt must be made to "cost out" each department or function in order to be able to control future expenditure and assess profitability, there are in this field many grey areas. Of these perhaps advertising is the most obvious. A typical provincial general practice will spend the major part of its advertising budget on "house agency" advertising, and relatively little, rightly or wrongly, on advertising its professional skills, yet we all know that one of the objects of all advertising is to inform the public of the firm's existence, give some idea as to its size and capabilities, in short to present a public image. It follows that even if 80 per cent of one's advertising costs are involved in advertising houses for sale, some of this 80 per cent could properly be charged against those other departments which benefit from the overall image created. Just how much should be so allocated would depend entirely on the circumstances and the nature of the other work being carried out in the office, and certainly I am not in a position to give any firm guide. Similarly, the general practice partner is likely to spend some of his time in house-agency work. He may be the partner responsible for this deparment, in which case he will spend the greater part of his time involved in it. But some time will have to be spent in general administration and in the conduct of the practice as a whole and not all his costs could be directly charged against the house agency department.

On the other hand he may be a partner doing in the main professional or commercial work but spending part of his time in general administration, some of which would directly affect the house agency side of the practice. He may become more directly involved there where, for example, a house vendor is a personal friend or business contact, or where a house is to be sold by auction, or land by tender. In such circumstances no one other than the partners working in that particular office could with any accuracy allocate costs to functions. All I can do is express the view that it should be done.

One of the advantages that solicitors' practices have derived from the use of computers is the accurate assessment of time spent and the ability this gives accurately to assess income and expenditure to separate departments or functions, and indeed to individual fee-earners. The difficulty of applying any time-recording basis of assessment accurately to an estate agency department that works on a contingency fee basis, is obvious.

However, in acknowledging the difficulty of time-recording I am in no way arguing against tight control and budgeting in the estate agency side of the practice.

In regard to budgeting, I again must generalise, being conscious that at one end of the scale one could have a sole principal, himself almost entirely devoted to house agency work, one negotiator and perhaps two girls. The records he would need to keep in order to know just what he is spending and what his income is likely to be from month to month would be relatively simple. At the other end of the scale, in the very large general practice office, the task would be a complex one and one that might already have been computerised, the program having been the subject of long, careful and detailed analysis, and the recording and extracting of data reduced to the simple exercise of disciplines.

I will, however, attempt to suggest the areas over which control could be exercised and the information that should be available to management. I am going to try to limit myself to the estate agency function, but I do not think there is a need to differentiate between house agency and commercial agency.

Income forecasting and cash-flow

The great majority of estate agency transactions go through three phases. First, an agreement between parties that is subject to contract. This would apply both to a house sale or a commercial letting. The second phase is the exchange of contracts, or the formal signing of the lease and its counterpart. The third and final phase will be completion of the transaction.

In the case of a sale by auction, or a sale by tender there may only be two relevant dates. The date when the transaction becomes binding on the parties, for example, the day of the auction if it is successful, and the day when it completes.

For the estate agent the completion date could be described as the date when he expects to be paid. For income-forecasting this process provides three useful items of information. When the transaction is first agreed between parties, the agent will know that there is the "possibility" of being paid and, based on the purchase price or rent agreed, he will know what that payment is likely to amount to, when and if it comes. When contracts are exchanged, he will know that that income is going to be due to him, and most practices would at this stage formally invoice the client; and lastly he is likely to know when he can expect payment, for if he does not already know the date when completion is to take place, this is information he should be able to obtain from the vendor's or lessor's solicitor.

I accept that, dependent to some extent on market conditions, many transactions agreed "subject to contract" never proceed and that the income likely to be received from such transactions is fairly nebulous. Some would argue, indeed some of my partners do, that it is too nebulous to be of value in forecasting. I, on the other hand, believe that management needs to know the level of potential income as far in advance as possible and in particular, if market conditions are changing either for better or worse, he wants the earliest possible indication of what is happening, either to restrict expenditure, in so far as he is able, or to increase it if he feels it justified.

In any event, the partner responsible and the manager of the department should know on a day-to-day basis what transactions have been agreed subject to contract, and what they are likely to be worth in commission income. He should also know what sales or transactions earlier agreed have "blown". If he does not keep separate records this information should be available to him directly from the office bulletin. It is not difficult to compile a monthly list of transactions so agreed and their value in terms of potential income, and to off-set against this both the sales recorded in an earlier month that have "blown", and the loss of potential revenue. Given that records will be kept of earlier years, or at least the preceding year, a comparison can be drawn.

In the multi-office practice it is questionable as to whether the information obtained from the record of subject to contract transactions is of sufficient value to justify the work involved in calling for returns and analysing them. If communications in the firm are good, the partners will from regular contact with each other and with office managers know what is going on in the market. On the other hand, if the firm has a computer, the amount of time and effort involved in

HOUSE SALES UNDER CONTRACT DURING

	Cumulative Direct Insts.						This Month	Value of Sales Under Contract		
	197 /		197 /		197			197 /	197 /	197 /
	Rec'd	Sold	Rec'd	Sold	Rec'd	Sold				
Chichester										
Selsey										
Bognor										
Portsmouth										
Havant										
Hayling Island										
Waterlooville										
Storrington										
Billingshurst										
Pulborough										
Horsham										
Hove										
Petersfield										
Littlehampton										
Worthing										
Southampton										
Park Gate										
Bitterne										
Wittering										

recording and computing this information will be negligible and almost certainly justified. Even if the information has to be compiled manually I personally regard the exercise as worthwhile.

The performance of the firm or office cannot, however, be measured only in terms of potential income. Management will want to know how many instructions have been received and how successful that office or the firm as a whole is in converting those instructions to completed transactions. In multiple agency areas the number of sole agencies obtained and the percentage of the total instructions they represent could also be relevant in assessing effectiveness. If a reasonably accurate assessment has been made of likely increases in expenditure over those incurred in the previous year, comparison of sales achieved expressed in terms of commission income in the same period of the preceding year would give a guide as to the likely profit or loss position.

I illustrate our own current monthly return pro forma but stressing that it records only transactions where contracts have been exchanged. It enables these responsible for management to compare the number of direct instructions received, the number of units sold and the income earned to date with the position at the same date in each of the two preceding years. We circulated widely among the senior staff on the sales side enabling them to compare the performance of their office with others. In itself it acts as an incentive.

What this pro forma does not give us is the anticipated date of payment. Although we find it adequate, those with a computer could very simply forecast future income much more accurately if approximate completion dates were known.

Staff motivation, assessment of work-loads and evaluation of performance are perhaps more marketing matters than budgetary, nevertheless much information gleaned from adequate monthly returns could be of real value in assessing the performance of the agency team. I have mentioned the proportion of sole agencies to total instructions, the number of instructions received, the number of properties sold, the number of sub-agency instructions received and the number sold; all these can be related either to individual negotiators in one office, or one office as opposed to another, to assess the work-load per negotiator and the relative levels of success achieved. The number of houses sold in each price-range would give management an indication as to where there may be room for future growth, or perhaps where the public image is wrong.

The number of instructions received, the number of units sold and the commission earned which can be related to known regional house-price increases, will all give an indication whether or not that office is achieving real growth or simply reflecting inflationary increases.

Negotiators must not be distracted from their principal tasks of taking instructions and selling. To this extent returns should be simple to compile and the number called for must be kept to a minimum, but at the same time it is vital that they do give the information necessary for management to carry out its tasks of assessing performance and forward planning.

Unlike a manufacturing industry, the estate agency practice cannot adjust the price of its product, the houses it has to sell, to make good an inadequate profit-margin, or to protect a profit-margin clearly shown by the monthly returns to be at risk. Improved performance is an obvious remedy, but however good the team and however well controlled and directed, the market can turn against it and it will be powerless, as King Canute was, to turn the tide back. A change in the rate of commissions charged might be the only answer. Much will depend upon what one's rivals are doing. Any partner or manager knowing his overall commission income will know what effect an increase from a flat rate of 2 per cent to say 2.25 per cent will mean in terms of increased income, provided, of course, that he is satisfied that it will not act as a deterrent to vendors. But I suggest he should know a great deal more than this. Ideally, he should know what his costs per instruction and per unit sold amount to and he must know the number of houses sold in each price-range (I do not suggest particular ranges, for these would clearly vary from one area or district to another). It may be that to increase commission rate at the bottom end of the market would be to deter vendors, but there may be room at the top end for a somewhat larger increase and only careful analysis of performance from records will enable management to make the decision likely to produce the increased income aimed for without deterring vendors in a particular sector.

There is little statistical evidence of the average performance of firms throughout the country related to their agency-function to enable me to give a realistic guide as to the sort of margins one should be looking to. Earlier I quoted profit margins per sale in comparing sole and multiple agency practice. These came from the Monopolies Commission Report, but this is now over ten years old and should, I think, not be relied upon. In any event although they tried conscientiously to separate estate agency income and expenditure from those related to the firms' other functions, the process was of necessity somewhat arbitrary.

The Price Commission Report of 1979 is much more recent. To this extent it can be relied upon, but on the other hand it made no attempt to isolate the estate agency function. Its findings on profitability may, however, be of some value to practising estate agents. The survey was based on financial information supplied by 266 firms, which the Commission broke down into three categories — single office firms, "small"; other firms with an income in 1978 of up to £½m, "medium"; and those with an income in 1978 exceeding £½m, "large". They commented that there were only a few large firms in the sample and this fact should be borne in mind in considering the Tables they produced. Regrettably, it was only the Table showing the performance of the large firms that gave comparable figures for 1976, 1977 and 1978. They gave only 1978 figures for the small and medium-sized firms.

Before looking at the Tables I think we should see what the Commission had to say about their terms of reference.

They first commented on house agency income as opposed to total income:

"Although on average 60 per cent of the income of small firms and about 55 per cent of that of medium-sized firms came from fees from sales of domestic property, there were considerable variations between individual firms; some derived all their income from domestic property sales, others relied heavily on other sources such as fees for surveys and valuations. Our terms of reference asked us to pay particular attention to the domestic property activities of estate agents. Many estate agents, however, have difficulty in allocating costs to their various activities and thus in isolating profit derived from the domestic property business. We examined the firms with a high proportion of domestic property sales and found that, on average, those firms were not more profitable than estate agents generally."

It may be dangerous to rely on this finding indicating that the income and expenditure statistics for the mixed practice are much the same as for the practice whose income from estate agency represents a very high proportion of total income. It is nevertheless an indication that this might well be the case. If this is so, then the Tables do give, if nothing more, an indication of the sort of expenditure levels incurred under their various headings.

One must accept that for the majority of estate agents in Britain 1978 was a successful year and for most of the country a year in which property values rose faster than expenditure.

The Commission's Tables expressed both income and expenditure and therefore profit, in actual as well as percentage terms. I have extracted only the latter.

Although the Table setting out the average income, expenditure and net profit for the larger firms also gave such statistics for the two preceding years, the percentages earned and spent under each heading varied so little from those produced for 1978, that it is unnecessary for me to set them out.

I am not suggesting that those of my readers who are responsible for budgeting in their own firms should take the Commission's finding as a guide to what they should be achieving; to do so would in effect be accepting no more than an average performance. They nevertheless may help in giving a guide against which to set one's own firm's

performance, and if one is going to do this then some of the
Commission's other comments may be of value.

Average percentage income, expenditure and net profit in 1978

INCOME	Small firms	Medium-sized firms	Large firms
Average number of offices	1.0	3.5	9.9
Fees from domestic agency	60	54.3	44.6
Other income	40	45.7	55.4
	100	100	100
EXPENDITURE			
Salaries and Wages	24.9	30.8	37.2
Advertising	10.9	11.6	9.9
Motor Vehicle expenses	6.5	6.9	5.2
Printing, Postage, Stationery and Telephone	6.5	7.4	6.7
Other expenses	18.5	16.1	18.5
Total	67.3	72.8	77.5
Net profit per principal	32.7	27.2	22.5

Note Small firms were single-office firms. Medium-sized firms were others with an income of up to £½ million, and large firms those with an income in excess of this figure

First they used as their measure of profitability net profit per
principal; by principal they meant directors as well as sole traders and
partners, and the net profit was struck before charging principals'
salaries, interest on principals' capital and taxation.

They noted that salaries and wages as a percentage of income reduced
with the size of the firm from 37.2 per cent in the large firms to only
24.9 per cent in the small one-office firms. This they attributed to a
greater proportion of those working in the small firms being principals
rather than employees.

They found some regional variations in profit per principal, when
they took the small and medium-sized firms together. In Scotland, the
North of England, the Midlands and in Wales profits were similar and
if we assume this figure to represent 100 per cent, profit per principal in
Greater London was higher at 116 per cent. In the South it was

appreciably lower at 76 per cent and in Northern Ireland lower still at approximately 65 per cent (these figures to the nearest 1 per cent).

The incidence of multiple agency they thought might have been partly responsible for the lower profit margins in the South as compared with the other regions in England and Wales.

Although the large firms showed, at 22.5 per cent, an appreciably lower profit margin than the smaller firms, at 32.7 per cent, what this represented in terms of income to the principals concerned varied greatly, but in reverse order. If one assumes the income per principal in the large firms to represent 100 per cent, the principal in the medium-size firm earned only just over half as much, at 52 per cent, and the principal in the small firm appreciably less again at 37 per cent.

The Commission's breakdown of average expenditure was into only five broad headings. Simplicity was no doubt the reason, for respondent firms were given little enough time in which to cope. I personally would not regard such a simple breakdown of expenditure as adequate for effective management and control. I would want to see a breakdown of salaries and wages, which presumably include commissions or other incentives paid, into guaranteed income on the one hand and incentive income on the other. I would like to see the costs of National Insurance and any in-house pension scheme extracted. Advertising I would like to see broken down as between commercial, residential and promotional, and into local and national. On the assumption that the Commission's figure is a net one, I would want to know the difference between gross and net, and how much of the total was recovered from clients. This particular evidence may indeed be very misleading, for in that they took their sample from across the country, it would have included many firms operating in regions where the majority of advertising costs are recoverable, and elsewhere it is the larger firms who find it easier to recover some of this expenditure.

Motor vehicle expenses, or if I might widen it, travelling expenses, need to be broken down, for particularly tight control is necessary here if these are to be contained. I would want to know how much went in depreciation, how much on petrol and oil, maintenance, repairs, and insurance, and I would want to be able to compare the costs of cars individually.

I would certainly want to see printing, postage and stationery separated from the costs of the telephone, for in an operating sense they are to an extent alternatives. If there is an in-house printing department I would want to see this separately costed, for one would want to make regular checks that it was in practice cost-effective against outside purchasing. Certainly to accept something between 16 per cent and 18.5 per cent as coming under the heading of "other expenses" would be totally unacceptable to me. Hidden in here must be administrative costs, such as the accounting staff, the professional indemnity insurance premium — surprisingly it appears nowhere else — rent and rates (any budgeting exercise should include an allowance for estimated open market rental value, even if the freehold is owned by the principals) and the elusive figure that could be attributed to "office expenses".

This may appear to be digressing from the subject of budgeting, which is in effect forecasting, into the field of management control, but I make no excuse, for budgeting without control would be a meaningless exercise.

If one is to set an achievable budget, one needs to be able to analyse the preceding year's expenses, not only into the headings I have suggested, for there are many others that some would consider appropriate — repairs and renewals for example. From this one would want to extract anything that was abnormal and non-recurring, or which ought to be costed out over a period. A substantial sum spent on re-furbishment should perhaps, for management purposes, be spread over a five-year period.

One has then to look into that preceding period and identify those heads of expenditure where increases took place during the period and therefore are not fully reflected. One may in fact be looking at historical data as opposed to data current at one's budget date.

Having broken down immediate past expenditure and adjusted to reflect current rates, one has got to project these throughout the budget year. Some may feel that recent experience of inflation renders a year too long a period, but I think anything less could again be meaningless. One may have to accept, however, the need to adjust the budget if a major change in likely expenditure under any one head takes place during the period. One has got to make a realistic forecast as to what is likely to happen during the year ahead. Some may feel it sufficient simply to apply the forecast inflation rate to one's estimated current costs, but to assume an increase of say 18 per cent, although it may accurately represent the rate at which expenditure is running 12 months hence, will not reflect the rate throughout the year. To make any arbitrary provision would be to acknowledge lack of control. There are certain heads of expenditure where control could effectively restrain expenditure and it is wrong to assume that all heads of expenditure will rise, for in practice this may well not be the case. A rent reviewed two years ago with five years remaining to the next review is not going to alter. Salaries and wages, possibly advertising costs, should be related to one's income target. If the latter is achieved, incentive payments to staff will no doubt increase, but the target is calculable at the beginning of the year. If market conditions are such that the target is not going to be achieved, advertising is one field where reductions can be made, though

I would not here argue one way or the other as to advisability of doing so; that is a marketing judgement.

I have no doubt that most firms already try to motivate their sales team by setting targets; many no doubt link incentive remuneration to those targets, and the great majority will monitor just what progress is being made in trying to achieve them. It is equally important that expenditure limits set do reflect one's prepared budget, and that actual expenditure is monitored. It is of the utmost importance that those who have any degree of control over expenditure know exactly what their individual budget is and are accountable for it.

To set sales targets and expenditure limits for a period, be it a year or less, is not sufficient, for income may not be received in a regular pattern; only those who practise in an area will be aware, for example, of seasonal sales patterns, and expenditure will not be incurred at a steady rate throughout the period. Some items will only be payable quarterly — one's liability to account for VAT is significant here; incentives to staff may be payable quarterly, or even only annually. The professional indemnity premium is probably another annual expense.

Cash-flow is a matter of vital concern to management. The likely pattern of income receipts and expenditure payments is capable of being forecast simply mathematically, by graph or by use of a computer.

Dependent upon one's own experience of the average time-delay in one's area between exchange of contracts and receipt of commission, it may help for one's monthly, and ultimately annual, sales return to run to a date preceding the commencement of one's budget year. Assuming an average interval of two months and a year-end date of the 31st March, one's sales return could run to 31st January.

I do not wish to minimise the difficulties either in setting sales objectives, in budgeting expenditure, and keeping to it, or indeed difficulties of accurately forecasting cash-flow. To the estate agent expenditure budgeting is probably the easiest part of the task. Analysing under each head of expenditure the preceding year's costs, adjusting to current levels and then forecasting, again under each head of expenditure, reflecting any known likely variation, is likely to produce a reasonably accurate result.

The Price Commission commented at some length on one question that is of concern to every estate agent. Having drawn the conclusion that the steady increase in the rate of home-ownership over the years 1951 to 1976 showed the estate agent to be operating in a growing market, they said this:

"In the short run, however, underlying growth is over-laid by considerable fluctuation in the volume of transactions. This uneven flow of business is characteristic of estate agency in most local markets. There is in the first place a seasonal pattern under which in many years house sales dip in the first quarter. But cyclical variation is the more important source of short-run fluctuation. Much of the time there is either a buyers' market or a sellers' market. At certain points a substantial supply of houses for sale is matched by demand made effective by the availability of adequate mortgage funds, and a surge in transactions occurs. These peak periods, which bring high income to most estate agents, typically only last a number of months."

They produced a graph, which I reproduce here showing the number of sales of second-hand houses financed by mortgages on a quarterly basis from 1970 to the third quarter of 1978.

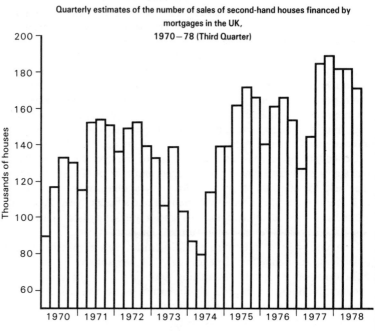

Quarterly estimates of the number of sales of second-hand houses financed by mortgages in the UK, 1970–78 (Third Quarter)

Source: Housing and Construction Statistics. Tables 36 (b), 39, 40 and 41(a) according to year.

This graph needs to be looked at with some caution, for it does not show transactions other than those financed by mortgages and it is believed that these other transactions account for about one quarter of all second-hand house sales. The second-hand market is likely to be less variable than the new and the transactions shown on the graph include certain transactions which are irrelevant to the estate agent, such as advances for house-improvement and topping-up loans. The graph therefore almost certainly shows an over-statement. It nevertheless illustrates the point on which I want to conclude this chapter.

It may well be right to motivate the sales team by setting a target based on the preceding year's performance, relating it to current house-values, making some allowance for an increase in values in the ensuing year and adding a margin for real growth. It would be totally unrealistic for those involved in the management of the practice to do this regardless of the market conditions at the time, or the agent's experience of the market. An appreciation of the factors that affect the market, how it is likely to react to those factors, what effect they will have, both on the likely number of transactions and on values, is vital if any forecast, as opposed to target, is to be realistic, and if one's cash-flow forecast in particular is not to prove embarrassingly unrealistic.

Twenty-one

The Estate Agent in the Development Field

> The agent's role — Basic knowledge required — Town
> planning — A developer's view on agents — Market
> research — Special sector considerations, residential,
> industrial, warehousing and offices — The need for
> site appraisals — The need to monitor the market —
> The agent's future involvement — Projected costs and
> values — Development appreciations — Other
> commercial property development considerations —
> Real growth development — Replacement
> development — Abnormal development costs — The
> profit margin — The future for property development

Few members of the public would identify the estate agent, whether
operating in the residential or commercial markets, as being involved in
the development process, other than in the sale or letting of the
completed product. Yet for the agent with the necessary enthusiasm,
flair and knowledge it is perhaps the most rewarding and constructive
field of activity, though I must stress that very few estate agents are
themselves involved as principals in development projects and many
would deprecate such involvement. We are concerned here with the
agent's role as an adviser to developer clients, his role in identifying
sites suitable for development and bringing them forward, and his
involvement in this field for the general promotion of his practice.

We must first consider the basic knowledge the agent will require if
he is to function effectively in this field. We must assume he already has
flair and enthusiasm, for he will certainly need both.

First he will need a detailed knowledge of his area; for the provincial
residential agent this may be just his own town and the rural area for
which it is the centre; for the commercial agent dealing with prime
shops it will be the significant shopping centres throughout Britain, or
in all probability those that lie within the region or area that is his
particular responsibility.

Similarly, the agent specialising in office or industrial development,
and one must not forget that this includes redevelopment, must know
where the industrial estates are, where sites suitable for development are

likely to be found, where older buildings exist that provide the opportunity to redevelop. It will not be enough to know the area thoroughly in the geographical sense, knowledge will need to be both deeper and wider.

He must be thoroughly conversant with planning policy in the area and throughout the region he is expected to cover. This knowledge he will have to relate to the nature of the development he wishes to bring about.

The Provincial practitioner is likely to be interested in everything from a site for, say, two houses, or an older house to convert into flats, to major shop, office or industrial development, but in the commercial context probably only in the immediate area covered by his firm.

The commercial agent operating nationally and acting for a major development company, an institution, or possibly both, may only be interested in the development of property investments that will on completion be worth not less than £250,000 or even more. The agent specialising in prime shops will only be interested in the prime and perhaps very good secondary shopping areas of the towns in which he is interested. Whatever the field of interest the principles will remain the same.

Since 1971 planning policy throughout most of the country has been in a state of flux, with relatively few of the intended County Structure Plans approved and some not even in final draft form, and with very few local plans in existence. In many areas one is relying on development plans and town maps prepared over a quarter of a century ago, and on the way these have been interpreted over the years, in particular the departures that have been made and the policy or change in policy that underlies these departures.

In this state of flux while planning authorities are developing new policies or have expressed them only in draft or interim form there is often little firm information on which the estate agent can rely. He must have such plans and supporting documents as exist available to him, but beyond this he must by pressing enquiries of planning authorities get a clear view as to their likely reaction to any development proposal he might identify and want to bring forward, whether it be residential or commercial.

Next the agent must have a sound knowledge of his market. Mr. Brian Grainger, F.R.I.C.S., F.S.V.A., a developer in his own right, in giving a paper at CALUS on "Marketing and Selling Houses from a Developer's Point of View" referred to market research as "the vital stage in the evolution of the development process". He broke this down into:—

The area and immediate locality; Is there full employment or unemployment? What communications are there from the potential site to places of employment, schools, amenities? Is competition strong or lacking?

The people (the potential buyers) Who are they? Their wage structure, earning capacity and buying capacity. How old are they? Where are they living? Size of family and tastes — what do they really want and need?

He laid particular emphasis on amenities, commenting that "People will not buy houses if facilities such as communications for the husband to go to work, shops and parks for the wives and schools for the children are not available". He further pointed out that "The small developer has to rely on what already exists." What he then said should cause practising agents concern: — "With his local knowledge, the local agent should be in his element and without peer. He ought to be able to help the developer on those points; however I find the help lacking at this stage for these reasons:

    i) The agent cannot see the wood for the trees. He is so closely involved in the locality and community that he has very rigid ideas about good and bad areas — probably for the wrong reasons.

    ii) If the agent is not offering a particular site he tends to be uninterested at this stage. Unless one is an old client very little help and information is forthcoming".

When it came to an assessment of the competition likely to be encountered during the development of the site, he said, "The local agent should have all the information at his finger tips", but, he asked, "Does he?"

From the developer's point of view Mr. Grainger saw it as essential to weigh up the opposition, actual and potential. Questions to be asked include: What type of houses are selling readily? Are more of these needed? What is needed and not being offered at the present time? What other developments are being planned by other companies and will therefore form direct competition at the start of building?

He then described a case where his company developed an estate in Buckinghamshire and where the homework had not been done properly. Builders on an adjoining site were building similar houses at a similar price but with a downstairs cloakroom, with the result that none of the company's houses sold until the opposition had sold all theirs.

I have dealt with these criticisms at some length for I know Mr Grainger and worked with him on the CALUS Estate Agency Study Group, and his opinion is one I respect, not least because he has experience on the other sides of the fence and is a member of both the leading professional bodies. This was not, however, the only reason. The sort of agent he describes, and it matters not that he was referring only to the residential market, is just the sort who will not succeed in this rewarding field.

The good estate agent involved in development work should not have to carry out market research as a specific exercise; it should for him be a constant and on-going exercise and he should at any time have "all the information at his finger tips", not only as to the matters referred to, sites being developed or about to start, but knowledge of any land that might come forward during the anticipated period of the development he is considering. Few sites can maintain a sales-rate much in excess of 50 units a year. If he is considering a site for a possible 250 units, allowing for the acquisition, design work, planning and initial infrastructure works, he is probably looking at a six-year period, and this demands a detailed knowledge of planning policy.

He should also have other background information. At what rate have new houses been built and sold in the area, and in what relative price groups, or of what approximate floor areas, and did this vary under different market conditions? The rate at which he can expect to sell is vital information to a developer, for on it will depend the percentage of overall development costs represented by the cost of finance, and cash flow. A serious error could mean failure of both the project and the company. Other questions that must be asked include the following:

"Are there any parts of the area where ground conditions are suspect, where, for example, other developers have encountered running sand or where the land has been 'filled'?"

"Are there parts of the area where the planners are likely to insist on abnormally high-quality materials which must be reflected in higher estimates of building costs?"

To summarise, if he is to succeed in the development field the estate agent must know the planning policies, have the confidence of the planning officers, and he must know and constantly monitor his market. He must have a well-informed view of how that market is likely to behave in the immediate future and he must know his area almost by the square yard to be aware of where opportunities might lie and where unusual difficulties might be encountered.

The agent interested in the residential market can fairly easily establish where the majority of his opportunities lie. Planning authorities have to maintain land availability studies and these are available for inspection. They will identify sites and give an indication as to the number of dwellings for which they are considered suitable. These sites can then be inspected and if development has not commenced, ownership be traced and an approach made.

To the reader interested only in the commercial market and maybe only one section of that, I would apologise for this apparent concentration on residential considerations, but many of the points raised are applicable to every market. A developer considering an industrial development will be concerned at the supply of skilled or, as the case might be, unskilled labour. Housing in the area will be relevant. He will want advice on known demand and as to whether or not there are established industries in the area cramped for space or known to wish to expand.

The office developer may not expect to find a local or entirely local demand for the space he is considering providing. He may well expect any agent bringing a proposition to him to have a detailed knowledge of other office developments carried out in the region and an opinion based on knowledge and experience of development of a similar kind as to what the likelihood is of being able to attract a suitable occupier to the town in question and, given that few are attracted to anything other than a completed or near completed building, how long it might take to find such an occupier.

He will expect his agent to know what quality of accommodation should be provided, whether it should be air-conditioned, lift-served or both, and how much car-parking should be provided to make the building an attractive proposition.

There are likely to be relatively few potential takers for such a building and he is therefore going to be more than usually sensitive to any potential competition. A company which bought a similar site in the town a year earlier, before site values escalated, which has its detailed planning consent and is about to make a start will have its accommodation available that much earlier, and in all probability its costs and funding arrangements will be such that it could afford initially to take 50p or even £1 a foot less than could the later company to come on the scene. The existence of such a threat, particularly in a small town, could render the proposition not only far too speculative but difficult to fund.

The agent wishing to be involved in development projects and as a result obtain houses to sell or space to let, cannot expect to succeed simply by sending brief particulars of sites available to the development companies he knows and hoping for the best.

We have considered the background knowledge he should have; how he should present a particular site to a developer is something we will consider in more detail.

Although I have said that the agent should be constantly monitoring his market, this will never remove the need, once a potential site has been identified, for more detailed research into that specific site, its potential and its difficulties. There is market research to be done in the context of the overall market in the area, and research that is "site specific". They are two stages in identifying a development project.

The Relationship between Agent and Prospective Developer

Here I must differentiate between the residential and the commercial market and I deal with the residential market first.

It is relatively rare in this market for developer clients to retain an agent's services in the finding and appraisal of sites for a direct fee, i.e., a fee related solely to acquisition, unless there is no possibility of the agent's services being required later. The agent's reward will often only come from selling the completed units, and most agents actively involved in this type of work will have a number of regular developer clients with whom they have an understanding that where they introduce a site they will subsequently be involved as selling agents, although the degree of involvement will vary. An agent who has put in a great deal of work in identifying, for example, a site in several ownerships, advising as to the value of the separate interests, discussed the form the development should take with the planners, negotiated the acquisitions and given detailed advice on matters such as density, type and size of unit to be built, the standard of fittings, selling prices and potential sales rate may well be justified in seeking remuneration for this work as well as enjoying the ongoing role as selling agent. He may have done more than this. If he acts regularly for a development company he should know what it costs them to build to a particular standard, what this basic cost would cover and what the infrastructure and other costs such as fencing and landscaping are likely to be. With this knowledge he could, and should have, let his client have a detailed appraisal as to how he sees the development working out at the end of the day.

On the other hand he may have done very little; just received particulars of land from a vendor's agent and sent it on with little or no comment. He is asking too much if he expects that developer to feel obligated to him when the houses come to be sold. The temptation for developers to sell direct is considerable; they save costs, they remove a third party from every transaction, they are in direct touch with their purchasers, feel a greater degree of control over the selling procedure and welcome direct contact with the market. These are no doubt some, if not all, of the reasons why the larger developers seldom employ agents.

As Brian Grainger put it: "I do complain that when I express interest in a site information is either unavailable or tends to be vague or inaccurate. Consequently, although I have to retain an agent I am obliged to make the full site investigation myself . . . This is outrageous . . . information on planning, services, road improvements and density should be available from the agent. It is not sufficient to send a location plan through the post and expect the builder or developer to do the rest".

A different situation arises where the agent actively involved in the new development field is the agent chosen by the owner of a development site to sell it for him. Any attempt to direct that land to one company or to a limited number of companies any of whom would re-employ him would involve failure in his duty to that vendor, unless, as is highly unlikely, he has the vendor's authority to offer it in this limited way. His duty is clear, he must do everything in his power to get the best possible price for the vendor and take his chance as to who might be the ultimate purchaser and as to whether or not he is subsequently instructed by him. It follows that the best chance of further involvement is to so impress the prospective purchaser with the standard of his service to his vendor client, with the way he presents the land, with the information he has available to him, by his knowledge of the district and by the help he is prepared to give them in making their own assessments that the successful bidder will "want" to retain his services and not feel obliged to, because few will feel this.

Development site appraisal and projected values

The ability realistically to appraise the development potential of a site is important, and not only to the agent wishing to be involved in new development work. It is important first in advising a client wishing to dispose of land as to the nature of the planning consent he should seek and as an aid in advising as to value. Care needs to be taken in the valuation context; as we noted earlier, much will depend on market circumstances and particularly in buoyant conditions many development companies will "take a view" as to likely increases both in their development costs and in anticipated market prices. For this reason, in the early and indeed very late 'seventies many agents made appraisals on current costs and values and were surprised to find their answer vastly exceeded in the market place. This was not, of course, confined to the residential market.

In the South, where I practise, during the period from 1976 to 1979 industrial rental values have nearly doubled, while office rents moved little. Office sites were hard to place and industrial sites not surprisingly realised prices that amazed even the experienced agents.

This begs the question as to whether or not an agent is justified in himself attempting, when making an appraisal, to project costs and values. If he does not do so in buoyant market conditions and his clients abide strictly by his advice, they will not acquire. We considered this point in the context of advising as to likely sale value, where I expressed the view that the agent should use his past and present knowledge of the market, and the economic circumstances that govern it, to do so. I do not hold this view when it comes to advising a development company on a possible purchase. By its very nature development always involves some degree of risk; the risk and the profit hoped for are related and both are the developer's; if he is to make the latter he must also accept the former. Having said that, the agent is entitled to offer advice as to how he believes the market will move. This is not contradictory, for the agent should in giving advice, and this includes submitting an appraisal, separate fact or views that can be shown to be based on factual evidence from views that are simply conjecture. He can do this in two ways. He can make his appraisal using current costs and values and in submitting it advise his client as to how he believes the market will move between then and when the completed building, or the first unit in a development of several, will be ready. Alternatively he can make his appraisal reflecting what he believes will happen and inform his client what assumptions he has made. "I have assumed a 10 per cent increase in building costs over current levels, but an increase in values over the next year of 20 per cent" or, in the commercial field: "As industrial premises are in such short supply, I have assumed rental values will rise over the next year from the current level of about £2 per sq. ft. to a minimum of £2.25. I also believe interest rates will harden and have capitalised to show a yield of 7 per cent as opposed to the 8 per cent one could anticipate now." Either way he is telling his client what assumptions he has made and how his answer relates to current evidence, leaving the client to decide whether he feels those assumptions to be realistic, and whether or not he is prepared to accept them in assessing what offer to make for the site.

Development, as we have seen, covers a very wide field and I do not think it practical in this book to deal in detail with the making of development appreciations. The residual method of valuation, to which they are similar, will be familiar to most valuers. It is, I think, sufficient to outline the principles involved, and in doing so one must bear in mind that not all Companies will assess potential profit in the same way or indeed look for the same margin of profit. The margin looked for will be related to risk and perhaps to volume, with the large builder-developer of low-cost housing anticipating a ready market and steady cash-flow being prepared to accept a much lower margin than, for example, the developer of a large office building who, having let the building contract, is committed to complete the work without knowing for certain how long it will take him to find a suitable occupier. Some would express profits as a percentage of given costs, others as a percentage of the final sum realised.

We have considered the knowledge the agent will need if he is to give constructive help and advice to a developer; if he is to go further and prepare an appreciation he will need knowledge of current building costs, the costs of road construction, of laying out parking areas and so

Appreciation

	£
Road costs, 400 feet @ £40	16,000
Conversion of existing house into six flats, 4,000 sq ft @ £15 per sq ft.	60,000
Allow for provision of lift	12,000
Allow for Garages, parking area and landscaping common grounds	12,000
Construction of 10 houses, each of 1,500 sq ft., 15,000 sq ft @ £20	300,000
Allow for Garages	20,000
Landscaping front gardens and fencing	8,000
Total construction costs	£428,000
Architects' fees to detailed planning consent only @2%	8,560
	£436,560
Finance Costs: allow one third development costs over 20 months @ 18% (145,520 × 1.66 years × 18%)	43,297
Total development costs	£479,857

Realisation

	£
6 flats at average of £35,000	210,000
10 houses at average £58,000	580,000
	£790,000
Less agents' and solicitors' costs @ 2½%	19,750
Net realised	£770,250
Less development costs	479,857
Available for initial purchase and profit	£290,393
Say site purchase @ £150,000	
Finance costs on site, say half over two years @ 18% £27,000	177,000
Profit	£113,393

Total Costs: £479,857 + £177,000 = £656,857.∴ profit, approximately 17% on costs.

on. He will need to know at what rate of interest the developer is likely to be able to obtain his building finance. If the development is going to be complex or long drawn out to prepare a cash-flow graph could help him in accurately assessing the finance costs.

Simply to illustrate the process which would apply to any form of development, be it residential or commercial, I set out a simple appreciation of a development of a large house into six flats and the construction of ten houses in its grounds. I have assumed that from completion of purchase it would take four months to obtain detailed planning consent and make a start, and for the sake of simplicity I have assumed that the development would take a further twenty months to complete, that the construction costs would be evenly spread over this period, and that the sale of each unit would complete as its construction was completed. In practice this would not be the case, for example, the majority of the road costs and the costs of drainage would be incurred at an early stage; if a more accurate assessment of finance costs was necessary, or if one needed to assess the maximum amount likely to be borrowed at any one time, a cash-flow graph would be necessary. One could plot likely expenditure and interest costs on a monthly basis, and likewise anticipated sales income.

In the commercial field some will be developing to hold as an investment and will be delighted if the anticipated initial rental income is sufficient to cover the finance or mortgage charges; if it in fact will "wash its face". As we have seen, this has become more and more difficult to achieve and the developer's role has tended to change. Such a company can and will normally take a long-term view, relying on subsequent rent-reviews to create "profit". The company that is trading as opposed to investing will be looking for an immediate profit, then want to move on the next project.

The construction costs I have used must not be taken by any reader as an accurate guide. Costs vary considerably, to me inexplicably, from area to area. They will vary from company to company. The large company providing cheap high-density housing anywhere in the country will, by using a few standard housing types, by bulk-buying and by mass-production of some component parts, be able to build at rates significantly below those of the small developer perhaps producing 50 units a year on a number of relatively small sites, demanding a great variety in house-types.

It does not follow that in every case the agent will need to produce appreciations of this type. In ideal circumstances he will be acting regularly for a number of companies, and he will know just what information each will need to draw its own conclusions. The major national companies in particular will wish to assess potential sites using their own criteria, all they will need are as many facts concerning the site as one can give them and, although they will invariably carry out their own market research, the agent who knows his job should be able to help.

The relevance of appreciations of this type to planning advice and valuation must not be forgotten. They may primarily be intended to project the outcome of a development, but they can also be seen as residual valuations of the site itself and as a means of establishing, not only the most economic form its development could take, but the relative degree of risk involved. A site with outline planning consent for residential development in a high-value neighbourhood may be equally suitable, in marketing terms, for large houses built to a very low density, or a block of flats. Another site might be capable of being developed with small detached houses to a density of, say, eight to the acre or with low-cost terraced housing at nearly twice that density. Similarly a site in the centre of a small town, for office development, might be equally suitable for development by way of shops with flats above. To the experienced agent the answer will in most cases be obvious, but there will be occasions when appreciations will help in assessing potential profit and degree of risk.

Other development considerations in the commercial market

So far we have been considering in effect the development of vacant sites by the conventional development company. The field in fact is wider than this. Paul Orchard-Lisle says this of "The Developer".

"It is the act of developing the property that classifies a person or body as "a developer" and it matters not what the nature of the organisation may be. Frequently property developers are owner-occupiers, financial institutions, banks or pension funds. It is the fact of development that brings them within the overall compass of 'property development'. Development does not necessarily mean the creation of new building on a virgin site. It can equally well involve the pulling down of an existing structure and its replacement, or the retention of a structure and the renovation of some or all of the interior. The extension of an established building is also development".

He went on to break down commercial development into two categories: *"Real growth development"*, which he defined as the development of new accommodation to house a new money-producing activity or the expansion of an existing business; and *"replacement development"*: the replacement of accommodation that has become outmoded, or outdated, by statutory controls, by physical obsolescence or new techniques in business or manufacturing processes.

Replacement development would include the creation of commercial buildings to house a new form of business or process, replacing an earlier one that has failed, but which will use the same or similar work force.

He illustrates this form of development by what happened in Northampton when the shoe trade contracted. "Without adding to the floor space that existed, the local authority provided for industrial development which now employs the original work force and which produces approximately the same spending power in the town".

He concluded with the comment — "It is this latter form of development that is likely to take place in a 'no growth' economy and which gives the lie to the suggestion that property development can only take place in a boom (or growth) period".

We have seen that development costs consist of four main items: site costs, construction costs, cost of finance and professional fees. These are common in one form or another to all development projects but simplest to assess in the context of low-rise residential projects. They are broad headings and in the context of commercial development we have to look more closely at extra costs and circumstances that should be provided for, particularly in a large project.

Land cost, if the site is clear of building, will be actual cost plus acquisition fees for the solicitor and retained agent, and stamp duty. If abnormal site conditions are expected there could be additional costs in a civil engineer's fees and the taking of trial holes or bores in order to assess likely abnormal construction costs.

If, as is often the case, the site has on it extensive but obsolete buildings, allowance must be made for site-clearance.

Not infrequently the site for a large project would have been acquired and put together piecemeal and it may well include some occupied buildings. An estimate must be made of the likely cost of not only acquiring any leasehold interests but compensating the lessees for the loss of any business that may be conducted on the site.

Unlike the low-rise residential field where the developer and builder are likely to be the same person or company, the construction of a commercial building is more likely, though not necessarily, to be carried out by an independent contractor, who may need to use one or more specialist sub-contractors. Considerably more experience and knowledge will be required in assessing total potential construction costs than is likely to be available to the estate agent. The help of a quantity surveyor will be required.

So far we have assumed finance costs to be the estimated amount of interest payable on capital directly invested in the project and on the money borrowed or that will be borrowed to complete it, but we may be dealing with a replacement development project and with a site already owned, that is rent-producing. Alternatively temporary accommodation may have to be secured at an abnormally high rent to enable the business to continue during the replacement period. These costs, or rent loss, may well exceed the notional interest that one would allow on "site value". If this is the case it is the higher figure that should be used.

In low rise residential development professional fees are likely to be limited to solicitor's costs in acquiring the site and conveying the completed units, architects' fees, which in many cases would only need to cover work to the detailed planning consent stage, and those of the estate agents (if any are used) on selling. Abnormal site conditions may have made it necessary to employ a civil engineer, but this is relatively rare.

A major commercial development will almost certainly need full supervision by the architect, the employment of a civil engineer and that of a quantity surveyor. Professional fees not only become more significant as a proportion of total costs, but will be payable, as in the case of the contractor, at stages through the development period. They will need to be allowed for in any cash-flow calculation.

Three other minor headings of costs need to be considered. A major commercial development may need promoting by advertising or other promotional activities, incurring costs that the letting or selling agent could not be expected to pay.

Where commercial premises are being developed speculatively it cannot always be assumed that a purchaser or lessee will be ready to occupy immediately the building is finished. Some allowance will need to be made to cover interest on costs during this vacant or "void" period. One cannot advise on the period that should be allowed for — it is closely related to overall risk — but the agent's advice as to the potential demand and what he sees as the degree of risk is clearly likely to be sought.

Last, few major projects go through "without a hitch". The contractor is unlikely to be on a fixed-price contract and variations are commonplace — some allowance must be made to cover contingencies.

The financing of the commercial market is considered briefly in another chapter, but where a development is being funded by way of some form of leaseback agreement with an institution, the developer's approximate margin could be arrived at by taking the total of development costs and converting this to an estimated annual rent charge by decapitalising to show the yield either agreed with the institution or which it is expected to accept. The margin between this annual rent charge and the agent's estimate of the open market rent likely to be obtained will express the profit margin in rental terms.

If the aim has been to make a profit on the outright sale of the completed investment then the estimated profit will of course be the difference between total estimated costs and the open market rental capitalised to reflect the yield assumed in making one's appreciation.

The Future for Development

Writing this early in 1980 with a current MLR of 17 per cent and little evidence of any growth in the economy, the future looks bleak, and in particular must it look bleak for those, and I am one of them, who practise in areas of severe planning restraint. Paul Orchard-Lisle clearly believes that replacement development will continue and that boom conditions are not necessarily a pre-requisite of development taking place. These conditions will certainly tax severely the active agent wishing to identify and bring forward projects to his developer clients.

I believe there is a lot to be done. Conditions will vary greatly from region to region and, within regions from area to area, and I can only give a guide as to the sort of opportunities I believe will be available in most areas.

On the residential front evidence shows that although the population is not increasing and even that over the country as a whole there is an adequate supply of houses, it also shows that the average size of household is decreasing and it follows that the number of family units needed is increasing. The number of elderly, as a percentage of population, is also increasing. At the same time young families are finding it harder than ever to make a start in home ownership. Again evidence suggests that the number of houses grossly under-occupied is also increasing at a time when maintenance and heating costs are escalating.

For these reasons I believe the 'eighties will show an increasing demand for "starter" homes of only two bedrooms; if they are built capable of easy extension to three, to accommodate a growing young family, so much the better. I believe we shall also see an intensification of the demand we have seen in the late 'seventies for flats, some of them very small indeed, to accommodate young couples, single-person households and the elderly, and these should be the residential developers' aim. I believe much of this development will not take place on "green field" sites but will be provided by conversion and by redevelopment to very high densities of the sites of some of the large houses that, it follows, are likely to become available.

On the industrial front Sir Keith Joseph perhaps gave the clue when being questioned about the future of British industry and the apparent failure of so many large companies. He stressed that at any time there were industries that were dying and industries that were opening up, and others that were expanding.

Many companies are occupying premises inadequate both in size and from obsolescence. Planning authorities at last appear to recognise the need to provide employment opportunities in rural communities. The quality of industrial relations varies enormously throughout the country and provides a spur to some to move from unstable to more stable areas. Nursery units, young expanding companies and even rural industry are fields to which we should be looking.

The warehousing and storage market appears a less attractive field in a "no growth" economy, but we have noted the influence of the transport and road systems and the attraction of major airports. It is unlikely that development will cease but only the agent who is well aware of developing pressures will be able to identify the opportunities that may become available.

Notwithstanding the pressure in some of our great city centres, the future for office development looks bleak and the decade opened with building costs increasing far faster than rental values in most areas. Higher transport costs and rental values in the city centres may bring renewed pressures for decentralisation and certainly there will be refurbishment opportunities.

In all sectors it is clear that viable development projects will be harder to find, the nature of risks more varied, margins narrower and costs likely to be harder to assess. In these circumstances the agent with determination, entrepreneurial flair and a real knowledge of his market place and construction costs will have an even more significant role to play in the future than he has in the past.

Twenty-Two

Financing the House Market — The Building Societies

Financing house purchase — The mortgagee, his rights — The agent as an adviser — Mortgage and insurance broking — The role of building societies, local authorities, insurance companies and banks — The repayment mortgage — The endowment mortgage — The need for insurance cover — With or without profits policies — Other sources of finance — The option mortgage scheme — House renovation grants

Early history of building societies — Susceptibility to interest rates — Resultant fluctuations in money supply, its effect on the market — Lending policy, owner occupiers and others — The surveyor's report and valuation — The role of the surveyor — Independent surveys

House-purchase is inevitably achieved in one of two ways. For the fortunate it is by an outright purchase for cash, for perhaps the majority of people it is with the help of a lesser or greater amount of borrowed money and sometimes very little of their own. Those lending money for house-purchase (the mortgagees), with very few exceptions seek to secure that loan by a mortgage deed that will specify the amount loaned, the date by which it has to be repaid and the way in which it is to be repaid, and prescribe a rate of interest, albeit that the mortgagee will in many cases have the power to vary that rate. One of the attractions from the house-purchaser's (the mortgagor's) point of view is that in normal circumstances the mortgagee will never be entitled to anything more than repayment of the original amount borrowed, and the interest on it, leaving the house-owner to benefit from any increase in the market value. The mortgagee does, however, have very specific rights if the mortgagor fails. He has the power, on giving notice, to foreclose, to take possession, and having done so he has a power of sale. This power of sale is not absolute, for the law puts him under an obligation to take all reasonable steps to secure a fair and proper price and he is accountable to the borrower (mortgagor) for any surplus realised on sale after recovering the costs of sale, the outstanding debt and any accrued interest. The obligations imposed on a mortgagee in possession are relevant to estate agents, as we shall see when considering methods of sale.

It is possible for a borrower to have more than one mortgage secured on the same house. After the "first" mortgage or charge there could be a "second" mortgage, and indeed a third. Such a situation is more frequent than many realise. A bank home-loan account is normally secured or charged against the property with the first mortgagee, who is said to have the "prior" charge, being notified of the second mortgagee's interest.

In that the first mortgagee who forecloses and sells to recover his debt has an obligation to the mortgagor, he has a similar obligation to any other mortgagee of whose interest in the property he has received notice.

In these circumstances the second mortgagee's position would appear, and might indeed be, perilous, but he does have a remedy. He can "redeem up" as a matter of right by repaying the first mortgagee what is owed by way of capital and interest, effectively merging the two charges and putting himself into the position of first mortgagee with control over the disposal of the property.

If the house agent is to be able to give a first-class service to prospective purchasers, he has got to understand and be fully conversant with the various sources of finance available to support house-purchase and the criteria that these sources follow in deciding on what types of security to lend and as to the amount that they will lend in relation not only to the value of the house concerned but to the borrower's income, or, to use the term more frequently employed, his "status". He must understand the tax implications and benefits, and, as the availability of funds varies from time to time, he must know where at any one particular moment, a prospective purchaser is most likely to get the funds he needs.

Some of the larger firms of estate agents have set up their own mortgage and insurance broking departments. Where this can be done it provides the opportunity to employ specialist staff and to give prospective purchasers a comprehensive service. Where this is not possible, thought should be given to the possibility of making one member of the agency team responsible for keeping up-to-date in this field, maintaining contacts and generally advising his colleagues, but however one sets about giving the service that is needed every negotiator must know the basic principles and be able to give initial advice and help to any prospective purchaser.

There will always be the difficult cases. The cases where the would-be borrower's income does not match up to his cash requirement. There are those with higher incomes and therefore paying a very high rate of tax who have alternatives open to them and may need advice that the average negotiator might feel incompetent to give.

Many firms, who have not set up their own departments, have established close links with independent firms of mortgage and insurance brokers, to whom they refer those whom they cannot help, or those whom they have identified as needing the advice of a specialist in the mortgage and life assurance field. Clearly if the advice can be given "in house" then the commission earned on the introduction of business, for example to a life assurance company, will be retained "in house" and the agent's overall receipts from that one particular sale can be substantially increased. Most independent mortgage and insurance broking firms will pay an introductory fee, and in that the standing of one's firm as estate agents should be the prime concern, it is clearly better, if one is in any doubt, to introduce one's prospective borrower to a well qualified and experienced specialist and avoid the risk of giving advice that might ultimately be seen by the borrower to have been unsound.

Some firms, not having their own departments, and rather than use brokers, have established links direct with life assurance companies. Provided some care is taken to ensure that the company is competitive in the mortgage field, this is to be encouraged. As important will be the calibre of the local manager or inspector of the society or company that is used in this way. The negotiator making an introduction will need to know that the person who will deal with the enquiry is someone in whom the prospective purchaser will have confidence, and that he will go out of his way to help, for this particular service often involves evening and week-end working.

What are the sources of finance? There are basically four institutional sources — building societies, local authorities, insurance companies and banks.

In 1968 the building societies and insurance companies between them provided no less than 95 per cent of the total advances made for house-purchase. Of this the building societies advanced 87.8 per cent and the insurance companies 7.2 per cent. The building societies clearly play the dominating role in financing the house market. The role of local authorities has never been of great significance, because central Government has "blown hot and cold" as to the extent to which they should be involved. Originally they were encouraged to enter into the market with loans of up to 100 per cent and on the older type of house. It follows that their commitment, such as it was, tended to be in the lowest price-ranges and initially was intended to supply mortgage finance in cases where building societies could not or would not make a large enough advance or any advance at all.

Local authority loans have, in contradistinction, tended to be more expensive in terms of interest than those from building societies, but like those of the life assurance societies their advances were normally at fixed interest rates. The building societies and local authorities both equated the amount borrowed and the overall interest to be charged with the term of the loan, which was then repayable at an even monthly rate throughout the term, but the building societies have had to adjust the overall monthly rate to reflect variations in interest rates and in particular the rate of interest they have had to pay to attract investors.

When they have done this, they have normally given the borrower the opportunity either to increase the repayment rate to maintain the same length of term, or to maintain his original rate of repayment and accept a longer or indefinite term. I write this only the day after the Building Societies Association approved an increase in their interest rate to an unprecedented 15 per cent and when the Association's Chairman admitted that considerable difficulty would be caused to many borrowers, and that in some cases the Societies might have to accept that the new monthly rate would be beyond some, with the short-term consequence that some advances would have to be allowed to increase rather than decrease.

Local authorities are not likely in the future to play a significant part in financing house-purchase with the Government anxious that they should reduce their lending commitments. In that both normal building society and local authority loans are intended steadily to be repaid throughout the period, they are generally referred to as "repayment mortgages".

The endowment mortgage works on a different principle. The building Society or life insurance company makes its loan for a specific period and does not seek repayment of that loan until the end of the term, charging interest only. The borrower, however, takes an endowment assurance policy on his life for the amount borrowed (this policy can be with or without profits and we shall discuss this point) and the policy is charged to the society or company. On maturity the policy will produce the sum necessary to redeem the mortgage and if it was a policy "with profits" the profits will accrue to the borrower.

Of late the banks, who traditionally have been opposed to lending "long", have entered into the mortgage market and in particular where the larger loans, those of £20,000 or more, are involved.

An owner/occupier can currently claim tax-relief on the interest he pays to a building society or indeed to any mortgagee, and the relief he obtains will be at his highest tax-rate. For anybody paying income-tax at the standard rate or above it, this help is significant and indeed it has been severely criticised and threatened by some politicians as being a subsidy to those who do not need it or should not have it. It should be noted that where the mortgage advance currently exceeds £25,000, interest payable on the sum by which this figure is exceeded cannot attract tax-relief, and relief is only available in respect of one's principal place of residence, or in respect of one provided for a dependant relative. This facility, whilst clearly helping many, puts those on low incomes at a relative disadvantage.

The Government introduced the Option Mortgage Scheme, which effectively gives the borrower a choice. He can either pay the building society the normal interest rate and claim his tax-relief on the amount, or he can opt to pay a reduced rate of interest, effectively the normal rate less tax relief at the standard rate. It is of considerable benefit for someone who believes his income will remain low and who is not paying enough standard rate tax to take full advantage of the allowances, but perhaps of less benefit to somebody for whom promotion is assured. It is in practice possible to switch from the option scheme to the normal building society method after four years, but only on the first day of April in any year. It is not as easy if one has taken a normal building society advance to switch it to an option scheme. The society's permission will be required and it will be necessary to show reduced financial circumstances.

Another feature of the Option Scheme is that the Government subsidises 50 per cent of the normal insurance guarantee premium required if the building society is to increase its advance to 95 per cent. This arrangement makes it technically possible to obtain an advance of 100 per cent of valuation up to £12,000.

The agent advising a prospective purchaser who is planning to take out a repayment mortgage in any of the ways we have discussed must stress to that purchaser one serious disadvantage and how it can be easily overcome. There is no protection by way of life assurance or in the case of permanent sickness.

If the bread-winner should die, his dependants will be responsible for the outstanding mortgage in full, and grave hardship could result. In the event of long illness or total incapacity the benefits which the family may be eligible for from the State may not be sufficient to maintain both the family and the mortgage. The family can be relatively cheaply protected against the contingency of death by a mortgage protection policy or by term life-cover. A mortgage protection policy is normally taken out for the amount borrowed and the actual sum payable in the event of death reduces year by year to reflect the amount that would still be outstanding on the mortgage. This is the cheapest way of protecting one's family, but there are dangers. The average life of a mortgage is only some $5\frac{1}{2}$ to 6 years. One of the reasons for this is an owner/occupier's selling one house, paying off the mortgage, buying another and taking another mortgage, normally for a higher sum. This would leave his original mortgage protection policy inadequate and make it necessary to take out another. If his health had become suspect there would be no guarantee that he could obtain the increased cover he would need.

Increasing interest rates present the other danger, for, as we have seen, where interest rates increase, most building societies will allow borrowers to extend the term if they cannot stand the increased repayment rate. This would carry the risk of a protection policy proving inadequate if not "topped up."

Dependent on age and state of health, insurance to provide income in the event of a long illness or total incapacity resulting from sickness or accident is relatively inexpensive.

There is I think little I need to add with regard to the endowment method. At its simplest it is a mortgage that will remain constant throughout the term, attracting interest but no repayments as such. Repayment will be achieved at the end of the day by the proceeds of a life insurance "endowment" policy that will be charged to the society, or if the mortgage is from the insurance company direct or the bank, held by them. The normal tax-relief on interest, except to the extent by which the loan exceeds £25,000, is available, but in addition tax-relief on the insurance premium is also allowed at half the standard income-tax rate. A word of caution: a high income earner may already have other complex insurance arrangements, and in particular could this apply if he is self-employed, and there is a ceiling on the amount of premium in any one year that can attract tax relief. At the end of this chapter I will set out tables comparing the various methods, but the policies available to support endowment mortgages are many and various, and it is at this stage that the estate agent without his own department specialising in this field will need the help either of a broker, or of a life assurance company which he knows to be competitive.

The with-profits endowment policy has obvious advantages, for not only will the borrower be protected against inflation to the extent that it will be reflected in the value of his house, he will at the end of the term get the benefits of the profits earned by his policy. Another word of warning. Some of the life assurance companies, being aware of this, will not, if they themselves are to be the mortgagees and thereby losing growth on the amount advanced, at the same time allow their borrower to share in their profits.

Low-cost endowment mortgages could be of particular help to those who anticipate future growth in earnings but at the outset are faced with a very tight housing budget. Schemes vary in detail, but a typical low-cost endowment mortgage for say £15,000 would provide life-cover (cover on premature death) of the full £15,000, but an actual sum assured of £7,500 on a with-profits basis relying on profits, not to produce a cash bonus at the end of the term, but to make up the difference between the amount borrowed and the initial sum assured.

Other sources of house finance

We have noted that the banks are beginning to interest themselves in this field, particularly at the top end of the market. For most of the last 20 to 25 years the pressure on the building societies has been such that they have been unable to meet all the demands placed on them by would-be borrowers. This pressure is likely to continue and one could expect to see the banks' involvement in the house finance field becoming a significant one.

It should not be forgotten that they have always played a role, but this historically has been by way of short or medium term lending, the Home Loan Account over a period of up to ten years being common. Insurance companies are also willing by way of second mortgages to "top up" the principal loan from a building society.

There are other sources of housing finance not significant in the overall context of "financing the market" but of which the good estate agent should be aware. Some companies, and the banks themselves are an obvious example, provide mortgages for their own staff, some private investors, normally reached through their solicitors or accountants, are prepared to lend money by way of mortgage, either on first or second charge.

The following tables have been prepared so that the various methods by which house-purchasers are normally financed can be compared. The interest rates and tax-rates used were those current when the calculations were prepared. In that the rates are likely to fluctuate, I have not attempted to adjust to reflect the rates current at the date of going to press.

It will be noted that the rate of interest adopted in the endowment scheme example is slightly higher than that of the normal building society loan; this is normal market practice.

It must be stressed that terms offered by life assurance societies, while unlikely to differ widely, do differ, and any borrower seeking to finance his first house-purchase, or agent seeking to help him, would be well advised to look at several quotations and examine them closely. When the time comes for the borrower to sell and purchase again, his overall position should be reviewed. He will be older, perhaps if he was not well advised in the first place, wiser, and he may be in a very different position as a tax-payer. (See table on page 340).

House Renovation Grants

The Housing Act 1974 provided various kinds of grant for the repair of

sound older houses to be made by Local Authorities, with Government assistance. It is sufficient for us to note the four types of grant available:
(i) *Improvement grants* for improving existing dwellings to a high standard or for converting properties into flats. The Council pay these at their discretion.
(ii) *Intermediate grants* for providing certain missing standard amenities in existing dwellings, coupled with essential repairs or replacements. Provided certain requirements are met the Council are obliged to pay.
(iii) *Special grants* for providing certain standard amenities for the overall benefit of houses in multiple occupation, payable at the discretion of the local authority.
(iv) *Repairs grants* for repairs and replacements to a dwelling which is in either a housing action area or a general improvement area, payable at the discretion of the local authority in cases of financial hardship.

The estate agent should have detailed knowledge of the grants available in his area and the Department of the Environment have prepared booklets, available from Local Authorities, setting out the types of grant available, the amounts that can be granted, how to apply, and the conditions attached to them. Although not of great significance in "financing the house market", their availability can have a marginal effect on values and therefore on the saleability of houses to which they would apply.

The Building Societies

The first building society is understood to have been founded in Birmingham in 1775. In those early days the societies were no more than groups of individuals who joined together to use their accumulated savings to buy land and build houses on it; each member paying the society a fixed monthly sum until all the members were housed, at which stage the society was wound up. As Mr. Henry Webb of the Nationwide Building Society said in a paper given at the Centre for Advanced Land Use Studies, "these were the original terminating societies".

Then came the realisation that there were many who either did not want to own their own house, or already did so, and who had money to invest. It may be recalled from our brief look at the development of privately owned housing in Britain, that in the latter part of the nineteenth century direct investment in private tenanted housing was for many small investors a traditional and safe way of protecting their own savings and obtaining a reasonable return. It was perhaps understandable that the same type of investor was prepared to invest money in the new societies. As the young societies started to attract these investments, the terminating societies that still existed, and new societies, developed into what we know and recognise to-day as the "permanent" building societies.

The movement grew rapidly. The first Building Society Act was passed in 1874 and by the beginning of the twentieth century the number of societies had reached 2,200, although "each was relatively small and local". Many societies to-day are still identified by the name of the town in which they originated.

During this century the pattern has changed considerably, for although the societies, now under the overall control of the Chief Registrar of Friendly Societies, have vastly increased their assets, and degree of involvement, by dissolution and mergers the actual number has reduced to less than 400, and in 1973, 72.5 per cent of the total assets were in the hands of the then 14 largest societies.

That the societies have continued to attract investment money sufficient to finance this growth is to some a matter of surprise, for the investor in the building society cannot hope to see growth in his investment in real terms. Nevertheless the societies, benefiting to some measure from tax concessions and in normal circumstances able to pay a relatively high rate of interest net of tax to their investors, have their attractions to those who do not pay tax at higher than the standard rate. In particular they remain an attractive investment for those investing relatively small sums and wanting both security and ready access to their savings.

In recent years the societies have come under a great deal of pressure, not only from the rapidly developing new investment media, such as unit trusts, but from the State. It is strange to reflect that while successive governments have paid lip-service to home ownership and the building societies, they have, because of their insatiable need to borrow, through many of their various national savings proposals, been in open competition with the societies for their traditional investors. Partly as a result of this, the societies have become very susceptible to the general level of interest rates. If they cannot compete in the market place, they cannot have the funds to lend to would-be mortgagors. At the same time there is a tendency when it is necessary for them to increase their interest rates both to borrowers and to investors, to maintain an adequate investment flow, for them to come under pressure from Government not to do so. Although the Conservative Party believes in a free market, such pressure was exerted by the Conservative Government in 1979. The societies held back, and estimate that it cost the movement something in the order of £40m. They held back believing that the then very high Minimum Lending Rate was a temporary measure, and they may have received some assurances to this effect, but in November the same year the Minimum Lending Rate leapt to 17 per cent and the societies were forced to increase the rate of interest charged to their borrowers to 15 per cent, with the effects we have already noted.

Again I may appear to have digressed, but there is a factor here of considerable importance to the practising estate agent. A change in interest rates involves a great deal of work on the part of the societies, work that may have been very nearly impossible to accomplish were it not for computers, but even with this aid, in 1979 it was estimated that the cost of making all the necessary adjustments and keeping borrowers informed of their changed repayment rates and so on, was in the order of £1m. This is one reason for the Societies' reluctance to react immediately to every change in MLR. Another is the need, as they see it, to keep levels of interest both paid and received as stable as possible. It follows that societies tend to hold back to see whether a significant change in the general level of interest rates proves to be temporary or is going to be sustained long enough to justify their following suit.

Constant changes in interest rates and the need to compete with other forms of investment, in particular the banks and national savings, has been the principal cause of wide fluctuation in the rate of investment into the societies. This produces periods when mortgages are relatively easy to secure, and almost immediately available, but also periods of mortgage famine, with societies forced strictly to control the amounts lent.

The estate agent needs to appreciate the effect that interest rates have on the supply of money available to the housing market, for it is one of the principal factors underlying the boom/slump pattern of the market during the late 'sixties and throughout the 'seventies. We will be considering market factors elsewhere, but in the context of the house market, it is the periods of mortgage famine that are of particular significance to the estate agent. When the conditions that lead to a mortgage famine exist there is a tendency for the rate of instructions to sell to increase, and for the market itself to stagnate. Costs rise and revenue falls. The agent who cannot anticipate the money flow into his market will neither be prepared for the boom, nor for the recession, and his fingers will be burnt.

The Societies' lending policy

From time to time the societies have attracted some criticsim for being over-selective in deciding to whom and on what sort of security to lend. None of the comments I would make can be specific, for although the movement as a whole might follow a general pattern, individual societies will have their own guide-lines and indeed these will from time to time vary. Criticism generally has been ill-informed. The societies must have two main aims. The first is to protect the interests of their investors. I would not claim to know the policy followed by individual societies throughout the last 25 years, but if this aim has led some from time to time to restrict the type of property on which they are prepared to lend, by age or by specifying houses as opposed to flats, they could hardly be criticised for that. It must also be remembered that many of those who invest with building societies are young persons saving with a view to buying their first home and doing so with the benefit of a loan from that society. If some societies have in times of mortgage famine limited advances, or given a degree of preference to such persons, again who could blame them?

Their second aim, and one must remember that they are non-profit making organisations, must be to help as many would-be house purchasers as possible. If this has led to some putting a ceiling on the amount they are prepared to lend to any one person, could this not, at times when funds are short, be seen as abundantly fair?

There are further considerations that should not be overlooked. First, societies have to maintain a given standard of liquidity and second they have to differentiate between normal and special advances. Currently the limit on any normal advance is £20,000. Any loans they might wish to make above this figure, or on, for example a non-traditional security (and an estate agent's freehold office would be such a security), has to be regarded as a special advance and these are controlled, in that societies cannot in any one year make special advances totalling more than 15 per cent of the total advances made in the preceding year. To this extent, therefore, the societies are not only controlled as to the maximum they can normally lend to any one borrower but at the same time are compelled to direct the vast majority of available funds into the house market, and of this total the vast majority goes to owner/occupiers. Henry Webb gives a figure of 97.9 per cent of total lending in 1973 "with remaining mortgage funds being allocated almost entirely to projects allied to owner-occupation such as building finance, housing societies, self-build groups, etc."

Since the Housing Act 1964 there has been close co-operation between the building societies and the Housing Corporation in funding developments by Housing Societies and co-ownership schemes. Housing Societies have been able to borrow up to 100 per cent of cost, half of this coming from the Housing Corporation and the other half from the building society movement. The part housing societies, or associations, will play in providing housing in the future remains to be seen, but those of us who have had experience of selling land to them realise the restraints imposed on them and it is difficult to believe that they will ever be able to make a really significant contribution.

Building societies have always been willing to help the self-build groups, but however admirable the enthusiasm of these groups, they have not made a notable contribution to the stock of new housing.

Given that the vast majority of the money available to the societies to lend goes to owner/occupiers, we are now concerned with the other criteria to which the societies look in deciding to whom and on what security to lend.

First we look to the property offered as security. There is little evidence to show an unduly restrictive approach by the societies. Again I turn to Henry Webb's paper, in which he gave a table analysing what was then recent lending and it showed that of all the houses mortgaged to them 20 per cent of properties were built before 1919; 18 per cent of properties were built between 1919 and 1939; 7 per cent of properties were built between 1940 and 1960; 26 per cent of properties were built between 1961 and 1973; 29 per cent were new.

Certainly this shows no obvious bias based on the date of construction. Mr Webb went on to say — "Contrary to popular belief, building societies are prepared to consider the whole spectrum of properties as security and will advance on private dwellings for owner-occupation within the whole housing market. These include houses, bungalows, flats and maisonettes, new, modern, modernised and even older (pre 1919) properties."

A building society is required by law to have each property offered as security surveyed by a professional qualified surveyor and most place great reliance on the reports and valuations they receive. The society and its surveyor will be concerned about one or two matters in particular. Locality and saleability are two of them. Locality because the society, like any other prudent body or individual lending a substantial amount of money against a security, will want to know that the value of that security is likely to be maintained during the period of the loan. It will want to be satisfied that if its borrower got into difficulties and had to sell the house, this could be readily achieved and in more dire circumstances, if they were forced as mortgagees to repossess, that the sale of the house would recoup the loan.

They will be concerned at the structural state. This is not to say that they are looking for the structurally perfect. The surveyor will be concerned to satisfy himself that there are no defects serious enough to cause rapid overall deterioration and a significant fall in value. He will also want to satisfy himself that any repairs that he considers essential and that require immediate attention if value is to be maintained, are carried out. He will make recommendations in this respect to the society, advising either a retention from any advance agreed until the work has been completed, or that the society obtain an undertaking from the borrower to carry out those works.

The surveyor and the society will both be concerned as to value. This does not necessarily mean simply that the price being paid for the house is fair. Perhaps the best guide as to the value of any house is what somebody is prepared to pay for it, but there is always somebody prepared to pay "over the odds" for something that suits them ideally and there are those lucky enough to buy something at less than full open market value, possibly from a relative or in the case of a sitting tenant from his landlord. The society will want to hear from the surveyor/valuer what price he believes could readily be obtained for that security in the open market.

It is one of the criticisms often levelled at building societies and at the way the house market operates in this country that although the borrower pays for it, the contents of the building society's surveyor's report are confidential and solely for the purpose of that society in considering the advance. Borrowers are expected to accept this and with it accept that the society is to have no responsibility for, or give any warranty as to, the condition of the property. This is a matter on which the Office of Fair Trading have recently expressed concern and urged action, and one major Society has already responded.

I suggest the reasons are obvious. The building society surveyor is not expected to carry out a fully detailed survey of the structure, but simply to satisfy himself as to the matters I have already outlined. If the surveyor's report were to be available to the prospective purchaser, there is the danger of giving an implied warranty both as to condition and as to value. This could lead to disputes with regard to undisclosed minor defects which had not, bearing in mind the object of his inspection, caused the society's surveyor any concern. It could also lead to purchasers quoting the report in an attempt to re-negotiate the purchase price. The building society would in effect become, just what it is not, an adviser to the purchaser. Its prime aim, as we have seen, is in practice to protect the interests of its investors. There is a clear difference in emphasis between what a purchaser would "like" to know about the house he is buying and what the society in its capacity "needs" to know.

An attempt is being made by the societies to answer the concern expressed by the Office of Fair Trading. Most societies now will advise purchasers wishing to have an independent structural survey and, if need be, valuation carried out to go to the society's own surveyor for this purpose, on the understanding that as that surveyor will be receiving two fees, there will be some overall saving. It is also suggested that where the purchaser wishes a particular surveyor to carry out his detailed structural survey, the society should use that surveyor.

There is a danger here, for the societies select the surveyors they are going to use, and close associations have been built up over the years. The societies are obliged to satisfy themselves as to the experience and qualifications of any surveyors they use. It follows that if the purchaser wishes to use a surveyor who is not already known to the society, time could be lost while the society satisfies itself that he is acceptable to them.

There is a belief that if the same surveyor carries out both functions, time will be saved. This is likely to prove an illusion. The average building society surveyor regards society work as urgent and is expected to do so. Because of its limitations the inspection carried out for a society is likely to take appreciably less time than a fully detailed survey of structural condition. Most surveyors in my experience would try to carry out a building society inspection and report on the day the instructions were received, but few would have their diaries so empty that they could immediately go out and carry out a full structural survey. The surveyor may have to make two visits, in which case the saving in time and costs is minimal, or he will delay preparing his report to the building society until he has been able to carry out the structural survey. This will slow down even further the process that is already the subject of much criticism.

Considering further the types of security the societies are prepared to accept, the majority will insist that where loans are to be made on flats or maisonettes, they are held on long lease, to ensure that the necessary rights of support and so on are there, and further that covenants controlling the use, maintenance of structure and common parts and indeed the behaviour of lessees, are capable of being enforced to protect the value of the security. They will also want to see that the asset remaining at the end of the repayment period is of significant value and for this reason they like to see 25 or 30 years of the lease unexpired at that time.

When lending on new property, the societies who are members of the Building Societies Association, are committed to lend only if the property carries a National House Building Council 10 year guarantee certificate against serious defect.

The purchaser wishing to borrow against the security of a very much older property, a timber-framed thatched cottage, for example, or against one of unconventional construction may have difficulties, not necessarily because the society itself will not lend as a matter of policy, but possibly because its surveyor has taken a view either as to a considerably increased risk of rapid deterioration in the structure, or as to difficulty in marketing, and either valued at well below the agreed price, thereby limiting the amount of advance that might be obtainable, or advised a limit to the length of term, thereby effectively increasing the repayment rate.

The other criteria used by the societies in assessing how much they are prepared to lend is the "status" of the would-be borrower. I cannot be specific about this, for policy will vary from society to society. Some may adapt their basic rules to reflect changes in interest rates and the resulting repayment levels while others will continue to look only to a multiple of the would-be borrower's income. In relating the amount they are prepared to lend to income the societies' object is to minimise the risk of default and the distress that this could cause. In particular the policy of societies with regard to the treatment of a wife's income varies. Some are prepared to offer an advance based on $2\frac{1}{4}$ times the husband's annual income plus one half of that of his wife. Others may go as far as to offer three times the husband's income plus the whole of the wife's. Policy also varies as to the treatment of non-guaranteed income such as overtime, commissions, bonuses, etc.

The societies will normally want to check the accuracy of any information given, either with the applicant's employers or in the case of self-employed borrowers with their accountants or by actually seeing audited accounts of the firm.

There is flexibility in the system and the good estate agent will know the policies followed by the societies represented in his own town and where best to go, in a given set of circumstances.

The societies are, not unnaturally, anxious to lend to borrowers who are likely to prove sound and to honour their commitment in all respects. Somebody with an existing track record as a borrower, or somebody who has shown the ability to save and invest regularly with their society are clearly in the strongest position.

The societies also limit the amount they are prepared to lend in relation to the purchase-price or the valuation figure, whichever is the lower. The normal maximum advance on a modern house is 80 per cent. For older houses, policy varies from one society to another and one cannot give a clear guide, other than an indication that if the society is prepared to lend at all, it will probably lend 60 per cent, if not more.

Also, one has to bear in mind the society's first responsibility to its investors, and it needs a margin, for if it were forced to re-possess and realise the asset, not only have the costs of doing so got to be borne, but there will be outstanding interest to recover, and if a borrower has got himself into difficulties the value of the house may have been depreciated by lack of maintenance. An 80 per cent advance can, however, with the approval of the society be increased to a maximum 95 per cent by an insurance company guaranteeing the difference. This guarantee would be arranged by the society, and the borrower would be charged a single premium in the order of £4 per cent on the difference between the basic advance and the total amount to be borrowed.

£15,000 MORTGAGE OVER 25 YEARS: MALE 29 YEARS OF AGE

Repayment Interest Rate 15%; Endowment 15 %; Option 10 %.

	METHOD A	METHOD B	METHOD C	METHOD D	METHOD E
	Government Option with (1) Mortgage Protection (5) Assurance	Capital Repayment with Mortgage Protection Assurance (5)	Low Cost Endowment (includes life cover)	Full Endowment without Profits (includes life cover)	Full Endowment with Profits (includes life cover)
Building Society payment (2)	143.10	193.50	190.65	190.65	190.65
Tax relief (4)	—	43.05	57.15	57.15	57.15
Net Building Society Cost (3)	143.10	150.45	133.50	133.50	133.50
Assurance Premium	3.50	3.50	27.35	33.05	57.35
Tax Relief (4)	0.61	0.61	4.79	5.78	10.04
Net Assurance Premium (5)	2.89	2.89	22.56	27.27	47.31
Total Net Monthly Cost	145.99	153.34	156.06	160.77	180.81
Estimated Tax Free Cash Lump Sum at End of Term (6)	NIL	NIL	£8,355	NIL	£35,340

NOTES (1) Government option — no tax relief on interest payments.

(2) In methods A and B the building society payment consists of elements of both capital and interest.

(3) Net monthly cost shown is the average figure over the term of the mortgage for method B.

(4) Tax relief calculated at 30% of interest payments and 17 % of premiums.

(5) Mortgage protection assurance is the cheapest form available, namely decreasing term assurance.

(6) Assuming that endowment bonuses are maintained at current rates.

Premium rates and bonuses used are those of the Legal & General Assurance Society Limited.

The lower the mortgage interest rate, the cheaper the low cost endowment method of repayment becomes in coparison to the capital repayment method.

The calculations have been made on the assumption that neither interest rates nor tax relief changes during the term of the mortgage.

Twenty-three

Financing the Commercial Market

The owner-occupier — The developer — Short and long term finance — The relationship between developer and investor — The Institutions and their aims — The Insurance Companies — Pension funds — The Banks

This is a major subject. Any close study would involve considering the links between the major financial institutions of this country and the economy itself, the overall investment policies of those institutions, the operation of the banking system, a knowledge of economics, a study of the many and varied forms of investment available, the factors that bear upon future value and performance, and so on. It would need a book in its own right.

I attempt no more than to give a brief outline of how I understand the market to be financed, which I hope will be of some assistance to general practitioners as and when they become involved with this particular section of the market.

In considering the financing of the residential market we were concerned in particular with the source of long-term mortgage finance. We were discussing a market place populated by owner-occupiers or potential owner-occupiers. Developers in that sector bought land, provided infrastructure works, built houses, sold them and moved on. We did not even consider how they were financed, believing it to be obvious; short term finance provided by the banks with the purchasers providing the "take out" and with each development proposition considered on its own merits in the light of banking policy at the time, and anticipated market conditions.

Financing the commercial market is much more complex. Although a significant proportion of this market is populated by owner-occupiers motivated by profit, the driving force underlying the market is in practice a significant proportion of the wealth of the people of this country represented by the insurance companies, the pension funds and the unit trusts who hold their savings and who themselves function in the property market as investors, and effectively as developers.

We propose here to consider the aims and financial requirements of those involved in the commercial market, first the owner-occupier, then the developer, the short-term financier, the long-term financier, and the investor.

We need only refer very briefly to the owner/occupier, the small industrialist, for example, the shop-keeper or the professional firm. It is arguable as to whether or not they should aspire to owning their own premises, the financial yields from which in terms of hypothetical rental value are likely to fall far short of the return the same capital would produce if directly invested in the expansion of their manufacturing process, the stock or merchandise sold, or into their own practices. This is not a debate we need enter into, for it is clear that many do choose to invest capital in their own premises, and whether they do so because they believe it gives their business security, because the investment is wise from a personal point of view, or simply because they see it as a means of acquiring capital as opposed to income is not our concern. If these owner-occupiers are to achieve their aim they need access to long-term mortgage funds. These traditionally have been available from insurance companies, who have been willing to make long-term investments, normally at fixed-interest rates. The banks also have been heavily involved, although on a somewhat shorter-term basis. In some cases firms or individuals have been able to borrow from the building societies, although, as we have seen, the amount they can lend by way of special advances has always been strictly limited.

Our study of financing the commercial market could well start with the developer, but remembering throughout the underlying role or influence of the institutions. Mr Milo Cripps, in a paper given for the Centre of Advanced Land Use Studies and discussing the developer, the short-term financier and the provider of long-term funds, said this:

"Twenty years ago their relationship fitted more or less tidily into an established pattern. Short-term finance was provided by banks against the security of a committed institutional take out; long term funds largely by insurance companies anxious to make fixed interest-rate investments on the security of a good covenant and attractive site. The developer usually combined the role of manufacturer and of long-term equity investor. He acted as impresario to the project from which he achieved without difficulty sufficient income to enable him to service a two-thirds valuation mortgage. His effort was directed to be sure that two-thirds of valuation equalled cost and ideally to enjoy from the first long rental period a substantial net income on his 100% equity."

One could put this another way and compare it with the house market. The house-builder relied on his eventual purchaser for his "take out". The commercial property developer looked not to a purchaser necessarily, but to the insurance company who would lend him enough money by way of long-term mortgage to finance his development. This was his "take out". Against this "take out" he could take his short-term development finance from the bank. He aimed to create an investment the initial yield from which would pay the interest on his mortgage. The development was said to "wash its face". He may or may not have had an initial profit by way of surplus annual income, but in that his mortgage would have been of a fixed amount and probably at a fixed rate of interest, any increases in the rent received arising from periodic reviews would be profit, and in that at any time he could sell on to an institution at a price based on capitalising the rent actually passing or anticipated, a potential capital profit was available to him if he wanted it.

This scene has changed. Dramatic increases in the value of commercial property, although they may result from nothing other than inflation, have made the traditional role of the long-term lender look remarkably unattractive, and conversely the profits of the developer/investor disproportionately high. Inevitably those who provided the money came to want a share in the cake, "the equity", notwithstanding that this carried a degree of risk with it.

With the change of scene the traditional roles played by the developers and the institutions have changed. Except in the more speculative of projects the developer can no longer look to holding 100 per cent of the equity, which will now have to be shared with the institution. As Milo Cripps put it:

"There has now arisen some inter-changeability of function between the participants. The cake is being sliced vertically rather than horizontally, in a general recognition that the icing is at the top. Increasingly, the finance on which the industry relies is provided by partners rather than by third parties, with third party finance tending to be available only from the banking system for short or medium term periods".

One other factor has made it increasingly difficult for developers to hold either all or even a substantial proportion of the equity. Pressure from the institutions wishing to acquire first-class commercial property investments has forced yields down, while in general terms interest rates have increased. Even if the developer could find long-term mortgage finance, and this has become much more difficult, faced with an interest rate of say 17 per cent and yields, as we have seen, as low as 5 or 6 per cent from prime property investments, he is unlikely to be able to fund or carry out a development project with any hope of it "washing its face". In short his outgoings will be substantially higher than income. What has been referred to as "a reverse yield gap".

Who are the institutions and what are they setting out to achieve? First the insurance companies and we are concerned here with the life companies and those general companies who effect life assurance business. These are the companies who have traditionally been committed to property investment and in recent years we have seen the growth of several new companies with a particular interest in the commercial property field. These companies were one of the main sources of long-term mortgage funds to the commercial property market and still play the most significant role in this field. Inflation has, however, affected them. The average man in the street traditionally saw life assurance as a means of protecting his family against premature death, as a means of saving either by way of an endowment policy towards his needs in old age, or for the general benefit of his family. In times when inflation was not a significant factor, he was prepared to secure by this means a fixed sum payable at a specific date, or at death. The company's commitment was known and they could therefore lend fixed sums at fixed rates of interest, balancing the two in the knowledge that they would be able to honour their undertaking under the policy. For the insured, however, inflation created the fear that as and when the proceeds of a policy were received they would, in relative terms, be valueless. This led to a substantial increase in the number of policies being taken out "with profits" and a need for the companies in their investment policy to protect themselves against the effecs of inflation to ensure that they would be able to honour their increased commitment. The reader will recall the attitude of these companies when lending direct on house-purchase and we have already commented in this chapter on the changes this has brought in their approach to financing property development, and indeed their investment in the commercial property field. They then are not only the providers of long-term finance but investors in their own right and in the latter context, in order to secure the right investments, they are prepared to consider providing the short-term finance as well.

Pension funds, and here we are talking about the self-administered funds, have interests very similar to those of the insurance companies. In that the pensions they commit themselves to provide will reflect the general level of earnings they too have got to ensure that their investment in the commercial property field performs in a way that will reflect the general inflationary trend. It follows that their approach to commercial property is very similar to that of the insurance companies. The pension funds, however, do not have, as insurance companies do, a still significant proportion of their cash inflow taken against limited and fixed liability, i.e. without profit policies. It follows that the pension funds are not significantly involved in long-term mortgage finance.

A relatively recent arrival on the scene are property bonds, which are to all intents and purposes property unit trusts, although linked to life assurance for the tax benefits that brings. Again their approach is similar to that of the insurance companies and pension funds.

Then the banks. First the clearing banks, and we have already noted their role in both the house market and in the owner/occupier commercial market. They traditionally are the providers of short term finance and certainly in the commercial property field, this remains their role.

The merchant banks' role does not differ greatly, but, by definition, they are attracted to higher risk situations, provided the rate of interest reflects the level of risk involved, and they are prepared to lend on a somewhat longer basis. Their role can perhaps be described as a more "active" one, for they are prepared, given the right circumstances, to participate and indeed might seek to do so as a condition of providing the funds required.

Although the banks have traditionally been the providers of short-term finance, as in the case of the house market, they are now more heavily involved in medium and indeed long-term finance.

It is perhaps the role of the developer that has changed most significantly. He no longer occupies the role attributed to him twenty years ago. He would then have been the "manufacturer", the risk-taker and the investor. It is now the first of these functions that is perhaps the most significant. As he was forced, for the reasons we have seen, to withdraw if not wholly at least partly from his role as an investor and proportionately his role as a risk-taker, the institutions have moved forward to take up the ground he has had to give up, to the extent that in some cases the developer has become little more than an adviser and project manager to the institutions, taking his share of the profits, proceeds or created value almost as a fee.

In discussing the developer's part in the financing of the commercial market, we must not overlook the fact that the owner-occupier or potential owner-occupier could be, when building a new factory, carrying out major extensions to existing property, refurbishing or redeveloping, just as much a "developer" as the development company. Paul Orchard-Lisle, readers will recall, underlined what he saw as the significance of this form of development in the years ahead.

We shall now consider the ways and means by which the various participants can work together to achieve their aim.

First as to the developer. He may be prepared, or indeed want, only to achieve out of a project a trading or manufacturing profit. He may simply seek to carry out the development permitted and to sell it on to an institution to create that profit. He may seek a short-term bank facility to finance the development process. Alternatively he may seek both short-term finance and his final "take out" with an institution. If he can achieve this then his short-term finance is likely to cost him less and his future is secured. Most institutions would want in these circumstances to see a pre-let, but not necessarily so if the calibre of the project were high enough. Clearly, the rate of interest they sought in any pre-funding or development finance would be related to the risk they were taking.

The performance of commercial property as an investment has, however, made most developers reluctant to abandon altogether their role as an investor, and given that they can rarely now hope to retain 100 per cent of the equity they will be concerned not only with funding the development process, but with retaining, no longer the top slice, but nevertheless a slice of the action. To consider the many ways in which this can be done is clearly beyond the scope of this book, but I would draw the interested reader's attention to "The Property Development Process" *and the articles of Milo Cripps and Norman Bowie on "Development Finance and Funding".

*Property Studies in the United Kingdom and Overseas No. 7. Published by the Centre for Advanced Land Use Studies, College of Estate Management, Reading.

Twenty-Four

Selling by Auction — The Estate Agent as an Auctioneer

The authority of the auctioneer — The need for precise instructions — Instructions as to reserve — Authority to sell — Authority to describe — Misdescription and misrepresentation related to selling by auction — Remedies for — Puffing and its dangers — Need for inspection by the auctioneer — Oral corrections — Non-disclosure — Need for care — Availability of documents

We have discussed sale by auction as one of the methods that can be adopted for the sale of real property, the circumstances under which its use should be considered, and where it would be inappropriate. We have also dealt with the preparation of particulars, and advertising, and certain related aspects of selling by private treaty. We now turn to further matters in connection with public auction that need attention.

First let us take the question of the authority of the auctioneer. The estate agent selling in the normal way by private treaty is seeking to effect an introduction between his vendor client and a purchaser willing to acquire the property concerned. It is an essential part of his task to negotiate the most favourable terms he can from his client's point of view, but he is not, unless specific authority has been given, entitled to commit his client by way of a binding contract.

When acting as an auctioneer, however, he is normally employed to bring about a legal binding contract for the sale of the property. As Murdoch puts it: "In the vast majority of cases ... an auctioneer will be specifically instructed to sell the vendor's property".

It is, as we have noted earlier, one of the benefits of selling by auction that, assuming the sale to be successful, a contract is established on the fall of the hammer. We referred to this as a benefit from the vendor's point of view, but many would-be purchasers would likewise see an advantage in buying at auction simply because they know that the auctioneer has an expressed or implied authority, albeit normally subject to a reserve price, to sell that property at that time to the highest bidder and to commit the vendor to that sale. From both parties' point of view it removes doubt.

The position is clear where the auctioneer has been given express authority to sell, but Murdoch first considered the extent to which an auctioneer may bind his client in the absence of express instructions.

He quotes Lord Edinburgh, CJ,: "If the principal send his commodity to a place, where it is the ordinary business of the person to whom it is confided to sell, it must be intended that the commodity was sent thither for the purpose of sale ... if one sends goods to an auction room, can it be supposed that he sent them thither merely for safe custody? Where the commodity is sent in such a way to such a place as to exhibit an apparent purpose of sale, the principal will be bound, and the purchaser safe."

It would follow from this that the purchaser will obtain good title even if the auctioneer acted in disobedience of instructions, but the matter is perhaps not as simple as that.

It should be stressed that what would appear to be the auctioneer's implied authority to sell is not unlimited. Instructions to sell by auction do not give an implied authority to sell by private treaty. To illustrate this: an auctioneer who, having failed to sell by auction, sold one month later to a purchaser who had been present at the auction failed in a claim for commission, because it was held that the sale that took place by private treaty lay outside the scope of his authority. Somewhat in contradiction, a purchaser who, following an abortive auction sale, bought privately at the reserve price was held bound by the contract. It was argued on the purchaser's behalf that the auctioneer had no authority to sell by private treaty, but the court held that it was the clear intention of the vendor to sell, provided the reserve price was obtained *(Bousfield v. Hodges)*.

The question of the vendor's authority is considered by Murdoch at length. There are one or two practical points that we should note here. It is customary, where the auction itself has proved abortive but one of those attending the sale, while still in the room, indicates a willingness to pay the reserve price, for the auctioneer to accept it, to vary the memorandum of sale, which, as we shall see later, normally forms part of the auction particulars, so that they are applicable to sale by private treaty and enter into a contract on the vendor's behalf. On one or two occasions I have gone further and have completed such an amended memorandum on the vendor's behalf later on the day of the auction, having returned to my office, but I stress that my authority to do so has never been questioned by the vendor. I would not personally go beyond this without taking further express instructions.

It is clearly the precise nature of one's initial instructions that would dictate the outcome of any action, and the auctioneer would be well advised to ensure that these are as specific as possible.

When the initial instructions are received they need do no more than deal with those matters that lead up to the sale itself, i.e., identifying the property, the interest that is to be sold, the amount of expenditure agreed, commission to be paid, the date of the sale, and that it will be subject to a reserve price, if that is the case. The instructions obtained immediately prior to the sale could be almost as important. Ideally, instructions as to a reserve price should be in writing, but very often these instructions are given verbally, sometimes minutes before the sale commences. Under these circumstances the auctioneer should ensure that there is a witness, either his own clerk, or the vendor's solicitor.

It is at this stage that the wise auctioneer will also seek express instructions as to how he is to proceed if the sale proves abortive. These may be to the effect that he has authority to sell by private treaty at the reserve price, or at a somewhat lower figure. Preferably the instructions should also be limited in time. For example, one's instructions may have come from solicitors elsewhere in the country. Instructions such as: "In the event of the reserve price of £45,000 not being reached and the sale proving abortive, you have authority to enter into a memorandum of sale by private treaty at any time within 72 hours of the sale, and at a price of not less than £42,500." Such instructions would leave the auctioneer's authority beyond doubt.

Despite the principle as stated by Lord Edinburgh, a vendor is not necessarily bound by an auctioneer who makes a mistake and who sells otherwise than on the terms expressly authorised. A vendor will not generally be bound at the fall of a hammer even if the memorandum of sale is completed, if that auctioneer had mistakenly sold at less than the reserve price, or to put it another way, on terms that he had no authority to accept.

The law on this point is complex. The general principle appears to be that provided the particulars of sale make it clear that the sale will be subject to a reserve price, or even "may" be subject to a reserve price, the vendor, having given the auctioneer instructions as to what the reserve price is to be, is not likely to be committed if the property is knocked down for less. The auctioneer making such a mistake may not, however, be "off the hook". In the case of *Fay v. Miller Wilkins and Co.* the conditions of sale reserved the right to fix the reserve price and the vendor stipulated £750; the auctioneer, however, knocked the property down for £600 and signed a memorandum ratifying the sale that was subsequently held as sufficient to satisfy Section 40 of the Law of Property 1925. The vendor was held not to be bound by the contract, for the purchaser, knowing of the possibility of a reserve being fixed, was put "on enquiry"; in choosing to bid not knowing whether or not the reserve had actually been fixed he took a risk and could not hold that vendor bound if the reserve price in fact exceeded the amount of the bid. The purchaser, however, recovered damages from the auctioneers on grounds of a breach of warranty of authority to sell.

The rule would appear to be that if an auctioneer, having knocked a property down at less than the reserve price, realises his mistake before the memorandum is signed, then declines to sign it, the vendor will not be bound, nor would the highest bidder have any effective remedy. If, however, the memorandum is concluded, the vendor might not be bound, but the purchaser might have a remedy against the auctioneer.

The golden rule for the auctioneer is to obtain if possible written instructions, not only as to the reserve price, but as to what authority he is to have, if the sale proves abortive, to conclude a sale by private treaty and to commit the vendor to such a sale by a written memorandum. Further it must be made clear in the auction particulars or the special conditions of sale that the property is to be subject to a reserve price, or, that it may be so sold.

In that the auctioneer has authority to sell, he has authority to describe the property he is to sell, in his particulars, his advertisements and when he is on the rostrum. Great care needs to be taken and here again we underline the importance of accuracy in one's auction particulars.

As Murdoch says: "Where information furnished by an auctioneer is inaccurate or insufficient, the legal liability is primarily that of the vendor, although the auctioneers may incur some personal liability. In any case the vendor who has lost a sale or who has had to pay compensation through the carelessness of his agent is entitled to be re-imbursed. It is therefore of the utmost importance that an auctioneer should not make any misleading statements, and if employed to draft the particulars on a sale of land that he should make full-disclosure of all necessary facts".

He then lists three distinct ways in which a vendor, through the auctioneer, may become liable to a purchaser — misdescription, non-disclosure and misrepresentation.

We will consider these only very briefly and I urge any practitioner regularly conducting sales by auction, or assisting in preparing for them, to read Murdoch on the subject.

Misdescription and misrepresentation have also been considered in the context of consumer protection legislation.

For our purposes, however, misdescription comes in two broad categories: substantial misdescription that could render the auction contract unenforceable against the purchaser, even if the vendor was willing to pay compensation; and misdescription that could adequately be remedied by the payment of compensation.

Two words of warning. A statement made on behalf of the vendor which effectively conceals the existence of an encumbrance to which the property is subject will render the contract unenforceable.

An auctioneer selling a public house and believing that a 'tying' covenant was unenforceable, sold it as a freehouse; he was wrong, the purchaser recovered his deposit, and avoided the contract.

Where a property is bought as an investment rather than for personal occupation, any inaccuracy in the stated rents or profits accruing from it will be fatal to the validity of the contract.

In a sale of 13 houses let to various tenants the aggregate annual rent was correctly stated, but from the particulars it appeared that the houses were let in pairs rather than singly. This misdescription was regarded as sufficiently substantial to enable the purchaser to recover his deposit.

Whether or not a false statement can adequately be remedied by the payment of compensation is largely a matter of degree: the test would appear to be "Is the purchaser getting substantially what he bargained for?"

The sitting tenant of a house described as having a depth of 46 feet when it was in fact 33 feet was held to have purchased what he expected and the contract was enforced against him, but at a reduced price.

In another case, however, 30 acres of building land was sold, $4\frac{1}{2}$ acres of which turned out to be the subject of undisclosed easements. This deficiency was held to be too great to be remedied by payment of compensation.

"Puffing" is permitted, but only to a degree. Murdoch states that in puffing a property by "stressing (and perhaps rather exaggerating) its good points, no liability is incurred while what is expressed is a matter of opinion rather than fact." In the case of *Watson v. Burton* 1956 the property was described as 'valuable and extensive premises . . . situated in a first-class position' and 'very suitable for development'. This, said Mr. Justice Wynn-Parry, was "What I may describe, with no disrespect, as a typical auctioneer's 'puff'."

This is a matter where care on behalf of the auctioneer is needed, not only in the preparation of particulars and advertisements, but in correspondence prior to a sale, and on the rostrum. There must be great care not only that one's particulars are accurate but that what is said in puffing can be taken as no more than an expression of opinion, however wrong. If a purchaser is to obtain a remedy he must show more than a difference of opinion. Again from Murdoch: "Thus it is merely a 'puff' to describe property as 'a residence fit for a family of distinction' or as a 'substantial and convenient dwelling house'. Where, however, a house is described as 'in good repair' or 'not damp' these are treated as statements of fact and, if they are untrue, the purchaser is entitled to compensation or to avoid the sale."

Again the auctioneer would be wise not to express an opinion if there is any risk that it might conflict with known facts. Where for example an hotel was described as let to "a most desirable tenant" the purchasers were able to rescind the contract when it could be shown the tenant was in arrear with the rent.

It is common practice in auction particulars, or more usually in the Special Conditions of Sale that are to form part of the auction contract, to provide a provision to the effect that any errors of description will not annul the sale, and either that "Any misdescriptions shall be the subject of compensation" or that no compensation would be payable.

The effect of such provisions must be considered uncertain. They are unlikely to be effective where substantial misdescription is involved.

It is sometimes necessary for an auctioneer to make oral corrections and I limit myself here simply to practical advice.

It may be that the auctioneer is not the person who prepared the sale and drafted the particulars and any such auctioneer must make his own inspection prior to the sale to satisfy himself as to accuracy. If it is necessary orally from the rostrum to correct an error or to announce, for example, that a fixture is to be removed, or to add to the written particulars, for example, the reservation of a right for the vendor to hold a sale of goods from the premises prior to completion, I make it a practice not only to make the oral correction but to state that the contract copies have been so altered and request all those present to alter their own copies, and I would not hesitate if, once the sale has started, somebody arrives late and then starts to bid, to repeat the procedure to avoid any risk of the successful bidder being unaware of the correction. By way of illustration, in the case of *Edwards and Daniel Sykes and Co. Ltd.,* the particulars of sale of a leasehold shop named the "annual rental" at which it was held. The purchaser of the reversion claimed to have taken this to mean that the tenant had a yearly tenancy, paying the rates, when in fact the tenancy was monthly at a weekly rent equivalent to the stated "annual rent" and the landlord paid the rates. The purchaser claimed compensation but failed when evidence was admitted to show that the true position had been clearly explained by the auctioneer, so that the purchaser could have been left in no real doubt as to what he was buying.

Non-Disclosure

The need for great care in the preparation of particulars of sale is obvious, but as Murdoch puts it "Merely refraining from making any positive mis-statement is not, however, necessarily sufficient to avoid legal liability. The contract for sale of land occupies a special position in English law in that the vendor is bound to disclose certain matters; if he does not, the contract is unenforceable."

We need not consider non-disclosure at length. We are concerned principally with defects in the vendor's title to land rather than defects in quality of the land, or to put it another way, with latent as opposed to patent defects.

As one authority has it: "I think he (the purchaser) is only liable to take the property subject to those defects that are patent to the eye, including those defects which are a necessary consequence of something which is patent to the eye".

Murdoch says: "It is an implied term in all contracts of a sale of land that except in so far as the purchaser is told otherwise he may expect to receive a fee simple free from any encumbrances which would not be revealed by reasonable examination of the property."

It is usual to find in Special Conditions of Sale a condition to the effect that the property is to be sold subject to "any rights, easements, quasi-easements, liabilities and public rights affecting the same".

Such a phrase would protect a vendor against an innocent non-disclosure, but it would not protect where the defect in the title was known or should have been known. The purchaser's rights are similar to those that would protect him against misrepresentation or misdescription.

Amongst those matters that could be relevant to the auctioneer estate agent are footpaths, and I can remember a lovely Georgian house with lawns sweeping down to the shores of a harbour, which were in fact bi-sected by a little-used but nevertheless public right of way which only somebody who knew the area intimately could have been aware of.

Notices could also be relevant; a repair notice, a dangerous structure notice, party-wall notice, a notice for the making-up of a private street, and so on. It is very important that whoever takes and drafts the particulars looks out for problems of this kind and if need be asks questions of the vendor, his solicitor, or the local authority.

We are concerned not only with freehold titles, for the vendor of a leasehold property is obliged to disclose any covenants which are "unusually onerous for a lease of that type" and it would be safe to regard as unusual any covenants beyond the obvious, those to pay rent, taxes, to repair, the lessor's right of entry to inspect and the lessee's right to quiet enjoyment.

Whilst the majority of purchasers or their solicitors will inspect a lease prior to a sale, I nevertheless think it right that the sale particulars themselves should draw attention to any unusual covenants. A butcher, for example, having received particulars of a shop that he thinks would be of interest and having travelled a distance to inspect will not be amused if he subsequently finds a covenant effectively preventing the premises being used for his own trade.

What is important is that the auctioneer should have available to him and for inspection all relevant documents, whether it be a copy of the lease, a schedule of restrictive covenants, a planning consent, a repair notice, etc. These must not only be available to him, they must be available for inspection by prospective purchasers, either at his office or that of the vendor's solicitor, and the particulars must state not only that the documents exist, but that they may be inspected, where and when.

Misrepresentation

We considered the Misrepresentation Act of 1967 and the Trade Descriptions Act of 1968 elsewhere and will recall the basic difference between misdescription and misrepresentation, the latter being "a false statement of fact made by one contracting party to another which, though not forming part of the contract, induces that party to enter into the contract".

Or again to quote Murdoch: "The description of a misrepresentation as a false statement which is not included in the contract serves to distinguish it from a mis-description which ... is an error in the contractual description of property for sale".

It is because of the non-contractual nature of misrepresentation that the estate agent is more at risk when selling by private treaty than he is when selling as an auctioneer, when misdescription becomes the greater hazard.

Twenty-Five

Selling by Auction — Preparation of Sale

The time required — Availability of the vendor — Fixing the reserve — The guide price — Preparation of particulars — Special considerations — Special Conditions of Sale — Confirming instructions — Selling prior to auction — An aide-mémoire — The upset price

The time required adequately to prepare a sale will vary considerably, dependent on the nature and calibre of the property to be sold, the way it is to be presented and the amount of advertising that is to be carried out, in other words the degree of exposure needed in order to ensure so far as possible the success of the sale. It may be, for example, when selling small residential investments in a town where there is a known market, that a sale could be mounted in as little as four weeks, with little to be gained by taking longer. On the other hand, the good country house that, if it is to be presented in the best possible light, would require the preparation of printed particulars with coloured photographs, and advertising in the National press and "Country Life," the house being of a calibre where most would-be purchasers would want to have a structural survey carried out, to try to mount a sale in much less than three months would be unwise.

We have discussed earlier the taking of instructions, but in regard to instructions by auction there are further observations that should be made.

First, although, hopefully, one would have reached rough agreement with the vendor as to the reserve price to be fixed, the final decision as to the figure to be adopted should be left, if not to the last moment, certainly until the last few days before the sale itself, so that it can be finalised in the light of the known interest. It is particularly important, therefore, to ensure that the vendor will be available at the appropriate time, or to know where he can be contacted and arrangements be made for final instructions to be taken. Although one of the objects of selling by auction is often to avoid quoting a specific price, purchasers often, and fairly, ask what sort of price is anticipated. For negotiators to adopt too low a figure in the hope of encouraging widespread interest could depress the market for the property and prevent one getting the best possible figure. Similarly, the adoption of too high a guide price could turn away prospective purchasers at a very early stage. If, for example, one was looking to a reserve of about £45,000, it would be unrealistic to try to generate interest amongst those for whom £40,000 is the absolute limit and it could have a deterrent effect to say that one was anticipating £50,000 or more. To say that one was expecting the property to realise a price in the middle or high 40s would leave one open to fix the reserve price, in the light of experience and knowledge gained while the property has been exposed to the market at anything between say £42,000 and £50,000. It is important that whatever is to be said be agreed with the vendor at the outset. Particular care needs to be taken when dealing with the question whether fixtures and fittings are to be included or excluded, for it must never be forgotten that one is preparing a contract document.

Again, dependent upon the nature of the property concerned, the actual date of the sale could be important. A small residential investment, a good commercial property or a site likely to be of interest to a development company will attract those to whom it is likely to be of interest irrespective of the time of year when it is offered and when the sale takes place, but to mount the sale of a good private house on a date when many will be away on holiday, or which would involve advertising at a time when this was likely, would be to run the risk of under-exposure, with disappointing consequences. If there is any doubt in the vendor's mind as to what he wants to leave or take, then those items are better not referred to. If, as sometimes is the case, the vendor will require his purchaser to take over certain items, such as curtains and carpets, then this has got to be made clear. One often sees it stated ". . . are to be taken over at valuation". This should be avoided. Ideally, a schedule of the items to be taken over should be prepared, with a definite price stated, whether this be arrived at by valuation or simply decided upon by the vendor.

The preparation of particulars has been discussed elsewhere but here one must deal with matters specifically related to particulars for a sale by auction.

Auction particulars should be prepared in four sections.

(1) *General Remarks and Stipulations:* The matters that could be dealt with under this heading are: *Situation:* A general description of the area, with distances from main centres, public transport facilities, schools, sporting and entertainment facilities, shops and so on. *Method of Sale:* This would apply particularly when one was selling in more than one lot. For example, a large house with planning consent for an additional house in the garden. The auctioneer may have advised that the whole be offered first as one lot, and then if this did not sell as two separate lots,

but further, in the event of the house itself not selling, that it would be unwise to proceed with the sale of the building plot. This will lead to a stipulation that "Lots 1 and 2 will first be offered as one lot, if unsold they will be offered separately. If Lot 1 fails to sell the vendor reserves the right to withdraw Lot 2." *Fixtures and Fittings:* This could deal with any specific requirements with regard to taking over certain items at valuation, but as a minimum and to avoid any misunderstanding it ought to state that "only such items as are specifically referred to in the particulars are included in the sale". This statement is quite clear, but again care should be taken not to mislead, and if any items that the average purchaser might expect to be included are in fact to be excluded, it is wise to say so. Garden ornaments and garden sheds would be a good example. *Local Authorities and Statutory Undertakers:* In preparing a sale by auction one is creating a situation where would-be purchasers and their solicitors have got to make their enquiries before they know whether or not they can secure the house or property they want at the right price, and they may well want to make searches or preliminary enquiries of the local authorities, oar make enquiries with regard to services. The names of the authorities and undertakers, their addresses and telephone numbers should be given.

Other matters that could be dealt with in this section are: Tenure, including details of leases, availability of documents such as planning consents, easements, way-leaves, rating assessments, viewing arrangements and directions as to how to find the property. Special circumstances might dictate the need to deal with other matters under this general heading.

(2) *Specific Details:* The second section of the auction particulars will contain the details of the property, giving a specific description, covering those matters not already dealt with under Situation: type and date of construction, style and appearance, a photograph, aspects, views, and so on. It is in this section the greatest care needs to be taken not to misdescribe.

(3) *Special Conditions of Sale:* I am told that in some parts of the country, it is common practice for these to take the form of a separate document and even on occasions simply to be read out in the auction room. I believe whenever possible they should form part of the auction particulars brochure. They will be prepared by the vendor's solicitor, they will normally refer to the National Conditions of Sale, and a copy of those Conditions should be available in the auctioneers' office. They will either set out or refer to any restrictive covenants or encumbrances: if this is simply a referral, putting a would-be purchaser "on notice", then copies of these should also be available. They must give a completion date, and it is particularly important for the auctioneer to ensure that they do state that the property will be, or may be, sold

<u>**MEMORANDUM**</u>

I

of

hereby acknowledge myself to be the Purchaser of the property described in the Particulars and Special Conditions

of Sale at the sum of £   and I have paid the sum of £   to the auctioneers, Messrs.

                    as a deposit and in part payment of the purchase money and I agree to pay the remainder thereof

and to complete the sale in accordance with the Particulars and Special Conditions of Sale.

DATED the   day of   1980

Purchase money	£	
Deposit	£	_____
Balance	£	

....
Purchaser

As agents for the Vendor we hereby confirm this sale and acknowledge receipt of the said deposit

....

Abstract of Title to be sent to:

subject to a reserve price and, in my opinion they should also reserve the right for the vendor to bid either by himself or by an agent.

(4) *The Memorandum:* A typical form of Memorandum is set out opposite.

The mechanics of the sale need to be dealt with. The auction particulars should state prominently either on the front cover or on a fly-leaf, the time and place at which the property is to be sold, remembering to add if appropriate "unless previously sold by private treaty". They should also give, since a prospective purchaser's solicitor may want to make enquiries, the name, address and telephone number of the vendor's solicitors.

Letters confirming auction instructions need particular care, for there are matters to be dealt with not necessarily required when confirming a sale by private treaty.

First one should send a preliminary draft of the general remarks, stipulations and particulars of sale, asking for confirmation that they comply with the facts and the vendor's wishes. Further one should ask, if one has not already done so, for details of any outgoings and any rights which others may enjoy over the property, with a view to minimising the risk of misdescription or non-disclosure on the part of the vendor.

The letter of confirmation should also deal with the auction expenses and timings. It is customary for an auctioneer, having regard to the amount of additional work involved in selling by this method and the interest that it is hoped this work will generate, to seek a period, following the sale, when he will continue as sole agent, and possibly, (and this might be one occasion when it would be justified), with sole selling rights. This must be clearly stipulated. There is always the possibility that a prospective purchaser not willing to take part in an auction, or not able to do so, will make a very good bid prior to the sale. As soon as one's particulars have been printed, one in effect has a draft contract. If there is any question of one's client not being available, it would be as well at the outset to establish one's authority to sell prior to the sale. One would similarly need to establish, as we earlier saw, what authority one has to sell by private treaty in the period immediately following an abortive sale.

The fact that one has received instructions to sell by auction should be reported to the vendor's solicitor as quickly as possible, and as a matter of courtesy one should try to establish with him, even before confirming one's instructions to the client, that the proposed date of sale is convenient to him and indeed, if there are any unusual circumstances or conditions, that the proposed arrangements and method of sale are acceptable. He should be asked for any information that is relevant and which could be ascertained from the Deeds or of which he has knowledge.

However much time one has allowed, preparation for the sale needs careful planning and most auctioneers find an *aide-mémoire* useful. The following was suggested by "Practice Notes for Estate Agents."

PROPERTY AUCTION PROFORMA
AIDE MEMOIRE

	Date	Initials
ON FIRST INSTRUCTIONS (additional to draft letters and memos)		
Book room by phone		
Send off draft advertisements to newspapers		
Book space for advertising with co-ordinating offices		
Order plans		
Order photographs		
Draft and circulate preliminary particulars if necessary		
Order proof poster		
Send letters to:		
Solicitors to prepare conditions of sale and giving dates		
Client confirming instructions in detail		
Printers with timings that have to be met		
Hotel or saleroom confirming reservation		
5 WEEKS PRIOR TO SALE		
Check that all:		
Plans		
Particulars and		
Conditions of sale		
Posters		
Photographs (blocks)		
are in hand and will be available on time.		
3 WEEKS PRIOR TO SALE		
Check that all posters and particulars are out and that other adjacent offices have particulars.		
1 WEEK PRIOR TO SALE		
Make arrangements with clients as to where and when reserve can be fixed.		
Detail someone to prepare room and act as auction clerk		
Circulate reminders to those interested.		

Before considering the conduct of the sale itself there are a few further points that could be made.

First, dealing with the situation I have just envisaged — the sale prior to auction. One would seldom sell by auction unless there were compelling reasons for doing so and I share the view expressed by Clifford Murphy, F.R.I.C.S., when he wrote on "The Art of Auctioneering" in "The Chartered Surveyor": "Once a property is advertised for sale by auction the matter should proceed accordingly. Many purchasers may be going to the expense of making searches, carrying out surveys and arranging finance for a particular property and it is unfair that they should not have the full opportunity of bidding. However, the auctioneer does not have the last word in this matter. He is duty bound to keep his cleint informed and to submit pre-auction offers, unless he is specifically instructed to the contrary. If the vendor instructs the auctioneer to accept an offer, the auctioneer has no alternative but to carry out such instructions."

In practice, if the auctioneer and his staff are doing their job properly, they should be liaising, if they are not themselves holding the key and accompanying all those who make inspections, with the vendor and with the vendor's solicitor, and should know at any stage prior to the sale just how many persons have viewed, who have had surveys or valuations carried out and whether or not the solicitors have had any preliminary enquiries from prospective purchasers or their solicitors. However attractive an offer might seem, if it is known that a number of would-be purchasers have expressed interest and spent money on preparing themselves for the sale it must be basically wrong to accept and sell without giving them an opportunity.

The interest shown is one of the factors to be borne in mind in fixing one's reserve — a point we will consider in a moment. If a sale prior to auction is clearly in the vendor's best interests, then everything possible should be done to inform other possible bidders of the vendor's intention. This will not always be possible, but at the very least all those known to have expressed interest and those who have been sent particulars should be told at the earliest possible moment that the house has been sold and the auction cancelled.

It is important to make the most of the time one has in the run-up to the sale and for this reason I like to see a preliminary advertisement appear immediately instructions have been received, and if need be even before the date of the sale is known. To inform the public, for example, that a specific house is to be sold by auction "in early May" is to give early warning to anyone who could be interested and give them a chance to make arrangements accordingly. Many auctioneers like to send a short reminder notice of a sale about a week before the date.

Earlier when looking at the circumstances when sale by auction should be considered, I stressed that the vendor must have in mind a realistic reserve. Clifford Murphy had this to say:

"The reserve is a most important factor and woe betide the auctioneer who accepts instructions, regardless of the reserve, merely to test the market and fill his 'catalogue'. One has to hold faith with both vendors and purchasers and it must be remembered that potential purchasers often spend considerable time and energy in investigating properties offered by auction. If such purchasers find that despite their efforts and willingness to bid to a fair price the property is withdrawn as unsold, they will not react favourably to the auctioneers who have wasted their time. There is also the Vendor's disappointment at an abortive auction."

He goes on to say: "Assuming that you are well acquainted with prevailing market conditions, locality and so on, you should advise your client to fix the reserve at about 10 per cent below your top valuation."

I would not necessarily disagree with this, for he clearly had in mind that the lower the reserve the sooner could the auctioneer indicate to those present at the sale that the property was "to be sold" or was "in the room" and there is, of course, no doubt that there are many who will hold back from bidding until such an indication, that the reserve has been reached, is given.

I believe there to be a number of factors that have a bearing on the level at which a reserve should be fixed. The level of interest is but one. Arguably, there is little to be gained by fixing a reserve at below the figure hoped for if very considerable interest has been shown. There is always the danger in fixing a reserve too low that one will only have one bidder and the property will be sold at a price below that which that bidder might have paid had a higher reserve been fixed. I have known a number of occasions when the concentrated effort that led up to the sale generated such post-sale interest that the property subsequently sold at a price higher than the reserve that was not reached in the room. Some persons feel too nervous to bid openly, others may earlier have dismissed the house as likely to fetch too much money for them and others just may not have been able to bid.

Much will depend on market conditions at the time. If the market is buoyant and prices are tending to increase, one could safely adopt a higher figure than one would in adverse market conditions.

The reason for selling is another factor that must influence both the auctioneer and the vendor. Failure to achieve a sale on the day may cause some inconvenience, but it could lead to the vendor losing the house he has set his heart on. The auctioneer must be prepared to give firm advice, and if I am talking to a vendor who does not agree with me I then advise that the reserve should be at the lowest level at which he would, that evening, feel relieved if not pleased, to have sold.

Although in Mr. Murphy's experience the highest prices are obtained where the reserve is fixed at a low level, he does add an important rider: "You must of course be assured that there is an adequate market for the property being offered and that it is safe to rely upon competitive bidding".

There will be occasions when one has to discuss and agree a reserve when one knows that there has been little interest shown and that there is a real possibility that one will not get any bids at the level considered realistic. One must face up to the fact that one's sale is likely to prove abortive and on this assumption consider what would be in the vendor's best interests. This may not be to withdraw the property at just one bid below the reserve figure, thus indicating the price likely to be quoted after the sale. There may be a case for fixing the reserve at a level that will give some flexibility, or indeed for the auctioneer having authority to bid on the vendor's behalf beyond the reserve price — in effect to have two reserves with the discretion as to which to use being left to the auctioneer. I do not believe he could in law do this if *both* the right for the vendor to bid and for a reserve price to be fixed had not been conditions of the sale.

Last, in discussing the fixing of a reserve, we should consider the possibility of selling with a declared reserve, or "up-set" price. This is not a practice that I would advocate except in very unusual circumstances. The auctioneer loses any opportunity by puffing or bidding on behalf of the vendor to generate enthusiasm. He can only ask for a bid at the up-set price; if he gets one he can proceed, if he does not he can only withdraw. Very occasionally one might meet circumstances where an up-set price will, when related to the description of the property, itself be a very real attraction to some who might otherwise not consider the property, and only in these circumstances, and provided the auctioneer is certain that there will be competition, should this course be considered.

Twenty-Six

Selling by Auction — Conduct of the Sale

Preparing the sale — The Auctions (Bidding Agreements) Act 1969 — Creating the right atmosphere — Briefing the clerk — Rights of the vendor — Puffing — Protecting the bidders — The right to withdraw — Damping the sale — Responsibilities of the clerk during the sale — The auctioneer's copy — Introduction to the sale — Dealing with amendments — Opening and regulating the bidding — The bidding sequence — Closing the bidding — Need for control — Care necessary not to give warranty — Authority to sign on behalf of the purchaser — Action after the sale — The private auction

Certain preparation work related to the conduct of the sale will be necessary. The auctioneer must try to ensure that the vendor's solicitor or his representative will be present; occasionally this will not be possible, in which case the auctioneer must himself be prepared to answer any questions of a legal nature that might be asked. He must personally check that he has available to him on the rostrum any relevant documents or plans, restrictive covenants, planning consents, public health notices, Rent Officer's Certificates, etc. Murdoch reminds us that the Auctioneers' Act 1847, Section 7, provides — "Every auctioneer, before beginning an auction, should affix or suspend, or cause to be affixed or suspended, a ticket or board containing his true and full christian and surname and residence, painted, printed or written in large letters publicly visible and legible in some conspicuous part of the room or place where the auction is held, so that all persons may easily read the same, and shall also keep such ticket or board so affixed or suspended during the whole time of such auction being held".

The subsequent Act of 1927 provides that a copy of that Act shall also be exhibited and this has now been extended to include the Auctions (Bidding Agreements) Act of 1969. My tablet is out of date by some 25 years and my sentimental attachment to it could at any time cost me a fine of £20.

The auctioneer must be concerned to create the right atmosphere in the saleroom. He must not only himself have confidence, he must generate an atmosphere of confidence amongst those present, in particular any likely bidders; confidence that the property or properties he is to offer are going to be sold. An auctioneer who has neither personally supervised the preparation of a sale, nor carried out an inspection of the property and carefully perused all relevant documents before he gets on to the rostrum, is not likely to be a confident man, nor is he likely to feel confident if he and his clerk face only one other person in the room. He must take steps, if need be, to ensure that sufficient members of his staff are present (they may well be required if there is more than one lot), a few friends and, not least, some of his competitors. The atmosphere must also be competitive, as Murdoch says — "The very nature of an auction presupposes a conflict of interest between on the one hand the bidders, who seek to purchase the property as cheaply as possible, and on the other hand the vendor, who wishes to obtain as much as he can... In taking any positive steps to achieve this object the bidders are hampered by the fact that they are in competition with each other, as well as with the vendor."

The auctioneer must ensure that his clerk is fully briefed as to what is expected of him, and ideally that clerk should be the person who has been most closely involved in all the earlier stages. The auctioneer should also get his sales staff to identify for him those prospective purchasers present and likely to bid. I normally make a note not only of their names, but where they are sitting. If during the course of the sale they can be referred to by name I believe they feel more closely involved, and it will remove any doubt in their mind as to whether or not it is their bid that you have taken. I think they like, if they are successful in purchasing, for that success to be known but the auctioneer must avoid such personal identification if it is likely to embarrass the individual concerned, and refrain if need be.

Before we deal with the actual conduct of the auction, we should consider the rights of those involved. The vendor will, in the great majority of cases, have imposed a reserve price and/or the right to bid. The latter gives more flexibility, but unless the auctioneer knows clearly what his vendor's intentions are and is sure that in the excitement of the occasion the vendor if bidding himself will not lose his head, he should work to a fixed reserve, or bid on the vendor's behalf himself.

It would appear clear that if neither right is openly reserved, the auctioneer cannot bid on the vendor's behalf, nor could the vendor bid for himself or appoint anyone else to do so.

The judgement in *Green v. Baverstock* makes this clear: "Upon a sale by auction where the highest bidder is to be the purchaser, the secret employment of a puffer by the vendor is a fraudulent act. The sale is vitiated by the fraud and void".

There is some uncertainty as to whether a vendor reserving a right to bid should also sell subject to a reserve, or whether the former would in itself be sufficient. Murdoch deals with this matter at some length, but concludes: "Whether or not it is strictly necessary, the prudent auctioneer will ensure that, wherever a right to bid is reserved, the particulars or conditions of sale also contain an express statement to the effect that the sale is subject to a reserve. It has been suggested that the reservation of the right to fix a reserve price would not be sufficient, as this would not inform bidders whether such a reserve had in fact been fixed; however, in other circumstances such a condition has been held sufficient to put a purchaser on inquiry and, it is submitted, the result would be the same in this case".

Another point should be stressed. Even with the right of the vendor to bid reserved, only one puffer can be used, and for this purpose the auctioneer bidding on behalf of the vendor is regarded to be a puffer. Neither the vendor nor anyone else can join in without running the risk of a purchaser, if he became aware of the circumstances, avoiding the sale. The habit of some auctioneers of getting somebody else to help the early bidding, below the reserve price, is wrong, and carries with it this risk.

The right of the auctioneer to withdraw the property from the sale needs commenting on only very briefly. This right is quite clear where the property has been offered subject to a reserve price and that reserve has not been reached. In the very unlikely event of a property being offered "without reserve" it is highly unlikely that the auctioneer could withdraw it from the sale, however low the highest bid, without incurring a liability to the would-be purchaser. "A vendor who offers property for sale by auction on the terms of printed conditions can be made liable to a member of the public who accepts the offer if those conditions be violated." (*Warlow v. Harrison*, 1858).

Conversely it would appear clear that any bidder can withdraw his bid before the fall of the hammer, and it follows that the auctioneer could not hold him to it, unless the property has been "knocked down", the rule being that it needs the consent of both parties to make the contract binding and that any bid constitutes nothing more than an offer on one side which is not binding until it has been accepted by the other, in the case of an auction by the fall of the hammer.

We have been considering mainly how the law protects the bidders. We should now look briefly at how it protects the vendor, although the bidder's opportunity for sharp practice is not as obvious. Murdoch quotes two cases under the heading of "Damping the Sale". In both the plaintiff had the property knocked down to him at a very low figure, as the result of the sale having been damped by others refraining from bidding, believing in both cases that the bid was not genuine but made by a puffer. In one case it was the defendant's solicitor in fact bidding for the plaintiff! In the other a personal friend of the defendant was bidding for himself. In both cases specific performance was denied to the plaintiff.

Every auctioneer will be familiar with the would-be purchaser who asks what he believes to be a very damaging question of the auctioneer immediately prior to the sale with the clear intention of damping the sale. This, of course, any person attending an auction sale can do, but he must not misrepresent. If he does and subsequently the property is knocked down to him, he will not necessarily be entitled to specific performance of his contract, and if he does not succeed in buying, he could have damages awarded against him, provided it could be shown that the statement made was untrue, that it was made maliciously with a dishonest or improper motive, and that the plaintiff had suffered financial loss as the result. (*Mayer v. Pluck* 1971.)

Most auctioneers will be aware of how "the ring" operates at chattel auctions. In short a group of dealers agree beforehand who of their number will bid for those lots that are jointly of interest, whilst the others agree to abstain, with the clear intent of damping the sale and of acquiring the lots below their proper value. Subsequently at what is called the "knock out", the lots would be re-auctioned amongst themselves and each would share in the cash surplus. The 1927 Act sought to deal with this practice, but the restraints it imposed were not only limited to "rings" in which dealers were involved, but did not apply to the sale of land. There is, therefore, nothing to prevent two or more would-be purchasers in our context reaching agreement between them as to who would bid and who would refrain, nor indeed would it be wrong for one person to pay another to refrain from bidding (*Heffer v. Martyn* 1867). On the face of it, it seems illogical that it should be illegal for a vendor to combine with others to force the price up, and yet be legal for would-be bidders to combine together to keep the price down. Lord Romilly M. R. expressed the view that "the vendor's real remedy in such a case is in fixing the reserved bidding".

We now consider the conduct of the sale itself and first the duties of the auctioneer's clerk. I commented earlier that ideally he should be the person who prepared the sale, therefore know the property concerned intimately. He should also be aware where any known likely bidders are placed in the room. He must know the reserve price and have it clearly marked in his copy of the particulars, and either he or the vendor's solicitor, as is appropriate, should have all relevant documents at hand.

During the sale he must carefully follow the bidding and note down all bids made, whether or not he knows them to have been made on behalf of the vendor. He must assist the auctioneer, who cannot look in every direction at once, ensuring that no bids are overlooked. He must follow carefully the auctioneer's bidding sequence and be ready to help or correct immediately if the auctioneer either loses that sequence, or clearly makes an error. If the auctioneer is to feel confident, he must have confidence in his clerk.

The auctioneer's copy of the particulars should be clearly marked as such, as should the clerk's. There should be readily available two copies for each lot clearly marked "Contract Copy". I like a folded foolscap sheet of plain paper fixed in my own, on which I can make notes during my pre-sale inspection. These notes should, either in full or in intelligible outline, set out what one wants to say at the commencement of the sale. First, if one is selling jointly with another firm, the name and address of the firm and, if there is a partner or representative present, his name. Also the name and address of the vendor's solicitors, the person who is representing them and whether or not he or she is a partner. Those features of the property to which you want to refer, and I try to avoid a detailed recital of the particulars which might be informative to those who have never seen the house and who have no intention of bidding but are of little value to those who are really concerned as potential bidders. What one is here trying to do is briefly and succinctly to stress the property's really saleable features. A mention of any documents one has available and which might be of interest to those in the room, together with an invitation to them to inspect. A reference to any special conditions of sale, to any restrictive covenants that need special comment, the date on which completion is to take place. In particular, and heavily underlined, any last-minute amendments you feel it necessary to make, and last but not least, "Any questions"?

Individual styles will vary from one auctioneer to another. Ebullient self-confidence and quiet assurance are both acceptable. If bidders are to bid readily they must feel as relaxed as possible in an atmosphere that can often be tense, and the auctioneer must use his own personality to try to achieve this.

The opening moment of the sale is in my experience by far the most difficult. At what level do you seek your first bid? It should be either above or below the reserve price, never at it! Selling my first house from the rostrum I made just this mistake. With a reserve of £4,500, I asked "Would somebody like to bid me £4,500?". A large and loud woman in the very front row said "I will". If there were any other bidders they were stunned into silence and I meekly knocked it down to her.

I find it difficult to give any firm guide-line about this, for so much will depend on the circumstances. There is no doubt that a clear opening bid from the room is of great value in getting a sale going, but, conversely, for the auctioneer to struggle too long to get one can get the sale off on exactly the wrong note. I normally seek a bid just above my reserve price, rapidly coming down to seek a bid perhaps 20 per cent below it. Given a reserve price of £50,000 one might initially seek a bid of £55,000 then seek to open at £45,000 and then £40,000. If one has not at that stage got an open bid one would open with a bid taken "off the wall", in fact a bid on behalf of the vendor.

If selling subject to the Nineteenth Edition of the National Conditions of Sale the auctioneer's right to regulate the bidding is provided for. If in any doubt one should check and get authority from the vendor. As to the size of the increased bids one should seek, only circumstances can dictate. Certainly circumstances will dictate the speed at which one moves towards one's reserve. If one is confident of selling, and given that it will be a very positive encouragement to announce that the property is in the room, the sooner one can get there, avoiding undue haste, the better. Under these conditions one could probably run up to or just below the reserve price quickly, if there is keen bidding from the room, there will be no need to hesitate, if there is not, I would normally break, take the opportunity to stress some feature of the house, "You couldn't hope to build a house of this size with this accommodation for anything like this sort of money". If I had been increasing the bids by £1,000 I would seek another rise of this amount, but then halve it, to give the impression that a new buyer had come into the room.

"I will take £500 if it will tempt you". The minimum amount of an increased bid will again depend on conditions at the time and to a very large degree on the auctioneer's instinct as to what is required to keep the sale going, or indeed as to whether he has reached the end of the road. One must take care to avoid reducing the size of increased bids too early. If one does this and one succeeds in getting a bid from the room, there will be resistance to any attempt to increase the amount of the jump again, and to advance several thousand pounds in bids of £250 is not only annoying for the auctioneer, but monotonous for those present.

The auctioneer must carefully judge the moment when he informs the room that the property is to be sold, or that it "Is in the room". There are occasions when it will be right to let this be known just as soon as you have a bid at the reserve, but if bidding is brisk and the reserve is clearly going to be exceeded by a considerable margin, one should, as long as one is getting genuine bids from the room, hold off until the bidding hesitates, then use the announcement to get it going again. It must never be forgotten that when you tell the room, by whatever phrase you use, that you have reached the reserve, you are in effect telling them that you as an auctioneer and valuer and your client felt it was a realistic price for the property and this could positively discourage some from bidding much further.

At the end always, close the bidding slowly, giving ample opportunity for a last-minute change of mind. This is particularly important if you sense or know that one of your bidders, desperately keen not to lose the property, is already bidding above the limit he set himself. A reminder that you are selling might help at this stage, and the question "Are you all sure you have finished?" can help to elicit that extra bid.

I cannot stress too strongly the importance of not only being in control of the room, but feeling that one is in control. If at any moment you feel you have lost control, slow down and regain it. This could be done by taking longer to identify the next bid, or to make it, if it is to be on behalf of the vendor, by checking with one's clerk as to where one has got, or by breaking the bidding to stress a feature of the property.

Throughout, the auctioneer should note down every bid made, and to enable him to keep to his bidding sequence he should do this even if the bids are his on behalf of the vendor.

Two last words of warning. First stressing a point made earlier, puffing is acceptable but one must avoid positive statements, for example as to value, or as to structural condition that could be taken as a warranty. Second, in one's capacity as an auctioneer, once one has knocked the property down, one has authority to act on behalf of the purchaser to the extent that one can sign the Memorandum of Sale on his behalf. There is some doubt as to how long the auctioneer can hold this authority and Clifford Murphy quite rightly advises that an auctioneer should never leave the rostrum until all contracts are signed. I personally do not interpret this literally, but I certainly never leave the saleroom itself until the memoranda are signed.

The commercial market may be a hard-hearted place, but, as I have stressed often, the residential market is an emotive one. If the bidding has been keen there are likely to be a number of desperately disappointed people in the room. If for no other reason than that they remain prospective purchasers some sympathy from the auctioneer might not be out of place. I like to make a comment to the effect that "After such spirited bidding I am only sorry that one can only sell to one purchaser". One should go further and have members of one's sales team present, to speak and give what reassurance they can to the unsuccessful bidders. In any event they should be there, for if the sale proves abortive, anyone who bid unsuccessfully should be spoken to, and if this cannot be done at the time a note of who was present should be made and they should be contacted to try to establish the extent to which they were interested in that particular property, and what their presence at that sale can tell of their own requirements.

The authority of the auctioneer following an abortive sale we have considered earlier, but clearly if the vendor's instructions have not already been obtained as to the action to be taken, this must be done immediately and with as comprehensive a report on the sale as possible; the number of bidders, the amount of the highest genuine bid, and advice as to what the result means in terms of value and as to future marketing policy.

Lastly, the success of a sale by public auction is an occasion from which the firm might be able to take some advantage. Not only is it a time for Press Releases, it may have given information that would enable one to speak more effectively to other vendors who are still holding out for prices that are too high, and it might be an indication to a number of prospective purchasers that their ideas of value are incorrect. In short, the information given by the successful sale could well be of use in generating activity elsewhere in that agent's market place.

Selling By Private Auction

I have never been involved in such an operation. Presumably if one were faced with the task it would be because for some reason or another the vendor wished the auction to be attended by invitees only. Maybe if a significant number expressed interest in a property or offered the asking price for it, it would be one way of bringing matters to a conclusion, or, if a vendor wanted his purchaser to come from a given group of people or companies it would be an alternative to selling by private treaty or tender. In any event, as I see it, the identity of those whom you would want to attend the auction will be known in advance. The same principles, given this limitation, would apply as in the case of public auctions. I try hard to imagine the circumstances under which such a sale could take place, to assess the practical differences from selling by public auction. The time available between getting instructions and the date of sale is likely to be appreciably less, the printing of special particulars and conditions of sale would almost certainly be unnecessary. The vendor's solicitor would need to prepare the conditions of sale and a form of a memorandum, and copies could be circulated with the agent's normal particulars to the invitees. There would presumably be no advertising to be carried out. In every other respect the conduct of the sale would be similar, although perhaps the auctioneer's approach could be somewhat less formal. If the sale was successful I assume he could not, as in the case of sale by public auction, disclose the name of the purchaser or the price paid without the authority of the parties.

Twenty-Seven

Selling by Tender

Preparation — Conditions of sale — Avoiding the unquantified tender — Treatment of the deposit — The opening of tenders — Informing the tenderers — Action to be taken if no tender acceptable — The need for frankness

Preparation of a sale by tender will differ little from that of a sale by public auction. The preparation of particulars, the request to the solicitors to prepare the conditions of sale, the advertising programme and the timing factor will all be similar. The conditions of sale will not vary greatly, although there are two provisions which it is essential to include.

First there should be a stipulation that the vendor does not undertake to accept the highest or any tender, protecting himself against having to take too low a figure, as, in the case of a public auction, he would do by fixing a reserve price, but, further, putting himself in a position where he can decide who the purchaser should be on criteria other than just price. This may well have been the reason why this method of sale was chosen initially.

Second, the conditions must specify the circumstances in which a binding contract for the sale and purchase of the property shall be constituted between the parties. In the past, when this method of sale has been used, some have tried to avoid tendering a specific amount by tendering "some £100 higher than the next highest tender received subject to a maximum of £...". For this reason it is advisable to stipulate that no tender will be entertained unless it is both unqualified and of a fixed specific amount.

Special thought needs to be given to the treatment of a deposit. A possible set of conditions, purely as an illustration is set out below. These visualise the successful tenderer being so informed, then having to pay his deposit within a specific time for the contract between him and the vendor to become enforceable. Very often, however, when this method of sale is used, tenderers are requested to enclose a deposit cheque with their form of tender, an undertaking being given on the vendor's behalf that unsuccessful bidders will have their deposits returned within a reasonable time after a decision has been taken.

In these circumstances such deposits would not normally be returned on the actual date the decision was taken, but immediately the successful tenderer's cheque had been cleared.

ILLUSTRATIVE SET OF CONDITIONS FOR TENDERING
(To be included in the Special Conditions of Sale)

1. Any person desiring to purchase the property shall complete and sign the Form of Tender in the Appendix hereto and shall send the completed and signed Tender together with the foregoing Particulars of Sale and these Special Conditions of Sale (still attached thereto) in a sealed envelope marked "Tender—Blackacre" to the vendor's agents, Messrs.....................of.....................so as to be received by them at that address not later than 12 noon on the...

2. The vendor's agent shall as soon as practicable thereafter (and in any case before the *........) inform the person whose tender it is proposed to accept by registered post addressed to such person by the name and address specified in his Tender that his Tender is accepted conditionally on the receipt by the vendor's agents within ...... days after the date of such letter (time in this respect being of the essence of the condition) either in cash or *by cheque* or banker's draft of a sum equal to 10% of the purchase price inserted in the said Tender and upon the receipt by the vendor's agents within such period as aforesaid of such sum as aforesaid a contract for the sale and purchase of the property shall be constituted between the vendor and the person whose Tender is so accepted (herinafter referred to as "the purchaser").

3. The vendor does not undertake to accept the highest or any Tender and only unqualified Tenders of fixed specific amounts will be entertained.

4. The said sum to be paid to the vendor's agents as aforesaid shall be treated as paid by the purchaser to them as stakeholders as a deposit and in part payment of the purchase price and forthwith after such payment the vendor's agents shall give to the purchaser an acknowledgement of its receipt.

5. The purchase shall be completed on the ....at the office of the vendor's solicitors, Messrs.................of...............and on that date the purchaser shall pay the balance of the purchase price.

*A date to be specified

I stress that the set of conditions illustrated above are not to be regarded as a precedent or model, for circumstances and requirements will vary and the conditions of tender must reflect them.

The time and place for the opening of tenders will have already been established. The latter should in my view be the offices of the vendor's solicitor, but even if this is not possible, he should be present. There is no obligation on the vendor or his agent to permit the bidders to attend when the tenders are opened. As it is possible that this method of sale was chosen was to give the vendor flexibility in selecting the purchaser he may choose not to accept the highest tender and embarrassment could be caused.

As we have seen, one of the disadvantages of this method of sale is its secrecy and the doubts it could cause as to fairness and impartiality. If the vendor is resolved to take the highest bid, subject only to the figure being acceptable to him, then there may be little to be lost by inviting tenderers to be present and the openness and frankness will remove doubts.

Assuming that the opening takes place "behind closed doors" it is most important that unsuccessful bidders be treated courteously and, in so far as the vendor's interests permit, with frankness. They should be notified of the vendor's decision just as quickly as possible. The successful bidder should be told that his tender is accepted subject only to the clearance of his cheque, or conditionally on the payment of the deposit called for by the tender conditions.

The unsuccessful bidders should be given as much information as it is proper and advisable to disclose. Certainly they should be told the number of tenders received. If the tender accepted was in fact the highest they should be told the property was sold for an amount in excess of their own tender and they should be told their numerical position in a list of tenderers arranged in descending order. The more that can be told, the surer they will be that the sale was properly and fairly conducted.

One needs to consider what action is to be taken in the event of no one tender being acceptable. It could be that the vendor will wish to withdraw the property from the market, but more likely he will have in mind a minimum figure that he is prepared to accept and wish to negotiate with one or more of the tenderers to see if terms acceptable to them can be negotiated. It is certain that any undue delay in notifying the tenderers as to the result of "the sale" or the vendor's intentions will lead to doubt and mistrust, not only of the vendor, but of the agent involved. Again one must be as frank as the situation allows. If the vendor wishes to withdraw the property from the market, the action to be taken is clear. If he has a minimum figure that he is prepared to take and if he is prepared to exchange contracts with the first person to make him an offer of that amount, again there is no difficulty.

If, on the other hand, he wishes to try to negotiate a deal with one or more, but not all of the parties, then some tact will be called for. It is suggested that the tenderers be told that no tender was acceptable, then where their own bid came in the numerical order and further be told that the agent's instructions are to negotiate with a specific tenderer with a view to trying to agree terms and that if agreement is not reached they will be so informed.

Again, as in a case of sale by auction, prospective purchasers are likely to ask for some guide as to the price expected. It is of the utmost importance, bearing in mind the suspicion that surrounds this method of sale, that the advice given is consistent.

Twenty-Eight

Estate Agency Abroad and Multiple Listing

Levels of owner-occupation — Comparison of
commission rates — The control of estate agency,
registration and qualification abroad — What
conclusions can be drawn — The role of agents in
conveyancing — Sole agencies — A Canadian firm
looked at — Relative attitudes in America and
Australia.
Multiple listing — Could it work in Britain —
Attempts to co-ordinate estate agency work in Britain
— The Northampton Group, Leicester Centre Point
Scheme, the National Network of Estate Agents and
Home Relocation Ltd — Implementing multiple listing
— Difficulties to be overcome — The use of a
computer — An unwarranted fear

Estate Agency Abroad & Multiple Listing

I open this chapter with misgivings. First because I wonder to what
extent any understanding of practices elsewhere in the world could be
of help to British practitioners, and secondly, because although I have
travelled fairly extensively in Europe, on most of those occasions estate
agency has been far from my mind. One is, however, aware that the
Monopolies Commission felt it appropriate that they should, in
considering the estate agent's role in the house-market, look at practices
overseas, and more recently the Price Commission did likewise. My late
senior partner toured North America specifically to study estate agency
methods and I am to an extent relying on memory of his experiences. I
have personally had opportunities of discussing operating methods with
practising estate agents visiting this country from Australia, New
Zealand and the United States. I also have available to me a report of a
colleague who visited Canada and, last but not least, I have the Price
Commission Report that devoted a chapter to overseas estate agency
which was based on a study carried out for them by The Economist's
Intelligence Unit, and on some studies they made of their own that
included discussions in the United States.

My initial doubts as to the relevance of overseas practice is borne out
to an extent by the marked differences from one country to another — in

charging methods, services provided, and with regard to other costs associated with house-selling. Other countries vary vastly in size, density of population, and distance between communities. Research found marked differences in levels of owner-occupancy, which in both Sweden and the Netherlands was at about 35 per cent. Strangely, Belgium was at about 61 per cent. It is believed to be appreciably higher in North America. The research also found that the estate agents' involvement in the market varied greatly. In Italy they were believed to handle only about 20 per cent of the house-maket, but in the Netherlands a surprisingly high 90 per cent.

In particular there were wide variances in the rates of commission charged, as illustrated by the following table.

Country	General Level of Charges %	Structure of ad valorem charge
U.S.A.	6-7	simple
Canada	5-7	simple
West Germany	5-6	simple
France	4-8	tapered
Italy	6	reported to be tapered
Belgium	3-5	tapered
Switzerland	3-5	mixed
New Zealand	2.5-5	tapered
Sweden	3-5	simple
Denmark	1.5-4.5	tapered
Spain	2-3	simple
Irish Republic (Dublin)	3.5-	simple
Irish Republic (elsewhere)	2.5	
United Kingdom	1.5-2.5	mixed
Netherlands	1-2	tapered
Norway	1-2	tapered

I have tried in looking at overseas practices to see if they give any guide as to the way estate agency might develop in this country and as to whether there are any obvious lessons to be learned and applied here.

First I looked at the degree to which estate agency elsewhere is controlled. In nearly all countries rates charged appear to conform to "norms", either through the influence of trade associations, presumably the equivalent of either our professional bodies or local associations (probably the latter) and they are controlled by law. Legal maximum charges are imposed in both France and the Irish Republic.

In New Zealand a statutory licensing authority sets the rate. In Belgium and the Netherlands national trade associations advise a scale fee. In both the United States and Canada rate-fixing is now illegal, but the Commission reports that "the standard charges have generally been maintained through informal mechanisms", so there is here a clear similarity to British practice.

Many of the governments concerned have recognised a need for regulation and control of estate agents and others are currently considering the possibility of imposing some form of control.

The practice of estate agency in the United States and Canada is of particular interest to me, for I believe the multiple listing systems which operate there could, if there were the will, operate here and bring about a significant improvement in the way estate agency is practised, but more of that later. It is, interesting in this context to note that in the States the licensing of agents is at present optional, but that the Federal Trade Commission is considering measures requiring estate agents' licensing, other measures relating to multiple listing systems, and the information that is to be disclosed to clients. Their interest seems to have stemmed from various cases brought against real estate associations or boards under the anti-trust laws, in particular relating to the operation of multiple listing systems.

If in a society that is believed to be a great deal freer than ours in the conduct of its business, multiple listing systems are giving rise to public concern, it is, regrettably, more likely that they would meet opposition here, although I personally would not believe it justified.

Elsewhere in Europe the degree of State involvement varies considerably. In Scandinavia, Denmark and Norway not only do estate agents have to have a government licence, applicants for such licences have to be qualified by passing set examinations. In Norway there is a limitation by way of age, a would-be estate agent having to be 25 before he could apply. Sweden was, at the time the enquiries were made, preparing legislation to bring in a degree of control, and this now may be an accomplished fact.

In Italy firms have to be registered and "professional staff must pass an oral examination", whatever that involves and whoever it is intended to cover! The professions there are reported to be pressing for a tightening-up of regulations, the imposition of a set training period and qualification by written examination, but "unofficial" agency activities are common in Italy.

In France an estate agent is legally obliged to hold a professional card and to do so requires a minimum educational qualification, a limited period of practical experience, a bank guarantee and "civic responsibility" insurance cover.

There is little or no government control in Belgium or Germany. In the former many unqualified operators are reported to act as agents and in the latter agents' work is done by the banks, by their equivalent of the building societies, and even by architects.

Coming nearer home, "auctioneering" appears to be a very much more clearly identified profession in the Irish Republic than it ever has been in Britain. The auctioneer's operations are subject to strict controls, they are licensed, they have to operate to a satisfactory standard, there are accounting rules, for example, separate banking arrangements of clients' moneys, and they have to deposit either a cash sum of £10,000 or an insurance bond for this amount with the High Court.

In all the countries from which the Prices Commission were able to get information, professional associations existed, but insufficient information is available to enable an assessment to be made as to their effectiveness in controlling either estate agency methods or the fees charged.

In the Netherlands, if the general level of charges reported, of 1 to 2 per cent, is correct, it is not dissimilar from the rates charged here if one allows for the fact, which I understand to be the case, that the agents there recover all advertising and out-of-pocket expenses, as they do in many parts of Northern England. I am interested in two particular aspects. Firstly, how they achieved a standing with the public that involves them in 90 per cent of all house transactions, for given that some transactions will always take place between related persons and personal friends, they must enjoy almost 100 per cent of the available market.

Secondly, I understand that in one of their major cities the agents co-operated to provide a city-wide computerised service.

I have noted with some interest that research showed in the Netherlands a common practice of charging both vendors and purchasers commission, although this practice was then being examined by the Ministry of Economic Affairs. Whether or not the 1 to 2 per cent shown in the Table represents what is payable only by the vendor I do not know.

In some German provinces again the agents' charges are frequently divided and so we are told that in a buoyant sellers' market the purchaser often has to pay the commission in full. In France commissions are sometimes split between vendor and purchaser.

No really meaningful conclusions can be reached from the general level of charging. We do not know, for example, how the number of agents practising in any one country relates to the estimated number of houses sold there in a year, nor do we know how the value of the average house elsewhere compares with values here. I do recall some considerable time ago seeing a comparison of the values of the small three-bedroomed family houses in most of the Western European countries. I also recall that at that time the average house in England was worth little more than half its West German equivalent at £15,000 to £29,000. The Netherlands were not far behind West Germany, and only in one country were houses cheaper than here and that was in the Irish Republic. Even if my memory is accurate, these figures are too old to be really meaningful, for they certainly will not reflect the rapid escalation in house-prices during 1977/78 in this country.

But it seems that any comparison of house values is likely to make the very much higher rates of commission charged on the Continent harder rather than easier to understand. The Price Commission felt, however, that the information available to them was sufficient for them to conclude that on international comparisons "charges by UK estate agents are amongst the lowest in the Western World".

If estate agents here can draw any conclusions from this evidence of charging rates overseas, they must be, first, that if agents' rising costs at home are not matched by rising values, and profits can only be maintained by increasing commission rates, there may be room to do so. I would not comment here whether this room exists at all price-levels. Secondly, I think one could conclude that if a more efficient way of operating the house-market exists or can be found, but only at a higher cost than at present, the room exists, if the public want the improvement in service, to charge for it.

There may be some connection not only between commission rates and values but between commission rates, the percentage of houses in owner-occupation and frequency of sale, but this can only be conjecture.

In recent years two subjects in particular have been discussed amongst estate agents, with the media and with solicitors, the merits of sole agency as opposed to multiple agency, and the question of the property shop, and whether we might have seen, had the solicitors lost their conveyancing monopoly, the establishment of centres where both agency and conveyancing work could be done at a composite fee. I therefore looked to see what was common practice elsewhere.

The operation of the market in North America we will consider separately, but elsewhere the Commission found:

"There is no standard practice regarding exclusive (sole) agencies in other countries. In Italy and Norway exclusive agreements are normal, usually for a fixed period of up to six months. In West Germany also there is a movement towards exclusive agreements. In other countries both exclusive and multiple agreements are common, but not surprisingly the exclusive agreement is said to be favoured by estate agents".

There is nothing meaningful to be gleaned from this, but, in finding that in all countries from which they had information the agents provided the same basic services as they do here, i.e., in checking the property, producing the particulars, contacting prospective purchasers, making arrangements and accompanying to view, the Commission also found that —

"In some countries agents become involved in the later stages of a property transaction. In France the agent prepares the sales agreement, the lawyers take over the conveyancing stages. In Norway, agents carry out the conveyancing work, whereas in Belgium the agent will accompany his client to the lawyer but will not become directly involved. In Sweden, agents perform the legal conveyancing function, as is the case in the U.S.A. and Canada. In Italy, not only do agents carry out conveyancing but they also provide direct loans for house-purchase".

In their conclusion the Commission said:

"It is the total cost for the whole transaction including conveyancing fees and Stamp Duties, which concerns the buyers and sellers of property, but these are outside our terms of reference."

Having regard to the recent "whitewash" of the solicitors' near-monopoly of conveyancing, with which I have no argument, it is most unlikely that we shall see property shops, as some feared, being established in England & Wales, and most unlikely that we shall, certainly for many years to come, see agents involved in conveyancing work as such. Overseas practice however again begs the question as to whether or not there is a case for agents in many, if not all, transactions taking matters through to the exchange of contracts preferably with the approval and support of the parties solicitors.

Although I want to consider North American practice more fully, in the context of possible future developments here, it is sufficient now to comment that in most areas of the United States and Canada the local associations or real estate boards administer multiple lists. In short, an agent receives either an exclusive or a multiple listing, of which he has to notify the board. If the property is to be multiple-listed, for which a somewhat higher commission is normally charged, then the board prepares details and circulates to all members of that board. The listing agent remains in control, but effectively any member of the board is able to offer a prospective purchaser the vast majority of houses in the area likely to be of interest. The system clearly has merits.

I would comment also on what I understand to be the basis on which sales or negotiating staff are normally employed by estate agents (Realtors) in North America, Australia and New Zealand. In Britain most agents pay such staff by way of a basic salary plus a commission or incentive payment, with the basic salary forming the major part of overall remuneration, and most of the partners I know in the larger well-established reputable firms would deprecate any change that would significantly increase the incentive element of remuneration, fearing that this would lead to oppressive methods, both in securing instructions and in selling. Elsewhere exactly the opposite view seems to be taken. For example, as we shall see, in Canada the realtor is considered to be the equivalent of the partner, his negotiating staff would be engaged on relatively short contracts, receive little or no basic remuneration and be rewarded by a very high commission rate on what the individual personally sells. It is worthy of note that a very much higher proportion of women are employed than in this country. I understand that the practice throughout much of the United States, Australia and New Zealand is similar.

It is clear that in most of the countries we have considered, the structure of estate agency is very similar to that in this country, highly fragmented, largely made up of sole practitioners and partnerships, a few companies and only few firms operating nationally, and even those only in the commercial field, the land agency field or at the very top end of the house-market. In recent years the position in North America has begun to change with the development of national real estate "brokerage" chains and franchising organisations. Again I think it appropriate to consider these matters when we take a look at the future, but they bode ill for the small firm and there are now clear indications that this is one way the profession could develop here in Britain.

North American Practice

Earlier, in considering the estate agent's role I stressed that, particularly in the residential field, this was primarily to act as an agent of the vendor, who became a "client". Further I stressed the importance of getting this relationship better understood by the property-owning public. The position in the United States and Canada is very different. Henry E. Hoagland, in "Real Estate Principles" and under the heading of "Brokerage" says this:

"The real estate business originates with brokerage. The broker is the negotiator who brings about the meeting of minds of the parties to a real estate transaction. The subject to be negotiated may be the sale, leasing, management or financing of rights in real estate. The real estate broker's operations are different from those of most businesses. He has no goods on his shelves, no samples to display. The only commodity he has to sell is service. He is not a buyer or a seller ... he is a negotiator ... oftentimes the seller has too high an opinion of his property. His asking price is higher than the market will pay. The buyer may err in the opposite direction. His bid price may be too low. The difference between the bid and the asked prices must be negotiated if a sale is to result. A go-between may sometimes effect a meeting of the minds more readily than if direct negotiation were undertaken ... The broker is more than a message boy in these visits. He studies each party to the transaction and tries to determine what concessions and adjustments will lead most directly to a successful conclusion."

The position is made abundantly clear, for although presumably the vendor will pay the broker, in no way is that broker acting specifically as the vendor's agent. He is looked upon as a third party, an intermediary, employed as such to bring about an agreement between the parties. As Cliff W. Krueger said in "Successful Real Estate Selling" — "selling is walking down a path of agreement".

Strangely, although there are many similarities between the practice of estate agency in North America and that in Australia, we find that in Australia the real estate man's relationship with the vendor is similar to our own. "Real Estate Practice in Australia", when dealing with the role of the real estate agent in the community, says: "These men often act first in the capacity of a consultant and after ascertaining the desires of their client and giving their best advice as to the course of action the client should pursue, may receive instructions to act for and on behalf of a client in following such a course; thus the consultant then becomes the agent of his client in future transactions on his client's behalf. This procedure is an everyday occurence in the business of a real estate agent."

There would appear to be another significant difference between practice in the United States on the one hand and practice here and in Australia on the other. Krueger specifically states that "appraisal is no part of brokerage". But from "Real Estate Practice in Australia", one sees not only the agent's relationship with his client underlined, but the need for basic knowledge and training stressed: "The concentrated efforts of the Real Estates Institutes of Australia over the last 40 years have also *promoted* in the public mind a recognition of the important function which the trained real estate man performs in the business community".

It is sad to reflect that the fragmented structure of estate agency in this country has effectively prevented any such concentration of effort.

"Real Estate Practice in Australia" continues: "The proper implementation of this role demands that a real estate agent should firstly be thoroughly trained in the many and varied duties of his calling." It then describes the courses that are available in every mainland state and continues — "The complex nature of real estate activities to-day demands a thorough basic knowledge of these operations", and in a following paragraph: "The role of the real estate man requires an up-to-date knowledge of city, suburban, provincial and country developmental trends. It requires continuous renewal of information and improved patterns in housing construction and design, in commercial development, industrial and rural expansion and the current costs of varying forms of buildings and general development. Current market values in all forms of real estate must form a continuous part of the up-to-date real estate man's knowledge". Many would have sympathy with this view.

In concluding this chapter I would like to look more closely at the actual structure of a Canadian firm of Realtors, for it may have some bearing on the future of estate agency in this country, particularly if one considers the implications of computerisng and the possibility of negotiators having V.D.U.s in their cars and homes! My comments are based on a report by Mr. John Vail following a visit to Canada.

The office itself was in a good-class residential suburb of one of the major cities. The offices were modern, in a prominent corner position, but without display windows, internally lavishly appointed with a waiting room "furnished like a drawingroom".

The firm consisted of four realtors (brokers or partners) and with them 70 agents (negotiators) all of whom worked independently. The office acted as the nerve centre for their operation, but the agents worked mainly from home and came to the office only to get their typing done, deal with the paper work involved in sales negotiated and to collect the information received daily from the local Real Estate Board.

The standard commission rate charged was 5 per cent or 6 per cent if the property was to be multiple-listed. If one of the agents, (negotiators) obtained instructions in his own right that property became his own personal listing and if he sold it he took 3 per cent and the firm only 2 per cent of the purchase price. If the firm received instructions then, on a rotating basis, these would be passed to and become the listing of one of the agents, and again commission would be shared.

There was an even more significant difference between practice there and here, for in that particular Canadian firm it was normal for any one agent to handle only five to ten properties at any one time, with the result that there were nearly 10,000 agents in that particular city two thirds of whom were women and the majority employed only on annual contract.

The function of the realtor partners was simply to control the business, deal with problems on contracts or mortgages and with administration, and although most of them originally started as agents they did not get involved "in the front line of property negotiation".

The colleague on whose visit I am reporting concluded: "There is no doubt that the vendors and purchasers receive a better service in Canada than they do in the U.K. ... the commissions are very high and when one considers the average house-price to be about $75,000 it is hardly surprising that both vendor and purchaser demand a better service."

A surveyor who went to live in the States, whose name I have no record of, wrote making observations on estate agency practice there that might be of interest. He commented on fixtures and fittings, where the general practice was to include in the sale of a house a great deal more than we would here, on the nature of their market, and in particular on mortgages. Many mortgages are at fixed rates of interest and the majority transferable, so the amount of the mortgage and the rate of interest charged could become a significant factor in assessing saleability and value. Among points he made are these: "Realtors help their clients by finding mortgages for buyers, and they also spend a lot more on advertising than you probably do, but they charge a flat 6 per cent of the price of the house (in some places $6\frac{1}{2}$ per cent) for their services. This rate incidentally is not fixed, and a hard-pushed realtor will handle a house for 4 per cent — but will then not put it in his local multiple-listing. You probably know about the multiple-listing system here. Most realtors belong to it and multiple-list most of their own listings, so in theory a prospective buyer can go to one realtor and be shown everything on the market. Customarily, the realtor who sells a competitor's house has to split the commission with him. Actually realtors work a lot harder to sell houses on their own lists".

We shall return to multiple listing at the end of this chapter, but there are two points I would like to make here. First, it would not appear mandatory in the States for every house to be multiple-listed and there seems to be some flexibility with regard to commission rates charged. I stress these points because from discussions I had many years ago with two local associations in an attempt to get them to consider multiple-listing, the question of "having" to multiple-list an instruction appeared a stumbling block to many, and it was part of the Nine Societies' case to the Monopolies Commission that the removal of a set scale of charges would restrict the degree to which agents could co-operate.

Our correspondent went on in a more general vain. "Realtors here are not as responsible as you are for what they sell. Very few of them are trained surveyors, and very few take the trouble to learn about the structure of houses. Yet, curiously, the majority of American home-buyers do not use lawyers to negotiate house sales for them! In Maryland, people thought we were crazy to use a lawyer, and although we got the best firm in the town where we were, they handled the transaction in a very slipshod way. Here (also in the U.S.) we found a much better lawyer, and he certainly went out of his way to see to it that we got what we were promised.

"The one thing the realtors and their sales people do here that you do not is show people round occupied properties. In most cases, in fact, they prefer to show them through properties when the owners are out, and they advise their clients how to make their houses as appealing as possible."

Finally, and bearing in mind that we heard earlier that Canadian realtors gave a better service than we do, he said:

"Taken altogether, the home buyer and seller both get better treatment from the British estate agent, than from the American realtor."

Multiple listing

We return to the major Canadian city to consider multiple-listing more closely. Although there may be variations in both Canada and the United States as between the operation in one real estate board's area and that in another, I understand that the basic principles are similar. To counter another argument that has been forcibly made, to the effect that "Multiple listing might work in North America where communities are further apart and much more clearly defined, but it would not work here," I would comment that my late partner's cousin practising in California, in order effectively to cover his area, was a member of about a dozen real estate boards. My immediate reaction was to think that this must have caused more problems than we experience, even in a major South Coast resort where multiple-agency is rife. I was, however, assured that this was not the case.

The Real Estate Board in the Canadian city was a non-profit making organisation and I believe this to be normal. It was the practice there for most property to be multiple listed through the Board "in which case a further 1 per cent was added to the commission charge, making this a flat rate of 6 per cent". This again would appear to indicate that the multiple-listing of property was not mandatory.

The Board enjoys a virtual monopoly in the city and it would seem that any firm of realtors setting up in business, not belonging to the Board and having access to its multiple listing-service, would have little chance of survival. The Board enforces a strict code of professional etiquette, not, our reporter says, "unlike the R.I.C.S. code", and all member firms of realtors and the agents employed by them are bound by the rules. Certainly in the States the National Association of Real Estate Boards lays down a code of ethics. The situation in North America would therefore appear to be similar to our own, with national bodies laying down a code and local bodies incorporating this into their own and, one suspects, adding to it if, in the local context, they think it necessary. The difference would appear to be that there local boards are associated with the National Board, but here, although there are a number of national bodies and many local associations their efforts are unco-ordinated.

The Board works on the basis of publishing lists daily and circulating to members the details of all properties listed within the preceding 48 hours. All listings are dealt with on a sole-agency basis, with multiple-agency instructions only occurring in "exceptional circumstances".

The agent taking particulars of a property sends brief details, similar to those given by us on a register card, to the Board. If these were communicated to the Board, say on Tuesday, on Wednesday the photographer covering that sector of the city would photograph the building and prepare a brief summary of the accommodation. On his return it would be type-set and printed and incorporated in the register sheets for that area the same day or following morning. The Board operated a very sophisticated printing department.

The agents working for the realtors would arrange with the Board to be sent the "particulars" of all properties within a given area. The Board used a sophisticated automatic selection system so that the sheets for specific areas were bundled together to form one block and then delivered to the office of the realtors concerned. If that firm had 12 agents working with it, it would receive 12 separate bundles of particulars which would be passed to the agents, which they then placed in their own loose-leaf registers. The sheet would give all the information necessary, such as viewing arrangements, for the agent to work on. A daily index or information sheet was also circulated, listing those properties that had been sold, the price obtained and the selling broker. It is interesting to note that as between the Board, the realtors and the agents there was full disclosure.

It is also interesting to note that it is not normal practice, certainly in that city, for firms of realtors to produce any more detailed particulars. The whole systems worked on no more than what we would call illustrated registers.

The Board also published a weekly newspaper available free of charge from purpose-built news-stands which could be seen on pavements throughout the city. I understand this to be fairly common practice throughout North America.

The Real Estate Board went yet further, advertising on local radio, television, and on the subways.

The multiple-listing system also covered industrial and commercial property, but it would appear from the report that this was dealt with far less thoroughly, with the largest firm of commercial realtors operating not only independently, but very effectively. A point of considerable interest for our commercial agents.

The last comment our reporter makes is that the Board's code of ethics is backed up by State Registration and that agents (negotiators) have to qualify, and the Real Estate Board itself provides courses for three to six months. If that agent wants to go on to become a realtor in his own right, then further courses have to be taken.

From another source I understand that Real Estate Boards lay down a time-limit within which details must be sent to them to minimise the risk of individual realtors and agents keeping their "goodies" under the desk.

Exclusive listings (sole agencies not to be multiple listed) are not uncommon but I believe many Boards insist that they are also notified of these. The system must not, however, be considered parallel to sole and multiple agency in this country. The exclusive listing, it is true, is not dissimilar from our sole agency situation, i.e., one agent receives instructions and handles that sale by himself. Yet where the agent is instructed to multiple list, he is still effectively appointed as sole agent but one obliged to appoint as sub-agents, within a very strict set of rules, other members of the Board.

The overall standard of service given does make our own fragmented service at first sight appear totally inadequate, but before we consider the possible adoption of multiple-listing in this country it would be well to realise the price the American property-owning public pay for that service — to all intents and purposes 300 per cent more than their British opposite numbers. Out of this the payments that have to be made to the Real Estate Board are not insignificant. In the City we have considered in 1976 each realtor was paying about £450, each agent (negotiator) about £30, to belong, and in addition each firm of realtors paid £6 for every property listed and a further £6 to have it advertised in the weekly newspaper. Certain economies are, however, obvious. Firms of realtors are not involved, as we are, in the preparation and circulation of particulars, nor do they or their agents, as I understand it, circulate particulars, however, brief, in the way we do. The service is much more direct and personal.

Attempts to Co-ordinate Estate Agency in Britain

It could be argued that one cannot, or should not, start to compare estate agency practice across the Atlantic with that here if the former costs three times as much, but I think it does give us a great deal to ponder on.

What has so far been done in this country to co-ordinate the efforts of agents? I cannot claim to know what goes on throughout the country but I think, through my involvement with the R.I.C.S. Estate Agency Committee, the Management Committee of the National Network, and through the many individuals and firms one has established contact with, that I would probably have heard of any significant new initiative.

I believe that in practice little thought has been given to the subject, and even less done. There are, however, exceptions.

A few years ago I visited Northampton to look at the work of "The Group". This consisted of eight Northampton firms, who had got together to "multiple-list". Having regard to the firms concerned, it certainly was a significant initiative and a co-operative effort that appeared to be working well. The number of firms in that town who remained outside the Group was, however, such that I, with all due respect to those involved, question whether it made any significant difference to the overall standard of service given to would-be purchasers. They could still not go to one agent and get a comprehensive list of all houses available likely to be of interest to them, although from one of the eight they could get a comprehensive list of those being handled by them. The Group had a centralised printing and stationery department, preparing not only particulars but notepaper and so on for each firm, which retained its individual identity in every sense, even in advertising, although they all appeared under the heading of "The Group".

I took considerable encouragement from this. I was aware of a much earlier attempt to establish multiple listing in Manchester, which from my enquiries appears to have failed, perhaps because those who were willing to participate did not represent a sufficient percentage of the total market-place, and perhaps because of apathy. Maybe the area was too large to give such an experiment a fair chance of success, and it could well have been that commission rates were at such a level that there just was not the money available to mount it on a sufficient scale.

It is true that my late partner and I made attempts in the late 'fifties to get two strong local associations in the South at least to try to get something going on these lines and that we failed. In Northampton, however, it appeared to be working and the member firms seemed happy with it.

Multiple-listing could be described as a vendor-orientated co-operative service, but in Leicester, the Leiceter and District Estate Agents' Association had gone the other way and established a service known as "Centre Point". Briefly, the establishing of a centre to which any would-be house purchaser could go, give details of his requirements and have them circulated to all members of the Centre Point service, which in this case I understand represented the great majority of the agents in the area. Similarly a member firm, not being able to suit a prospective purchaser, could circulate details of his requirements to the others. I am told that no commission-sharing was involved. It was an arrangement set up by the agents aimed simply at giving a better service to would-be purchasers and in the process answering one of the main criticisms of the service given by estate agents in this country.

It may be significant that both Northampton and Leicester are sole-agency areas and I accept that the establishment of multiple listing in multiple agency areas would be difficult and to establish a service such as Centre Point probably impossible.

It would be wrong in considering co-operative methods of practice to ignore sub-agency. The extent to which sub-agents are appointed varies greatly from town to town. I know that in some South coast towns (multiple agency area) an agent receiving direct instructions, but knowing he is not a sole agent, will try to appoint as many sub-agents as he can as quickly as he can, to forestall any other agent being appointed direct. Again with respect to those involved, it is, as I see it, unco-ordinated, time-consuming and largely ineffective, for most agents just cannot deal efficiently with the amount of paper that circulates.

The National Network of Estate Agents and Home Relocation Ltd, are both relatively recent arrivals, and both sought to establish a network of agents throughout Britain aimed at helping, in particular, vendors and purchasers who wanted to move from one part of the country to another. As a member of one, I know a great deal about it, but perhaps not surprisingly, not a lot about the other. There is no doubt in my mind, or I think in the minds of the great majority of agents involved in the National Network of Estate Agents, that it is certainly working. It now has over 600 associated offices in Britain and certainly has the will to go on to bigger things.

Neither body, however, sets out to solve the problem of providing a better collective service by the agents in any one town or district. Multiple listing appears to me to provide the most likely solution, and we must ask the question of whether it could work here.

Could Multiple Listing work in Britain?

The answer is "Yes it could" and its introduction could be greatly helped by the use of computers. There would, however, be many genuine problems to be overcome and just as many prejudices. It would, as I have commented earlier, be easier to establish in a sole-agency area, but I do not think the difficulties in a multiple-agency area insuperable and I would like to examine how it could be established in one town.

I picture a South coast town I know well. It has a total population of some 60,000 persons and something approaching 40 estate agents' offices. It has two characteristics that I think important if an experiment in multiple-listing is to succeed. The boundaries of Worthing and District are fairly clearly defined, as are neighbourhoods within it and, most important, it has a strong and effective local association to which the great majority belong. Furthermore, it is a town where, perhaps for the reasons given earlier, the appointment of sub-agents is a regular feature of the market place and all the agents are accustomed to a significant part of their overall income being shared with other agents. To this extent, to attempt to establish a multiple listing service would be doing no more than attempting to make much more efficient and much more effective, from both the agents' and the public's points of view, a service which at least in embryo form already exists. One would have to accept at the outset that there are those who would want to remain outside, whether from a wish to retain their complete independence, a lack of faith, or an unwillingness to subscribe towards the initial costs involved.

One would hope that the larger firms would prove the catalyst, although, and I have not made a detailed study of the firms concerned, I believe that in Northampton it was in the main the medium-sized firms that got together in the Group.

One would hope that the number of firms prepared to join the experiment would be sufficient for the use of a computer bureau to be considered at the outset. One of the great difficulties to be overcome in the early stages would be reaching agreement as to common formats, register slips, daily bulletins, particulars and so on. The question would have to be asked not necessarily collectively, but in each firm as to whether particulars in their current form would continue to be used, or whether vendors and purchasers would be prepared to accept particulars unillustrated, in the form of computer print-outs, and of what quality these should be.

Early rules would have to be set, particularly to overcome the multiple agency question. For example, there would probably have to be a rule that once a member firm had notified the centre (the computer) that it had received instructions in respect of a specific house nobody else could multiple list it, although they could, if present practice was to continue, accept direct instructions from the vendor. Each firm and preferably each office would need a visual display unit and a printer, although the speed and quality of that printer could depend on individual requirements. Decisions would have to be made as to whether or not the computer was to be used on a "real time" basis or on a "batch" time basis. Cost would be likely to dictate the latter, certainly in the early stages. This would mean that each office would only go into the computer at specific times, perhaps first thing in the morning or last thing at night to "input" the variations resulting from the firm's own activities during the day and to retrieve new listings, price variations and so on resulting from the activities of other members.

One would hope that time and use would ultimately justify either the centre owning its own computer, or being able to afford "real time" on a bureau, so that each office at any time in the working day could have direct access. At this stage the register could be updated and negotiators could actually use the computer to search the register, as opposed to having to maintain their own.

There would be many other difficulties, both of a technical and a psychological nature, to be overcome, but I am convinced they would prove surmountable given the will.

A last word from our reporter on the Canadian scene: "The Real Estate Board is a most impressive set-up by virtue of its total dominance of the market. However, if such an organisation could be got underway in the U.K. it would undoubtedly be taken over by the government with the civil service or local authorities ... which could obviously result in disintegration of the system."

I think this an unwarranted fear. Those local authorities in the past who have attempted to establish an estate agency service have failed and the political climate has changed. I accept that it can change again, but I think the Price Commission Report will have taken some of the heat off the agents, particularly from well-informed quarters. I think the problem could be looked at the other way. A far more efficient service given by the agents would be a deterrent to those who would like to compete for whatever motive and further, if the agents do not take steps to make good their shortcomings, would this not leave temptation in the way, not only of the Government or local authorities, but commercial interests who might see either social or considerable financial gain to be made and the computer as a means of making it?

Twenty-Nine

Thoughts About The Future

**The public image again — A lovely morning spoilt —
Estate agents' commission an inordinate amount? —
The media's lack of knowledge — The Price
Commission's findings — The need to inform the
public — The loss of an opportunity — A challenge to
local associations — The need to consider the future in
the context of criticisms — Misunderstanding of the
agent's role — Broker or agent? — The view of the
professional bodies — Could the profession split? —
Could American practice show the way? — Do we face
chains or franchising — Are there significant signs of
change — Too many agents and relative profitablity —
The factors that could bring change — The
professional approach predominant for how long? The
possible conflict — The need to defend the professional
approach — The professional bodies — Government
and the media
Criteria considered — Sole agency "the better way"
— Improving the service to purchasers — Thin ice and
rigidity — Charges a deterrent in lower price ranges —
The need to innovate — Who will lead? — The
standing and future of the commercial estate agent —
Hope for the future**

I have for a long time now looked forward to this moment. It is
Saturday, February 23, 1980, and I sit at my worktable looking out
across the waters of the Camel Estuary. Here in Cornwall it is a lovely
early spring morning, or at least it was until I read to-day's "Daily
Telegraph". A short article on page 2 reports that the "Colchester
Evening Gazette" was refusing to publish advertisements inserted by a
Mrs. Julie Fuller. Mrs. Fuller had just opened a new shop called
"House Hunters" and claimed that she would be able to sell a house for
as little as £42 "in most cases". The plan apparently was that she would
charge a registration fee of £2 plus £40 for promoting the house for four
weeks, and if it failed to sell, the house would be offered for a further
twelve weeks for £120 and thereafter for nothing. She not surprisingly
had the support of Mr. Kenneth Weetch, Labour M.P. for Ipswich and
founder of the National Freedom for House-Owners campaign, which

seeks to fight what he calls the "three evils" of the property market — Stamp Duty, solicitors' fees and estate agents' fees. Mrs. Fuller has, of course, every right to do as she pleases, although it is hard to see how at that level of charging she could really do any more for a vendor than he could do for himself. She does not concern me and if she concerns the agents in Colchester to the extent that they, as Mr. Weetch is reported to believe, brought pressure upon the newspaper to refuse her advetisements I think this is regrettable. Mrs. Fuller is not the reason my day has become cloudy. That I found in the editor's column on page 16, under the heading, "The Cost of Moving".

Commenting that "exhortations to greater mobility of labour are countered by massive incentives to immobility and disincentives to mobility", the editor goes on to criticise the fact that home-owners who would move are subject to charges equal to over 5 per cent of the cost of a home. It is, he said, "customary to pillory conveyancing charges as the main culprit, but in fact they are much less than either estate agents' fees or Stamp Duty." He went on to attack Stamp Duty, which he described as an iniquity and one which falls on "every citizen who buys his own home, as if to penalise him for daring to opt for self-sufficiency". Few would disagree with this, for the Tax Man is the one person who takes a cut out of the majority of property transactions for giving no service whatsoever.

The article went on to describe the rate of estate agents' commission as an "inordinate amount". This one is hardened to, but what I found shocking, and indeed disgraceful, was when he then commented: "There is room for the Monopolies Commission and the Office of Fair Trading to look into this. They will need to resist lobbying and obstruction from professional vested interests — as our property correspondent's report indicates".

Is it really possible that the editor of one of our greatest national dailies and his property correspondent could both be unaware of the reference to the Monopolies Commission and their Report of ten years ago, and the Report of the Price Commission into the same subject published only in 1979, which found very little to criticise, and are they really unaware of the fact that the Commission was appreciative of the help and co-operation they had had from practising agents and the professional bodies?

Even given that they were totally ignorant of these matters, is it really credible that somebody in a position of such responsibility could suggest a reference to the Monopolies Commission or the Office of Fair Trading (which has taken over the responsibilities of the Price Commission) without checking whether or not the issue concerned had previously been referred to them?

Having eased the mind somewhat by getting that down, one has to recall that although the Consumer Survey carried out for the Commission in June of '79 showed that most persons who had used estate agents were satisfied with the service they got, many vendors regarded it as poor value for money. It will be recalled that the Commission concluded: "We believe that agents could do more to inform the public of the services they offer. As a first step in this direction we would like to see each agent display prominently in his office the services he provides and the terms on which they are offered".

However ill-informed the article, the editor expresses a view that many share. It will not be enough for the agents to shelter under the Monopolies Commission's statement to the effect that they can find no evidence of excessive profits, or the virtual whitewash given them by the Price Commission, for if the editor of the "Daily Telegraph" and his property correspondent are both unaware of the latter's report, who, other than the agents themselves and members of the disbanded Price Commission, will know anything about it or its contents?

This is perhaps a good place to start looking at the future of the profession.

What can agents do to get across to the public their role in society, the services they can give, their costs, the fact that their profits are not excessive, the fact that their commission rates are effectively less than almost anywhere else in the world, and the fact not only that approximately 70 per cent of house-vendors use their services, but that the majority are satisfied with them?

The majority of estate agent members of the Royal Institution had hoped that they, together with members of the Incorporated Society and with the backing of the two bodies, could take a joint initiative and promote the image of the "qualified estate agent". Their wish to do so has for the time being been thwarted by the General Council of the Institution. Many general practitioners deeply regret the decision and see it as the loss of a real opportunity.

This book is, however, about the practice of estate agency and however much encouragement one has had from members of the Institution, one cannot overlook the interests of those who are members of neither the Institution nor the Incorporated Society, but who are practising estate agents the majority of whom follow the Code of Conduct of their own professional body or that of their local association.

Earlier chapters of this book described how estate agency is controlled in this country and referred to the significance, certainly in some areas, of local associations and the localised nature particularly of residential agency work. If the leading professional bodies cannot and will not get together jointly to promote the interests of their members, then this responsibility must fall on local associations and on individual firms, for it is difficult to see how any one of the professional bodies could effectively exert real influence on its own.

In the context of trying to improve the general public image of the estate agent and ways in which the services given can be improved, one is concerned almost entirely with "house agency", for it is this one section of the profession's work that has attracted nearly all the criticism and with which the public identifies it. In the commercial sector there is no evidence to show that the agents are held in anything other than high regard by the interests they serve.

In concluding this study of the practice of estate agency and looking into the future I want to be both critical and constructive. I much earlier said: "If criticisms have been justified, there must be room for improvement. Recognition of faults is an essential step towards finding remedies".

I want to consider various directions in which the profession, and I use this word deliberately, may go, the challenges it might have to face, and in particular how the service it gives both in the context of residential and commercial estate agency can or might be improved, thereby reducing criticism and enhancing image.

Closely linked with the Price Commission's conclusion that we, the agents, could do more to inform the public of the services we offer, is what I see as the urgent need to inform what we must regard in this matter as a largely ignorant public as to our role, and we have got to resolve in our own minds the issue as to whether estate agency is or is not a professional occupation, albeit one that involves an element of "salesmanship".

The Consumers' Association clearly saw the agent's role as one of brokerage and we recall that they made the assumption "that the main 'function' of the general practitioner is the bringing together of vendors and prospective purchasers, lessors and prospective tenants and nogotiating between parties". This is precisely how both the American writer, Henry E. Hoagland, at that time Professor of Business Finance at the College of Commerce and Administration at the Ohio State University, and Cliff W. Krueger, a realtor who graduated as an economist, saw the American realtor's role. It is not the role that, I venture to suggest, the great majority of British estate agents want to regard themselves as playing, nor would it appear to be the role the Australian agents play.

In that the Royal Institution of Chartered Surveyors and the Incorporated Society of Valuers and Auctioneers see their members as professional men and women, and in that by far the majority of practising estate agents in this country are members of one or the other or both of these bodies, one could assume that the majority of practising agents see themselves as carrying out a professional function.

Admittedly the National Association, although very much smaller than the two main bodies, takes a more commercially-oriented view, and I quote from the guidance notes to its Rules of Conduct: "It places no restriction on promotional literature as such, believing there is a proper place for this in an activity that manifestly has commercial aspects". Yet they in Rule 10 say that "A firm shall use all due diligence in looking after its *'clients' '* business and shall take all reasonable steps to protect and promote the 'clients' ' interests as are practicable, without improper conduct and unfairness to others." If they do not see themselves as professional men in the sense that their chartered or incorporated colleagues do, they certainly do not see themselves as brokers, and from studying their examination syllabus published in July of 1978 one senses a movement towards professionalism. Indeed, describing the examination structure, they say that those students who successfully complete their course are eligible for "professional associateship", and further that "the professional qualification is carried through all the corporate grades for the Association".

There can be little doubt therefore that the vast majority of practising agents in Britain see themselves as always acting for one party or another in property transactions, never as brokers, and recognise some professional qualification as if not essential at least desirable. Perhaps, before we can consider how we might try to get this across to the public, it would be wise to consider whether or not in the foreseeable future the position could change. With all three professional bodies and the vast majority of practising estate agents presumably committed, it follows that where local associations exist they are also likely to be committed to the professional agency rather than the brokerage view. Just how could a position of such strength be changed?

Philip Whitehead, believed as long ago as 1965 that change would come and that we would see a split within the profession of the land with those carrying out purely professional roles going one way, and those responsible for the commercial role of selling and buying going the other. He believed this would come about for two reasons.

First that the commercial aspects of agency would attract substantial commercial or institutional investment and go multiple, and secondly, that the operation of the market would be made greatly more efficient, less personal and less professional by the computer. He did not believe that such a split would occur in the commercial sector of the market, holding that in this sector professional work, and in particular valuation, and agency were irrevocably linked. He did believe that once separated away, agents in the residential sector would move towards brokerage, partly because their professional status would have been eroded, but more importantly because he felt the public largely already believed this to be their role.

Fifteen years later it has not happened, but one would ask what changes have taken place and whether they do indicate a likely break at some future time.

In doing so I first look back across the Atlantic, accepting that the way the North America realtors see their role and work will not necessarily affect what happens here. Indeed one of the reasons for considering earlier the growth of the profession was to show how deep-rooted was its professionalism and that any dramatic change in the foreseeable future was unlikely. I look first at the Canadian firm which we considered earlier.

There it would appear that the realtors (partners) have separated themselves away from the selling function, but they remain under the same roof. Their salespersons' role was very different from that of the British negotiator and it is most unlikely, I suggest, that we in this country would ever come to operate their way. Although we are told they gave a very much better service, it is difficult to see how the gap in quality, with the possible exception of effective multiple listing, could be that great. Indeed I find it impossible to imagine what improvements could be made in the standard of service here that would make the British house-owner, already disgruntled at the level of estate agents' charges, happy to pay two or three times more.

Looking more widely at North American practice — does it have any relevance for us? Certainly I believe multiple listing could, and I shall be enlarging on this, and I believe franchising poses a threat.

The Price Commission having found that in each of the countries in which they were able to obtain detailed information, estate agency has traditionally been a fragmented industry dominated by sole traders and partnerships, commented that in North America the position had begun to change rapidly in recent years with the growth of (a) national real estate brokerage chains and (b) franchising organisations.

They commented on both. First that the main force behind the emergence of national chains had been the existence of economies of scale in advertising and promotion. These economies have become increasingly important as families have become more mobile; local brokers have been less able to rely on referred and repeat business, and advertising has become a more vital source of trade.

The franchise movement, it said, represented a response by small brokers to increased competition from national and regional chains. Each franchise apparently pays initial franchising fees of anything between $1,000 and $10,000 plus annual charges calculated as a percentage of gross income. In return for this the brokers receive (a) the benefit of national advertising, (b) training at the schools run by the franchising companies, (c) access to particulars of the properties listed with other firms under the franchise umbrella.

Their final comment was that many U.S. brokers believed that the structural changes taking place in the industry were such that in another five years 70 to 80 per cent of the sales of single family homes will be controlled by fewer than ten big companies.

Could it happen here? I refrain from mentioning names. Many firms are no larger in terms of offices or total staff than they were 15 years ago, but some have continued to grow, in the main by opening branch offices. This growth has largely reflected not only the local nature of the property market, but the strength of the local press in property advertising. Few firms have shown a readiness to open branch offices at a distance and in areas where existing offices could not give them support in the media. Notwithstanding this, the growth of some firms has been significant. One in the South now has over 70 offices. Their spread could not be described as national or perhaps even regional; it certainly has not reached the stage where it could be described as a national estate agency chain, nor is it a franchising organisation.

Another has adopted a somewhat different pattern of growth, being prepared to open offices at a considerable distance from each other, giving coverage of much of the South and South-west. It could perhaps be described as an estate agency chain purely because of the geographical area covered, but it could not be described as a franchising organisation, although there are some similarities. These firms are by no means alone in growth.

A significant factor might well be the variations the Commission found in the income per principal in the small, medium and large firms. Many would argue that big is not beautiful, but there can be no doubt that the larger a firm becomes, provided it is efficiently managed, the more it can spend on promoting its image, the more profit is available to the principals to expand further and faster, the more readily can it invest in the expensive exercise of computerising if, as we shall discuss later, computers have a significant role to play. Interestingly, neither of the firms referred to have so far computerised, although many smaller ones are in the process of doing so.

The rapid growth of what is still a relatively small firm in the North-east with institutional backing, using a computer and a well-known personality to promote it on television could be a significant development. There is very little other evidence as yet of major commercial or institutional concerns becoming involved, but attempts are being made to establish franchises.

The Commission's findings showed the average sole principal in the small firms to be earning no more than I know some employees are earning in the larger firms and even the average principal in the medium-sized firm was not much better off, and in both cases before any allowance had been made for interest on the principal's capital or for the risk element. We must remember that the survey on which the Commission based its findings was carried out at a time when estate agency in Britain was prosperous.

We have, therefore, in my opinion a situation that could lead, if not to an explosion, to rapid change. Any firm already large enough to have a national or regional image has the potential to grow either into a chain or to seek to establish a franchising operation. Curiously, firms with national names might find the latter the more difficult, for traditionally they are associated only with the higher priced section of the market and at the same time many have little to gain by remaining self-employed other than retaining their independence.

These then are the factors or circumstances that could allow rapid change to take place — no effective control on entry; as yet no control on standards of competence; unco-ordinated professional bodies; misunderstanding of the agent's role by the public and the media; increasing costs and narrowing margins (the problems of the smaller firm); the increasing power of the media; the greater efficiency computerisation will bring; and the ever-increasing need for working capital.

I sense if not winds of change breezes that could strengthen.

In the short-term I do not believe even the sort of changes I see as being possible will necessarily alter the way estate agency as such is practised. For the foreseeable future I see the professional approach predominating. The long-term danger is that some firms will grow to such a size that the directors or partners could not realise the value of their shares or release their working capital without going into public ownership or selling to outside commercial interests. This could bring them into conflict with the professional bodies, but every man has his price and if firms do pass into public ownership the new directors may not be enamoured of the niceties of professionalism and codes of conduct.

Despite the traditional differences, despite the much more localised nature of estate agency markets here in Britain and despite the apparently entrenched position of the professional approach, what is happening across the Atlantic may be relevant and certainly should concern us.

If the breeze increases to a wind, it is the house-agency function that is going to be blown out through the door and it is then that the traditional approach could give way to brokerage. Those with leanings towards house-agency may well have to give up membership of their professional bodies and be blown out with their function. Regrettably, I suspect there are some members of the Royal Institution who would welcome this. The majority I am sure would not. Whether such change once started could be arrested, I doubt.

If the professional bodies, their members and those who practise estate agency in this country want to see house-agency remain in the hands of professional persons and want to continue to have regard for the professional ethic, they must take a very much more active interest, preferably jointly, in protecting and promoting the interests of their members who work in this field and in instructing the public. If the public can clearly see the professional as opposed to brokerage issue, I am convinced they would prefer the former. If this view became very firmly and widely entrenched there is at least a chance that whatever changes might come, the role of the estate agent in Britain would not change.

As a very first step the professional bodies must take steps to try to ensure that the Government, the media and organisations such as the Consumers' Association are not only better informed than they would appear to be, but positively encouraged to support the professional approach. The Secretary of State has very considerable powers under the Estate Agents Act and must be encouraged to use them to preserve what I see as an approach very much in the public interest.

I now go on to consider the other criticisms that we noted much earlier, to see just what could be done to bring about improvements in these specific areas.

The criticisms levelled against agents we dealt with when we looked at their role and public image, and we did so in some detail and considered their implications. A few general observations seem called for.

If we separate the criticisms into two groups, the specific and the general, and deal first with the latter, it will be recalled that some agents did not set out the basis on which fees were to be charged; some gave unsound advice as to value; others were considered to have sought quick sales at a low price and others circulated particulars that bore no relationship to the purchaser's requirements. The remedy here must be in the hands of individual firms. If circulation of particulars is indiscriminate or simply sufficiently inaccurate to irritate, then office systems have got to be looked at and data-processing methods considered. As valuation in the house-market is certainly an art and not a science, inaccurate advice with regard to value will always be present. I suggest that if one were able to identify and question the critics, the criticisms or the great majority of them were made at a time when property values were escalating. I think it is possibly a fair criticism of many agents that they do not react quickly enough to changes in the market that can be both sudden and significant, and gazumping is, of course, a product of under-pricing. A greater awareness, certainly on the part of the partners in the business as to what is happening in the economy, what is likely to happen, and greater thought given to those factors that bring about a rapid change in market conditions would do something to help, as would regular discussion between partners and managers and their negotiators. In short, better training of staff and more alert management.

There is a tendency, which those responsible for management must recognise, on the part of negotiators to rely on immediate past evidence. It is readily available, it is concrete, why look ahead and conjecture? The quick sale at a low price is a closely related criticism. Close liaison between vendor, agent or negotiator and more frankness may help. One must accept, however, that "low price" may mean no more than that the price the agent advised the vendor to accept was less than the vendor had hoped for, however unrealistically. Even the best advice is not always palatable.

To some extent these criticisms can be related to multiple agency practice, for the reasons we considered when looking at the alternative forms of agency. The general move towards sole agency practice in the South has to be welcomed, and every possible encouragement must continue to be given, by the professional bodies, the local associations and by partners and managers within individual firms, to continue this tendency, and we should not hesitate to stress that the Consumers' Association itself found: "By instructing one agent only you have a far higher chance of a quick sale — you make the situation worse for yourself the more agents you instruct".

Their recommendations that vendors should instruct one agent only, not giving him sole selling rights, and possibly limiting his agency to two or at the most three months, must be stressed.

The specific criticism that purchasers have to go the rounds if they are to get a comprehensive list of the properties likely to be of interest to them was made, and it is one that has been made on a number of occasions. This is a criticism that could be linked to the early general criticism levelled by the Consumers' Association that the service given by estate agents is inadequate and that it is "not an efficient method of bringing buyers and sellers together".

Something could be done about this. Multiple listing has proved acceptable throughout North America and in Australia. We have considered its use here and how it could be established. The solution is very firmly in the hands of local associations, or the agents in any one locality who could, given the will, do something very positive to improve the service given, and in doing so give practitioners a measure of protection against the sort of changes I see as possible if not probable.

The other general criticisms can be quickly summarised. First, the criticisms on which we have already touched, to the effect that a lot of people do not realise that the estate agent acts for "the seller" and that in this area "the ice is thin and the situation unsatisfactory". The only remedy open is for the professional bodies, local associations and individual firms through the national and local media and their own public relations hand-outs to make sure their role in the market place is put across. Would it be too much to ask that every firm should have, in some form or another, a guide to purchasers, that could be handed or sent to them at the time the initial inquiry is made, stressing this point above all others?

The next general criticism on which I would like to comment is that of rigidity and the suspicion of closed shop attitudes.

The mere existence of the professional bodies and local associations is bound to give the impression of rigidity and closed shops and this would be exaggerated if the professional bodies used their Codes of Conduct to prohibit what the media and the public would see as healthy competition. If local associations are reluctant to admit newcomers, or exerted undue pressure on members, they again could be seen to be inhibiting competition. To bring pressure on the media to the disadvantage of competitors is clearly unacceptable.

There is here a very real anomaly, for I believe much of the criticism that has been made comes from the fragmentation that exists, but the improvements that I see as desirable, such as a greater degree of co-operation between agents, multiple listing and a more universally adopted code of practice, are only likely to come about if there is more uniformity and rigidity rather than less.

The principal general criticism, which has come from all quarters, from the Consumers' Association, the media and the public who have used agents' services, is that charges are too high in relation to the service given. It would be all to easy to point to the level of charging elsewhere in the Western world and say "What good boys we are". As I commented earlier in this chapter, we can point to the findings of both the Monopolies Commission and the Price Commission and say that we have been vindicated, but that would clearly get us nowhere, for these findings already have been ignored, perhaps because the professional bodies, the associations and individual firms were not themselves sufficiently interested in them to have spread the message. The proof of the pudding is in the eating and the fact remains that in the South some 30 per cent of vendors "go it alone" and this percentage increases in the North, where price levels tend to be lower.

This is clear evidence that the level of charging, certainly in the lower price-ranges, is such that it is deterring a significant number of vendors. I believe we have got to try to find ways of operating this sector of the market more efficiently and in a way that would enable costs and commission rates to be reduced in relative terms. If we are going to do this then we must look to the use of data-processing, micro and mini computers, and we must consider the relevance of many "sacred cows" such as individually produced particulars, the circulation of particulars in their current form, the type of staff employed and their remuneration, the possibility of giving partial services. Lastly, we must continue the move towards sole agency in the South and the adoption of multiple listing systems with the aim of minimising abortive work, achieving greater efficiency and giving better value in terms of service for money.

John Greve asked the question — "Are there too many agents?" Could our charges be too high simply because, as he put it, "there are too many agents, each of whom sell too few houses to permit a more reasonable commission to be charged".

There is no answer to this; the level of profitability in the smaller firms is perhaps an indication that the question is fair. We recall that the Monopolies Commission were very anxious to see that the proposed Estate Agents Registration Council should not impose restraints that would have made it more difficult for new agents to open, even restraints related to competence. Just as long as any person can call him or herself an estate agent, surveyor, auctioneer and valuer without either qualification or experience, for just as long as there are those willing to try, the present situation will continue.

It is a situation that must relate to the general criticisms of an inefficient and too expensive service. If there is an answer, it is not in the hands of the professional bodies, the associations or the agents, it is now firmly in the hands of the Secretary of State.

To summarise, I believe there are ways and means whereby the operation of the residential market in this country can be significantly improved. The professional bodies could give a lead in promoting ideas and in research, but I believe the practical improvements must come from the local associations and individual practitioners. If anything is to be achieved it will need a lot of goodwill, and give and take, by individuals, for whatever changes are proposed, the larger firms will tend to see them as benefiting the smaller, and vice versa.

What is the future in the commercial market? With experience limited to provincial practice, if I were to make any forecast, it could be seen as impertinent or naive or both. In practice, most of the significant commercial agency work is in the hands of relatively few of the larger firms, and most of these based in London or the major cities. Given a healthy economy, I think they have little fear of the future. Because of what the majority of practitioners see as both the desirability and inevitability of the agency and professional aspects of commercial practice continuing to go hand in hand, fragmentation is not likely to be a fear. They enjoy a relationship of trust with their clients that their residential opposite numbers envy, but perhaps the variety and continuity of their work is an explanation for this. They have shown themselves to be conscious of the need to promote their image and the commercial aspect of their practices, hence the quality of their public relations work and advertising, perhaps reflecting an ability and willingness to employ, or use the services of, experts in these fields. They have certainly shown a willingness to make full use of modern techniques. Many have computerised, and this will continue. Some might see the computer as a threat, with data banks able to produce valuations for a few minutes' work, and accessibility to lists of available property to be had through View Data or Prestel, in which the Royal Institution is involved, as likely to erode their position in the market. If such fears exist, I believe them to be ill-founded, for I do not believe even in this practical and unemotive field the computer would ever be more than a valuable aid. I do not believe it will ever erode the need for sound professional judgment. It will not identify or create development situations, nor will it ever provide the entrepreneurial skills necessary to the effective commercial property agent.

It is true that some of the Institutions have built up their own property sections, and some may see this as a threat. Again I think any fears are likely to prove unfounded, for the Institution that went "in house" would in doing so remove itself from the market place and put itself at a distinct disadvantage compared with those who continued to rely on the varied services their chosen agents have provided for them in the past. The Institutions will continue to grow and however much one regrets the passing of the small traders in the High Streets retailing will move more and more into national and regional chains. This movement will continue to increase rather than decrease the strength of the major commercial agency practices. Their success will, of course, remain relative to the national well-being, but again most of the firms involved are well geared to monitor and interpret the economy and its effects in real estate terms.

If there is any improvement to be made in the operation of the commercial property market, and I believe there is, it is in the Provinces and in the field of secondary and tertiary investments and owner-occupation. Most commercial work in the Provinces is dealt with by the medium and larger (in the Provincial sense) firms. How well it is done in those parts of the country that I do not myself know well, I cannot say, but in many firms I believe one will find it dealt with scrappily and inefficiently, if for no other reason than because it is seen as secondary to the principal role of professional men and in agency terms less important than the residential field.

I think the provincial general practice doing a limited amount of commercial work does face a danger, for there is a tendency for this work to polarise. In the average larger provincial town, it is perhaps unlikely that as house agents such firms can exercise a strong influence much beyond, say, a ten-mile radius (I accept that this must vary considerable, dependent upon population densities). The provincial firms with a well organised commercial department could extend their influence over a vastly wider area. I venture to suggest some directions in which firms might look to see whether or not improvements can be made. First, in their public relations, and the general promotion of their identity with the commercial market, which need not, in my opinion, conflict with their other roles. Second, by establishing much closer contacts with local industrialists, office-occupiers and smaller retailers. They should know, for example, which industries are prospering, which are likely to need more space, and so on. They could also perhaps do more by way of circulation of annual property market reports direct to commercial property users in their area. They should be in a position to know their area more intimately than any major firm acting nationally could hope to do. I think there is room for creating links and strengthening existing links with the major national commercial firms and through them with the Institutions they represent, and so act more effectively as eyes and ears.

I would like to end on a note of optimism.

I have no statistics available to me, but one cannot but be encouraged by the growth in the provision by the universities, colleges and polytechnics of full-time education facilities. (I would not argue here as to whether this is the only or best means of qualifying.) I am likewise encouraged by the calibre and bearing of most of the students who are graduating and qualifying and by the fact that many of them, who not long ago would have regarded estate agency work as beneath their dignity, are getting enthusiastically involved. This will strengthen the professional role of the estate agent in this country and will make it that much more difficult for those who would see a rapid slide into pure commercialism and brokerage as the opportunity to become involved and accelerate the change. I am sure that change would be contrary to the public interest.

I believe there are areas where significant improvements could be made, but I also believe that estate agents play a very useful role in our society, and that in the main the consumer surveys that have been carried out support me in this view. I further believe that in property marketing the British public is better served by the profession of the land than perhaps it realises.

Index